In an effort to maintain the deep emotional content of this book some excerpts written by Sarah Lee have not been edited for grammar.

These excerpts are written in her own words to allow the reader a more intimate understanding and shared cathartic experience of Ping Lian's life; as "Mummy" has experienced it. Entries from her personal journal show her name and year of entry.

SELF PORTRAIT 15201: PING LIAN YEAK WITH HIS NEIGHBOR'S ROOSTER IN MALAYSIA 2005

Painted in 2015 at Studio Artes in Sydney, Australia.

PING LIAN YEAK, WWW.PINGLIAN.COM
**Born in Malaysia – 18 November 1993
Residing in Sydney, Australia, since May 2006
Prodigious savant artist (Autistic)**

"*I Want To Be* ARTIST"

An Autistic Savant's Voice and
A Mother's Dream
Transformed onto Canvas

SARAH SH LEE

Edited by
DR. ROSA C. MARTINEZ

"I Want To Be Artist"
An Autistic Savant's Voice and A Mother's Dream Transformed onto Canvas
Sarah SH Lee

Copyright © 2017 Sarah SH Lee (Siew Hong Lee)

All rights reserved. This book or parts thereof may not be reproduced in any form, stored in any retrieval system, or transmitted in any form by any means—electronic, mechanical, photocopy, recording, or otherwise—without prior written permission of the author.

ISBN: 978-0-6480354-1-1

First Print 2017

Sarah SH Lee (PO Box 161, Roseville, NSW, 2069, Australia)

About Front Cover Photo
Ping Lian Yeak playing with his neighbour's rooster in Malaysia in 2005

Front cover designer
Sarah SH Lee & Jamie Soon (Malaysia)

Disclaimer
Some names and identifying details have been changed to protect the privacy of individuals.

CONTENTS

Foreword 1 An Inspiring "Miraculous Journey"......................................vii
Foreword 2 Ping Lian Yeak xi
Acknowledgement and Dynamics leading to the
 "birth" of this book..xiii
Introduction xxi

PART I
MY SON WITH AUTISM

Chapter 1 Ping Lian Says: "I Want To Be Artist"..1
Chapter 2 I Have a Special Son – My Awakening..................................27
Chapter 3 Getting Started With My Special Son..................................51
Chapter 4 Taking Action - Commit, Achieve and Be Happy 69
Chapter 5 Mummy Needs Motivation and
 Ping Lian Needs Motivation Too 107

PART II
PING LIAN'S ARTISTIC JOURNEY

Chapter 6 Ping Lian's Future and His Livelihood 129
Chapter 7 Year 2002 – Our Dream: To Develop Ping Lian to
 Be An Artist..141
Chapter 8 Ways and Means To Achieve Our Dream -
 Ping Lian Says "I Want To Be Artist" 163
Chapter 9 Renewal of Our Dream and Vision To "I'm a Dreamer".........189

PART III
LIFE ALTERING CHANGES

Chapter 10 Daddy In Memory 207
Chapter 11 The Joy of Achieving/Realizing a Dream 249
Chapter 12 "Come Here!"... Rooster 291

PART IV
PING LIAN ENTERS A NEW PHASE OF LIFE

Chapter 13 My Journey – USA and Dream To Go To Disney Land 311
Chapter 14 My Journey – Uprooted To Sydney, Australia 349
Chapter 15 My Journey – Malaysia & New Upgraded Dream 403
Chapter 16 What Does the Future Hold...? 427

Important Note 439

Epilogue Four years after the book was completed –
New updates: Summary Update 2015/2016.......................441

About the Author...447

About the Editor 451

SUMMARY INFORMATION OF PING LIAN YEAK -
My Artistic Journey 453

FOREWORD 1

An Inspiring "Miraculous Journey"
Dr. Darold A. Treffert

Children don't come with an owner's manual. So every parent is on their own when it comes to day to day operation, fuel, schedule for various fluid 'changes', overall care & maintenance and 'what-to-do-if' troubleshooting. That's a good thing because then each parent can form their own style of childrearing, individualized to each differently shaped soul given to them for tender, loving care.

And children with disabilities don't come with an owner's manual either. So once again the parent is left to develop their own style of dealing with that child, hopefully concentrating as much on strengths as on any deficits, and with the knowledge that love is a good therapist too.

I had the privilege of meeting Ping Lian and his family when they made the formidable trip across the world to Fond du Lac, Wisconsin, USA in 2007 for an art exhibit I had assembled called "Windows of Genius: Artwork of the Prodigious Savant". Ping Lian was a star at the exhibition, captivating the audience with his in-person "live and in color", instant, on-site production of beautiful artwork. If there is such a thing as perpetual motion in art, Ping Lian qualifies. He was the colorful, literally, energizer bunny of drawing and painting.

But what I also saw on-site, and in this book, was another beautiful work-in-progress—a mother with great patience, ingenuity, determination, optimism, pride, untiring spirit, perseverance, discipline, faith, hope and a dream carefully and lovingly helping to discover, tend, nourish, and then bring to full bloom whatever special gifts her child have might have, however buried and hidden they at first might have been.

This book then is an owner's manual of sorts, providing a chronicle of what did work— stylized but painfully slowly, for this mother, Sarah Lee, for her son Ping Lian in helping him on the road toward realizing his full potential as an artist. But even more importantly, helping him also to attain the best communication and social skills he could on the road toward eventually being as independent as possible.

In my work with savants I advise parents, teachers, therapists and whomever has contact with these special people to "train the talent" because with that comes better communication, social abilities and independent daily living skills. So this book is also an instruction manual for "training the talent" containing a multitude of useful 'for instances' from real life experience. For Sarah Lee Ping Lian's "I want to be an artist' wish was an achievable goal with his God-given special abilities. Obstacles were temporary opportunities to be overcome. A trip to the United States for an exhibit? Where does one get the funds? You ask an international courier company to help cover the costs of transporting the artworks to the United States and you ask the local airline to provide the tickets for such a worthy venture. And both proudly agree. Is it too high a goal to have Ping Lian's artwork on exhibit at the United Nations Headquarters in New York City or to have a permanent showcase of Ping Lian's works at the Art Commune in Malaysia? No. It is another opportunity, and with perseverance it happened.

Sarah Lee terms this a "miraculous journey". And indeed it is. Books by other parents about the journey from childhood to adult for their son or daughter with disabilities are usually retrospective recollections after the fact. But this book, because of the careful journal entries and copies of e mail and other correspondence kept diligently by Sarah Lee, as the journey happened, allows the reader to accompany she and her son on this journey contemporaneously tiny step by tiny step along the way. Mother acknowledges the change from blame and burden to privilege and "purpose". Other parents have shared with me that same transition, but none quite so personally and eloquently as Sarah Lee does in this book.

This book of course contains some of Ping Lian's remarkable drawings and paintings including some of my favorites. But it also contains some insights into 'the rest of the story' behind many of those works. And here we can see that Ping Lian is not just replicating what he sees like a copy machine, but instead he displays feelings and emotion such as humor, sometimes sadness, but mostly joy. Who says autistic persons are flat and without emotions? A careful look at Ping Lian's works dispels that myth. Further, in my journey with savants, I have seen a rather predictable but remarkable transition over time. They usually start with replication often with astounding precision. But then gradually improvisation occurs with a slight addition or deletion from a real-life scene. And finally creation of something entirely new occurs as the pinnacle of that remarkable transition. And Ping Lian is well along the way of that predictable passage. More surprises and fulfillment to follow.

We don't know the cause of autism. Hopefully some day we will. But this I do know. That within each child with autism, no matter how withdrawn and isolated he or she might be, there exists an "island of intactness" and it is our task, and opportunity, as parents, teachers or therapists to find that 'island of intactness', just as Sarah Lee did, and then tend it, reinforce it and 'train' it because with that comes improvement overall. For some that 'island of intactness' is an 'island of genius'—the prodigious savant—as it is with Ping Lian. The special ability, whatever it is, and however small or massive, is not a frivolous, "gee whiz, look at that" quirk or curiosity. It is the very language of that autistic person speaking out to us if we are astute enough to recognize it and inventive enough to 'train it'.

Until we know the cause of autism we will not be able to prevent it or cure it. But like Sarah Lee, our plea for a 'cure' can be modified instead to a dedication to 'help'. And this book is a manual on helping. The goal is not a cure, but instead the goal is to help each autistic person achieve his or her full potential and the highest social, communication and independent daily living skills as possible. In Ping Lian's case he went from a young boy who was non-verbal, with limited verbal skills, to being an artist at age 15 with his own art gallery. While that full measure may not be possible for every child with autism, such progress is possible in part at least in every instance and this book hopefully will inspire every parent to embark on that same journey of optimism and love for their child just a Sarah Lee did for hers. The results attest convincingly to the manner and worth of such a journey.

Darold A. Treffert, M.D.
www.savantsyndrome.com   www.daroldtreffert.com

Dr. Darold Treffert, *is Clinical Professor of Psychiatry at the University of Wisconsin School of Medicine in the U.S. He has worked with savants and researched this rare condition for nearly 50 years, and was a consultant on the award-winning movie 'Rain Man', in which Dustin Hoffman plays the role of an autistic savant.* His most recent publication, "Islands of Genius: The Bountiful Mind of the Autistic, Acquired and Sudden Savant", was published by Jessica Kingsley, Inc. in April 2010 in both the United States and England. It recently won gold in the Psychology/Mental Health Category at the 2011 Independent Publisher Book Awards and silver in the Psychology Category at the ForeWord 2011 Book of the Year Awards…. His earlier book, "*Extraordinary People:* Understanding the Savant Syndrome" was the first work to comprehensively summarize what is known about this fascinating condition, originally described a century ago, and to introduce the reader to a number of present day prodigious savants. In 2016, The Treffert Center opened on the campus of St. Agnes Hospital in Fond du Lac.

FOREWORD 2
Ping Lian Yeak
John McDonald

In his writings on *l'Art Brut* – 'Outsider Art' being the English-language term - Jean Dubuffet made a passionate case for those artists who remain outside of the institutional mainstreams. "Those works created from solitude and from pure and authentic creative impulses – where the worries of competition, acclaim and social promotion do not interfere – are, because of these very facts, more precious than the productions of professionals."

This description could have been made for Ping Lian Yeak, whose elaborate paintings and drawings are produced within a bubble of concentration that many mainstream artists might envy. We know enough about autism nowadays to understand that Ping Lian's condition is both a disability and an ability. Regardless of the difficulties he experiences with other tasks, when Ping Lian has a pencil or brush in hand he is alone with his motif, free from distractions and anxieties.

Many would-be artists have talent but lack the discipline necessary to make work of a consistently high standard. Ping Lian is a natural artist who responds to a motif with a complete lack of self-consciousness. When he paints the Sydney Opera House he is not thinking about all the other artists who have been there before him. He is not trying to compete with the Opera House pictures of well-known painters such as William Dobell or Brett Whiteley. His only concern is to capture the most vivid record of his chosen subject.

But perhaps it's not quite so simple. Because Ping Lian's verbal skills are limited he may be unable to discuss his ideas and motivations, but that does not mean he works in a purely mechanical fashion. In this book Sarah Lee points out the hidden faces and other figures found in many of her son's drawings, such as a *Swimming Pool* picture of 2004. Although speech may not come easily to Ping Lian his works testify to a lively imagination and a vibrant inner life. In many pieces he is not simply recording, but inventing. This ability to transform the everyday into the marvellous is a sign of the true artist. Technical ability can be learned, but imagination comes from deep within.

At first acquaintance with Ping Lian's work one is struck by its tremendous sense of detail and the wondrous, wristy line he employs. That line, so fluid and confident is Ping Lian's trademark – his unique signature style. One can learn a lot about an artist from the way he or she draws. Each drawing entails a complex interaction between eye, mind and hand. The lines of communication may be clumsy at the beginning, but with practice it becomes a matter of pure instinct. Ping Lian has arrived at that point where drawing has become a second language through which he conveys his thoughts and feelings. His cheerfulness and openness of heart are apparent at a glance, especially in his drawings of animals.

There can be no doubt that Ping Lian owes a debt to his 'tiger mother', Sarah, who recognised his talent at an early age and worked so tirelessly to help him develop his artistic facility. One need not share Sarah's faith in either God or motivational literature to realise she has found a set of techniques that have brought out the best in her son. She may prefer to give credit to the Supreme Being but it is her unconditional love, devotion and support that have turned this "poor boy" into an artist of formidable powers.

John McDonald is art critic for the Sydney Morning Herald & film critic for the Australian Financial Review

www.johnmcdonald.net.au

ACKNOWLEDGEMENT AND DYNAMICS LEADING TO THE "BIRTH" OF THIS BOOK

This book would not exist NOW without the encouragement and support of this special, amazing and inspirational lady- Dr. Rosa C. Martinez from New York, USA (Ping Lian and I call her Dr Rosa).

After Ping Lian's New York exhibition in 2006, I had been in touch with Dr. Rosa through email closely. Through my journey with Ping Lian, I had taken Dr. Rosa as my mentor, my friend and my very special partner in Ping Lian's Journey. She is so dear and special to us and no words can describe our gratefulness to her. She is considered as Ping Lian and my special angel that God sent to us, to help us walk through this special journey of Ping Lian's. I believe she is also a special angel to many other autistic people and their families too. I am so grateful that in life, I can get to know such a wonderful and amazing person like her… even more wondrous, is that she lives oceans apart from us. Yet, we still can be so connected and she still can continuously, tirelessly support us and help us over the past few years without asking for anything in return. … How beautiful is it, that in this world… though people may be far apart… they can still connect, support and encourage one another in such an amazing way? Read more in the story of the next few chapters … and you will know how special Dr. Rosa is in our life's journey… and how she contributed so tremendously toward who Ping Lian is today… People always tell me that I am so admirable for the way I have brought Ping Lian to where he is today… but my reply is always the same.. Ping Lian and I would never be "so good " ... without the support of our many special God sent angels. Dr Rosa C. Martinez is definitely one of those angels, and is the very special one. We will also, always be grateful to Dr. Darold Treffert and Yvonne Hon... two more very special, God sent angels, plus many more angels in our journey.

This book started when one day I emailed Dr. Rosa to share with her that *something* was troubling me...... and I sensed something "big" was going to happen in my life. However, this time it was different...it was about me (meaning the focus was on me) and not just about Ping Lian... I was concerned about that and doubted if I was able to cope or even willing to cope.....I then shared some short stories I wrote about some of Ping Lian's art works and she offered to edit them for me...(In fact almost everything I wrote, she helped me to edit; and without any fees, ...she did it for free). Dr. Rosa was so interested in everything I wrote, and so eager to hear more, that she recommended and prompted me to write a book! Thus, ...the birth of this book.

I always knew that Ping would have a very unique journey. I knew that one day Ping Lian's unique story would be written into a book. "… One Day, someone will come to me to write the book about my son";.... But I always thought I would wait and that ONE DAY when I am old and have some time, I will tell the story to someone and he or she will write the book.

But, on 6-6-2006, I emailed Dr Rosa …"......This evening my thoughts just kept going around and around. I am unsettled by a sense that something big is going to happen for me & Ping Lian, but I do not know What or When... It seems to be related to us being here at Sydney.... It is not the first time I have these feelings, but lately it just keeps getting stronger..... I just feel that one day Ping Lian will be an "important/special" person, and me too..... but I ask myself, why ME? I am not that special... though I am confident in my own way. I just can't believe that "I" too may become

Acknowledgement and Dynamics leading to the "birth" of this book xv

important ..., but yet I see this blurred picture about myself in the future and I have so much doubt that how can it be Me too... I just ask How could it be...and What is it about... anyway as much as I felt bothered by this......I feel good that I am able to put it aside after sharing this with u..."

In another email to her...:"....Too many things happen in such special way & I realize that my intuitive/ sensing feelings are getting stronger.... I always ask lately, "What is God actually leading me & Ping Lian to? What does He plan for us?...."

One of Dr. Rosa's replies:

> ".... this has prompted another idea in my mind. Ping Lian has so many works. Why not publish his own book of art works as well?...... It would also be wonderful to include all of your excerpts. Your thoughts and "dreams". Sarah, this is a best seller! I believe this may be where your intuition of fame comes in. You are such an inspiration and an inspirational writer. You were meant to pen this story with your words and Ping Lian's pictures..."
>
> "....you should write the story on your own... Yes! You can do it....You can do it on your own, and do it right NOW! I will support you and help you with the book..."

Her short and simple mail had touched me, inspired me, motivated me and moved me. So, I discussed it with my daughter... and I replied to Dr. Rosa, "...I shared your suggestion with Cher (my youngest daughter), surprisingly she agreed that we do indeed have an interesting story to tell. Even though she knew that I am weak at my English language, she asks me to go for it ... at such young age (15), she said "Yes! Dr Rosa is right, you should write it yourself NOW! And you don't need to wait till one day when you are old... and have time...". And ... I am even more surprise, she said the same thing...said it could be a best seller too. I did not tell her that you said the same thing. Surprise! Surprise! It seems to be I must go for it. – The story of Ping Lian's art works and journey…"

That is how the book came about and it took me and Dr. Rosa together six years to complete the whole book (completed in 2012). I am so very grateful to Dr Rosa. I did it… with the help and support of Dr Rosa. Though it took 6 years… and I am not that old yet.

Throughout the process of writing this book, Dr Rosa has been more than an Editor… My whole family is very grateful to her for her support in our journey with Ping Lian and the birth of this book.

I would also like to take this opportunity to thank other individuals and organizations who have been very special in our lives, who have impacted our lives and have supported and encouraged us. My love and hugs go to all of you who have been part of our journey … … and I would like to specifically mention a few below:

- My parent, mother in law (all already passed away) and my late husband – Thanks for everything you have done for me. I believe you are all smiling from heaven seeing what Ping Lian and I have come to achieve thus far. Special thanks to my Mom for nurturing me into a beautiful kind lady with wisdom, pride, dignity, love and compassion. Special thanks to my late husband for constantly exposing me to positive thinking and personal development reading materials.
- My daughters Sher Lyn and Cher Lyn– thanks for all of your endless understanding and support and thank you for forgiving my seemingly "neglect" to you; .. and thanks for loving and caring for Ping Lian… etc
- My sisters, brothers and brothers in law and sisters in law…and nieces and nephews- Thanks for you all are always there for me whenever I need you.

- Dr Laurence Becker… Thank you for bringing the most wonderful lady; Dr Rosa C. Martinez into Ping Lian's life and mine as well.
- Catherine Chew – Thanks for imparting your wisdom, vision and your continuous prayers for Ping Lian and my family in our journey. Also thanks for guiding me and leading me on my journey in trusting God, have Faith in God and constantly reminding me to look up to and be obedient to God's Plan and Purpose for Ping Lian and myself.
- All the Organizations that have supported or sponsored us - to name a few: JP Morgan, Malaysia Airlines, ABWM(Association of British Women in Malaysia), DHL, Crown Relocations, MPSJ Malaysia (Subang Jaya Municipal Council), Shell Malaysia, Tourism Malaysia, (**SHFA**) **Sydney Harbour Foreshore Authority (special thanks to the team from The Rocks Markets),** SP Setian Foundation, Albukhary Foundation, Strokes of Genius, Inc (SOG)) plus many more.
- Thanks to Tan Sri Liew Kee Sin, Datuk Eddy Leong & their friends. Thanks to Pak Yap Lim Sen. Your support has changed Ping Lian's life and indirectly changed my family life as well.
- Temple Grandin- Thanks to your story and books. The first autism book I read was about you. Your story has inspired me a lot. So positive, insightful, beautiful and full of hope….and the knowledge and wisdom I gained from your story has given me so much confidence, courage and hope, that I have managed to use wisely in my journey with Ping Lian. All this has contributed to what Ping Lian has attained to date.
- Thanks to all of Ping Lian's teachers, therapists and art collectors.
- Pr4A and friends and members from Pr4A… Thanks for your valuable time in sharing your knowledge about autism when I first came to know about autism… and sharing with me on What is

ABA (Applied Behavior Analysis)… thanks to ABA program … this helped to teach me how to start off my 'teaching/nurturing" of Ping Lian; at a time when he seemed to be my "terrible" and "hopeless" Ping Lian.

- My deepest gratitude is extended to Dr. Rosa C. Martinez, Yvonne Hon, Dr. Darold Treffert and *myself!* As you read this book, the reasons for these praises will be evident.
- Thanks to Dr. Darold Treffert – Thanks for being my mentor. Thanks for everything you have done and continue to do for us; thanks for your encouragement, guidance and leadership, etc … and thanks for sharing your knowledge and wisdom with us (His contributions to this journey are clearly outlined and when you read the book you will know what I am thanking him for). Thank you for your book and your research, from which I have truly benefited. Ping Lian would not have the success he celebrates today without you… the first expert I come to know and to learn from and who encouraged me…You and Dr. Rosa have both kept me inspired and excited about Ping Lian's Journey. Thank you both for being my mentors.
- Thanks to Yvonne Hon, your family and The Art Commune. … Aunty Yvonne, you are a super woman. We appreciate you and admire you. Thanks for setting up the gallery for Ping Lian at Malaysia. Thanks for many more things you do for us/ Ping Lian. No words can describe my gratefulness to you and your family. Thanks to Billy Leong and The Settlement Hotel for taking over the permanent showcase of Ping Lian's art in Melaka Malaysia.
- Thanks to Dr Darold Treffert and John Macdonald for such beautiful and complimentary forewords.
- Many, many thanks to my beautiful baby, Ping Lian Yeak. Regardless of his age… he and his sisters will always be "my babies". Regardless

of who Ping Lian is, as long as he is happy and I am happy, that has always been enough for me. Yes, he is now a tall and handsome adult but still in much area he seem to have the mind of a small boy with autism and intellectual disabilities, and he still enjoys being "my baby."

- ..."Ping Lian, because of you, your sisters and I have become better people. We are more loving, more compassionate, more understanding and are very patient individuals. Through you, we have experienced a more meaningful, purposeful and amazing life. Without your amazing character ... this book would never exist. Without your amazing journey I would be unaware of the true meaning of life. That is why this book is so important and I am compelled to share this wealth of knowledge.

There are those who feel sorry about what we as a family have had to endure, and the sacrifice to me personally. Quite frankly, I took what was handed to me and figured "life goes on" as usual. Since I viewed my life as "normal", for my family, it became "our normal". As a whole, I did not really feel sorry for myself, although when I looked back as I was writing this book, I often dropped a tear. Living it, was one thing, but reliving it and putting it down in writing so permanently etched in front of me, often resulted in sadness and crying. However, now I rejoice in the fact that Ping Lian has grown to become such a wonderful young adult. Ping Lian, you have made life easier and happier for me with each passing day.... As you are now such a loving, caring, grateful, patient and helpful son to me, you have become my best company.

I thank God for His LOVE, wisdom, guidance, favor, grace, abundant provisions, blessing and protection. I also thank God for giving me the privilege of living in such a purposeful and meaningful life; although at times it has been extremely tough.

"Thank you" to many more individuals and organizations who are not mentioned individually here for being part of Ping Lian's life and for having a positive impact on our family.

Thanks to all the good and positive messages of encouragement that I have received in my life from all people. Special thanks for all the messages of Love, Peace, Kindness and Hope…

Last but not least, I thank myself, through God for my hard work and perseverance… and my many "sacrifices" - throughout many facets of my life…including having given up my initial passion to work in a field that I enjoyed and excelled in. That career was bringing much bigger financial rewards. It was a faster and easier means of life. However, now I am happy with my decision and happy with my "sacrifices". I have come to realize that my initial "so-called" scarifies for my children have lead me to understand a deeper meaning and purpose of life …My initial sacrifices… later became what I loved. They even turned out to be what I really wanted. With regard to writing this book, due to my weakness in the English language, every paragraph and chapter in this book took so long for me to write. I read and write very slowly in English. Completing this entire book was in fact yet another struggle for me. I sacrificed a lot of my social and leisure time… but finally, seeing the book completed… brings me so much joy, satisfaction and a feeling of achievement. With this satisfaction, however comes an uneasiness when I think of the many facets of my personal life that are now public. The sacrifice was my privacy. I will soon feel "naked" in front of someone who has read this book. Yet, knowing that I have accomplished this publication, this "calling" that I was meant to "pen"; I truly hope that our story can help many. The "so-called sacrifices" were well worth it.

" I love you all… you all are so special to me!"

INTRODUCTION
Dr. Rosa C. Martinez

This book is a non-fictional account of the inspirational journey of a young boy with severe autism and an extremely low IQ who has been empowered by his single, widowed mother to become a successful artist and a well behaved young man who exhibits empathy and affection. This journey is about helplessness, fear, death, desperation, love, courage and the faith of a family, all culminating in a triumphant journey.

Ping Lian Yeak was born in Malaysia on November 18, 1993. At the age of three, came the seemingly defeating diagnosis of autism. As a toddler Ping Lian was non verbal, hyperactive, living in his own world, not showing affection or awareness of danger, unable to hold a pencil to write or to use a scissor to cut.

"I Want To Be Artist": An Autistic Savant's Voice and A Mother's Dream Transformed Onto Canvas is the story of a mother's desperate struggle to get her autistic son to "*see*" her; to "*love*" his family and to be a contributing member to society. This "journey" was carefully recorded in Sarah Lee's journal, where she wrote her innermost thoughts as an outlet for her emotions. Readers will be fortunate to capture not just the turmoil but the "life lessons" and strategies created out of Sarah Lee's desperation that have led to her son's success.

In an effort to maintain the deep emotional content of this book some excerpts written by Sarah Lee have not been edited for grammar. These excerpts are written in her own words to allow the reader a more intimate understanding and shared cathartic experience of Ping Lian's life; as "Mummy" has experienced it. Throughout the book, entries from her personal journal show her name and year of entry.

Also, please note that the title "I Want To Be Artist" – may be considered grammatically incorrect. However, it is written as it was spoken by the artist Ping Lian. Due to his autism, Ping Lian does not use articles such as the word "an" artist. Some of his mother's spoken language is also purposely shortened in order to make it easier for Ping Lian to understand the spoken words.

- March 2003 - Ping Lian's mother wrote in her journal - *"I want to develop Ping Lian to be an Artist, I know he will be an Artist one day"*….. And I get Ping Lian to say *"I Want to be an Artist"* every day as a way to "brainwash" him….
- *Feb 2004 - Ping Lian's father passed away due to a sudden heart attack. Ping Lian not only lost his dad but his only male friend. His Mum was left to raise her 3 children (10 year old Ping Lian, 12 year old Cher, 16 year old Sherlyn) and to care for their 79 year old grandmother.*
- November 2004 - Ping Lian's work, "Ubudiah Mosque I "was donated to Riding for the Disabled Association, Malaysia charity auction. It sold for MYR 100,000.00. 100% of the proceeds were donated. (Ping Lian was 11 years old!)
- May 2006 – Ping Lian's mom chose to uproot her family and move to Sydney and start a life there with no existing friends or relatives.

This book is a must read *internationally*. Autism occurs globally across all nationalities. Prevalence rates in just the U.S. have increased from 1 in 10,000 births in the 1970's to 1 in 55 in the current year. The contents of this book can easily be translated into various languages to reach a global population. Autism carries different meanings in different societies. However the notion of *enabling* and *training* a talent coupled with instilling love is not a bullet point you may come across in any cultures definition

or methodology when "treating" autism. For example: "In urban areas of South Korea, some families of children with developmental delays will go to great lengths to avoid a diagnosis of *chapae*, or autism. They think of it as a genetic mark of shame on the entire family, and a major obstacle to all of their children's chances of finding suitable spouses. The stigma is so intense that some Korean clinicians intentionally misdiagnose these children with *aechak changae*, or reactive detachment disorder — social withdrawal that is caused by extreme parental abuse or neglect."
http://sfari.org/news-and-opinion/news/2011/researchers-track-down-autism-rates-across-the-globe

Most importantly, this book is not solely intended to be of interest to families, parents, teachers, and professionals in the autism community, but also of interest to the general public.

This book focuses on the strategies used to "educate" a young boy with autism. Although his mother, Sarah Lee was guided by instinct, many of her approaches are comparable to the strategies that are empirically based scientific principles of behavior. Universities would benefit by including this book on their required reading list to educate future educators about the "abilities" of special education youngsters in contrast to the disabilities.

This book is not just about autism. It is a compelling story of faith and triumph, full of insightful advice that may transport any reader from a state of hopelessness to one of positive outcomes. Sarah Lee focused all of her energy on what she learned from personal development speakers and books and used it to mould a positive future for herself and her family. The content is a message of one mother's triumph for developing a skill, training a talent and developing good character in her autistic son, who possessed only one interest,… drawing! It describes in detail the journey from a boy who appeared "disconnected" from the world (including his mother) to a boy who now experiences sentiment and love. It describes the journey of a boy who had poor fine motor skills, to a boy who becomes a renowned artist and is highly recognized in the United States. The main focus of the book is how this mother followed her instincts and successfully "trained the talent" in her severely autistic youngster enabling him to develop a passion and skill with the aim of resulting in his own livelihood. The mother speaks of her ignorance of the "autism" diagnosis and the scarcity of resources in Malaysia. Thus the target audience includes families on the autism spectrum, siblings, teachers, art instructors, therapists, professionals and the general public. This is the story of a mother who decided to forgo her successful career as a senior sales and marketing manager, sold her house to support her family, nurtured the interests of her severely autistic son and thus succeeded in bringing her son's artistic talent to the United States including the United Nations, Carnegie Hall, NY Chelsea's art mecca and more! Most chapters include a "motivational quote" written by Sarah Lee which she created, posted and lived by. The book has components that steer the reader towards life coaching and self-help skills. All this is written in an endearing, delightful and infectious manner by Sarah Lee. It is a joy to read and should appeal to a wide audience. In general, this is a positive and inspiring family story that is hard to put down once you start reading.

There are many books on individuals with autism; artworks by individuals with autism; personal stories of individuals with autism, etc. This story however, is presented from a very different perspective. The book does not simply showcase the art. "I Want To Be Artist" – showcases the inspirational path to ability and love. It showcases the power of *dreams* and how ones determination can change a situation that appears *Impossible*, to become *Possible*. Sarah Lee engages us in a journey that originates in hopelessness and culminates in celebrating victories.

This book is different because it is NOT just about teaching a skill. No other book (to my knowledge) is about teaching and instilling emotions! Ping Lian was taught to love others, to have a sense of community, to love to paint and to have pride! These qualities are not mechanical responses to any specific antecedents, but rather they are genuine "emotions" that are obvious in his everyday actions.

This mother writes about "how" she "trained" the talent in her son. It may very well be the first book that discusses the parents' journey regarding "how" she trained the talent. Sarah Lee successfully "brainwashed" her son to succeed in *her* dream for him. "Brainwashed" is the term used by Sarah Lee light-heartedly, yet compellingly. She attended personal development seminars and adapted them to suit her needs in "training" her son to have an interest in art and to be a good helper at home. The book describes her beliefs, her isolation and her endless pursuit resulting in "....an Artist and a good helper at home". In addition it is not just a book about her son's art, but includes the story behind each artwork. For every single artwork of this prolific youngster, there is an amazing story.

Due to his mother's perseverance, Ping Lian has matured into an obedient, hardworking, and grateful young adult. Ping Lian continues to have very limited communication and social skills but art has provided him with an outlet of expression and opportunities to be an integrated, contributing member of society. Today, Ping Lian is a talented artist full of love and affection, living a purposeful and meaningful life with his Mom and sisters. His unique style of bold strokes and cheerful color in his artworks has won over many art enthusiasts and collectors.

Sarah Lee continues to strongly maintain a positive outlook and is committed to her philosophy that "happiness is a conscious choice". Find out from the book how she was able to achieve that freedom to be happy despite all of the barriers.

Reading this book will no doubt change many mindsets and expose you to the possibilities of unlocking, training and fostering a skill set that exists within each of us, including those of an individual with autism. You will discover the power of your own inner strength as the most important asset and tool essential for further development in your child as well as in yourself. The book is not a list of essential techniques to master, but rather a narrative of one mother's unconventional approach to make her son develop from a youngster with extremely limited fine motor skills into a fine artist. Sarah Lee dug deep into her soul to create "abilities" in her son Ping Lian.

Throughout the book you will also encounter many slogans or catchy phrases quoted or written by Sarah Lee. These were the quotes that served as some of Sarah Lee's motivators and aided her to continually move forward even when she was catapulted ten steps backward. One of the more common quotes that Sarah Lee often utilized was the "kill 2 birds with one stone" (accomplish two tasks with one effort) philosophy.

Throughout the text you may see the following bird symbol, denoting her use of this particular strategy at a specific point in her life.

Dr. Rosa C. Martinez, Ph.D., BCBA-D is the President and founder of Strokes of Genius, Inc
www.strokesofgeniusinc.org

PART I
MY SON WITH AUTISM

CHAPTER 1
Ping Lian Says: "I Want To Be Artist"

PING LIAN AT THE AGE OF 9

"I want to be artist" said Ping Lian, loud, clear and with confidence. He was nine years old and still had very limited communication skills. Unprompted, he would usually respond to questions using only one or two words. Yet, he responded "I want to be artist" loud and clear! This could be the longest sentence Ping Lian has ever spoken so confidently and spontaneously.

Ping Lian had uniqueness in his voice and mannerisms whenever he said "I want to be artist". Our family enjoyed this very much and really looked forward to hearing and watching how cute he looked when he said it.

While in our living room, I asked Ping Lian "Who do you want to be when you grow up?" Ping Lian answered "I want to be artist". I would prompt him by modeling strong body gestures like lifting up my arms with my fists closed tight. I would raise my arms high, as if to show muscle and to portray strength. I would show Ping Lian that I am "able" and "powerful" and pair these gestures with a positive joyful tone of voice. Often times my daughters, Cher and Sherlyn would laugh at me. Cher would say "Mummy, Ping Lian does not know what 'artist' means". Sherlyn would say "Mummy, Ping Lian does not understand the meaning of …'when you grow up'!"

Whenever I asked Ping Lian "Who is artist?" he would respond "Artist use paint brush". When I asked "What does artist do?" he would answer "Artist use paint brush." I used pictures of an artist painting, in order to help teach Ping Lian to repeat these responses. The vocal responses were taught by using scripted responses during his ABA (applied behavior analysis) discrete trial drills[1] for the particular programs of "Who" and "What?" As I would point to a picture, each drill was to be as follows: Question: "Who is he?" and Ping Lian should answer "artist", "What does artist do?" ….."Artist paint picture"; "What does artist use to paint?"………. "Artist use paint brush".

I had been teaching these drills for quite some time already, but Ping Lian was not getting it! Whenever I asked him questions related to the artist, his answer was always "Artist use paint brush". Ping Lian did not really understand the concept of "who" or "what", but he would always try his best to respond appropriately through memorization.

Ping Lian does not really understand the meaning of abstract words such as "when", "yesterday", "today" or "tomorrow". He does not understand concepts such as "past" and "future". He does however have a consistent understanding for the specific words "later" and "wait". "Later" is like a *magic* word that I can use effectively when I need Ping Lian to show patience by waiting his turn or to "wait" to receive something he desires.

For over five years I had also attempted to teach Ping Lian the days of the week. I would drill him constantly with "Monday through Sunday" and "yesterday, today and tomorrow". Although he has learned to recite the days of the week in sequence, and he can say "after Monday is Tuesday", "after Tuesday is Wednesday" these words have no meaning for Ping Lian. He will recite the days of the week melodiously as if singing, but when I say

---

1   Discrete trial training (DTT) is a method of teaching in which the adult uses adult- directed, massed trial instruction, reinforcers chosen for their strength, and clear contingencies and repetition to teach new skills.

to him "Today is Monday, What day is tomorrow?" he cannot answer. If I tell him that we are going shopping "tomorrow", he does not understand. It is now obvious to me that Ping Lian has been unable to understand these questions because he lacks an understanding of the abstract terms and does not have a sense of past and future yet. My daughters know very well the frustration I have experienced in being unable to get Ping Lian to grasp such concepts. They would repeatedly say to me "Mummy, he doesn't understand *what 'artist' means* and he does not understand the meaning of *when you grow up*!"

> To achieve the so called "Impossible" requires the spirit to…Dare to Dream, Believe, Make Decisions, and to Take Immediate Action along with a Burning Desire to achieve it

Still, my response to my daughters was always the same…. "Yes. I know he does not understand this, but it does not matter right now". They both tell me "Mom! You are just 'brain wash' him", and I tell them "Yes, I am. That is my purpose. To 'brain wash' him and to hope that one day he can understand. I am 'brain washing' him to become an artist one day!" My husband, Min Seng Yeak would laugh and say "Your Mom is crazy" and we would all laugh. Anyway, this exchange would always put us all in a "crazy" but happy mood. At times I would actually ask myself "Am I really crazy, wanting to 'brain wash' my son into something he does not really understand?"

It has been a long journey from the time when Ping Lian was unable to hold a pencil to write, or even to use crayons to color. At present, not only does he write, but he has a special interest and is very skilled at drawing. Ping Lian had finally outgrown tracing and was suddenly showing a real interest in scribbling and drawing independently. His interest and willingness was so meticulous and passionate that it appeared to be an obsession. Ping Lian loved drawing and he enjoyed going to his art classes very much. Ping Lian's deep motivation and interest in drawing lead me to the following viewpoint… "Who cares if he understands or not. I will just continue to 'brain wash' him and hope that one day he will love being an artist. Isn't it possible that simply by him continually saying it maybe someday he will understand and will actually want to be an artist?"

Thus, I continued trying to use my own approach to prepare Ping Lian to work toward becoming an artist, knowing that people may laugh at me and the "little white lie" that I have planted in his mind as well as in mine. That is Ok to me, I am happy to have this 'white lie'. At the very least this "little white lie" keeps us happy and gives us hope. Who knows, maybe these thoughts will become embedded in Ping Lian's subconscious mind and a miracle might happen, or maybe God will hear Ping Lian say "I want to be artist" so often, that He will grant Ping Lian a miracle.

A good friend of mine once advised me to weigh the worst case scenario when having difficulty making a decision. "What do you have to lose?" she would say. I told myself that the worst case scenario might be that Ping Lian will never be an artist. Yet, looking at the brighter side of this "white lie" scenario… our family enjoys many happy times; acting crazy, playing games, sharing laughter and being ridiculous. It provides a hope that keeps me happy for the time being. It adds something positive, something to look forward to.

> Sometimes it is fun to have "crazy" thoughts & it is fun and happy to be "crazy"

Chapter 1: Ping Lian Says: "I Want To Be Artist"

"Sometimes it is fun to have "crazy" thoughts & it is fun and happy to be "crazy". This statement had become a good motivator for me to instill more effort in Ping Lian. It provided a justification for the investment of my time, energy and money in this area. On the flipside, the worst outcome might be; that I am happy that Ping Lian has developed a hobby he loves; an outlet to express himself, and something meaningful to keep him occupied. In any case, I am not that pessimistic. In the back of my mind I knew that with my 'brain washing' approach, the special interests Ping Lian already possessed and the special training provided to him at such a young age might not necessarily result in Ping Lian becoming a "recognized artist". Still, the worst case scenario could be that he may one day become a "road side artist".

At the time – I thought "I have the patience to wait for 5, 10 or maybe even 20 years. I am prepared to accept the worst case scenario in that I will be happy if Ping Lian only achieves the status of a "road side artist". So long as art can serve as an appropriate leisure skill for him when he grows up, that would still be a great outcome. I have always believed that something is better than nothing. Ping Lian has plenty of time to work on this goal of recognition as an artist. In ten more years he will still only be 19 years old." So, without hesitation, I move on to "brain wash" him with this "white lie" and look forward to the best for him while I am also prepared to accept the worst.

So, when I ask Ping Lian "*Who* do you want to be when you grow up?"…. "I want to be artist" is a beautiful response! After all, watching him draw and paint, I know that he loves it. I remain optimistic. So asking Ping Lian "Who do you want to be when you grow up?" had become our daily and happy time "brain washing" game.

In our living room these games are still going on with Ping Lian. I ask him again "Who do you want to be when you grow up?" Ping Lian will once again say "I want to be artist", loud and clear. I would hug him and kiss him and say "You are a clever boy". To make it interesting, I would vary my rewards to him, sometimes playing "give me five", while other times carrying him around and playing jumping games. Many times in order to try to get him to love and enjoy saying "I want to be artist" or to answer my question quickly and spontaneously, I would play a "special horse riding" game with him as a reward. With my hands and my knees on the floor, I would act as a horse and let him sit on my back. Ping Lian would remain seated on my back and "ride" for several rounds. He absolutely loved these games we played.

During these times our living room was always so full of joy and laughter. Sherlyn, Cher and Min Seng would watch and laugh. Sometimes, Cher and Sherlyn also wanted to ride on me. Although Sherlyn was really too old and too big, I couldn't let her feel left out. I would give her a few seconds of a quick "horsie" ride. Sometimes Ping Lian and Cher couldn't even wait their turn and I would have the two of them on my back at the same time. They just loved these games. I think back to how crazy it was for me, that after a hard day of work at the office, I would come home to play "horsie" to make them happy in an attempt to get Ping Lian to love to say "I want to be artist". I sometimes wondered where did I get my energy from! Anyway even though it was hard and tiring, I did enjoy this part of my life a lot. The anticipated thought of rewards to come for Ping Lian's future as an artist has always been worth it.

During these earlier years, I suppose that Ping Lian did not really understand the actual meaning of the terms "I want to be artist" and "when I grow up". However, I am convinced that today (2007) Ping Lian knows what it means to be an artist and his responses are purposeful and have meaning. I can see the pride in his eyes and his eagerness to have others view what he has created when he paints. It has been a long journey from the time when Ping Lian was unable to hold a pencil to write. He has outgrown tracing. He can now write and he can now paint with exceptional strokes.

Chapter 1: Ping Lian Says: "I Want To Be Artist" 7

PICTURE DRAWN BY PING LIAN IN
2002 AT THE AGE OF 8

Ping Lian half drew and half traced this drawing.

"05411 MY DOG II"

This is our family dog, Crystal. She is a golden retriever. Although we only have one dog; Ping Lian painted Crystal with three different expressions. Ping Lian had painted a few pieces of "My Dog" with one or two happy faces but yet another one that appeared not so happy, perhaps stubborn and in darker colors. Crystal died from rat poisoning on March 8, 2006. Ping Lian misses his dog very much and asks "Where is Crystal?" I tell him that Crystal had gone for a "long sleep". This is how I previously described the death of my husband to Ping Lian and the death of my mother-in-law. I told Ping Lian that Daddy and Ah-Mah went for a "long sleep". After Ping Lian's Daddy and grandmother passed away, Ping Lian appeared to understand the meaning of "long sleep". Yet after the many times of explaining to him that Crystal had gone for a "long sleep", Ping Lian would still continually ask "Where is Crystal?"

The last time Ping Lian saw Crystal, she was very sick and Cher was taking her to the veterinarian. Since then, Crystal never came back. In an effort to avoid the emotional situation for Ping Lian, I did not allow him to go to Crystal's burial. During that time Sherlyn was already attending Sydney University in Australia and I had just had some surgery and needed to stay home. Instead, a few of Sherlyn's friends accompanied Cher to Crystal's burial.

05411 MY DOG II - 56X76CM, ACRYLIC ON PAPER
PING LIAN PAINTED IN 2005 AT THE AGE OF 11

Look at "05411 My Dog II". Have you ever seen such a colorful Golden Retriever? When Ping Lian says again "I want to be artist", what do you think? Do you think at this stage he understands the meaning of artist?

Soon after, with my husband and my mother-in-law no longer with us, I made a decision to move from Malaysia to Sydney, Australia. In the midst of our preparations to uproot and move to Sydney, as Crown Relocations was packing our furniture, belongings and Ping Lian paintings, Ping Lian once again began asking with perseverance "Where's Crystal?" and I continually replied "Crystal went for long sleep". Regardless of my attempts to relate Crystal's death to the death of Ping Lian's father and his grandmother, Ping Lian continued to ask the same question again and again and again. I really did not know what message he was trying to convey to me. Still, later as we approached our actual departure date (6th May 2006) and Ping Lian realized our house was being emptied and our luggage was packed, he began getting more anxious. "Where is Crystal?" he persisted while continually pointing toward the outside of the house and saying "There, there". His escalating anxiety was clear. I felt so sorry that I did not know what he really wanted to say. I have tried very hard to make sense of his communication attempts. Despite the infinite times I explained to him about Crystal's death and tried leading him to tell me what he wanted, the result was always the same. He would only repeat these two phrases again and again. "Where is Crystal?", "There, there".

This continued for many days. At that time, I was very busy and emotionally overwhelmed with moving. Ping Lian kept coming to me and asking the same question again and again. I finally felt very irritated and told him to leave me alone. He eventually stopped, probably due to his understanding that I did not know what he wanted to tell me. He finally gave up asking but I have always felt so bad that Ping Lian could not express what he wanted to tell me and I felt guilty and sorry that I did not understand my son. I thought "… could it be that due to his lack of communication skills, saying 'Where is Crystal' is his way of communicating that he misses and is thinking of Crystal?" I just don't know what else he wants to convey to me. At this stage, Ping Lian is still not able to talk about his feelings and frustrations, nor is he able to answer questions like "Why?"

I could only guess what Ping Lian intended when he kept saying "Where is Crystal?"

- Maybe he wanted to tell me that we visited Daddy and Ah-Mah at the cemetery and we visited many relatives and friends before leaving for Sydney, but we did not visitCrystal.
- Maybe because he did not see Crystal's burial, he did not really understand the meaning of death and "long sleep" for Crystal. Possibly he thought that Crystal was not yet dead and he was just looking for Crystal to say bye-bye to her before we move.
- Maybe he was just asking "Are we taking Crystal along to Sydney?"
- Maybe he wanted to tell me to "Please take Crystal to Sydney"
- Maybe he was trying to remind me that I forgot to take Crystal.
- Maybe he simply wanted to convey the simple message "I miss Crystal."

My poor Ping Lian! I am so sorry that I really do not know what it is that you so desperately were trying to tell me … but however I do know from your paintings of "My Dog" series, that you experienced much emotion. Looking at your paintings, I have come to realize and understand that you are aware that Crystal is at times tame, happy, cheeky, stubborn or unhappy. I am blessed when I see your paintings. In your paintings I see how much you "do understand, experience and know about emotion."

PING LIAN DRAWING AND PAINTING OUR FAMILY DOG
IN 2005 AT THE AGE OF 11

05420 MY DOG IV – PAINTED IN 2005

05410 MY DOG I - 50X61CM, ACRYLIC ON CANVAS - PAINTED AT THE AGE OF 11

This is Ping Lian's dog Crystal. He painted one dog with two expressions. "At times my dog is stubborn, angry and unhappy because at times everybody is too busy with their life and no one seems to bother with Crystal." "At times my dog is so happy and cheeky because we give him attention. He is just happy and invites you to play with him." "Do you notice that my dog's eye is following you in whichever direction you are going?" Looking at this dog painting, I am sure that Ping Lian knows/ understands about feelings (2005).

SUNFLOWER PAINTINGS - 2005

05504 – SUNFLOWERS I

05505 – SUNFLOWERS II

05506 - SUNFLOWERS III

Ever since Ping Lian was able to trace and sketch, his favorite subjects have been sunflowers, hippos, the Statue of Liberty, the Eiffel Tower and horses. His painting, "Sunflower I" was the result of our encouraging Ping Lian to use acrylic paints without providing his usual water and brush. As anyone with a child on the autism spectrum knows – changing the routine can be a devastating experience. Flexibility and change did not come easy for Ping Lian.

In December of 2005, his art instructor Mr. Tan, from "My Favorite Art House" believed it was time for Ping Lian to move on in his art technique regarding use of medium. Instead of the watercolor materials, Ping Lian was given acrylic paints and a painting blade. We decided that since it would be Ping Lian's first time using acrylics at "My Favorite Art House" without a brush and water that selecting his favorite subject to paint would make this transition easier for him to accept and hopefully an enjoyable experience. At first, Ping Lian was uneasy and not at all happy. He stared at the acrylic paints, the blade and the paint cloth and repeatedly said "water, water, water". The usual struggle resulting from a change in routine now ensued. We explained to Ping Lian that "Today is different". He would only have a blade and paint, "no brush" and "no water." We explained to him that he can use the cloth to clean the blade to replace the water.

Ping Lian would usually come to his art classes in a calm and obedient state. He would not idly get up from his seat, nor spend time walking around. However, on this day he would not follow the art teacher's instructions or even my directions. He kept trying to run off to the toilet to get water and searched for brushes throughout the classroom. It was necessary to call him back several times. Ping Lian was very quick and very persistent so I needed to run after him and consistently bring him back to his seat. After several such episodes and much struggling, I gave him an ultimatum. Either "no art class today" or "go for it" and use what you have. Ping Lian finally started to paint. After what at first seemed to be the start of an endless futile battle, he finally chose to settle down and to accept what was presented to him to paint with. I was really very amazed with the new decrease in the duration of his "stubbornness". I attribute the speed with which he accepted the ultimatum and adapted to the changes to his love of painting.

Ping Lian loves his art classes. I see a happy and confident person in him when he draws and paints. Given the fact that we took away his "routine" work materials and presented a totally new set up, we were all very surprised with the outcome of Ping Lian's first acrylic painting without the use of a brush and water. This art lesson turned out to be a life lesson for Ping Lian. It paved the way for another new break through for Ping Lian in both, his artistic skills and his social responses to changes in life. After seeing his Sunflower I we encouraged him to paint more, resulting in Sunflower II and III as a series. Ping Lian put forth such positive energy in painting this way and he really enjoyed it.

It is no longer a struggle for him when the table is set without the water and brushes. Ping Lian has accepted this change and I hope that he continues to learn and accept that life is not always the "same". This was really a milestone for Ping Lian, as he will always encounter changes in life and need to adapt to certain situations he may encounter.

I always tell him "Not every day is the same; "Every day has changes"; and "Every day is different." My hope has always been that "life lessons" as I call them, will aid Ping Lian to make breakthroughs not only in his art but in his day to day life experiences.

As difficult as it has been to change already established routines for Ping Lian, eventually the end results make it all worthwhile. When it comes to changes, there are no excuses – and I would not say to myself that because he is autistic I will make things more comfortable and easier for him. I can see he is trying hard to accept and adapt to the changes in life. I do not support the idea that because he is autistic, we need to adapt to him all the time. Since Ping Lian was very young (including situations that had nothing to do with art), I always took advantage of "possible opportunities" to purposely create changes for Ping Lian. I would purposely attempt to break his developed habits and routines. It has always been a priority for me to try and teach him to be more flexible and to learn to adapt to changes.

Forcing such changes in Ping Lian's daily life has definitely resulted in his increased ability to cope with changes more positively. Ping Lian is older now (2006) and it has been apparent to me for some time now that Ping Lian is trying very hard to cope with many "big changes" in his life. Ping Lian still loves to play with his sisters; however those opportunities have greatly decreased. Especially after Min Seng passed away, Cher and Sherlyn have less frequent interactions and have different types of interactions with Ping Lian than they did when they were all younger. His sisters have their own emotional situations to deal with now. They are busy with their own lives and their own friends and Ping Lian has learned to cope with this change as well.

PING LIAN AT THE AGE OF 12:

While continuing to focus on Ping Lian's artwork and overall development, I have had to come up with different ways to engage, reinforce and motivate him. As he grows older and taller he can no longer ride on my back. However, I must continue to be very animated when I am teaching him. To teach Ping Lian the difference between a good artist and an outstanding artist, I have paired different body images with each phrase. A "poor artist" is depicted with weak body posture and a weak tone of voice. An "outstanding artist" is depicted as one standing tall, strong and powerful with a loud, yet positive tone of voice. I would ask Ping Lian "Do you want to be a poor artist or an outstanding artist?" while pairing these statements

10th Oct 2005- Photo of Ping Lian just before turning 12 and just before the art works were sent to New York for exhibition - Photo by kidchanstudio.com

with the corresponding body gestures. I would then guide him to choose the "powerful" choice by leading him and acknowledging acceptance by showing a joyful mood when he chooses the" powerful" one. Once Ping Lian was able to make the distinction or at least the choice vocally and respond "outstanding" I replaced the word poor with the word "good"

keeping the gestures the same. When I ask him "Do you want to be a good artist (paired with weak gestures) or an outstanding artist (paired with strong gestures) he selects the "strong-outstanding" artist!

In our living room, the "brain washing" training sessions go on as I ask Ping Lian: *"Who do you want to be when you grow up?" Ping Lian says: "I want to be artist". I ask again: "Good artist or outstanding artist"; Ping Lian says: "Outstanding artist". I shout joyfully: Oh, yes. You are a clever boy. You are an outstanding artist!"*

At this stage my joyful responses to his answers and my acceptance are the best rewards for Ping Lian. I no longer need to be a "horse" and play "horsie" games with him.

Ping Lian also prays clearly "I want to be outstanding artist". Later, when I ask "Who do you want to be when you grow up?" "I want to be *outstanding* artist"!, he answers clearly, loudly and confidently.

Does Ping Lian really understand the word "outstanding"? I do not know. Probably not, but again I expect that one day he will know and understand. For now at least he relates outstanding to powerful and positive, and when given the choices, he can make the selection. I am pretty sure that he relates outstanding to powerful and positive and he understands that the answer that makes Mummy happy is "outstanding", and therefore it is the correct choice. For now it does not matter how much he understands about what *outstanding artist* really means. What matters is that at least he can differentiate that "outstanding" is better and more powerful than "good" and he is aware that Mummy will love "outstanding" more than "good". For now that is enough for me.

Ping Lian has always been told by others that he is good in art. I have always praised him and told him that he is good "all the time."

> Life is competitive, good is never good enough, so it is best to aim higher when you think you are more able

I am amazed! Gradually I have discovered images within images in 06501 Sunflowers IV. This is the second time Ping Lian uses oil to paint. Many pieces of Ping Lian's art works encompass hidden aspects and forms, not initially seen or noticed upon first view. Someone also brought to my attention the additional images seen in this Sunflowers painting. My elder sister and I both noticed the beautiful face at the right hand corner around the third flower (counting from the left). Later I found a white bird with a green bead at top left side on top of the first flower; a horse head at the lower left hand side beside the vase; a standing horse at the right hand side just below the third flower- the horse is quite similar to standing horses at 04323 Horses IX (refer to www.pinglian.com Gallery 2004 II). One day, a child looking at this painting, pointed at the picture and shouted to her Daddy indicating that there was a dog face at the lower right hand corner. Do you see that? Just beside the right hand side of the vase, is a combination of yellow flowers plus two smaller flowers on top of it. It took me weeks to use my imagination to accept that it is a dog face.

Is this work done by an "outstanding artist"? Has Ping Lian achieved the status of an outstanding artist already at only the young age of 11 or

12? Has Ping Lian come to understand the meaning of *outstanding*? I guess only he knows.

> God is always good, he will provide and do his part, but we need to do our part too – Have Faith, Dare to Dream, set Goals and have willingness to take action in order to ACHIEVE!

PING LIAN AT THE AGE OF 13:

Ping Lian is 13 years old now. I no longer let my children sit on my back to play "Horse riding games"; Ping Lian still loves to say "I want to be artist". When asked "Who do you want to be when you grow up?" Ping Lian says "I want to be artist" or sometimes he will say "I want to be outstanding artist." loud, clear and spontaneously. As a family, we hold strength in prayer.

When I tell Ping Lian that it is prayer time and ask him to pray, he often times says something like this: "My dear God, please help me speak well, understand things well, concentrate in class, pay attention to my work, draw well, paint well, be a great artist, outstanding artist... Thank you God……."

Has Ping Lian achieved the status of an "outstanding artist"? Does he finally know the meaning of "outstanding artist" through his "Artistic Journey"? Does he understand the meaning of "grown up"? He is still not quite able to tell me directly. Let's see what he has drawn or paintedand the details of his story in the following chapters. Maybe then you can answer these questions for me.

**06501 SUNFLOWERS IV – OIL ON CANVAS
PAINTED IN MAY 2006, AT THE AGE OF 12**

Sunflower IV is only the second time Ping Lian ever used oil paint. How many faces do you see within the flower? I see one beautiful gentle face and one serious stern face. In this picture do you also see some additional animals (2 horses, a dog, a bird)? Was this work done by an "Outstanding Artist"?

It Does not matter
WHO YOU ARE NOW
IT IS
WHO YOU WANT TO BE
AND
WHO YOU BECOME
THAT MATTERS
Make Decisions
And
Take Action

Sarah St Lee

CHAPTER 2
I Have a Special Son – My Awakening

Ping Lian does not talk, he is hyperactive, jumping around daily and possesses no sense of danger or awareness of his surroundings. These are generally typical characteristics of someone with autism. Ping Lian does not require much sleep. He is especially hyper at night while *we* sleep. He will jump on me or on his sisters until he is exhausted and then only will he sleep. I think back, and frankly I do not know how I was able to exist through those times. I just remember that I screamed at him a lot at midnight. At that time I did not know what autism was and I did not know that Ping Lian was an autistic boy. I was thinking that maybe boys are more naughty and hyper than girls and that he would grow out of this soon; as my friends son did. Witnessing my friend's son's behavior caused me to be more ignorant and I rationalized Ping Lian's behavior to a point of indifference, eventually denying his problem. I just waited and hoped that one day Ping Lian would be okay. Many of my friends and colleagues gave me the same advice referring to their own experiences. I consistently heard things like "Don't worry, boys usually speak later than girls" or "He'll grow out of it just like my son did". After hearing so many positive stories, I began to feel good and hopeful yet deep in my heart I still felt worried. With no precise measures to take, life just went on as usual. I just waited and hoped for "The Day" to come when Ping Lian would be okay. I now realize that this is not a dream. This is day dreaming. I wait and wait, but

"The Day" never comes. I finally came to understand that I needed to face the reality of *autism*.

MY IGNORANCE, DENIAL AND INDIFFERENCE

Since Ping Lian was very young, I suspected that he was different from my other children. I have always liked to play one simple game with my children when they were still babies. I would grab their fingers and pull them up. When I played these games with my daughters, both girls would definitely respond and try to get up and of course their responses grew stronger as they matured. When I played this same game with Ping Lian as a baby, he had no response. Even as he grew months older, when I tried engaging him with these types of games, he had no response. I wondered "Could it be because he is a boy he is different, or is something wrong with him??!!". This thought haunted me on and off, as I often would put such thoughts aside. When I took Ping Lian for his routine immunizations, a few times I voiced my concerns to Ping Lian's pediatrician. Once or twice I even showed the games to the pediatrician and explained to him that Ping Lian did not respond. Ping Lian would not get excited by my stimulation attempts and he would remain calm.

Ping Lian was not always hyperactive. I can remember when my domestic helper would carry him ever so calmly before I left for work. This image of my son is etched forever in a beautiful photo I once took of him as he sat up by the side of the lake. He was only 10 months old. I remember my husband and I calling him, but Ping Lian did not respond. To Ping Lian we were transparent. It felt as though he was looking through us. I called him many times until I convinced myself that he noticed me.

Still, the photo turned out to be so beautiful. At this point Ping Lian also still slept well and often fell asleep quite early. I usually put him to sleep in a small bed in my room so I could have more time with him before I went to sleep around 12 midnight. I would then carry him to my domestic helper's room, who by then had already fallen asleep. I can't quite pinpoint a time frame, but somewhere between the ages of one and three Ping Lian started to show hyperactive behavior and sleepless patterns.

PING LIAN YEAK- SEPTEMBER 1994

Yet, even with all of these concerns my pediatrician checked Ping Lian physically, turned him around and said "Ping Lian eats well, looks good and is physically fit". He concluded "Not to worry, Ping Lian has no problems".

Ping Lian would not respond to me by pointing to the sky when I asked "Where is the star and moon?" My other two girls loved these games when they were of similar age. My girls loved when I carried them facing the sky and counted the stars. They also loved when I praised them as "clever"... but Ping Lian was not interested in my counting the stars or calling him clever. I thought all babies and toddlers loved games and praise. How come my Ping Lian was not interested in any of this? Worse of all, most of the time he would treat me as if I were invisible. Often times, calling his name had no result. I can remember when Ping Lian was just a few months old, every morning my domestic helper carried him and sent me off to work. I would say bye-bye to Ping Lian, get in the car, reverse my car, stop in front of the house and call his name again to say bye- bye. However, he still did not look at me. I always felt, he could not be bothered by me and he expressed a kind of look (which I do not know how to describe). I usually tried calling him many times until he seemed to notice me calling him, but even then he had no readable response on his face. It appeared as if he had expression, yet he did not appear to be hyperactive at these times either. My domestic helper would always say that he was shy and that maybe because I go to work early in the morning and come back in the late evening (6 or 7 pm) that Ping Lian is angry with me. Although that seemed to make sense to me, I didn't really think he could be so smart at that age. When I would come back from work, Ping Lian still treated me as transparent and could not be bothered when I called his name. My work schedule was the same when my daughters were younger and yet neither of them were ever angry with me. On the contrary, they were so excited and happy when they would see me get home from work. I was so disappointed that to Ping Lian I was still invisible.

Ping Lian had no interest in responding to whatever I talked to him about. In the back of my mind, I kept asking, why would he behave like this? I felt disappointed that Ping Lian was ignoring me. Ping Lian was also not interested in the toys that my two girls loved. I wondered "How come all children love toys, but not him." I would engage my children in play activities and Ping Lian would not show interest. I would read a book to Cher, and Ping Lian would come join us, sit down for a brief moment and then take away the book and walk off.

Chapter 2: I Have a Special Son – My Awakening

At the age where most children start calling mummy and daddy etc, he would not speak. He never called "Mummy" or "Daddy". I only remember that he did say my dog's name often- "Twinkle" - a small little dog, Australia Silky. He just said the dog's name, but he was not calling the dog (I never came to know why or how he learned to call my dog). Also one day I heard him mumble "Sedap" when I gave him the durian[2] (Sedap means "Yummy" as in "tastes good" in Malay's Language. My domestic helper speaks to Ping Lian in Malay language. I was so happy that he expressed something that he experienced, something "real", but I only heard him say it once. Anyway that showed me that he can talk. I wonder how come he can say the dog's name and when I try to get him to call daddy and mummy, he refuses to?

Min Seng and I continue contemplating: "Does he have a problem?"….. but from the surface he looks so good; he is such a handsome boy; he does not look *retarded*[3] and he eats so well". My domestic helper had taught Ping Lian some eating manners. He has better table manners than his sisters. He also has fantastic gross motor skills. He would climb everywhere in the house and walk along all edges with no problem. I always brought up my concerns about him to my friends and relatives but they all advised me not to worry because hyperactivity and speaking late are common occurrences in some children. They advised me to be patient, to wait and see and one day he would settle down and start talking. Anyway my pediatrician concurred. He also advised that Ping Lian had no problem since he could say a word or two. That advice was all I needed to start justifying Ping Lian's behavior. So, "what's the worry?" I do not know why I did not bring Ping Lian for a second opinion. Possibly I became a procrastinator scared to face the reality of a diagnosis and maybe I fostered an attitude of indifference in the hopes that

---

2 Durian is a fruit revered in Malaysia as the "King of Fruits". It is distinctive for its large size, unique odor and a formidable thorn-covered husk
3 Today use of the word 'retarded' is considered derogatory, offensive and politically incorrect. However, it is used here as it was acceptably used in the past to convey a limitation in intellect

one day he would be okay ....or maybe I was just too involved with my office job. Maybe with each day, passing by so quickly I did not even 'notice that he was already turning three years old.

That's when I started to panic. "Ping Lian is three years old!" I decided to send him to Montessori[4] Kindergarten. I hoped that he might change and settle down in kindergarten. Some of my friends' children have hyperactivity problems, but they appeared to settle down after they attended the kindergarten program.

At the kindergarten Ping Lian was running wild. He did not like being there. He even tried to climb over the fence and attempted to get away a few times. At a precise moment, during one of those episodes, was when I really knew that Ping Lian definitely had a problem. I couldn't wait any longer, so I went back to the same pediatrician again and this time he agreed that Ping Lian had a problem and referred Ping Lian to a neurologist.

I AM OVERJOYED - MY SON'S BRAIN HAS NO PROBLEM

As I walked out of the hospital, I am relieved and overjoyed with the results of Ping Lian's brain examinations. I am so happy and can't wait to reach home to announce this to Min Seng, so I call him the moment I walk out from the hospital. "Hi Yeak! Is so good....Doctor say your son's brain has no problem. He is not retarded". The whole morning I kept telling myself "Please don't tell me my son's brain has a problem. Please don't tell me that he is retarded". I am so happy and I sense that Min Seng at the other end

---

4   The *Montessori Method* is an educational philosophy and was originally developed in the late 19th century by educator Maria Montessori. Many Montessori schools are preschool or elementary school in level, but there are some Montessori programs that begin with infants or end at 12th grade.

Chapter 2: I Have a Special Son – My Awakening

of the phone is relieved too. I continue to relay the wonderful diagnostic information…. "Doctor says Ping Lian has Attention Deficit Hyperactive Disorder with autistic features and he just needs occupational therapy and speech therapy!".

I was so ignorant that I still did not realize that I was in deep trouble. It was my belief then that Ping Lian only had a "problem" if his brain tests would have revealed something wrong with his brain or if the doctor would have informed me that he was retarded. I focused on the direct meaning of the words and made my own interpretations. Attention deficit means not enough attention, it is a small matter. Anyway, we see many children with attention problems but they will eventually be okay once they are no longer hyperactive. "Ping Lian is hyperactive", that was obvious. I did not need a doctor to tell me that, and we can see that hyperactivity in children is common. It is definitely not a big issue; they all outgrow it soon enough. My best friend's child was my proof. He was very hyperactive as a toddler, but by the time he entered primary school, he was such a wonderful obedient boy.

The doctor did not explain much to me about the diagnosis or if he did, I guess I did not understand. I focused so much on Ping Lian's brain results that I did not pay attention. Also in reality I guess I was unable to really focus as Ping Lian was busy walking around exploring the clinic. I was not given any pamphlet or article to read about Attention Deficit or Autism. At this time internet connections were not common for most of the Malaysian homes and small businesses, thus we did not have this type of access to do any research either.

With regard to the extended diagnosis of "with autistic features", I had never come across the term "autistic" in my life before and the doctor did not emphasize it. Since it was "just a feature" I also did not focus on it. Since it was not the main emphasis of the diagnosis, I put it aside. I jumped to my own conclusion that Ping Lian did not have a major problem…after all, his brain has no problem and he is not retarded. What else can be more serious than that?

Now I was happy. Given this pretense of a joyful mood I focused my attention on the results of Ping Lian's brain tests and the rationalization that he had no problem. Ahead of us lie positive outcomes and he will eventually progress just like my friend's son did, just maybe a little later! My colleagues at the office were anxiously awaiting my news from the doctor. They were also worried for me and anticipating my son's brain test results. After they heard from me that Ping Lian's brain had no problem and that he *only* had an attention deficit, they all congratulated me. I did not realize that in fact Ping Lian was autistic which is a serious disorder and that I was entering into a huge problem that would affect the lives of my entire family forever.

> The worse situation was - "Not knowing what it is you don't know"

When the doctor told me that Ping Lian will need occupational therapy and speech therapy I was puzzled. What is this occupational therapy? It is also the first time in my life I heard about occupational therapy. "What does Ping Lian's problem have to do with occupation?" I asked the doctor what is occupational therapy and he referred me to a lady in the hospital who was an occupational therapist. Ping Lian started going to occupational therapy at the public hospital once every two weeks. However, he was unable to sit through an occupational therapy session. We had to seat him in a high chair meant for dining (with safety belt that *tied* him to the chair like an infant/toddler's eating high chair) in order to keep him seated for an actual session. The occupational therapist guided him to do very simple tasks.

Chapter 2: I Have a Special Son – My Awakening

I asked the doctor if we could delay the speech therapy. Since Ping Lian wouldn't even sit down for a few minutes, how was he supposed to sit through the speech therapy sessions? The doctor said that Ping Lian is already slightly beyond three years old and showing extremely limited speech, so he definitely needs the speech therapy as soon as possible. Although I doubted that Ping Lian would sit through a session, I decided if this is going to help him to talk I would send him for the speech therapy. The doctor gave me a list of more than ten speech therapy providers and asked me to copy down the names and to call them for an appointment. I asked him since he knew Ping Lian's situation, would he recommend one or two of the speech therapists suitable for Ping Lian's condition, but he said he could not do that.

Meanwhile, Ping Lian continued to demonstrate his hyperactivity and mischievousness during the course of this discussion with the doctor. I did not have any peace while talking to the doctor at all. Ping Lian played with the water in the sink, grabbed things from the table, climbed up and down on the bed and pulled the sheets off the bed. At one point while I am still talking to the doctor about speech therapy, Ping Lian turned his attention toward the dustbin. He was fascinated with the dustbin paddle and started playing by opening and closing the dustbin. The doctor and I became very worried that Ping Lian might grab a used needle from inside the dustbin. Neither of us was able to redirect Ping Lian's fascination with the dustbin so I promptly took him and left the hospital.

Both Min Seng and I agreed that Ping Lian needed to learn to speak soon. However, common sense told us that there was no point wasting time and money for speech therapy when Ping Lian can't even sit down for a few minutes. The doctor at the hospital couldn't even control him! So we both gave up on the idea and decided to wait until we can get Ping Lian to sit down for at least a few minutes. Then only, would we contact the speech therapist. Meanwhile I gained some knowledge from the occupational therapist in getting Ping Lian to sit down and do some very simple tasks. However for me, each attempt was a big struggle to get him to sit down and pay attention to a task. It was so very hard, frustrating and drained me of all energy. We did not know of any alternative or better way to train him to sit down and be obedient.

Min Seng and I are still considering doing nothing and hoping that a "miracle" will happen and Ping Lian will just settle down as he grows older. Then we can take him for speech therapy. In the back of my mind though, I still hoped that one day he may just start talking—after all his brain tests showed that he had "no problem with his brain".

No one explained to me the actual meaning of Ping Lian's diagnosis and no one offered me guidance on how to look up information to gain knowledge about this diagnosis. No one warned me of the seriousness of this diagnosis, nor of the impact it would have on our lives in the future. Min Seng and I took no initiative to look up such information. Secretly, we both felt that since his brain had no problem, he had no problem and we both just waited. Even when I speak about Ping Lian's diagnosis, I only talk about attention deficit and hyperactivity. I do not elaborate or talk about autism; mostly because we had no knowledge base about this "feature". We were very ignorant about what we were in for. We continued on with our daily life routines unaware that our ignorance and indifference to Ping Lian's problems were wasting valuable time and opportunities for early intervention.

There are times when I still feel guilty about my choice to ignore, deny and remain unresponsive to these issues. My husband and I are both university educated, but we had never heard of "autism". I guess Min Seng equally harnessed feelings of guilt and resentment, as he later always mentioned that every parent should know about autism before they become a parent.

In the year 2004, upon taking Ping Lian for a medical checkup at the private clinic intending to purchase medical insurance; when I mentioned that he was "autistic" the doctor asked me what that meant! I explained what autism was (as I understood it); yet at the same time I appreciated his humbleness as he asked me to come back again the next day to give him the opportunity to research about autism. Frankly, I was amazed and at the same time suddenly feeling, not so guilty about my own ignorance.

"FIGHTING SPEECH THERAPY" - WE ALL GIVE UP!

We were advised to return to the hospital for regular monthly visits. Each time the doctor asked me the same question "Have you gotten a speech therapist for Ping Lian?" Each time I gave him the same answer, "He can't even sit down for few minutes, what can speech therapy do for him?" and the doctor would still urge me to do it.

Ping Lian is now approaching four years old and he still doesn't talk. Nothing much has changed for him other than he does not run wild in kindergarten anymore. I have started feeling worried and guilty again for not doing anything.

One day my boss introduced me to his friend who had just come back from overseas (a speech therapy graduate). She was a very nice and caring lady. I decided to give it a try! Min Seng still insisted it was a waste of time but I told him we would at least try. The speech therapist had a beautiful office. Ping Lian was so fascinated with the decorations in her office that he kept grabbing things here and there. Ping Lian even climbed up on the table and some shelves to reach a glass jug filled with handmade colorful paper stars that sat on the very top shelf. The speech therapist and I just couldn't control him. We struggled to get him to sit down. It was as if the three of us were having a big fight in the room for an hour. We finally gave up and the speech therapist did not want to take my consultation fee payment. Due to the time spent trying to keep Ping Lian from climbing from chair to table, etc. we did not have much time to even discuss Ping Lian's problems. Just before I left her office, she told me to come back after Ping Lian has learned to sit and settle down. This was something I had known all along. What I didn't know was "how?" How was I supposed to get him to sit still? Did everyone just mean that when the boy grew older he would just sit down?? I had been waiting for many years already. I thought "She did not teach me how to get him to sit down", or "Ping Lian is so hyper that there is no chance for her to teach me how to get Ping Lian to sit down". So this time we really gave up. I had done what I needed to do as recommended by the hospital doctor and it is true enough that Min Seng and I are right; nothing much can be done!! So we have nothing to do but to wait. Wait for *one day* when maybe Ping Lian will be good like other children and be able to sit down. Then we will go to speech therapy.

ADAPT TO THE TORTURE AND ACCEPT THE SUFFERING

When Ping Lian began exhibiting sleeplessness, hyperactivity, unsafe and unpredictable behavior we put him in our room to sleep with us. Ping Lian enjoyed one game every night….. Jumping on us when we fell asleep! He would jump on us until he was tired and until I was tired of screaming at him. Then only would he quiet down and go to sleep. Many times this went on beyond midnight until 1 or to 2:00 in the morning. Night was always so hard for us. Nonetheless, the next morning we both were able to get up, go to work and put aside the suffering from the previous evening.

Ping Lian spent the daytime hours with the domestic helper and my mother in law. Day in, day out, life would go on as usual. In the evening the torture and suffering ordeal would start all over again. Many times when I think back to those episodes, I just wonder how Min Seng and I endured those tough nights and tough times. If I had to be put back in the same situations again, I don't think I would be able to take it now. Anyway, no matter how difficult each night was, life went on like "normal" the next morning. Amazingly I was able to maintain and even excel at my job performance in the office.

Through these experiences I have realized that when presented with adverse situations and no choices to avoid them; accepting them helps our bodies to adjust and trains us to adapt to the necessary routines. We (my family) embraced our situations as "normal" for us. We are in fact stronger than what we think. I have found that my body and mental abilities adjust to the situation accordingly. I have also learned that if we do not make decisions and take action to make changes, time will just slip us by without notice. Each day will pass and with each passing of the day we will miss many good opportunities. Min Seng and I have both felt guilty for wasting time, as we now all know that early intervention is crucial for the development of individuals with autistm. I now know that Ping Lian could be much more advanced in his personal development if we had taken effective action much earlier and much quicker.

SPEECH THERAPY WAKE ME UP AND "WHY ME???!!"

I was introduced to a second speech therapist by a friend. She also could not control Ping Lian, but she did understand my situation. She advised me not to sit and wait. She said that we needed to take the necessary actions to help Ping Lian "immediately". She also stated that one 45 minute occupational therapy session every forth night for Ping Lian, would not be enough. She proceeded to recommend me to a private occupational therapist for intensive therapy and advised us to come back to her in one to two months time.

We sent Ping Lian for intensive occupational therapy. Ping Lian was doing well. The therapist was highly experienced and she managed to control Ping Lian well and get him to really sit down and perform some simple tasks. I was amazed to see that Ping Lian did not need to sit on those "high chairs". I learned many techniques through watching her work with Ping Lian, enabling me to get Ping Lian to do similar tasks at home.

After a two month period we went back to the speech therapist. I was so relieved to see that this time the speech therapist was able to control him. After a while of Ping Lian going for speech and occupational therapy, he improved so much that I was able to set up some routines at home to get him to do simple tasks. This still required much effort and some struggles for him to complete the "Planned Tasks". I was also able to set up a routine for story time. I would tell Ping Lian simple stories in my own simple words based on simple pictures from a book. He was able to sit down for 15 minutes for the story telling (with my demonstrating and correlating a lot of actions to attract his attention). Simple stories like "The girl is laughing", and then I would laugh loudly and point my finger to the picture of the girls laughing. On the next page…"The girl is crying" and I would have to pretend to cry.

One specific picture book "Share with Us - Letters, Numbers, Words, and Animals" by Karen O'Callaghan[5] had attracted Ping Lian very much. He enjoyed the book with the simple stories I would create according to the pictures. We would now have *"Story Timeeee"* every morning before I went to work. Every morning I used the same book, the same story and read it at the same time. Ping Lian was able to sit with me until he heard the sound of the horn of the transporter car that came to pick him up to go to Kindergarten. I felt this improvement and development in Ping Lian's emotional growth as such a grand success. At this stage, I assumed

---

5   Karen O'Callaghan - Publisher: Brimax Books, 1984

that Ping Lian had succeeded so much, that with the additional help of speech therapy, he would be able to speak up soon. Ping Lian will be okay soon, after all, he is not deaf and dumb. He just needs someone to help him to learn to focus and speak up. My main concern was regarding his inattentiveness and hyperactivity. What I did not know was that I was actually going into a second stage of *ignorance*.

I was so happy that I had learned a lot with regard to ways to teach Ping Lian. I believed that the speech therapy would "rescue" him and... I could now go back to focusing on my career again. I got my retired sister and my brother in law to take Ping Lian to his speech therapy sessions. Once a month I would take leave from work to be able to take Ping Lian to his speech therapy sessions, check and observe his progress and to learn some new techniques to teach Ping Lian at home. In the meantime Ping Lian continued to attend his occupational therapy sessions as well. I also trained my brother-in-law to be able to work with Ping Lian. Since he was Chinese educated and spoke limited English he was unable to work with Ping Lian on his speech goals. Instead I trained my brother-in-law so that he could get Ping Lian to sit and focus on writing tasks. He would sit with Ping Lian and do simple tracing activities. Ping Lian spent much time tracing daily.

A few months later, the speech therapist came down on me hard; very hard. Apparently, she could not understand nor accept my laid back attitude towards Ping Lian any longer. One day she "hammered" me right on my head to "wake me up". I am always grateful to her for "aggressive" approach. She was the force that pushed me to change and make me start thinking seriously about *how* and *what* to do to help Ping Lian. Together, a combination of these series of occurrences led me to commit and to take immediate action!! However the speech therapists bluntness greatly contributed to my understanding of the urgency to help Ping Lian. I came to the realization that ...to "commit and to take immediate action is of the utmost importance."

Today, I still remember that "wake up call" very clearly. It continues to impact upon me daily. The therapist said "Do something for your son. Do not think that what we do here once or twice a week will heal your son. It is not enough. You need to give him intensive therapy and you need to focus on his behavior modification. You need to set your goals to aim for him to be accepted into a mainstream school. You are running out of time. You only have one to two years to work toward this. What we do here will not be sufficient to be able to achieve that. You need to get him to do at home intensively what I am teaching him here. There is no point in having Ping Lian come here every week and repeat the same task". She continued "Do you want to put your son in a "special needs" school or in a *normal* school? Go take a look at the schools and decide where you want your son to go… and what you need to do for your son…"

The thought that Ping Lian would not be cured of his "hyperactivity with autistic features" after receiving professional treatment (speech therapy and occupational therapy) was never a thought I entertained. When someone is sick, and given medicine, they eventually heal. Now I thought…"What? He will not learn and improve just from speech therapy and be able to speak soon? … So what is the speech therapy for?..... I thought the purpose of speech therapy was to teach a person to talk and that it would just be a matter of time before they will be able to talk! Normally, once children start talking they will talk non-stop. My Ping Lian is not deaf and dumb and his brain tests do not suggest his brain has any problems………. When will Ping Lian be healed?" During this long discussion with the speech therapist, I was suddenly overcome with a feeling of sadness. She spoke to me about autism, related problems of autism and shared some early intervention success stories.

After such a heavy *hammering* from the speech therapist, Min Seng and I finally took the initiative to do something for our son. Our first goal was to know more about "What is autism". Min Seng bought a computer with

Chapter 2: I Have a Special Son – My Awakening

internet connection capabilities for use at home. I was not at all familiar with this type of technology but having turned to the internet for resources helped me to learn quickly. Connecting to the internet was extremely slow and tedious but it helped us tremendously. At first Min Seng would do the research and print up the articles for me to read. We searched "ADHD and Autism". We were slapped in the face with the obvious realization that our Ping Lian was an autistic boy! He does not *have autistic features. He IS AUTISTIC!* We both felt extremely guilty and sorry that we had not been responsible parents to Ping Lian.

EXTRACT OF THE SPEECH- LANGUAGE ASSESSMENT REPORT:

2 Nov 1997 (Ping Lian at the age of 3 years 11 months)

Ping Lian was seen for a speech- language evaluation on 24-10-1997 and 31-10-1997. Mrs. Yeak was concerned about Ping Lian's ability to "express himself" and his behavior. Ping Lian's hearing had not been formally tested but his hearing appears functional. Mrs. Yeak stated that Ping Lian did not produce much vocalization when he was a baby and babbling was not noted at the expected age. She also notices that his eye contact was reduced even then and that he did not usually respond when his name was called. He produced his first word- the name of the family dog- when he was about 2 years old. His spontaneous speech at this time consisted mainly of single words and stock phrases such as "I don't want". Ping Lian has two older sisters aged 10 and 6. The home languages are English and Mandarin. He attends a kindergarten 5 times per week. Ping Lian goes to a baby sitter during the day.

Initial Impressions: Ping Lian was a restless child and was inclined to challenge the adult's commands to sit or to come with phrase such as " I don't want"

Assessment: The assessment of Ping Lian's speech- language skills was carried out using observations, parent reports and informal probes.

continuation:

Oral Peripheral Examination: The structure and functions of the oral musculature were within normal limits. Mrs. Yeak stated that he did not have any problem with eating or with his swallowing. No drooling was noted.

Communication: Ping Lian used hand pulling to request for things. He pushed or threw away things to indicate refusal. Sometimes he would draw attention to some object by pointing but this was infrequent. He did not usually respond when his name was called. Sometimes he would say "Auntie" to get his aunt to get an item for him. Jargon was frequently heard.

Receptive and expressive Language: Ping Lian could sort blocks according to form but had more difficulty with color. He could identify and name some body parts, common objects and toy animals. He showed some understanding of the meaning of same. A word check indicated that at this time, Ping Lian had an expressive vocabulary of about 60 words.

Attention and memory: Ping Lian's attention was extremely short. He needed cueing to complete short tasks.

Imitation: Ping Lian imitated some speech postures and speech sounds when requested.

Play Skills: Ping Lian liked to play with toy animals. Otherwise his play skills remain reduced.

Eye Contact: Eye contact was present but reduced. He needed cueing to look at the person talking with him.

Other Observation and Comments: Ping Lian had many negative behaviors; he kicked at the door and he threw things about. His mother reported that he would sometimes bite and scream.

Clinical Impression: Ping Lian presents with moderate to severe speech-language delay characterized by deficits in receptive and expressive language skills and reduced pragmatic (social interaction) skills. In addition he presented with attention deficit and hyperactive traits. Ping Lian's ability to comply was negligible at this time.

Extract below some of the recommendations by speech therapy:

- Ping Lian ability to comply should be increase before speech therapy is initiated. Mrs Yeak will consult an occupational therapist on this matters.
- Mrs Yeak should try to address the behavior problem immediately.
- It is also recommended that a psychologist be consult regarding Ping Lian's behaviors.

WE FINALLY KNEW WHAT WAS IN STORE FOR US...

After reading some articles which stated that autism could be a lifelong problem and knowing what may be in store for us, both Min Seng and I grew scared and helpless. We knew that life was going to be hard, possibly bringing lots of suffering and sacrifice for Min Seng, myself, Ping Lian and my two girls in the future. I asked God "WHY ME???!! Why my Ping Lian???!! Why do you want us to suffer?...Why have you chosen me?... It is so unfair??!!... What have we done wrong??!!" We asked ourselves all these questions while thinking how both Min Seng and I are kind and helpful people. We are not selfish and we are a sharing people and trustworthy people. Min Seng is an only son and his mother has lived with us since we have been together. She always expressed her wishes and love for me to have a boy to be her grandson. Well, she has one now! She is well known as a kind and nice lady by all people who know her. Why? Why? How come good people are given such severe pain??!! It is not fair!!!!! and why now? The timing is not right." There are so many questions but no answers. I am frustrated and mostly angry.

Life was never the same after really understanding autism. My "dream" of life ruptured once I realized Ping Lian was indeed an autistic child. It was painful to know that I could no longer continue my dream. I felt like an outcast, an exile and kept asking "Why? Why have I been chosen?"

> Just need to accept that life can be unfair at times, no point in wasting energy to find out "Why?"

REALIZATION AND HOPE

Asking God "WHY?" and harboring anger over "WHY Me?" will never help Ping Lian and he is only getting worse. I have already wasted enough of Ping Lian's time. I now felt that I had no other choice than to accept the truth and do something for him to change the *situation*. There can only be one simple reason "He is my son and I can't run away. No one can replace me to do something for him. What choice do I have?"

There is NO choice and only one option lies before me.. To accept the reality that he is an autistic boy. He will be my burden for the rest of my life, and he will destroy my beautiful *dream*. I am learning to accept that as truth and have decided to adjust our lifestyles to help Ping Lian. Still, I am very clear that I will take control of the level of *destruction* and that I will not accept that Ping Lian can destroy my future and the future of my daughters. I will do my best to minimize the burdens destined upon us. How? I do not yet know.....but I will find out as we go on! The most important thing I know is that, the only way I can reduce future suffering is to do something NOW for him!! I just need to re-adjust my dream. I started to focus my energy on what I can do to help him, and I decided to base that focus on what I want for Ping Lian in the future. I then started to list my goals for him.

Coincidently while I am at this stage of deciding what should be our next move, Min Seng printed an article from the internet. The title of the article was *"An Inside View of Autism"*, by Temple Grandin[6]. It was around 14 pages long. After reading this article, I also came to realize that, Dr. Temple Grandin was autistic. I was shocked that she could be so brilliant yet be autistic. I was very much inspired by the article. I read the article

---

6   An Inside View of Autism 1996, Temple Grandin, Ph.D. Assistant Professor Colorado State University Fort Collins, CO 80523, USA

many times. Dr. Temple Grandin had given me HOPE. My overall view of autistic people took on an immediate shift. There *was* hope.

> Hope motivates a person to take action, work harder and persevere

I decided that Dr. Temple Grandin would be my inspiration for Ping Lian. I told myself that if I gave Dr. Temple Grandin full points - 100 points (value system described later) and work hard with Ping Lian, than he *can* achieve! Yet, I dared not dream that Ping Lian could be so brilliant and good like Dr. Grandin (to get 100 points) but if my Ping Lian can achieve just a certain percentage like Dr Temple Grandin, I would be happy. I did not set my target % - I just knew that the more I worked with Ping Lian, the higher his percentage of success would be.

Dr. Grandin's writings also inspired me to persist in looking out for Ping Lian's special talent and skills. In my journey of teaching and guiding Ping Lian to achieve different sets of goals at different stages of his life, whenever I encounter "give up moments", there is always a voice inside me that says "Ping Lian has HOPE" and "Ping Lian will be "SOMEBODY". This voice crucially drives me on my "roller-coaster" journey of Ping Lian's development.

Around this time, I also coincidently came to know about PR4A[7] (a parent support group formed by a few parents each with an autistic child). While at the shopping complex one of my sister's old friends approached me and asked if I recognized him. This gentleman, although hesitant for

---

7   PR4A (Parents' Resource for Autism Malaysia) - A group of parents having kids with autism and related disorders; with the common objective of sourcing for the latest and most successful methods for the treatment of autism to help achieve their best potential. 51-3 Jalan Radin Anum, Bandar Baru Seri Petaling, Kuala Lumpur Malaysia 57000

fear of offending me apologized in advance for his following comments. He told me that my son has a problem and I should do something for him as soon as possible. I told him that I know all this but that I do not know HOW to help him. He told me about PR4A and he gave me the contact of a PR4A member saying I may learn something from them. He is such a wonderful man. From a cultural perspective, in Malaysia, this kind of act may get people to perceive him as "A Busy Body". Yet his "busy body" concern helped my son and me. This interaction brought me to yet another turning point in my life with Ping Lian. It eventually also lead me toward a reduction of stress and suffering. Through PR4A I learned about ABA (Applied Behavior Analysis) techniques. I also gained access to many good reading materials and books about autism and ABA. PR4A has a group of wonderful parents willing to share their knowledge, experience and resources. Many of the resources were purchased by individual parents, on their own, bought overseas and some were downloaded from the internet. Some of the parents shared costs to employ experts of ABA from overseas to help their autistic children in Malaysia and then they shared what they learned from the experts with other parents. Some of the parents even went to the extent of making a demo to show a group of parents how to teach their own child by using ABA techniques. I started reading and learning more about autism. There was so much to learn. I felt as if I was running out of time and was eager to learn more about autism so I could start helping Ping Lian more effectively as soon as possible. I have always been very hard working and an eager learner, yet I don't believe I have ever studied so hard in my entire life. This required and inspired more diligence in me than even necessary for my University placement exam and course of study!

I feel that I have learned and now understand so much about autism and ABA. I apply what I learn about ABA whenever I am teaching Ping Lian. His progress is quicker than we have ever experienced before and with much less effort and energy on my part. With the use of my limited knowledge of ABA, both, Ping Lian's frustration level as well as mine have decreased. It is the first time I have felt so good, even having a thorough understanding of what autism really is.

I am especially grateful to a few of the PR4A pioneering members for helping me to understand autism and ABA. I strongly believe that all parents need to have this type of organization as a support and resource system. Their assistance has made the world of difference for my family. I also, later employed Chin Chin (a college student) to implement an ABA program for Ping Lian at home. From this point on I had finally learned how to communicate with Ping Lian. I am able to manage Ping Lian's behavior much more effectively which has resulted in hearing much less screaming coming out of my house.

God is so good. I am so glad that I was finally led to move from ignorance, denial, realization and guilt toward acceptance and new hope. I am so happy that I have been able to move out of these negative cycles and move forward.

> A simple helpful gesture may bring a huge impact to create a great difference in another person's life

CHAPTER 3
Getting Started With My Special Son

INTRODUCTION: SETTING GOALS

Ping Lian had so many problem areas that needed to be addressed. In order for me to even attempt to try and cope with them I began to list a few major goals for him:

- Behavior modification- I must be able to control him. He must be obedient and able to sit down to finish a task.
- Ping Lian must be able to communicate- to talk and to deal with people- I have yet to hear him call mummy & daddy spontaneously without prompting.
- Ping Lian must be able to trace, copy, write and read but with the understanding that I do not expect him to understand what he is reading for the time being.
- Ping Lian must experience normal school life like other children have -putting him in mainstream school for at least one to two years.
- Most important of all - Ping Lian must have feelings for me and for others

Ping Lian appeared to have no feelings for others. He lived in his own world. I call him…but he does not pay attention to me. I am angry with him…but he doesn't care, although I imagine he does not understand what being angry is. Ping Lian could not be bothered. Even if I scold him…there is no self esteem. He just does not care about what is going on around him or how other people feel. He just does what he wants. He also has no sense of danger. Once he has an opportunity, he will run out of the house and disappear. I lost him a few times when relatives had come to stay with me. Whether at home or at the shopping complex, just a few seconds of not watching him has resulted in our losing him. Once, when he was with Min Seng and Cher at the shopping complex, and although he was seated in the shopping trolley; in the instant that Min Seng and Cher just turned around to get the ice-cream, he disappeared! Min Seng and Cher panicked. Cher headed in one direction and Min Seng went in the opposite direction to find him. Cher was only 5 or 6 years old at the time. My poor girl, who at such a young age is supposed to still need our care and supervision while in a shopping complex, at this moment needed to take on the responsibility and stress of looking for her brother. Finally, Cher found her brother at the nearby bakery enjoying the bread he took from a shelf, as if the whole world was just him alone.

I know that it will be difficult to achieve all of the goals I outlined for him, especially if Ping Lian does not care or experience how we feel about him. His lack of "feeling" and sharing emotion will be the biggest obstacle to overcome. Therefore my first priority and most important goal is that Ping Lian must have feeling. I decided to focus all of my energy to search and find ways to achieve this most important goal.

The doubt slowly began to haunt me. "Am I being unrealistic?" "Am I setting too many goals for Ping Lian?" No! These are all basic survival skills. Will these goals be easy to achieve? The answer is still "No"! Will I able to achieve so many goals in such a short period? I really do not know, but I do know that these are basic skills that he MUST HAVE! Ping Lian is already four years old. In just another one and a half years he will need to be either in a mainstream school or in a special needs school for people with all types of disabilities. I am very worried!

GETTING STARTED

Understanding autism seemed like an extremely long cycle, that in reality was never ending. Accepting the truth of autism meant changing my life style in order to proceed. It was of course easier to set goals than it will be to reach them. Even though I know there is hope, even though I know I must do it and know full well that it is my responsibility, the discipline and determination is just not enough to keep me going for the foreseen extended period. It will be a long and tough process.

There are two persons within me. There is the *positive* me and then there is the *negative me*. The two personalities often conflict. The feeling of commitment to persevere and achieve was really hard to maintain. It took so much hard work, discipline and sacrifice as the temptations of our life before autism surrounded me. I was just not committed enough or willing to let go of the many areas of my life which I enjoyed and treasured. I also needed to spend time with my other two girls. My main limitation is that there will never be enough time for everything and everyone. Unfortunately, at the same time we are burdened with huge financial commitments. Due to this situation, l can't let go of my job 100%. I need to help Min Seng in our family financial commitment or he may go bankrupt. I just can't focus and find that I am working on the goals for Ping Lian half heartedly as I continue to procrastinate and say "TOMORROW, tomorrow I will….".

> Never deceive yourself with "tomorrow, I will", there is always another tomorrow, it is just a temporary comfort

Whenever the opportunity arises I find an excuse to get side-tracked and I once again say "TOMORROW, I will". Before I know it, days, weeks and months have quickly slipped by. This cycle of focus from commitment to feigned relaxation continues for sometime" I use the term "feigned" relaxation because for us there was no such thing as total relaxation. Ping Lian required constant vigilance and energy. However, losing focus of my goals to work toward teaching Ping Lian did not ever mean losing focus of Ping Lian. His behavior did not allow that for at least one second. I existed day to day on this emotional roller coaster ride… up and happy when I was disciplined and focused, yet guilty and feeling low when I knew I was uncommitted.

Imaginative and free spirited are words that very strongly portray my personality. As I picture Ping Lian in the future all grown up, I feel petrified. I dare not imagine facing my severely autistic son as someone without feeling and regard for others for the rest of my life. Pondering the *burdensome* effects of autism on my freedom, and on the lives of my daughters for the rest of our lives brought immense fear and worry. When I imagine that one day Min Seng nor I will be around and no one will take care of Ping Lian, the fear becomes insurmountable. Many times I weep from deep within as my tears drop. Many times, as I think of what the future holds for Ping Lian, my heart cries out, "My poor boy……I can't bear thinking of your future… How? How?….".

The fact that I have full heartedly accepted that Ping Lian is autistic and accept him full heartedly does not mean that I can deny or ignore the imminent greater *destruction* this may bring to our family life now and in the future. Ping Lian and my two girls are still young. The *destruction* autism brings to our lives now is still acceptable and bearable. Yet, I know the worst is yet to come.

> If we can balance our fear with hope, then it is good to have FEAR, as fear is a strong drive and reminder to get us to move forward toward a more positive outlook

I know that the only way I can change the future for my daughters' and myself, is to change Ping Lian NOW! That means in order to *rescue* my daughters' lives and my life, the only approach is to *rescue* Ping Lian first. I know that I need to do my best possible by changing Ping Lian NOW! If I cannot avoid the destruction autism may bring to our lives in the future, at least I can do my best NOW to minimize the destruction. Undertaking of this rescue mission requires my focus and determination now, before it is too late and the destruction intensifies. I justify my rescue mission by continually telling myself that whatever I do NOW is not just for the benefit of Ping Lian but is also for the entire family's benefit. I do feel guilty for neglecting my daughters, especially Cher who is still so young….but there is so much to handle and so little time!

I constantly remind myself that Ping Lian is *my* son and it is *my* life-long responsibility to care for him. The reality was obvious…There is no way I can run away and escape. I must act NOW before it is too late. The question for me became: "more pain NOW, or more intense and longer pain in the future??" I believed the final motivation to really get me started and willing to accept the upcoming sacrifices unconditionally was "fear"."

Thus, I continue to read and gain more knowledge about autism. I attend conferences and seminars about autism at Kuala Lumpur and learn more about autism through the internet. I read success stories about autistic people and also some not so successful, unpleasant stories about autistic people. I know that I need to know both sides of the story of autism. The negative stories served as scare tactics to remind me to keep focusing on the immediate goals for Ping Lian and force me to let go of my immediate pleasures. I also relied on these negative stories to remind me of the poor future outcomes if I were to lose focus. The positive stories served to justify that Ping Lian is worth any and all sacrifices that my family must endure. They also help me to better understand the possible abilities for Ping

Lian. With these constant reminders, I manage to get more committed to reaching the goals I have set for my son.

For Ping Lian to achieve *any* goal, I must break down the goal into many small simple steps. My expectations for Ping Lian are getting higher and the tasks and demands are getting harder. Mostly, my anticipation for Ping Lian to progress to the next level immediately after having just advanced a step results in more frustration. I cannot help but to contrast Ping Lian's rate of progress to that of my girls. For example teaching Ping Lian a very simple task requires hours and hours of my input while encountering many difficulties and obstacles, yet, with my daughters tasks were automatically learned without my ever having had to actually teach them. Happy moments of teaching usually last for only very short periods. There is still a lot for him to catch up on and a long way to go. As time passes, it is getting more obvious that Ping Lian's ability level is low and that every step needs to be taught separately in order for him to make progress. Seldom was the case that once he knew something, he would automatically know the next step. I am starting to ask "How long is this going to take and how long can I go on like this?" Fear has started to eat me up again and the *hope* was starting to fade. I knew that it was going to be a long and tough journey but I didn't really know how tough. Most of the time my fears and frustrations were greater than my hopes. This is not healthy and I have started to wonder how I would maintain my Faith and HOPE. Without faith I could not maintain my commitment. I also wondered if the journey (for me) was just too long. The journey was getting tougher and I began to believe that it just might outlast me. Fear, as it turned out could not be my final motivation for proceeding on this journey.

As my faith dwindled, the burdens intensified. I really do not want to live my life this way and there has to be a better way to make this journey happier and more fruitful. Happiness is a choice that you make happen. However my optimism was difficult to maintain as each day brought forth yet another challenging encounter with autism. "What can I do to make our journey pleasant and enjoyable when I have an autistic son"?

"THINK & GROW RICH" – BY NAPOLEON HILL
– DESIRE PERFORM THE "IMPOSSIBLE"

Achievement of any goal encompasses more than understanding a technique or methodology. Method and technique can be learned from books, the internet, conferences, seminars and other parents. To learn how to sustain my motivation to achieve the goals and maintain a positive mental attitude toward all this, requires yet another approach. I need to learn how to make this sought after journey, with positive emotions in tact and without resentments. I know that I must embark on yet another search to discover "HOW". In *fact, even now, (2007) I am still in the process of Experimenting and searching how to better succeed!!*

I love the book by Napoleon Hill - "Think & Grow Rich".[8] This book was introduced to me many years ago by Min Seng as a "must read book". This book had such tremendous impact upon the changes I made in my life. It contributed immensely to my current thinking patterns. I used the book as a guide for my career and to train my sales team. The book has helped me to achieve many of my sales targets and to win many overseas incentive trips. I decided to read it again. I was most touched by the chapter about "Desire: Perform the Impossible". Following is a brief excerpt from the text:

> In this chapter, "the author tells about how he transplants his burning desire into his son's mind; the desire to hear and speak and live as a normal person. His son came to the world

---

8 Think and Grow Rich, Napoleon Hill (Hawthorn Books,1972)

without any physical sign of ears and the doctor admitted, the child might be deaf and mute for life. The author finds a way to transplant into his child's mind his own burning desire for ways and means of conveying sound to his brain without the aid of ears." I also remain inspired by another sentence where he states " I would fill his mind so completely with a burning desire to hear that nature would, by methods of her own, translate it into physical reality"[9]*..... In one section he says that "I discovered that he could hear me quite clearly when I spoke with my lips touching his mastoid bone, at the base of the skull... so I went to work creating stories designed to develop in him self- reliance, imagination and a keen desire to hear and to be normal"....*

At the end, his method of "programming" the child's mind was bearing fruits. His lifelong desire for normal hearing had become a reality.

Without any reservations, I believe in him and try my best to follow what Napoleon Hill did. I attempted to "transplant" all of my goals for Ping Lian, so that they would become Ping Lian's goals. I believe with this "transplant" of goals technique, we will have a better chance of success as I do not feel I am working alone on the goals, because in this case, Ping Lian would be working with me as opposed to my working *on* Ping Lian.

I read the chapter again and again. I must have read it more than twenty times. Whenever I set a new goal for Ping Lian, I reread parts of this book and when I am feeling down I would read it again. I followed the author's lead and began to transplant my *Dream* and my goals into Ping Lian to make them Ping Lian's Dream and goals. So much precious knowledge has stemmed from this book regarding faith, autosuggestions

---

9   Hill, p.42

and the subconscious mind. The following words became a big inspiration for me: "*...every adversity brings with it the seed of an equivalent advantage*". My *Faith* is growing again.

THE MORE I DO, THE MORE I WILL GET

After all the struggling, searching and reading, I have also come to the conclusion that the following is a universal rule: "*The more I do, the more I will get.*" The only unknown is how much I will get. My philosophy is that it does not matter *how much* I get. Sometimes something is better than nothing. So with these thoughts in mind I will proceed regardless of what adverse situations I may be facing with Ping Lian. I now approach the journey of teaching and guiding Ping Lian, as if preparing for an exam in school. I set up a point system where 100 points is the best and maximum score. The more I focus as I expect myself to, the more points I will earn. However, I would view *any* score as a success. The point was simply to do the best that I could with my limited resources at any given time. So long as I spent time teaching Ping Lian, I would be happy. So 70, 50 or even 30 points meant I was moving in the right direction. There is no such thing as failing in my *exam* with Ping Lian. Even a few little points are an achievement and therefore a victory. With this point system I began to enjoy every little step toward progress with Ping Lian. Secretly, I thought "Who knows, if I do my best I may be lucky enough that one day I may have a surprising result from Ping Lian…Maybe even 100 points as a bonus like Napoleon Hill's son."

I started to record how many hours I spent with Ping Lian each week. I enjoyed calculating the total hours that I spend with him. I also started to focus more on the quantity of my efforts as opposed to the quality of Ping Lian's progress. I no longer put the emphasis on how much or how effective was the time I spent with him. How much he progresses during the time, is not my priority anymore. As long as I did my best during those hours I spent with him, I was happy. Any little improvement by Ping Lian was a joyous achievement. That is enough to me. I also started recording the amount of time that the employed teacher spent working with Ping Lian. Calculating these hours was very rewarding to me. I felt comfort knowing so much time and effort was being put in each week. Not focusing on how much Ping Lian had improved from those hours, alleviated some of the stress and discouragement.

From an expert or educators point of view, my *teaching* approach may be deemed incorrect, but it definitely kept me positive and motivated me daily to move on. The simple fact that Ping Lian could spend x number of hours with me was already quite an achievement on its' own.

> Happiness is a choice, be content but not complacent and always work and look forward for the better times to come

As my Faith began to re-emerge and strengthen, my journey proceeded with happier times. To remain happy, I learned to appreciate. I learned to be happy with whatever I have now while looking forward and working toward, what *can* be better.

GET TO KNOW GOD

Later on I felt blessed that *"I have been able to know God, I open my heart for God and allow God to come into my life. I have God to depend and rely on. I do not just depend on my self. With the knowledge I gained from the book 'Think and Grow Rich' and the Faith that I have in God's grace, my growing Faith in Ping Lian's abilities, and my increased knowledge and experience about autism, I have gotten off of that emotional rollercoaster. I am focused and I have started my happy journey with Ping Lian."*

> Knowledge, Decision, Action, and Determination are crucial in determining what kind of life you are going to live

THOUGHTS FROM MY PING LIAN JOURNAL ENTRIES (EXTRACTS)

Written on Feb 2004 (Just after Yeak passed away)

> Initially Ping Lian lived in his own world and had no feeling for others. Ping Lian also would not allow us to hug him. He did not like to be touched. It was almost impossible to kiss him. At this time, recall that my main goal for Ping Lian was that he must have love and feelings for others. I tell myself, if he can't talk; it is not a big problem, but if he has no feelings of love, that is a big problem. Without love, life will have no meaning and he will be a dangerous person in the future. I can't and I will not be able to live with a person who has no love or feeling. So I set my goal

that he must have feelings. I did everything possible to make sure that he could experience "feelings".

So, every night I put him to sleep in between Min Seng and myself. We turned on the gentle brain stimulation music every night before Ping Lian slept and even right through until after he was asleep. In the morning before he would wake up we would turn on the music again.

We hugged him and touched him when he was half asleep and after he fell asleep. We also took every other opportunity to hug and touch him. I would talk to Ping Lian as he slept or just before he would waken and tell him how and what I wanted him to be. As he lay half awake I would apply "Autosuggestion Technique". Ping Lian would not listen when he was awake so I took advantage of this approach to speak to him when he was half asleep/ half awake. After all, what did I have to lose? He didn't listen when he was awake, why not try this? I was desperate. I just hoped and prayed that the message would get into his subconscious mind.

I would touch him, hug him, kiss him and tell him I love him over and over again. I would tell him how I wanted him to be and how I wanted him to behave in very simple language. I don't really remember exactly what other things Min Seng and I did or said or even for how long. I do remember that one day at the supermarket, one little girl was crying and Ping Lian just started running toward that little girl at a very fast speed. As I looked toward the girl's parents I saw a look of fear for their daughter come across their faces. They must have thought at that moment that Ping Lian wanted to hurt the girl...but I saw Ping Lian's face full of care, concern and worry for the girl. He was not going to hurt the girl but he wanted to console her and care for her. At that moment, I just knew that "HE HAS GOT IT!". I am so happy!!!! Min Seng is so happy.

Now, despite his autism, he has so much love, care and concern for others (Even though at this time, he still did not show his love and care in an appropriate way, I knew that he felt love). Nowadays he is very good at reading people's feelings and interpreting their body language. He can read when I am happy, upset, angry or not happy. He can read my body language if it says I am not satisfied or very happy with his performance. He can "sense" someone who cares for him or someone who cannot be bothered or is not interested in him. He always hugs a person spontaneously if he senses that the person really does care for him. This is also his way of showing his love or like of a person. At time I feel that he seems to instinctually know who cares for him.

He is a loving, obedient, obliging and grateful boy now. Every night before he sleeps I will say "I love you Ping Lian', and Ping Lian will say "I love you mummy". Many times I will give him a kiss and he will give me a kiss. And we go to sleep.

Ping Lian still has limited communication & social skills and so I continue upon my journey to strive for better.............

Look at the way Ping Lian leans on "Mummy".... so lovingly, obedient and content. You would never think that at some stage of his life, you couldn't even touch him or hug him and that he existed only in his own world with no feeling for others. Isn't he so blessed? ~ Photo taken Dec.2004

SUBWAY

Reading 3
Authentic Reading Experience
Islands of GENIUS
The Bountiful Mind of the Autistic, Acquired, and Sudden Savant
Darold A. Treffert
Foreword by Daniel Tammet

"Initially I had no clue that he was an aspiring outstanding artist"

Sarah GH Lee

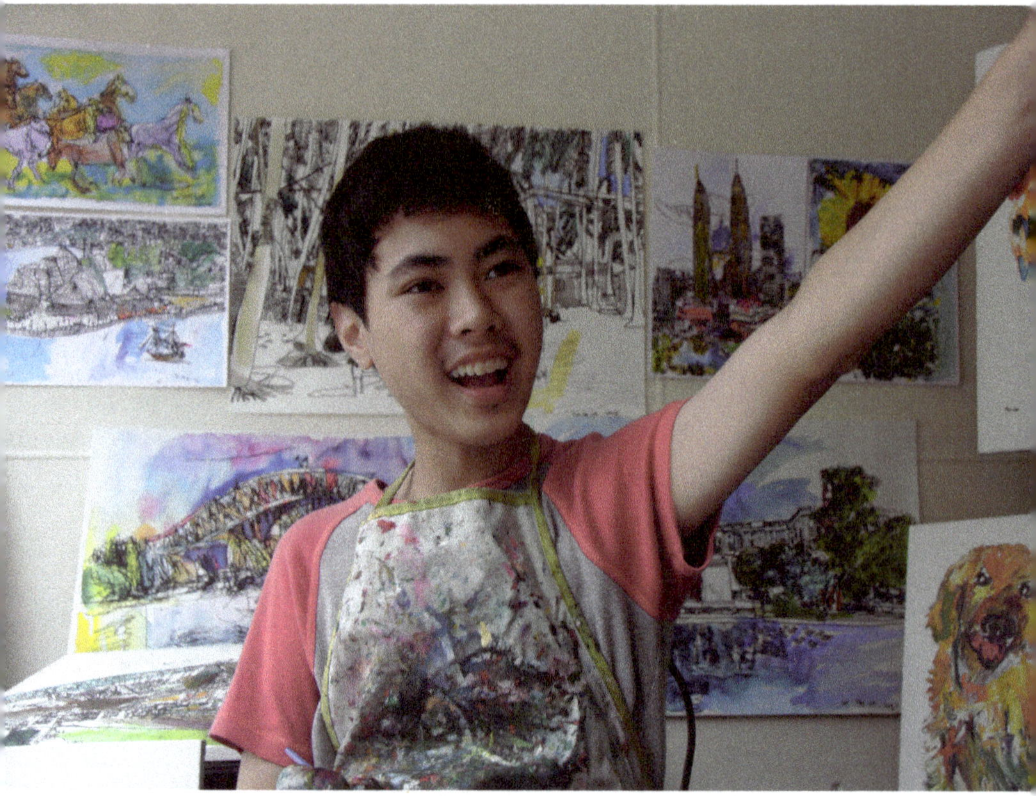

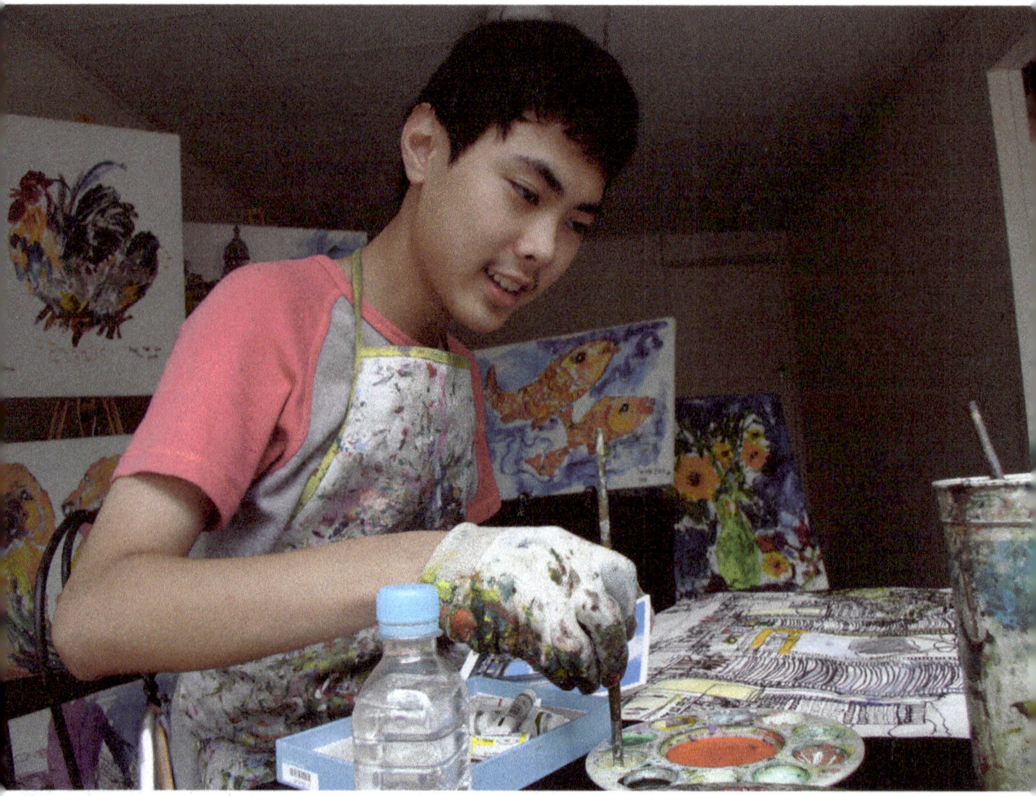

CHAPTER 4
Taking Action - Commit, Achieve and Be Happy

EXTRACT FROM MY PING LIAN JOURNAL ENTRIES:

Written on June 1998 (Ping Lian at age 4 year 7 months)

After 3 months of discussions with William (my employer), he finally allowed me the flexibility I needed at work. I am permitted to take 2 half days off per week to work with Ping Lian at home. In the mornings, I now have the flexibility to go into the office late and also the flexibility to extend my lunch hour if needed. This allows me to split my time to teach Ping Lian, in the morning before I going into the office (before Ping Lian leaves for Kindergarten class), during lunch time (my office was near my house, so I would rush home during lunch time to teach Ping Lian for a short session.) and at the night. I was so happy that William was finally amenable to this agreement. Otherwise, I would have had to resign and find a part time job. William said he was leaving it up to me, stating that I should plan my time and delegate additional work to my team. As long as the teams

I was responsible for could meet our sales targets every month, he was amenable to adapting my hours. I was very grateful that William's decision was in support of my needs during this time. I felt so relieved of the pressure and the additional stress that was created worrying about getting a new part time job, working in a new environment and barely making ends meet. William also said that my commissions from the sales team were not to be affected. This was wonderful. I no longer had to worry about getting a new part time job which would have meant a substantially lower income. The financial commitment was already just too much to bear, especially since the shares market had not recovered and in general was still very slow. Min Seng is still working on selling some properties to help finance several "bad investment" properties. Our reserve cash flow is dwindling and his attempts to collect on the debts owed us from his friends is unsuccessful. Still, with all of this happening, I am just so happy that from this month on, I will be able to have more time with Ping Lian.

SPEECH –LANGUAGE PROGRESS REPORT:

Date: 6-6-98 (Ping Lian at the age of 4 years 7 months)

Ping Lian was first seen in October 1997 for evaluation for speech-language skills. He presents with language disorder characterized by deficits in receptive and expressive language skills,

Therapy goals focus on increasing:
1. Ability to follow simple instruction, 2) Attention span, 3)receptive and expressive language skills, and 4) pragmatic skills, and 5) establishing the sound f,,v, z, ch and j. Semi- structure tasks and drills were used in therapy. Therapy was conducted in English.

Progress:

1. Ping Lian follows simple instructions with some cueing. He will usually comply with instructions to sit down.
2. Ping Lian can complete short tasks of about 5 to 7 minutes with minimal cueing. He needs more cueing in auditory attention tasks.
3. Ping Lian's receptive language has increased significantly to indicate more common objects in the environment and in picture books and food items. His naming skill has also improved to include common nouns and actions, colors and shapes. He can respond appropriately to where question with responses such as there and here. 4) Ping Lian can take turns in simple turn taking activities and to use some simple social phrases when requested to 6) Ping Lian can produce v and j and ch with about 80% accuracy. The production of the sound f is still unstable.

Summary:

Ping Lian makes significant progress during this period of treatment.

Recommendations:

It is recommended that Ping Lian continue with speech- language therapy focusing on increasing the auditory attention and memory, receptive and expressive language skills and following 2- step instructions.

Mrs. Yeak has been very supportive of Ping Lian and has been carrying out more language stimulation and reinforcement teaching at home.

SPEECH – LANGUAGE PROGRESS REPORT:

Ping Lian at the age of 4 years 11 months: (Oct 1998)

Progress:

1. Generally, Ping Lian's ability to comply has improved further. He will attempt to imitate actions or follow instructions but can only follow through with simple 2-step instructions about half the time.
2. Ping Lian's auditory attention skills have not improved significantly although he is now beginning to recall one element from a simple sentence he has just listened to.

SPEECH – LANGUAGE PROGRESS REPORT (CONTINUATION):

3. His receptive vocabulary in terms of name for nouns and verbs continues to increase. However he still has difficulty with labels pertaining to concepts and grammar such as prepositions and modifiers. He is beginning to respond more appropriately to simple Yes/No questions. His naming skills continue to improve and he is about 80% accurate in naming tasks. He is beginning to use 2-word utterances such as " eat bread", " brush teeth" spontaneously to describe pictures.
4. He still needs cuing in activities targeting pragmatic skills.

Summary:

Ping Lian has made some progress in most of the target skills but progress has not been as significant as hoped for. Short auditory attention continues to be a major difficulty.

....

KINDERGARTEN - AN OBEDIENT BOY

I was so glad that the administrative staff and teachers from Peter & Jane's Montessori Kindergarten were very supportive. If anything, I was most appreciative that at least my Ping Lian had a place to go. He started to love attending the program and he no longer ran all over the place while there. Ping Lian had become an obedient boy when at kindergarten. He was able to follow very basic instructions by imitating what the other children did in class. He would sit down when they sat and he would get up to line up when they did. Ping Lian had finally started to sit quietly throughout the class session with much less occasions of getting up and wandering around. He had also become toilet trained! I was very happy with his progress.

Ping Lian was still not speaking well and he continued to have very limited communication and social skills. We communicated with him by emphasising a few basic functional words to get him to follow instructions. For example we used "later" to get Ping Lian to wait, or to stall him when he wanted something. To teach him new words I start by pairing a word that has a similar meaning to one which he already fully understood. If I want to get Ping Lian to understand "wait", I will say to Ping Lian "Later, wait". After he gets used to the word "wait", then I will fade the word "later" and just say "wait". I use the new word in isolation (i.e., in this example – wait) only when Ping Lian has demonstrated that he understands and is able to respond to it appropriately. We share our style of communicating with Ping Lian with all of his teachers. His teachers attempted to follow through using this same tactic.

While I was very happy that Ping Lian had learned to sit still and to follow the very simple and basic actions of his peers, I was still saddened whenever I visited the classroom to observe him. As I would see him seated amongst his peers, I wanted to shed tears. He was "still" isolated "within" the group. The children would all be seated on the classroom floor and were engaged with some activity. Although Ping Lian was with them, he was "not engaged". The atmosphere appeared to be a happy one, as Ping Lian sat on the floor quietly. Ping Lian did not respond to what the teacher was saying. It was like Ping Lian was in his own world. When the teacher would say something, all of the children (all except my Ping Lian) would cheer and clap. Ping Lian appeared blank and emotionless. He would remain quiet; never look at the teacher, expressionless and without clapping. There was no single sign of any influence upon him from this joyful environment. The other children would clap and talk to one another. They "shared" their joy and responded to what their teacher was saying. I proceeded to wonder *"Why can't you be like the other children? Why don't you get involved and enjoy the happy moments?"* Ping Lian was indeed "among" them but he was not "with" them. Although he was physically present, his peers were non-existent for him and he in turn appeared to be non-existent to them. Yet, when Ping Lian observed everyone get up and line up to move to the next location, I watched as he stood up and followed the crowd. I insisted *"He knows what is happening around him"*. I wondered how he feels knowing that none of the children seemed to notice his existence! *"Does he feel left out? Did he feel rejected?"* At that moment, as I choked in an attempt to hold back my tears and control the throbbing knot in my throat, tears streamed down my face. Whenever I visited the class, this similar scene resulted in my heart crying out *"My poor boy, this is a happy and joyful moment. Why do you seem to not be there? When can you start to get involved and share the joy? Even if you cannot get involved and share with the other children, I will be happy just to see you enjoy the moment and the environment, even if it's by yourself I just want to see you 'IN'!"* I would walk out of the kindergarten class, crying inside with my heart bleeding. I just wished he could be happy and involved like the other children.

IMITATION SKILLS: "FOLLOW OTHER PEOPLE"

As I see that Ping Lian is still very much living in his own world and unaware or indifferent to what happens around him, I note that he is also *not* learning through observation how to socialize with the people. I decided to focus on teaching him to excel in this area. I wanted to get him to imitate and to learn from the children in his kindergarten. Learning from the "normal" children in kindergarten could be one of the fastest ways for Ping Lian to learn to be as normal as possible. I began to constantly use the phrase "follow other people" to get Ping Lian to follow others by imitation. This is also one of the ways I taught him to be aware of his surroundings in hopes of getting him to be more interactive and involved.

In order to make sure that Ping Lian actually applied his imitation skills by following what other children did in the class, I kept drilling him on imitation skills at home. I continually used the phrases "follow other people" or 'follow Mummy". Whenever I sent him to school or any other activities, I would constantly reminded him "Follow other people". The moment I would get into the car I would ask him "What Ping Lian do in the class?", and I would immediately answer the question myself (for him). In a happy and confident tone I would respond "follow other people do" or I would respond "Ping Lian follow other people. Ok!" I would then pause and repeat this question and answer adding "Yes!! Clever boy!" I would repeat this variation of questioning and answering myself aloud, many times until we reached our destination. This approach seemed to encourage Ping Lian while also reminding him of what to do next. It kept him thinking and gave him something to do. I used this same technique to teach Ping Lian everything and anything. Initially I would state a question and then repeatedly recite the answer myself until Ping Lian was able to repeat what I said. I often wondered if Ping Lian actually understood the words. "Does he understand?" No one can tell me the answer, not even Ping Lian. However, I didn't want to limit my expectations, so I tried not to focus on that.

There was no theory or model to my approach. It was my technique of "madness" and commitment. I just knew that if I kept saying and doing the same thing, "*one day*" Ping Lian would *know it*. For the moment, what mattered most was that I try. I only had one option… that was to keep trying until he understood. I believed, that one day…. one day, with all this hard work…. he would understand and he *will* do it!!

Sometime in the year 2000, I started getting constant complaints from the church's Sunday school children. "Aunty,[10] Ping Lian keeps following

---

10 In Malaysian culture children call all married women "aunty" and all married men "uncle", as a sign of respect. It is considered to be a show of good manners. I still call any one much older than me aunty & uncle.

everything I do…..". This was the best *complaint* I could ever have heard! Not until 2007, was it evident that Ping Lian's participation in the church was no longer pure imitation. He worshipped along with the rest of us. As I witnessed Ping Lian stand, jump and clap at the appropriate times during the service, I knew that he was not simply copying the actions of others. He was not imitating …he was "involved", participating and enjoying himself at the service. It appeared that finally, my "madness" was paying off!

PING LIAN MUST BE ABLE TO READ

By the age of 5 Ping Lian was still not speaking spontaneously. It took so much training and effort on my part just to get him to imitate and to say a short phrase. Even with all this training he had only learned to say very few phrases and would very rarely say them anyway. Ping Lian would say "I want apple" or "want water" with some prompting.

Speaking and reading became another prime area of focus for me to teach Ping Lian. I decided that while teaching him to imitate speaking, I would also teach him to read. Everyone must learn to read, autistic or not. How much he may understand from his reading didn't matter to me. I believed that *"One day"* he will understand!" I started teaching Ping Lian to read by using the "Lady Bird: Key Words Reading Scheme".[11] I made flash cards with words copied directly from the first book. Once Ping Lian was able to read and recognize all the words from the home-made flash cards of the first book, I attempted getting him to read the same words as they appeared directly from the book without the flashcards. Ping Lian did indeed eventually learn to read the words directly from the book. We

---

11   Ladybird Key Words Reading Scheme. By: W Murray
     Copyright: Ladybird BOOKS LTD MCMLXXIX Ladybird Book Loughborough

Chapter 4: Taking Action - Commit, Achieve and Be Happy   77

then moved forward using the same procedure for the next book and eventually it was no longer necessary to use the home made flash cards at all. I introduced 5 different books, while intermittently going back to previously mastered books for additional practice and retention of the words and phrases. I continually gave him the same books to read and Ping Lian was reading every day. He also started to appreciate my reading other simple books to him. In January of 1999 I employed Miss Rita to come to our house to teach Ping Lian to read using phonics. In order to help Ping Lian to focus more during his reading and his ABA drills, I turned to Ritalin. Ritalin was a medication recommended for treating hypractivity and impulse control.

At the onset, the Ritalin really seemed to help Ping Lian during his reading sessions. He definitely appeared much more focused than in the past. He was reading more quickly and for longer durations. Ping Lian had been on and off of Ritalin during different stages of his life. In general he would be put on Ritalin for several months and then have a drug "holiday" for a few months before starting Ritalin again. At some point I noticed that I no longer noticed any significant differences in Ping Lian's behavior or rate of progress whether he was on Ritalin or off of it, so I stopped giving it to him.

Although I was aware that Ping Lian did not understand the meaning of what he was able to read, I rationalized that if he could read the same basic simple books repeatedly over and over again; *"one day"* his understanding of the simple words and phrases would come. As for the more difficult words, my hope remained strong. There must have been some reason to my *madness*. Too much was involved. It was just too hard and required so much energy to teach him that I had to believe wholeheartedly that Ping Lian would learn to read! There would definitely be a positive effect down the road *one day*!

I hoped that the repetition of these words and phrases would lead to a quicker and fuller understanding of their meaning as they related to his daily life. We began to make a conscious effort to use these phrases in our every day family interactions in order to connect some observable and functional meaning to the words for Ping Lian.

Ping Lian still did not speak spontaneously, nor did he pay attention or understand me if I spoke to him in long sentences. There is still so much that he does not understand. Reading appears to have become a way to impart knowledge to him and also an appropriate way to keep him occupied. Ping Lian still does not engage in appropriate play, nor is he interested in watching television or childrens video programs. His occasional independent interest in reading provides me with a much needed break from the tiring and energy-draining process of my daily teaching routines.

Given Ping Lian's obvious deficits, I always tried to balance my expectations of him. While I had accepted and admitted to myself that he was autistic, I did not treat him as a disabled child all the time. As a matter of fact, I tended to plan for him according to my expectations of a typically developing child, a "normal" child. Deep in my heart, my gut feeling was that *one day* when he is ready to "open up" and start understanding the world, he will be able to depend on reading for knowledge. The enthusiasm I felt toward teaching my autistic son to read was not shared by my friends. I had an immediate circle of friends who together as a group along with me had gained so much knowledge by educating ourselves through reading about autism and ABA. These friends however advised me that reading should *not* be a priority for Ping Lian. "There is no point in getting him to read if he does not understand." The general consensus of advice was that I should focus on getting Ping Lian to speak. Due to the family's financial commitments it was still necessary for me to work to help support the family. Mother of three, needing to spend most of my time teaching Ping Lian, I really did not have much time for researching topics such as "what" and "how" was best way to teach a child who has autism. Whatever I did read I attempted to apply immediately thinking: "this is good and it will work!" I would take "Action" immediately. A few of the autistic families with whom I had become acquainted had engaged US and Australian consultants in Malaysia to develop programs for their children. The parents would follow through either by hiring a therapist to work in their homes or they resigned from their jobs to help teach their own child full time. Ping Lian was not so lucky. I could not afford to resign from my job or to hire a consultant. Given my situation, these were not reasonable options. My only recourse was to depend upon my own maternal instincts. The decision of "how" and "what" to best teach Ping Lian was based on my intuitiveness.

Most importantly, my vision for Ping Lian "NOW" was based on his future. I planned for him based on my expectations for him to have a "normal" future. I focused my energy and efforts in getting him to read regardless of what others advised me. I thought about the many deaf, dumb and even blind persons who lead quite normal lives. My priority became not *how much* Ping Lian can *speak*, but *how much* he could *understand* life.

By the year 2007, it was obvious to me that Ping Lian had gained some understanding of the world around him. I was no longer "alone" in this quest to teach him about life and the world. Ping Lian himself was trying to make sense of his surroundings.

I am still in the process and continue in my approach to teach Ping Lian to understand life and the world. I have learned that autism carries with it a very different meaning for each affected family. Resources, supports, knowledge, school programs, technologies; …. even awareness vary across individual families, communities, governments, regions, and countries. So just as every individual autistic child is so different, unfortunately so are the resources available. From awareness regarding autism to governmental support the differences are vast across communities and across countries. Thus, I have taken on the position that there are no set rules for "teaching an autistic child". If you can't afford or manage to implement one recommended technique or program then you should proceed with another plan. Everything needs to have a balance, and adjustments are imminent. I will always need my plan, based upon Ping Lian's progress and any changes in our availability of resources. The fact that my priorities may not be viewed as common priorities by others, is just another notch in the autism spectrum. As parents, we need to use whatever knowledge we have attained through our shared life experiences coupled with what we have learned from experts and formulate our own path toward advancement for our individual children. Guidance is all that we are offered. A parent must then take that guidance along with their own wisdom (the wisdom that only a parent can have), adjust the template and then decide what is best for their own child. This was and always has been my frame of mind. I then invested all of my energy ….in taking *"Action"* for Ping Lian! I had no more time for additional research. I only had time for taking immediate *"Action"*. I also did not have the financial means to employ professional therapists or knowledgeable consultants. My budget was only enough for me to employ someone, like a university student who needed some part time income, to work with Ping Lian at home. This is where I invested any and all additional monies.

Of course I wanted Ping Lian to learn to speak, talk, and communicate. However, I decided to proceed in my desire to teach him to read without "waiting" until he could speak. I thought *"What if Ping Lian takes 'forever' to start talking?" It is not necessary to wait until Ping Lian talks to teach him to read!"* So with the reasonably limited knowledge that I had gained regarding autism and my limited finances…I proceeded with confidence that I could help my son. I would do whatever I could and believed that if you *" never try, you never know"*. In retrospect I learned that teaching Ping Lian to read was actually so much easier than teaching him to speak.

PING LIAN PARTIALLY EMERGES FROM "HIS OWN WORLD"

Ping Lian had progressed into an obedient boy who was much more aware of his surroundings. We no longer needed to struggle with him when we took him to the shopping complex. He no longer ran away to grab other peoples food and drinks. We no longer needed to hold his hand tightly and keep him close.

One day (August 1999) I realised that Ping Lian seemed to be more aware and involved in what was going on in our lives. We were leaving the shopping complex, and while walking back to the car, I suggested that we stop at the bathroom first. Of course, I know that Min Seng and my daughters were attentive to my words. Ping Lian (as always) did not seem to be aware. His eyes, his mind and his emotions had always been so disconnected from our conversations. Yet, this time Ping Lian reacted to my exact words. He was the first to respond by walking straight to the toilet. I was so surprised. I didn't tell him specifically that we were going to the toilet. Nor did I ask him if he wanted to go to the toilet. He had never walked into the shopping complex toilet (or any public toilet) unless I specifically said to him in a simple phrase "go to toilet", or unless his father simply took him into the toilet. From that point on, I realised that even though Ping Lian may appear as if he is "not with us" or not listening, he *is sometimes* actually "aware" of what is happening. I started to observe Ping Lian more closely. Although he rarely responded to others appropriately, I knew he had begun to absorb some basic things and have an understanding of his immediate environment. I started to feel that there was some emotional and social interaction developing at last!

Once Ping Lian learned to read, I was able to teach him to do worksheets by combining pictures and simple phrases. The worksheets involved tasks related to daily living skills and even some simple science.

I would read them to him and provide some basic instructional prompts in order for him to complete the worksheets. For example: I taught Ping Lian to connect the words and pictures symbolizing "when it is raining" to other words and pictures such as "you need an umbrella." Through the use of all these pictures, it became clear that Ping Lian did understand quite a bit about daily living.

As Ping Lian's reading and worksheet skills progressed his vocal communication skills were still extremely limited. At the age of 6, he was still not responding appropriately to basic requests. I could take nothing for granted. Even a simple 'yes" or "no" response to a basic question was not forthcoming from Ping Lian. For example, Ping Lian loved lolli-pops. I would hold a lolli-pop in front of him and ask "Do you want this?". Although Ping Lian wanted the *lolli* he would respond "no". These were very frustrating lessons (for both of us) because although I knew Ping Lian meant "Yes" because he did indeed want the item, I did not give it to him when he answered "no".

After mastering the basic reading and worksheet exercises, he still required my prompting to make a correct choice vocally. This was always very baffling to me, since the skills required to complete the worksheets (in contrast) seemed to require much higher-level thinking skills. Ping Lian eventually understood that his response to a Yes/No question held specific consequences. Ultimately, he began to process the information. The calculation and thought processes were evident on his face and actions. I could visibly see Ping Lian repeat the question "Do you want lolli, yes or no?", process the question, pause and then respond "yes". It was many years before Ping Lian could make such a choice independently.

I was proud that I decided not to adhere to the recommendations of others who had advised me against "wasting" time trying to teach my autistic son to read. Having made reading a priority, Ping Lian is not only learning to read, but also developing critical thinking skills.

By the year 2004 communication between us was so much better and easier. Although I was fully aware of all the time and energy myself and others had devoted to teaching Ping Lian, I was still so amazed whenever a day came in which a glimmer of independent functioning and understanding were evident. Still, questions had to be phrased in a specific format enabling Ping Lian to express a preference. For example I would have to say "Do you want to stay or do you want to go off?" Given this form of questioning Ping Lian will express his preference of "stay" or his preference to "go". He was definitely not just echoing the first or last choice given. Given three choices to make a preference, Ping Lian would still appropriately select the one that he actually wanted to do. His willingness and engagement once he made a "choice" was clear indication that the choice was indeed his "preference" at the time. I could not however simply ask Ping Lian "What do you want?" He did not appear to comprehend open ended questions. In 2007 - this is still how we typically communicate with Ping Lian.

I was overjoyed and proud with the progress that Ping Lian had made thus far. He could now understand most basic daily living skills. Even more thrilling to me was the fact that we had started to understand one anothers needs more clearly. Although his understanding was at a very low and basic level, it made a huge difference. Ping Lian was "thinking critically", and now I worried that *"There was still so much for him to learn about life, so much for him to learn to be able to integrate into society independently. We still had such a long way to go,…… a very long way to go. How much will Ping Lian be able to achieve in the future?"* I still do not have these answers. All I know is that I will reach for the stars and never limit him.

Knowing that Ping Lian has feelings for us; is able to read emotions; cares what is happening around him and can establish basic communication overwhelmingly feeds my hope for his potential. Since around 2004, Ping Lian no longer looked through me as if I were transparent. He is an involved member of the family. He loves to be around children, although he does not join them in play. He does not know how to engage, play or participate with other children, but he does show interest, awareness and enjoyment. He likes sitting near other children. When his sister is playing with her many cousins, Ping Lian is sure to remain close by. We are happy that Ping Lian has taken the initiative and made the decision to be "In". Even though there are still times Ping Lian obviously remains "in his own world", this has decreased tremendously.

Ping Lian was 10 years old when his Daddy passed away in February of 2004. I really no longer had the time and energy to continue to sit down and do table drills and worksheets with him. I even stopped reading to him. A few months after Min Seng passed away my domestic helpers (Mylyn) father also got sick. Mylyn, who was also under tremendous stress, eventually quit. For a very long time I felt unlucky. I was unable to get a good helper willing and able to assist me with teaching Ping Lian. In search of something to occupy Ping Lian who was now just wasting his time, I remembered a book that I had put away. It was called "The Original Social Story Book"[12] I had purchased the book a long time ago, and had put it away for a later date when Ping Lian would be *ready for the book*. Now was the time! Since I had no time to read with him, I tried to get him to read it by himself without me sitting beside him guiding him and teaching him. I tried to get him to read a few chapters every day and I just hoped that he would learn something from the book on his own. If nothing else, at least reading the book would keep him appropriately occupied. Ping Lian managed to finish reading the entire book within just a few months. It was 208 chapters (each chapter was a brief story of 1 or 2 pages in length). He may not have understood all of the stories, or even have read them correctly but he was definitely engaged and occupying his time in a functional way.

---

12   The Original Social Story Book, Editor: Carol Grey; Jenison Public Schools (1993)

I was just happy that he was able to do this independently. What a great moment that was. It was such an achievement for Ping Lian. The social stories didn't even have pictures. From that time on, I continued to give him this book to read (especially when I was occupied with something else and did not have time for him). He had possibly read specific chapters of this book more than three times.

Three years later (2007) I was still depending on this book to create some "appropriate" occupation of time for Ping Lian. Like any other child, Ping Lian did not always do as I wanted him to. However, Ping Lian's instances of refusal were welcome moments of independent thought. On occasion when I would give Ping Lian the Social Story book to read, he would refuse it by selecting a different one. Sometimes I would insist that Ping Lian read specific chapters again in the social story book because I wanted him to learn the content of a specific chapter. Ping Lian would complain by saying "read bear book" – to indicate that he wanted a different book. Other times he would accept the social story book and then proceed to take another book without my approval. Whenever he did this I actually experienced happiness. I thought *"He is so cute"* and in my heart I laughed.. *"Hey! He is not like a puppet anymore. He knows what he wants now and he knows how to go get it. He is not like a puppet that just does what I tell him"*. By the same token I begin to think that this may show that he has become bored with this book. Would boredom be possible if there was no understanding of the content? Anyway, I continue to wait for that *"one day"* when Ping Lian will tell me about what he has read. We will continue to work hard and to pray that this will one day become a reality!

Ping Lian was now 13 years old. He chooses reading as an activity and he selects books on his own. He indeed appears to enjoy reading, however I still do not know how much of what he reads he actually understands.

PING LIAN LEARNS FROM TV AND VIDEO

The search for areas that interest Ping Lian has been a most difficult task. I have been waiting a very, very long time for Ping Lian to develop an interest in watching television or videos. I had previously purchased a variety of CD's ranging from "Magic English" to "Sesame Street", "Richard Scary" to "Nursery Rhymes",etc. I bought so many just to see if any of them would strike his fancy. For very long time, Ping Lian showed absolutely no interest. I continually tried to engage him but to no avail. From the time Ping Lian was three years old, I instructed our domestic helper everyday to leave the educational video/CD on for many hours even if Ping Lian left or ran out of the room. It occurred to me that if the video is always on with childrens educational program or nursery rhyme videos, although Ping Lian may not be watching, he can hear it. Perhaps some sounds and words from the program will get into his mind or brain. Perhaps, one day a particular segment will catch his attention. After many years to my delight, Ping Lian however slowly, began paying more and more attention to the television. He eventually began to actually watch whatever video was playing for longer and longer periods of time. This finally developed into an appropriate leisure activity for Ping Lian as well. At some point Ping Lian was able to enjoy all the videos. He even began asking for help to get the videos on. I recall the excited feelings of success when my persevering "madness" to leave the videos on, although no one was watching resulted in yet another breakthrough. Ping Lian was focused and would sit and enjoy watching a video on the television. This provided the availability of yet another tool with which to teach Ping Lian. He also eventually (at age 10) started requesting to buy some of his "favorite" videos. I began using the purchase of new CD's as a reward for him for "jobs" well done, and good participation and behavior.

EXTRACT FROM PING LIAN JOURNAL ENTRIES:

Written on August 1999 (Ping Lian at age 5 year 9 months)

August 1999: Ping Lian had good progress

- Ping Lian has suddenly become very motivated to learn, very good attention and attentive. He is more independent with his task/works. He is able to write his own name now.
- He started to communicate with me. He couldn't read some of the new words in his school book and he came to me and pointed to the words!!!!! Hey! This is good progress...the first time he is asking for help on his own initiative with his "Home Work"[13]. I am happy! (Previously, when Ping Lian gets stuck, he would just sit there, stop and do nothing. If I did not take initiative to go to him to guide him, he would sit there for a very long time and do nothing).
- Do work in front of TV:
- I purposely got Ping Lian to work in front of the TV in the living room instead of at the table in the bedroom. All family members were watching TV. Ping Lian read the numbers aloud from his dot to dot book. He read from 1 to 30, then he connected the sequence by dots. After that I got him to color then. Wow! He started to use different colors on the picture. I am so happy. But I am even happier when he asked me "Black colour?" He said "Black colour?" a few times. In my heart I cried "My poor boy! I do not know for sure what you wanted to say...but I am happy that you try to communicate

---

13 "Home works Time" is a key phrase I have used with Ping Lian from the onset of all of our teaching sessions to prepare him for drills and all other instructional sessions at home. Whenever I would say "Home works Time" Ping Lian knew what was expected of him. Still today, I use this same term as it is really effective to get him focused to work.

- ..."... This is all first time!!!
- It is the first time he can do work in such a focused manner in front of the TV and complete his work. It is the first time he uses different colors on one page. How encouraging and exciting...It is the first time he spontaneously and independently asks me for an opinion in "words" about his coloring. I am so happy even though I do not know his exact question. Was he asking if this was black? or... if he should use black? Right now, I don't care how much I can understand him, He ask "black color?"!!! that is good enough ....etc.

(Note: Before this day Ping Lian completed each page with only one color regardless of my constant efforts to get him to use different colors at different parts of the objects he was supposed to color in. He always refused and he preferred to use only one color for each picture. This was the first time Ping Lian used different colors to color a picture on a single page. At this stage we still did not have any plan or idea that he would be involved in art).

- I am just happy that Ping Lian on his own tried to give me a message for the very first time!!.... He said "Miss Rita", "Miss Rita". I did not understand what he wanted to tell me. I only know that he is trying to say something in relation to his teacher Miss Rita. So I reply to him, "Today is Thursday, tomorrow is Friday. On Saturday only Ping Lian go to Miss Rita School". To my surprise, Ping Lian said "Miss Rita, train".
- I remembered then that on this Saturday, Miss Rita was going on a school field trip train ride, and there was to be no class for Ping Lian. I think Ping Lian was trying to tell me:
- Miss Rita is going for a train ride. Maybe he try to tell me: There is no class on Saturday, because Miss Rita is going for a train ride... or maybe he wanted to says that... He wanted to go for the train ride? or maybe!.... maybe?...... maybe?.... MAYBE!!!!!?? I

tried to get him to tell me more but he didn't or couldn't. Ping Lian ran off and gave up because I did not understand what he wanted to say.

- In my heart I cry again, "Oh! My poor boy, I do not know what you are trying to say to me…but I am happy that you take the initiative to communicate; trying to tell me what happened at school, or just trying to talk about Miss Rita. Even though all the words may not come out, I am happy that you try to " Talk" to me now. I am happy that you are more "involved" in life. I am happy that you know what is happening……etc.
- This month is really a good month, so many good happenings in Ping Lian's life. I am so happy with his progress. He has achieved so much in such a short period. I am so happy to see all these new signs. This tells me that we have a lot more to hope for. He has the potential!…etc.

PING LIAN'S DRAWINGS OF MUMMY

03202 MY MUMMY - NOV 2003

Ping Lian draws "Mummy" tired and full of stress. Yes! It is true. I am so stressed and tired on this day. I just wanted to know how Ping Lian would draw me. So I quickly got him to sketch me even though I was thoroughly exhausted.

04203 MY MUMMY - JAN 2004

I had just gotten my hair done. Ping Lian was not use to me with my new hairstyle. He kept touching my hair. I am in a happy mood, as I do feel that I look good and look younger with this new hairstyle. I asked Ping Lian to "draw Mummy" and he did! Doesn't the drawing actually show Mummy happier and younger? That is how I felt!

PING LIAN DRAWS MUMMY AND CHER ON CHRISTMAS EVE 2004

04216 HAPPY BIRTHDAY MUMMY – DECEMBER 2004

"Hey! Ping Lian it's Christmas Eve and we are not going to sleep so early. Tomorrow is Mummy's birthday, Please draw Mummy now for Mummy's birthday present, OK!" (It's actually well passed midnight. The fact is we have not yet gone to sleep and it is already the 25th, but because we have not yet gone to sleep, I cannot say it is already Christmas Day - Ping Lian would not understand.

Ping Lian enthusiastically gets ready to draw me and I say "Ping Lian, I want a beautiful and sexy Mummy". "Ping Lian, please draw mummy beautiful and sexy OK!"

It is past 12 midnight and we just returned from watching the 12 pm Christmas Eve fire works. He seems to understand what I am telling him. He is just so engrossed in drawing Mummy. "Did he understand what beautiful meant for a lady? Did he draw Mummy beautiful and sexy?" We are so happy and amazed in watching his enthusiasm and the energy he put into this drawing.

Note: In fact Ping Lian drew mummy as seated on a chair but he did not draw the chair.

04217 MY DEAR SISTER, CHER – DECEMBER 2004

Cher also gets amazed with his energy, and we love what he has just drawn. She gets so excited that she also wanted Ping Lian to draw her "beautiful and sexy". Cher said "Ping Lian draw Cher beautiful and sexy like Mummy OK!" And he did! It is the first time he ever drew Cher.

Cher is very close to Ping Lian, she cares and loves him a lot. Ping Lian has been taking advantage of Cher since very young – for the past few years. Cher has always given in because of his autism. Cher has grown up now. She is not a child anymore. She is in high school. The passing of her Daddy changed her a lot. She does not play with Ping Lian the way she used to. She prefers more private time and she does not allow Ping Lian to take advantage of her anymore. On this day, Ping Lian is so starved for Cher's attention and so he is happy and excited. He energetically draws Cher with even perhaps more energy than when he drew Mummy. I can see him feel satisfied and happy. By the time all was done, it was passed 3 A.M. You can imagine what kind of mood Ping Lian was in!!!

Don't these pictures confirm my belief that Ping Lian is no longer just living "in his own world"? Don't they show that Ping Lian understands? ….that he can read the emotions of Mummy and his sister?

STANDARD ONE

"My Ping Lian must go to mainstream school. He must experience school just like "normal" children ….for at least one to two years." *"I only have one year left to work toward this goal of mainstreaming Ping Lian".* My main focus is now to teach him skills that will enable him to survive in school and in large crowds.

My determination for Ping Lian to experience the mainstream school has always been great. This has created an urgency for me to work on Ping Lian's behavior and his basic survival skills within the school environment. I have a fixed time frame within which to work toward improving his many areas of weakness so that he can survive in a mainstream school. The compelling thought of sending Ping Lian to a mainstream school has served as a reminder and discipline system for me to work even harder. I continually remind myself…. *"If not now, it will be too late, and then Ping Lian will have no chance. I am running out of time. I only have one year left to work toward this goal."* In fact, this reminder prompted me to prioritize everything else in my life. I no longer considered such decisions as "sacrifices" for me, although they were still sacrifices for my daughters. They are the ones who suffered. Especially Cher, my youngest daughter. Cher is only two years older than Ping Lian. Just recently (in 2006) she shared with me that at one stage of her life, when she was very young, she felt like she had no Mummy. My heart broke upon hearing her say those words.

Although I always tried to balance my time, Ping Lian was so needy. It was impossible to give all of my children equal time when Ping Lian demanded so much of it. However, the price to my daughters has obviously been a costly and severe one. My ultimate goal has always been for Ping Lian be as "normal" as possible. I just wanted him to be like every other kid and to experience school as they would. I did not want him to miss out on this part of life.

School could be a safe place for him where he could learn about life. It could be a natural environment in which Ping Lian can learn to cope with crowds and changes. I thought that if he could gain the experience and ability to "survive" at the mainstream school, it would be much easier for me to teach him to relate and to survive in the "real world".

I envisioned him learning appropriate behavior from his peers. I knew very well that if I did not get him into the main stream school in Malaysia for Standard One[14] that he would *never* have another opportunity in the future. Also at Standard One, children are still young and naive, so it is safer and easier for Ping Lian to "survive" there. Looking at Ping Lian's needs as a whole, I decided my focus would be to get him into the mainstream school. I was fully aware that Ping Lian would not be able to cope academically in such a setting, but my primary focus now was on his socialization opportunities, not his academic achievement. Yet, to be truly honest… in the back of my mind I did have hopes that he might suddenly progress and be able to cope with the academics as well.

During this time my teaching drills at home with Ping Lian had shifted focus toward behavior modification in an effort to get Ping Lian to be accepted into the school. I simply wanted Ping Lian to learn to go to the right toilet; line up for assembly; sit through the classroom session; learn to copy from the board; go to the canteen, behave appropriately in the canteen; transition when necessary; know where or which class he is in; return to class after recess; …The list goes on. There is no better place in Kuala Lumpur that I can find for him to learn these most basic survival skills. I planned to teach what I could at home and he would learn to apply these skills within the school environment.

I had visited a few schools, including those which included special needs classes for the mentally challenged. I became even more certain and

---
14 Standard One in Malaysia refers to Grade One – the first year after kindergarten.

convinced that my decision to get Ping Lian into a mainstream school was definitely the right decision. I was pleased that this had been my plan for him from the beginning. I finally felt that SRJK Taman Sea[15] was the best for Ping Lian. The head master was very understanding and supportive. A few months before the new school year started, I told her about Ping Lian's autism. I made sure to explain to her as frankly as I could, Ping Lian's weaknesses as well as his strengths. I mentioned how obedient and loving Ping Lian was. I also mentioned that I would continue to work with him on his behavior and that if she did not accept Ping Lian into the mainstream school, my Ping Lian would have no place to go. I would rather continue to teach him at home full-time than enroll him in any of the public special needs classes I visited and I couldn't afford a private program.

Without allowing her time to give me an answer I proceeded *"I do not expect much of Ping Lian in the area of academic achievement. I do not expect much from the school either... I just need for you to accept him. To give him a chance to try and to support him to learn to "survive" in school and to learn some life lessons. I only request your permission to allow me to be in school to observe him until morning assembly is over and allow me or my helper to come in during recess time to help him." (At this time, In Malaysia the regular public school system did not allow parents, or any aides to come in as shadows for students, nor did the school provide aids for any students.)*

The head master turned out to be very supportive and Ping Lian was accepted into the mainstream school. Although Ping Lian was generally well-behaved, I was extremely concerned about the crowded school environment which was about to become a totally new experience for him. I worried about the negative impact that it may have on Ping Lian's behavior. I recalled instances where my friend's child being "kicked out" within the first or second week of school. I envisioned the possibility of

---

15 SRJK Taman Sea is a mainstream school in Malaysia.

Ping Lian's behavior being unsatisfactory and him being "kicked out" immediately. However, the head master was so caring and she trusted me when I said that Ping Lian was well behaved in the home environment.

We came to the agreement that, if in the beginning of the school year Ping Lian's behavior proved to be unsatisfactory they would consider that the misbehavior may be due to the new environment and would give Ping Lian additional time to adapt. The head master promised to let Ping Lian try for a while. I was so happy that I finally had a "normal" school for Ping Lian.

Immediately, I engaged in some pro-active steps to avoid the possibility of Ping Lian ever being kicked out of the school. Everyday, for a week, and weeks before school started, I got Ping Lian to dress up with his school uniform and his school bag. We pretended to go to school. It was still school holiday time and so there were no children in the school. The school was quiet. This was the best time to train him, expose him and get him familiar with the schools surroundings. We took Ping Lian to the actual classroom that he was scheduled to attend. We drilled him and taught him to copy from the blackboard. Chin Chin and I took turns pretending to be the classroom teacher providing Ping Lian with specific instructions. Everyday, for one week, we spent two hours in the classroom practicing with Ping Lian.

On 17 Jan 2000, at the age of 6, Ping Lian officially attended his first day of regular school. His class teacher and I were amazed by Ping Lian's overall behavior in the class. The classroom teacher was very supportive and she tried to explain to the children in the class about Ping Lian's condition. She asked her students to assist her in helping and supporting Ping Lian.

Together the teacher and I explained to the class that *"We have a special child in our class. He is Ping Lian and he is different from all of you. He does not speak like you, he does not understand things like you do, and he does not respond to things like you do."* I continued to explain ...."*but... Ping Lian actually wants to be like all of you but he is not as lucky as you. You learn many things very quickly and you can do them automatically. Ping Lian needs to try very, very hard to learn things. Even to say a simple word is a very hard thing for him to do. He needs to work extra hard to practice how to say something. Aunty knows that Ping Lian also wants to have friends like you, but he is just unlucky. He do not know how to make friends. He is still learning. For all of you, talking and making friends is so easy, but for Ping Lian it is so difficult. Ping Lian is a good and obedient boy! Ping Lian actually feels good when you accept him, when you are nice to him and when you are with him... even if he does not show it. You are all so lucky, but he is not. Can you all help him, teach him and give him support?!!"* Watching the children's faces as they paid such close attention to me and my words, I continued .... *"When you care for Ping Lian, he may sometimes not respond. It may seem like he cannot be bothered by you but please do not get upset. He is actually very happy and in his heart he is thankful to you. He just does not know how to show it. So, please do not feel bad if Ping Lian does not respond to you. Just continue to be nice to him. He knows when you are nice to him and he will be happy about it. We are all so lucky, we can speak well, play well and have friends.... but Ping Lian does not have all of these things. He is a special boy. So let us help him! OK! We are lucky people. I know all of you will be very helpful and I know all of you can do this. Aunty and Ping Lian will be very thankful to you for helping and supporting Ping Lian"*

We repeated this information over and over again to the children from his class as well as to the children in other classes. I also recited this as a story at the school canteen during recess time to children sitting around Ping Lian. I also purposely sent Ping Lian to school very early, so he would have more opportunities to mix around with other kids. I would then repeat this story again, in an effort to ensure his success and to help him. I was trying to ensure his safety in the school by getting as much help and support as possible from his peers. It was fortunate to see that Ping

Lian was always surrounded by so many children at recess time and even before the start of school. The children from his class and the general school were so supportive. Every morning I would hear reports of how Ping Lian was doing, and what the children had done for Ping Lian. Many children seemed proud when they were recognized for helping Ping Lian. Sometimes I would just stay back, relax, watch and enjoy how they actually fought to be the "one" who would help Ping Lian. In reality, sometimes they helped too much. I actually had to tell the children to allow Ping Lian to do some things for himself. For example I had to ask the children to let Ping Lian carry his own school bag! My Ping Lian just loved to go to school.

In the midst of all this "good" there were a few rare occasions reported to me where Ping Lian was being disturbed and teased by some students. In general this was very rare and occurred with children that were not in Ping Lian's class and who did not understand Ping Lian's condition. Whenever I heard such a report I requested to meet with the class of the "teasing" child to tell my story. After sharing with the children that they were.... *"...so lucky, they could speak, they could play but Ping Lian could not do these things yet. He is not so lucky like you. He is a special boy. He likes friends but does not know how to make friends. Please do not disturb him! You are luckier than him. Please help him. ...or you can let me know who disturbs him, and I (Aunty) will talk to them"*.

After hearing my story, the children who were teasing Ping Lian stopped bothering him immediately. There was however one particular child who was not at all affected by my story. He enjoyed the attention he received for teasing Ping Lian. Apparently he also enjoyed the attention I provided by speaking to him one on one about Ping Lian. Later, I decided to ignore this other child even though I knew he continued teasing and disturbing Ping Lian. I decided, so long as he wasn't hurting my Ping Lian, I could ignore him. Even, in my presence this young boy did not hesitate to tease my son. After a while, on several occasions this boy actually came very close to me, looking for my attention. I would say to him "You disturb Ping Lian, I don't want to talk to you. I don't like you" and I give him a very "cold face". I would then immediately and purposely turn around toward the other children, smile warmly and speak warmly to them. I would thank them and praise them for helping Ping Lian. I pretended not to see the boy who teased Ping Lian. Surprisingly enough, after a short period, I did not hear any more complaints about this boy disturbing Ping Lian. Ping Lian was so protected and supported by his classmates and the other school children, that possibly this "bully" experienced the rejection from his own peers as a result of bullying Ping Lian. Also, now that I was ignoring him instead of giving him additional attention he stopped. Anyway, Ping Lian was getting a tremendous amount of help and support from the children and teachers in school. He was just so blessed.

Finally, neither Miss Chin Chin nor I needed to attend the recess to help and oversee Ping Lian. We let him learn and develop to the next level of independence. I proceeded on to my next step of learning for Ping Lian by approaching the school bus driver. I spoke to him about Ping Lian's condition and with the drivers help was able to teach Ping Lian to come back home from school by school bus (private school bus). Once or twice he almost got onto the wrong school bus, but the children in school helped direct him to the right bus.

I was so happy that Ping Lian survived well in the mainstream school. He was finally able to experience so much of school life. He had successfully learned and "survived" in large crowded areas and in new environments with other children, with "normal" children! He enjoyed the attention and the warm friendships offered by his peers. Ping Lian still needed to acquire many skills to enable him to "survive" in the "real world". After one and a half years in the mainstream school, I felt it was time for Ping Lian to move on. He had experienced enough school life and had gained "socialization" and coping skills for daily living. It was time for Ping Lian to leave. He had progressed tremendously in the area of daily living skills, although academically, he was still unable to cope.

I sensed an urgency for Ping Lian to advance in other directions and other areas for basic survival. I would now focus on those areas that I had temporarily placed on hold. In September of 2001, I took him out of the mainstream school. At this point I began to home school Ping Lian and also enrolled him in a program for special needs children (Emmanuel Care Center[16]) where he would receive supplementary instruction for 5 to 6 hours per week. Unfortunately resources were very low at the available program and 5-6 hours weekly was all that Ping Lian could get. At the time, this was actually the maximum number of hours that could be provided because there were too many *autistic children in attendance*. Later on Ping Lian also attended Kumon[17] once a week for the Math Program.

EXTRACTS FROM DIARY: (NOV. / DEC. 1999 AND JAN 2000)

Nov. 1999

- I find that Ping Lian learns about words much faster and also understands much better. but his other areas of progress appear to be stagnant. I am quite worried for next year he needs to start his "standard one" at main stream school. I doubt he can cope, but I tell myself that he will be OK. I am hoping for a miracle……
- Lately I tell him very often that miracle is in him….etc.

---

16 Emmanuel Care Center (ECC) was set up on 18 Sept 2000, under the Social Concerns Ministry of Emmanuel Methodist Church in Peteling Jaya. ECC provide supplementary classes to primary school children with special needs.
17 Kumon: www.kumon.com

Dec. 1999
- While I was downstairs and Ping Lian was upstairs, I asked him to take my black jacket for me (which was on my bed). He was able to get it for me. I am so happy that he can do it. Ping Lian progressed another level again and he is more aware/responsive of what's happening and also more "verbal".
- Continue on drilling him with activities he needs to cope with in the school and in the class, including "location drill" in the school.
- Start applying Autosuggestions technique again, I start talking to Ping Lian before he wakes. Preparing him to get ready for the school……..and I also tell him he will behave well at school …also tell him what he need to do at school ….and say he will make it………………………………………….etc.

Jan. 2000: Ping Lian at the age of 6 years 2 months
- Very happy - School started on 17-01-2000.
- Ping Lian went to school with half tablet of Ritalin. The doctor advised me to give Ping Lian one tablet, but Ping Lian was so lucky he only needed half a tablet to have a positive and noticeable effect.
- Weeks before school started we went to school to show and teach Ping Lian the actual site and class that he would be attending. We trained Ping Lian in the actual class. Ping Lian was able to follow instructions. Chin Chin and I are so happy. Chin Chin pretended to be the teacher of the class. Ping Lian was able to copy from the board spontaneously. When we asked to pass the book to the teacher, he did it too! When we asked pick up a specific book or activity book, he was also able. We are both very happy!
- We taught him where the canteen and the toilet were. We taught him to differentiate between the girls and boys toilet and we taught him that he cannot go to the girls' toilet.

Chapter 4: Taking Action - Commit, Achieve and Be Happy

Continued Jan. 2000

- We asked Ping Lian "What class are you in?" he answered " ONE YAKIN" .. We are Happy ……………………………………….etc.
- We trained him at the school for a few sessions before school actually started.
- The first day in school, Mrs Ong (his class teacher) and I were surprised and very happy with Ping Lian's good behavior. He was very well behaved, able to line up, sit in the class, able to follow simple directions to copy from the board and do some simple works in class.
- Wei Ling (Ping Lian's classmate) is very helpful and supportive. Ping Lian sits beside her and Ping Lian appears to be scared of her. He listens to her instructions or her body language which reminds him to pay attention in the class. Ping Lian always imitates and follows Wei Ling in the class works and he imitates her actions in the class.
- If I can't go to canteen to help Ping Lian during recess time, Chin Chin will go and help him. Every day she take Ping Lian home. After lunch and short rest, Chin Chin teach Ping Lian for two hours or more on specific ABA drills. Ping Lian takes another half tablet of Ritalin before Chin Chin's class. Ping Lian is so hard working that even after 5 to 6 hours in school, he can still cope and is willing to focus
- Once when Chin Chin told him "Ping Lian do work, look and listen to teacher", he covered his ears with both hands. This was the first time she saw him do this. "He is so cute", she commented
- Ping Lian was able to say Monday to Friday and January to December but he does not understand what it means ……………………………………….etc.

PING LIAN AT AGE 11
Photo by www.kidchanstudio.com

CHAPTER 5
Mummy Needs Motivation and Ping Lian Needs Motivation Too

SPEECH –LANGUAGE PROGRESS REPORT

> **Jan.6, 1999 (Ping Lian at the age of 5 years 7 months):**
> - Ping Lian has considerable difficulty with auditory-based tasks. His ability to perform 2-step commands remains at 60% accuracy. ……. Ping Lian frequently echoes key words or phrases in a question format instead of giving an answer.
> - His ability to categorize common objects has improved but he has difficulty transferring this skill according to changes in the question. For example, he can respond to "What is a zebra?" but has difficulty with "Name one animal?" …. His understanding of Yes/No questions continues to improve. However he still needs cueing to respond to "When" and "Who" questions….
> - His ability to respond when spoken to, has increased although his responses are not always verbal. He is beginning to express some wants spontaneously using short phrases such as "read book" to indicate he wants to do some work with the clinician. ……
> - Generally Ping Lian has made some progress in some of the target skills. His ability to attend to more demanding auditory stimuli continues to pose a challenge.

SPEECH –LANGUAGE PROGRESS REPORT
(continuation)

Jan.12, 1999 (Ping Lian at the age of 6 years 0 months):
- Ping Lian's reading comprehension skills have improved significantly.
- Towards the end of October, he could answer simple Wh questions based on the written text.
- Ping Lian attempts to communicate wants spontaneously. He is beginning to use more 2-word combinations but it is not easy to understand what he wants unless the person knows him well. Ping Lian is beginning to understand tasks required of him more easily. However, his attention is inconsistent.
- Generally Ping Lian has made progress in the target skills. Most significant was the improvement in the way Ping Lian responds to and interacts with the clinician and the plant (mother) during therapy.
- Ping Lian has overcome a lot of difficulties since he started intervention in December 1997. Mrs Yeak has been very supportive of him and this has helped Ping Lian tremendously. It has been very pleasant working with them.

PING LIAN'S MOTIVATIONAL MATERIALS

After Ping Lian was able to read, I created and designed my own special "Motivational Materials" specifically for use to teach Ping Lian. I printed those Motivation Materials and hung them in the living room, Ping Lian's room, my room and my domestic helper's room. Chin Chin had resigned, so I had employed a graduate lady from the Philippines, Mylyn to help me with my housework. She also served as Ping Lian's home tutor. These motivational materials were to serve as tools which I could apply to the autosuggestions and subconscious techniques which I learned from Napoleon Hill's book and other success and motivational seminars. With my limited knowledge, through trial and error I attempted to apply those learned strategies and techniques on Ping Lian. I created two similar but separate motivational materials, each with a different emphasis. One motivational material emphasized "I CAN"; while the other emphasized "I WANT".

The purpose of "I CAN" was to motivate Ping Lian by reminding him that if he tries hard he CAN do what he wants to do. It also created positive reinforcement reminding him that he is capable. The purpose of "I WANT was to create and foster desire for achieving certain goals. It also served to remind Ping Lian what his goals were.

I applied a color coding system to the text of the motivational materials, because there were too many words. The color codes served as a guide to the order of emphasis and the impact of the specific words. I selected and prioritized specific phrases. I printed the high priority words and phrases in BOLD RED. These were the words that were to be of primary focus for Ping Lian. He was to learn these words immediately. I wanted to drill the bold red words *"thought"* and *"Dream"* into his brain immediately. The phrases which I selected for secondary emphasis were color coded in black and in green. I immediately began to teach Ping Lian the red words. Ping Lian read this Motivational Material before and after each "Homework Time" session. I knew very well that many of the words in his Motivational Material were much too difficult for him to understand. Regardless, it was what I wanted him to achieve, so I just wrote it down, and let him read it. I was ready to "brain wash" him as my other children called it. As an auto suggestive and subconscious technique, my hope has always been that one day he will not only understand the words but also he will try hard to achieve their meaning.

I can talk

I will talk
      Spontaneously

Not good – is ok.
          Try again

I will be good

God always help me

I know I can
      talk well

Clever Boy

I want to talk well
   Listen well
Understand things well
   Play well
Concentrate in my work
   Pay attention in everything I do

Not good – Is ok
         Try again
I will be good

God always help me   I AM A CLEVER BOY

I later realized that these Motivational Materials had a very strong impact on Ping Lian's journey to overall learning. For example, as I delivered a direction to Ping Lian "It's Homework Timeee" usually in a sing song tone, Ping Lian would prepare for his lessons, knowing what was expected of him. At times Ping Lian would become frustrated, especially during these "Homework Time" sessions if he was unable to perform a given task independently. He appeared to lose confidence and would proceed to bite his shirt or get up and start jumping. I selected such opportunities as this one to introduce and emphasize the RED motivational phrase. I would point to the large red print and read "Not good - **Is Ok!** Try again, **I will be good!**" I then would have Ping Lian repeat it and read it. Sometimes I also asked him to continue to read or say: "God always help me" and then I would say "…and you are a **clever boy**" or I had him repeat "…and I am **clever boy**". Using this method, on many occasions Ping Lian immediately calmed down. I remember thinking to myself *"Hey, It works!"*

As Ping Lian matures, he has become more conscious of doing well in his tasks. The "Not good - Is Ok! Try again, I will be good!" phrases have been amazing magic words for Ping Lian, resulting in him being able to relax and calm down. Full of pride and patting myself on the back for what I had been able to accomplish, I thought aloud..... *"Ha! Isn't it good to let him learn reading?"*

Ping Lian ultimately learned to better cope and accept situations in which he felt unhappy or dissatisfied with his own performance by relying on his newly learned motivational terminology. He actually began to apply the phrases without further use of the actual written motivational materials! I no longer needed to rely on the written text and simply prompted Ping Lian to say " Not good…". I would pause and he would continue by saying " Is OK"! I would say " Try again" and prompt him to say the following with me.... "I will be good"! Sometimes I added " Yeh! Ping Lian is a clever boy", melodiously. This process eventually resulted in Ping Lian immediately calming himself down and regaining the confidence to try again. The ability to rely and implement the motivational techniques described, regardless of environment or situation were key factors in Ping Lian's ability to remain positive. This inherent positive approach to dealing with obstacles aided Ping Lian to maintain a happy personality. Maintaining a positive attitude, coupled with hope, such as is indicated in phrases such as "Not Good, is OK, Try Again", "I will be good", "I am a clever boy" have successfully proven here to promote a healthy attitude. The key ingredients are acceptance and forgiveness for oneself as well as toward others.

As the years have passed and I see my Ping Lian has grown to be very hard working, persistent and happy, I believe these motivational techniques are embedded in his brain and that he will continue to motivate himself in the face of obstacles. Perhaps this is the reason I am always told that he is such a "happy boy".

PING LIAN'S MOTIVATIONAL STORY

Usually before we actually start an instructional session, Ping Lian is made aware of his reward in advance for performing a "good job". I usually give him chocolate, cookies, or take him shopping, or to the play ground or just go outdoors - anywhere. He loves to go out. For these rewards Ping Lian will sit down to complete a session. Sometimes Ping Lian will complete a task just for the sake of getting the reward. At other times he seems to push himself that extra mile. I don't really know what motivates him to do so, but it appears to come from within himself. As he is autistic, he does not communicate well, and worst of all, he is still very much "living in his own world". I really do not know what he is thinking.

One day, half way through a teaching session, I felt the need to motivate him further. I wanted to see him put more of his heart in the session and so I created a very personalized motivational story just for him. I said to myself "What if he does understand and can identify with his own story? "My Story"? In order for Ping Lian to have some level of understanding of the motivational story I knew it would have to be simple. The task to create a simple motivational story, yet one that can have an impact on him, was not an easy one. Suddenly I had an idea. I told him *"Ping Lian, do you want to drive car like Daddy?"* I was unsure what Ping Lian could really understand so of course I used my gestures and acted as if I was driving at the same time that I posed the question. I held onto the invisible steering wheel, complete with making the car sounds and I answered the question myself - "Yes!" Then I said *"If Ping Lian want to drive car like Daddy, Ping Lian must work hard to be a clever boy"*, *"Only a clever boy can drive car like Daddy"*. Ping Lian appeared to understand. I was really amazed! I don't know what Ping Lian actually related to from my skit. It may have been that to him "Daddy drive car"- meant that he could go out; or maybe the familiar key word phrases "work hard" and "clever boy" affected him. Maybe he even really understood and wanted to be "able to one day drive a car!"

Anyway, how or why it appeared to have an effect on him did not matter. What mattered most was that it worked! As long as it works, it is a good story. From that day on, I just proceeded to use that same story. As time passed, eventually whenever I would say "Do you want to drive car like Daddy?" Ping Lian immediately responded by becoming very attentive and focused working happily.

So this has been my motivational story for Ping Lian. Sometimes I make the story longer. I might say something like "When Ping Lian grows up, Ping Lian want to drive car like Daddy?" I have made sure to begin to introduce the concept of "grows up" because I do not want Ping Lian to think he can drive a car immediately. I take caution knowing I am speaking to my autistic son. He is still a very young boy and I must be careful of what I say since I do not know what is in his mind. Sometimes I just make the story very simple," If you want to drive car like Daddy, you must work hard and be a clever boy". This story really seems to have an impact upon Ping Lian. He actually works harder and shows much effort to do well.

As Ping Lian grows more aware with the surroundings and is getting more mature, the story seems to be even more effective. Sometimes I can see him immediately becoming very motivated to work after he hears the story again. Frankly, after so many years, even today (2007) I am still unsure about how much Ping Lian really understands or even what he is looking forward to. The stories however, definitely continue to generate happy outcomes for Ping Lian. At the same time, I also constantly remind Ping Lian that "Ping Lian is special boy, Ping Lian is different, and so Ping Lian must work harder than other people to be clever". Many times I add "*Then* Ping Lian can drive car. OK?" This is just my trial and error type of methodology... Same story but put it in many ways because I do not know which words he understands most or how much he understands of these phrases. As time passes, these phrases embedded in stories still have a positive effect without me tell him the long stories. I just need to tell him "Ping Lian is special; Ping Lian must work harder to be clever boy". I emphasize "harder than other people OK!" Anyway, I guess maybe he knew that he is special and that he needs to work harder than others. Many times I know that Ping Lian does actually work and try much harder than most typical kids.

My friends and relatives express concerns that I give and push Ping Lian too much and that I cause him stress. There were times when Ping Lian was getting instructional programming seemingly non- stop all day with combinations of some easier tasks and some more difficult tasks. He had some breaks in between and many different part-time home teachers. There were very few full- time home teachers or therapists available and they were also very expensive. I always rationalized my "madness" and drive by telling myself, "Ping Lian is a special child. He needs to work harder than others. This is life. Life is never fair." What was most challenging and most important was to make the process interesting enough for Ping Lian so that he would be happy, motivated and have an ability to cope. Maybe I have successfully "brain washed" him to the point that he has developed a mental attitude to accept this situation. Or maybe he has developed his own drive and is willing and motivated to go the extra mile, sitting long hours every day to be a clever boy. Most importantly, he is still happy while he is going through the process. I believe the motivational story and the motivational materials have been very effective with Ping Lian. Many times I hear the voice of Mabel Goh (Ping Lian's teacher at Kumon) when she told me that, Ping Lian tries harder than the other (normal) kids in the center. She would always provide me with feed back informing me that she would sometimes use Ping Lian to motivate the other children in the class. She would tell them "Ping Lian is a special boy but he is trying so hard just to learn simple mathematics, but you are all so lucky,….." etc.

So, as for how much Ping Lian can cope with, and whether I am "giving" or "pushing" Ping Lian too much…… I guess it is pretty "relative". Every day that we "stress our muscles" a little, will one day benefit us. Anyway I have also learned from the books and seminars that "no pain -no gain!"

One day, Min Seng felt so touched by Ping Lian's hard working attitude that he wrote a prayer note for Cher to help to pray for her brother. This is what it said:

Talk To God

Lord, my brother Ping Lian has lived
without understanding as normal children do.
He has tried very hard to learn and
speak every day for long hours.
Now, what is become of him?
He must have you. Come help him.
Break your vow of silence.
Heal him, Lord.

Ping Lian, a boy who was initially living in his own world; not bothered about how I feel, not caring what was going on, having no self esteem, not caring if I scolded or screamed at him, ... has grown to care so much about how I feel. Sometimes a simple glance from me, results in him refocusing on his task, simply because he knows that I want him to, and because he is motivated to learn! Knowing that Ping Lian cares how I feel and how I see him makes me more than happy. How much he has already mastered or learned; how clever he is or can be, is now secondary. Ping Lian still has many limited abilities across all areas, but as long as he is happy and can maintain his motivation to learn, I know he possesses the potential to live and learn throughout his entire life.

At this point, I remind myself not to get settled with content. Very soon Ping Lian will no longer be a boy, but a man! As he develops he is becoming more aware. I see him getting more sensitive to how people understand him and accept him. *"Would these motivational stories and materials still have a positive effect on him as he grows up"?* That is yet to be seen. As a mother I am concerned about how he sees the world and how the world sees him and accepts him. I have started to wonder how long these motivational stories and materials will last? I need to get prepared and to search and adjust other methods and means to motivate him, again!! It is a never ending journey!

> In the process of achieving your goals and dreams, whenever you meet obstacles/ resistance and feel frustrated; just persist and remember that - Not good- Is Ok! **TRY AGAIN,** I will be good

EXTRACTS FROM MY PING LIAN JOURNAL ENTRIES:

Written on 3rd Oct 1999 (Ping Lian at age 5 year 11 months)

- I review Ping Lian's performance, I am very happy- Ping Lian doing well, improve a lot for the past few months. He has grown more mature now.
- I get him to practice copy from the board all by him self (without me sitting beside him) while I am watching TV at the other room with me checking him constantly. He did not do so well- few line of words, for normal children, may take less than 5 to 10 minute to finish it but Ping Lian had sit in front of the board for more them 45 minute still not finished yet. He copy, stop, and copy stop, his mind seem to wander round. Sometime I peek on him, some time I remind him. I am so tended to sit down beside him, them he will finished very fast, but I can't as by January, he need to be all by himself when he go to school. Many times when I check, I am almost run out off patient! But later, I think, at least he know and understand what I want him to do/expected from him and he is trying- This time, he is so obedience that he sit there all the time, he did not run away, he did not walk to my room at all, he did not jump to the bed. I start appreciate his trying progress and feel happy that he is aware of my expectation, he know that he can't get up because he had not finished his task— But I wonder when I do not sit beside him, why it take him so long to perform the task he already able? Why he can't focus whenever I do not sit beside him? I can't sit beside him all my life!!!! Doesn't he want to quickly finish the task, and then he can go for his reward? What has "Autism" done to him?

- I decide to leave him alone and not checking him to see what will go on and I try this- "Ping Lian, mummy watching TV- There! OK! - When Ping Lian finished, give mummy and say – I had finished!" I said again " I had finished! OK!". I go back to continue my TV program, it is quite for a while, no sound and noise from the other room. I wonder what is going on!! When I go back to check on him again- I feel like crying and laughing!
- My poor Ping Lian, he has already fallen asleep on the chair with his head on the table. Poor boy! He is really trying hard and be obedience. The bed is just beside him; he did not get up and hop on to the bed. I feel so happy and at the same time so sorry.
- Hear me coming in, he wake up, he look at me, his expression show that he look so guilty and worry, I feel even sorrier. And I tell him that "Ping Lian is clever boy! Is OK! Good try! Mummy so happy!" and I told him again "Not good! Is OK! Try again!"........ and I sit beside him, he continue copy and finished it quickly- I am happy, Ping Lian is happy.

(Note: Until today, 2007, as I am writing this chapter, the image of this scene – Ping Lian fallen asleep on the chair and trying very hard, the guilty look etc is still etched in my mind).

- I read "Baking a cake" with him, he like it and I had just finished make cake with him.
- He had complete reading Peter & Jane book (5b) today.
- We did a lot today.

DOESN'T THIS INDICATE THAT PING LIAN IS A HAPPY BOY?

04302 HAPPY FAMILY I (PAINTED IN 2004)

Look at the family of the horse, they are all happy and smiling, some are even laughing. Do you think it requires being a happy person to draw this? I doubt how an unhappy person can express such a happy and joyful expression of horses. So, do you think Ping Lian is a happy boy?

Chapter 5 : Mummy Needs Motivation and Ping Lian Needs Motivation Too   121

05405 HAPPY FAMILY II (PAINTED IN 2005)

Look at the happy and joyful chicks and the happy daddy and mummy chick. I guess Ping Lian is happy. Even if he drew this based on some other reference, if he is not happy, I don't think he can express the happiness and the joy in the picture so well; so lively and real.

A PERSONAL REFLECTION AND INSIGHT FROM "ONE OF A KIND" WEIRDO!

I am constantly aiming and looking for a way to have "outcomes" outweigh the effort that I put in. I do not believe that "One stone can kill two birds". I believe and aim higher as in "One stone can kill *many* birds". Given my limited time and limited financial resources, I need to be more efficient and effective. In my quest to aim high, I have come to the realization that things like "mental power" are crucial components to a child's success. Based on my own personal experiences with my son, I know that a general knowledge of the existing research regarding "what", "how" and "why" to teach autistic children is not good enough. I believe the process by which we can be more effective and achieve more successful outcomes will be easier if parents use positive mental power, coupled with a strong desire to achieve. Better yet, transfer that desire to their own child's mind and make it their child's desire. It can definitely be much easier if we work with them and not on them. As parents we need to work hard, but we must also work smart. This philosophy is what is referred to as "mental power". Whenever I attempted to share this *mental power* with other parents who had a child with autism, they generally did not understand or they were convinced that I was a "one of a kind" weirdo!

After Ping Lian's successful "survival" in a mainstream school, I was asked by one of the parents to share my experiences at a parent support group meeting. I was to talk about (a) goal-setting, (b) how to approach a mainstream school, (c) preparing your child for the new school process, (d) the obstacles encountered once at the school, and (e) steps taken to overcome the obstacles. I was very excited and ready to share my successful insights of Ping Lian's journey with other parents. Everyone was attentive, interested, enthusiastic and eager to listen. The attentiveness and eagerness of the audience was short lived. Once I discussed my approach of possessing "mental power" coupled with a " burning desire to achieve" I felt the atmosphere change quickly. I proceeded to share my thoughts on the importance of a parent's ability to transplant these burning desires into their own child's mind and transforming their parental expectations to become their child's goals. In my experience, nurturing those desires, to achieve them would result in more positive outcomes. Mostly, the parents were taken aback by my comments and basically decided that I was a one-of a –kind weirdo! As I pulled out a photocopy of part of the chapter "Desire" - Desire to Perform the "Impossible" from Napoleon Hill's book- " Think & Growth Rich" to share….people started losing interest. Some of them started smiling and even giggled, while others tried to cut short my presentation by talking over me. In general, once the majority of the audience was aware that the information was from a book about becoming "rich", they felt I was way off topic. This is supposed to be a forum about autism not about "sales"! They were only interested in knowing about what happened in school and how.

I persisted on sharing this belief that to me has made such a difference in our lives. I wanted everyone to benefit the way I felt that I had benefited. I felt strongly that to teach our autistic children we first need to teach ourselves how to acquire a positive mental attitude and to instil this burning desire to achieve our goals in our kids. The best I could do was to tell them that I am not an expert but I encouraged them to just be open minded. I urged them to read this book or at least this one particular chapter, which was about the authors son's experiences. I ensured them that they may find inspiring and helpful information for their own children. Although the information was not received with open mindedness, I was very eager to share my approaches and beliefs with this group. They were very knowledgeable about autism and I initially learned so much about autism, ABA, etc. directly from them. I will always be grateful to them for sharing their knowledge which helped me to help my son tremendously. Committed to sharing my experiences in hopes to maybe help others, I proceeded telling the group how this particular book had benefited me in dealing with Ping Lian and helped my family to come this far in achieving some of our goals. The most important influence having been the successful transition regarding Ping Lian's affect from one of "no feelings and living in his own world" to becoming such a loveable, obedient, obliging and grateful boy who can now survive in a mainstream school. A few parents did actually comment and asked, "How I keep myself so well and happy when I have an autistic boy at home?" (In fact I did not tell them that not only did I have an autistic boy at home, but I was currently under a tremendous stressful financial situation.). I did not give up and I continued in my hopes that they would see benefits as I have benefited. As I continued, stressing the fact that the book and the references to "rich" are not just talk about money, and not just motivational techniques for sales people

(Note: at the time I was working as a manager in sales and marketing).

Some of the group started laughing and I also felt some strange looks directed at me. I had photo copied many sets of the chapter "Desire to Perform the Impossible" and I encouraged them to take a copy as a free gift from me. Although I stressed that they should "just try to read it (only 8 pages) and that it may prove helpful to them", it was very disappointing to see that by the end of the meeting, I think not one person had taken a copy.

That meeting will always remain fresh in my mind. I remember feeling so badly and instantly thinking to myself… "You think I am funny and weird and you do not believe me???…. One day when Ping Lian is doing very well or he becomes somebody, then you will know what I am talking about… then you will not laugh at me!" I also was feeling shocked and surprised at myself for thinking that way at that moment. At that particular time we had only achieved a few of the goals I have mentioned thus far for

Chapter 5 : Mummy Needs Motivation and Ping Lian Needs Motivation Too   125

Ping Lian. The day of this support group presentation I did not yet have a single clue that Ping Lian would be a talented artist. This presentation was during the year 2000, and Ping Lian only began to draw and sketch independently by mid 2002.

> Our determination together with our autistic child's determination are crucial to achieve the goals we have set for them

PING LIAN'S SELF-PORTRAITS

03203 PING LIAN LOOKING AT THE MIRROR - PAINTED IN 2003

Does he look happy? Is he a happy child?

This is the initial drawing of Ping Lian after his start taking art lessons with teacher Bee Ling. He draws it with teacher Bee Ling sitting beside him reminding him and guiding him along- to get him to pay attention to darker and lighter portions - teaching him how to control his strength to get the different effects of the shadowing. Ping Lian loves teacher Bee Ling and he loves her class. Isn't this a look of focus and determination… and happy?

PART II
PINGLIAN'S ARTISTIC JOURNEY

CHAPTER 6
Ping Lian's Future and His Livelihood

As Ping Lian progressed, I started to focus on his livelihood. "What can the future possibly hold for my autistic son?" My thoughts were consumed with what I should plan for him. "How will he develop to be independent when he grows up?", "Who will he be?" I began a constant search reviewing possibilities for employment and what type of job might be best for Ping Lian in the future.

My initial plan for Ping Lian's livelihood was "custodial" types of services. "He could clean!" "If I find a 'safe environment' Ping Lian can be trained to clean!" However, as Ping Lian progressed further, I began entertaining thoughts of him employed as a gardener instead. "He can work in a nursery or maybe even a farm!" Then, I became even more ambitious. "I could get a few parents to work together to open a Café for our autistic children!" "We could open a Chinese Dim Sum[18] restaurant!" Thoughts of becoming an outstanding artist had not yet occurred.

---

18   Dim Sum is a traditional Chinese cuisine in which small portions of a variety of foods, including an assortment of steamed or fried dumplings, are served in succession.

YEAR 2000 WHEN PING LIAN WAS 6 YEARS OLD:

I am very happy with Ping Lian's progress over the last two years. He has made significant gains in his achievement levels within such a short period of time. His greatest progress has been in his behaviour and his affect. He has developed emotions or at least developed the ability to express feelings and awareness for his family and for others. My happiness is however coupled with my concerns and reality that he still has such a long way to go to be able to integrate into the community and the "real world". His main problem is still his limited social and communication abilities, given his deficiency in cognitive skills, and his low IQ level.

On occasion I would bump into a parent whom I had originally met at the hospital two years ago. It was always so satisfying to hear comments from them such as "Wow, Your Ping Lian has improved so much!" "Two years ago when we first meet, he was so.........." The most satisfying achievement is when others see Ping Lian show *"feelings"*. Ping Lian has developed obedience. He has become a loveable boy, who appears to be quite aware of his surroundings. He cares how we feel and he is starting to enjoy being with people, especially his sisters and cousins. I have nine brothers and a sister. When we have family gatherings Ping Lian is surrounded by more than thirty cousins. He enjoys the gatherings and enjoys being with us, not just amongst us.

I have forgotten since when, but for quite a while now, every night before we sleep, we will have a "special good night routine". I will say "Good night Ping Lian" and Ping Lian will say "good night mummy". Then I say "I love you Ping Lian" and he will say "I love you mummy". Then I kiss him and he will kiss me and we go to sleep. Every night, it's the same sequence and the same phrases.

How much of these routine phrases Ping Lian actually understands, as with everything else I am unsure. I sense that he understands love much better than before and that he loves me more and more. He tries very hard to do something or to work hard to please me. When he eats something, he sometime takes the initiative to save or offer some for me, and sometimes he even offers me a bite before he finishes all of it. He also sometimes saves some nice tidbits for Cher and Sherlyn. Ping Lian also displays through his behaviour that he is aware of what is right and wrong. He displays guilt if he has done something wrong, or if he has not done something that was expected of him. These may sound simplistic, as for most children they are behaviors a parent takes for granted. However, for my Ping Lian, these behaviors are milestones.

Many years ago, I often played games with Ping Lian by asking him "Do you love mummy?" If he said *yes*, I would exaggeratedly show my joy, hug him and say "I love you Ping Lian". If he answered *no*, I would show my sad face and pretend to cry loudly. I often peeked to view his reaction. Then I would ask him again "Do you love mummy?" I repeated these actions again and again and again, until he would say "Yes!" Sometimes instead of asking him directly, I just kept pretending to cry, mumbling "Do you love mummy?", "Do Ping Lian love mummy?" Often when he saw me "crying" so sadly, he would then pause and repeat my question by asking himself "Do you love mummy?" and then answer himself "Yes!" At this point I always break out with joy and laughter and shout " Ya! I love you too" and hug him, and kiss him many times. (In fact when Cher and Sherlyn were younger, I loved to play this with them too). There was a time when playing such "pretend" games had no effect on Ping Lian. He would just walk away. He didn't care how I felt. Even when I pretended to cry loudly, Ping Lian showed no response. I would be left feeling so alone, disappointed and heartbroken and the pretend crying would become real tears.

From the days when Ping Lian showed no feeling for me, to now showing love and care for me, I am so very proud of our achievements. To develop a loving character in an autistic boy is not an easy task. Looking at this as my personal achievement, I have become more confident and have developed even more faith in Napoleon Hill's book - Desire to perform the "impossible". Thus, I now start getting more daring, ambitious and confident in my plan for Ping Lian. Who will he become one day?

PING LIAN'S LIVELIHOOD
I am most happy if Ping Lian can be a cleaner

Written when Ping Lian was 6 years old, in year 2000:

When Ping Lian was three years old (or possibly even younger) he demonstrated many inappropriate negative behaviors like kicking, biting other people, hyperactiveness, running wild and throwing things. He showed no regard or consideration for others in his immediate environment. Over the years, it appears that his autism has become less severe and that his overall level of functioning has improved. He is obedient, smarter, and aware of his surrounding and relates much better with people than before. I would not refer to him as low functioning now. As I became more confident in his abilities I shifted the way I was thinking about his future. I now needed to set some new, more challenging goals for him.

I have always felt very strongly that Ping Lian must be able to hold a job when he grows up. He must be able to occupy his time appropriately and productively. I did not want to see him as 100% dependent upon his family members. I started to think about what might happen to Ping Lian when Min Seng and I would both be gone. The thought of Ping Lian being reliant and dependent as a burden to his sisters was worrisome. I wanted Ping Lian to at least be able to provide partial financial independence for himself. I knew that in order to achieve any success in this area for Ping Lian, I needed to plan for him while he was still young. Training him while he was still young would make it easier to guide and influence him. If Ping Lian could hold down a job in the future, it would not only reduce the family's financial burden, but it would be good for his self esteem. I refused to envision him as a "parasite" or an adult with nothing to contribute to his community or to society at large.

During these times Ping Lian had still not developed any particular hobbies. I told myself that there was no way that when Ping Lian grew up he was going to do nothing! He must have something meaningful to do! Given the limited awareness, support and resources about autism in Malaysia; opportunities for getting reasonable support from the government appeared non-existent. Everything was up to me and Ping Lian. I set out to make his future plan and to "dream" for him because he was autistic and could not do it himself. "Who will he be?" "What will be his future livelihood?" "What should I plan for him?" "Who will he become?"

From my personal experiences with my son, and some of the case studies I had come across in my research on autism, I knew that "non-compliance" was a major issue. I felt the urgency that anything I would like to plan for Ping Lian would have to start NOW! "Start now while he is still young! I can teach him, control him, influence him and plan for him! I can provide training, instil interest and motivation, and polish his skills from a young age!"

Since Ping Lian was still very young, I still possessed thoughts that he would one day be "normal". Although I had high expectations for him, I also knew very well, that I still needed to be prepared for a possible worst case scenario. "What if he will never be 'normal'?... What if he remains autistic?... If I wait until he is a teenager, it may be too difficult and too late to teach him anything new!... He may become use to a lifestyle of dependency with no drive and no goals..."

So at this stage, I started to focus on goals for his livelihood. I needed a plan, a specific plan in order to set suitable goals for my son. As Ping Lian showed improvements in his imitation skills and was able to follow some simple instructions I began to entertain the possibility of specific jobs for him. My domestic helper started getting him to learn cleaning at home. I thought we could start by teaching him to clean in the house. With the help of my domestic worker, we began teaching Ping Lian specific cleaning chores. For example, cleaning the glass windows and glass doors. This provided good training for jobs by teaching him imitation skills, following directions, increasing auditory skills and if nothing else; provided Ping Lian with some exercise. Even if one day, Ping Lian would not have a cleaning job; he would be able to use his skills in his own activities of daily living. The skills being taught would definitely be functional for him in the long run. There was nothing to lose, "One stone kills many birds"! I then began to ponder the possible environments where Ping Lian might be able to clean. I needed to consider safety first.

My fourth sister (Alice) attended a big church in Kuala Lumpur. She was always inviting me and Ping Lian to go to her church. I believed that church was important and also a good place to take children to learn and worship, but I did not have the discipline to go to church every Sunday. During the past few years, I would only go to church once a year. I would go faithfully on Christmas Day, which was also my birthday. I began to consider my sister's invitation to attend church. Ping Lian had no friends. Perhaps he could make some friends from the church. This might also provide a good opportunity for Ping Lian to learn from typical children. He could learn integration and social skills too. If I take him now, while he is young, he can start building up a network of friends and so one day when I am gone, he may have extra support and community from the church. Most important of all, I told myself that because Ping Lian is autistic, he needs God even more than I do. He needs to go to church to learn more about God. The decision was made. It was time for us to go to church!

In January of 2000 when Ping Lian was age 6, my sister took me and

Ping Lian to Calvary Church in Kuala Lumpur. Calvary is a big church and from the very first day that we went there, I felt really good. Contrary to my expectations, the Sunday school teachers were very understanding and supportive. They happily accepted Ping Lian in the class and offered to pay special attention to him. The first two to three Sundays I remained in the Sunday school classes with Ping Lian. Once the teachers felt confident that they were familiar enough with Ping Lian, they encouraged me to leave and go to attend the service underway at the main hall. I left knowing that Ping Lian was very much enjoying going to church every Sunday.

At that time my faith was not strong. Frankly I joined the Church because of the possible benefits I envisioned for Ping Lian. This was worth my spending a Sunday morning in Church. Ultimately, however I am glad that I finally developed the discipline to attend church regularly every Sunday. I am so grateful to my sister who for all these years never gave up on us and was persistent in encouraging me to go to church.

It wasn't long before I started thinking that Calvary church would be a good and safe environment for Ping Lian to clean when he grew up. Wouldn't it be wonderful? This could indeed be the safest plce for Ping Lian to have a cleaning job! If my Ping Lian continues to attend this church from youth through adulthood, he will know the church well and the church people will know him well! However (as was my nature), I automatically reversed the possibilities, thinking "What could be the worst case scenario?" I decided that the outcomes would still be positive ones. If the church will not have a place for him as a "cleaner" at least Ping Lian will have grown up with many other bright and loving boys who attend the church. He will have developed some friendships and some of these young boys will have grown to be successful businessman. They may have a big factory or an office that may need to be cleaned. So, the church in the long run can provide love, care, support, and friends and maybe even a job opportunity for Ping Lian in his adulthood!

As I shared these thoughts with Min Seng, he laughed and said I was "crazy" and that I should do whatever I wanted. I was unsure if his laughter was saying that I was over ambitious or under ambitious. I decided not to ask him to clarify and to go about my specific plan. I did not want to get discouraged. My faith with God was not strong yet. I hoped to someday be a Christian but for now I was on a mission. I did not want to get shaken…. as long as He did not object, we would continue going to Church and I was happy.

Note: So, initially my commitment to attend church was based on my hopes for Ping Lian. Ping Lian is the one who had made me develop the discipline and commitment to go to church every Sunday. I knew that I needed God in many areas. I needed God to help me with my Faith and motivation. I needed God for a miracle healing. As I continued going to church every Sunday, I came to know God even more. My love to God grew strong. Now, (2007) every Sunday I go to church with Ping Lian and Cher. Ping Lian loves to go to church, but I love to go to church too. I always feel good after returning from a church service. I have grown to love God even more and my family has many times experienced God's grace in our lives.

FARMWORK, NURSERY, OR DIM SUM RESTAURANT
Year 2002 when Ping Lian was 8 years old:

Two years later (2002) as Ping Lian had progressed further, I started thinking more ambitiously. Perhaps I should train him to work in a nursery or maybe at a small farm. I started contemplating about one day moving to the country, but not be too far from Kuala Lumpur. I must be close enough so that when my daughters grow up, we can still see each other regularly. Obviously, I assumed that they would most likely stay on in Kuala Lumpur, as the job market here in Malaysia is mainly available at Kuala Lumpur. It has always been my hope that they live together or nearby when they are grown. I actually started checking on the cost of land at a radius within a one hour drive from Kuala Lumpur to see if one day, I might be able to afford such a purchase. Gardening could prove to be a very good trade for Ping Lian. With training, he might develop a real interest in this area and become good at it. If he can pick up gardening skills, this could become a hobby and his future livelihood. Also it can be so interesting to see and learn how things grow. He can see his own achievement in the growth process over time from a seed to a plant, blooming flowers, etc. Best of all Ping Lian can start to learn from his Daddy right now. He can learn to cut the grass in our garden and also enjoy spending time working with Daddy.

In October of 2002 I received a promotion at work and so I decided to use the additional income to find a bigger rental house with a bigger garden. Ping Lian was now eight years old. Our family was also looking forward to additional outdoor space for Ping Lian to be able to engage in more play outdoor activities, like ball and badminton. Once we actually made this move to a bigger house with a bigger garden Ping Lian learned how to cut the grass. I bought two big scissors for cutting grass and as Daddy or the domestic helper used one scissor; Ping Lian imitated and cut grass with the other. He loved cutting the grass.

During this same time frame, one day while I was having breakfast with my family at a Chinese Dim Sum restaurant, I realised that none of the waitresses spoke to us. The waitress simply presented us with a variety of small plates of food on a tray for us to select what we wanted. My first thoughts were "Wow, for this type of restaurant, people who serve food do not need to talk much!" I started thinking that if Ping Lian continues to show progress, this might be a suitable job for him. He has limited communication and social skills and this might be a good fit for people with autism. My mind raced with thoughts of what I should do next. Perhaps I can partner with a few parents to open a small Dim Sum restaurant where our children can be employed in the future. I shared my thoughts with Min Seng immediately and asked for his opinion. He kept laughing and said I have too many ideas. I told him we needed to do some research and explore all the possibilities and then decide which job and environment might suit Ping Lian best. I start thinking of how to go about it. "How should I cultivate his interest and polish his skills from a young age in making Dim Sum? …Which autistic child parent should I share this thought with, with the hope that their child will be a potential future partner of the restaurant?" I presented the idea of opening a Chinese Dim Sum restaurant to a few parents that I had gotten to know from my parent network. The parent network was a group of parents that would sometimes get together for workshops and also socially for picnics or holiday events. I suggested we could start by simply getting our autistic children to play games and teach activities such as making *dim sum* with Play Doh. We could all train the skills needed and later on, a few of us may want to partner to open an actual business together. In general, the parent consensus appeared to be fear of the unknown factors. Will my child progress? Will my child be able to cope? Will my child be interested? These were all valid concerns but should not be reasons to abandon hope. The more training and knowledge we provide for our children the more opportunities we create for them! At least if we start to take action 'early' we can build hope toward increasing their possibilities for the future. I felt that in the long run, even if only one or two parents remained to pursue this – that would be all that was needed to make a partnership. I continued to say that if we trained our kids while they were still young, who knows – they may have a sibling who would show interest and might grow up wanting to be a business partner. They could even continue the business when we are all gone, but our autistic children will have a livelihood!

The general idea was well received. However, the majority view was that the plan was too far in the future to discuss now. Some felt it was beyond ambitious, and others felt it was too much work to consider. Not only do we need to worry about teaching them restaurant skills, but we have to worry about their behaviour and their social skills. Still, my views were set in concrete. As stated earlier in a chapter "Life is like preparing for an exam, the more we prepare the higher we can score. If we are not prepared, we may score zero points. Worst case scenario – Our children will have learned valuable daily living skills, even if they do not work in a restaurant. Maybe even, one day when we are gone… our children will have learned to be able to prepare meals for themselves. Training can only widen the opportunities and lead to learning additional skills in even more areas. What do we have to lose? I can't think of any loss, but the benefits can be numerous. Set positive goals and aim high. *"Never try, never know"*.

A few short months after this discussion, while still contemplating bringing the nursery, farm or restaurant plan to fruition there was a remarkable change in Ping Lian's motor skill ability. He had grown out of tracing and began drawing free-hand. I had actually been thinking for some time now about sending Ping Lian for art classes. I tended to procrastinate about this and did not take action because Ping Lian had previously been thrown out of a basic drawing class. This was very hurtful to me especially since the instructor of the art class was a therapist for children with autism. The class itself was a basic drawing class for typical children, and they accepted Ping Lian in the class with me as a shadow. Ping Lian was fairly well behaved, relatively calm and had not exhibited any severe challenging behaviour in this class. Still the teacher said that Ping Lian was affecting the other children's learning. This was a very negative experience for me as well as for Ping Lian. I began to work with Ping Lian myself, teaching him to trace and to draw. I wondered how someone who is supposed to be an educator for children with autism could turn away my son. This rejection hurt deeply and out of fear of experiencing this again, I procrastinated. So I sat on it and did nothing about it. But I am glad and thank God that I did not sit on it for too long. I decided that if an autism *specialist* couldn't accept my autistic son, I would seek an art teacher who had no knowledge of autism instead!

CHAPTER 7

Year 2002 – Our Dream: To Develop Ping Lian to Be An Artist

As a young child, Ping Lian demonstrated poor fine motor control. In order to strengthen and develop his fine motor skills, his home schooling co-curriculum included tracing and coloring activities. These activities also served as a way to fill his time since Ping Lian was unable to engage in play activities. Ping Lian also had very poor imitation skills. In order to develop these skills, we focused on physically guiding him to trace lines and objects, stroke by stroke.

Innocently, these types of activities ultimately served as a catalyst for discovering and developing Ping Lian's exceptional art talent.

MY GOAL – "PING LIAN MUST BE ABLE TO WRITE"

In Kindergarten, all of Ping Lian's classmates were able to do basic writing and able to use a scissor for cutting. Ping Lian was unable to do either. He couldn't hold a pencil or a scissor functionally. Ping Lian's grip was weak so he was unable to scribble, trace or open and close a scissor properly for cutting. His pencil grip seemed hopeless and it made me very worried. I began to help him by holding his hand while using colored pencils to color large pictures and progressed to holding his hand to trace and to draw lines on paper.

At the time, of course I knew nothing about fine motor control, so I did not attribute his inability to perform such basic tasks to "motor weakness". Eventually with the guidance and advice of Ping Lian's occupational therapist (Miss Teo), we were able to get Ping Lian to do some exercises to strengthen his fine motor skills. The therapist recommended tracing a variety of simple lines daily to enhance these skills. In order to make the tracing activities more fun I began to insert other activities such as helping Ping Lian to trace my hand, his hand, my foot, his foot. While adding some fun to the sometimes monotonous "line tracing" activities, this also served as additional learning opportunities to teach about the body parts, etc.

It was many, many long hours, days and months before Ping Lian could finally trace a simple line on his own without my holding and guiding his hand. Once Ping Lian was able to trace a simple line independently, I began to draw a variety of simple line patterns on A4 size paper and had Ping Lian trace on top of the line patterns that I had drawn. In order to save time for myself, instead of repeatedly drawing a variety of line patterns on different sets of A4 size paper, I gave Ping Lian a box of colored pencils and taught him to trace the same set of line patterns by using 12 different colors over each line. Thus, for every single line pattern that I drew, Ping Lian drew twelve! Not only did this add a little more interest for Ping Lian, but it took him longer to complete. The more I could occupy Ping Lian's time constructively and independently, the more I was also freeing up a little more of my time. Each day Ping Lian spent longer and longer time periods tracing. In fact, he spent hours each day doing tracing exercises and *enjoying* it.

Since Ping Lian was unable to engage himself in play activities or other constructive activities, these tracing activities became a blessing. Ping Lian showed no interest in educational video programs, toys or books. These were very difficult times for our family, especially during the time that our domestic helper had resigned and the times I did not have a home teacher or therapist for Ping Lian.

My mother in-law was unable to cope with Ping Lian, mostly due to his hyperactivity. My elder sister and retired brother in-law would often come to help out and spend time with Ping Lian once he arrived home from Kindergarten. However, Ping Lian spent most of this after school time walking up and down all over the house, climbing and jumping everywhere, opening drawers and engaging in his self-stimulatory behaviors. It was painful to see him wasting precious time. Neither my sister, nor my brother spoke English well enough to deliver ABA instruction drills to Ping Lian. I asked them both to try to occupy Ping Lian with the tracing activities.

After so many months of simple line tracing activities, I felt Ping Lian was finally ready to progress to tracing more sophisticated lines. He started tracing letters and numbers using the same twelve color pencil technique previously mentioned. At some point I realized that during these tracing activities Ping Lian was always so *focused* and so *calm*. This was not at all typical for Ping Lian.

Whenever I had to go to work, or just out; I made sure to instruct the person in care of Ping Lian to provide him with tracing activities to ensure that Ping Lian would be cooperative and engaged appropriately.

As Ping Lian's tracing skills advanced, I introduced stencils to teach letters and numbers. The stencils were a guide toward independent writing for him. After a few months, Ping Lian was finally able to write alphabets and numbers freely. I continued to encourage him to trace pictures and also to color. I included the use of stencils for tracing objects such as simple animal and flower drawings. Ping Lian eventually became independent at using the stencils to independently trace pictures. The time spent on his daily activities was now expanded as they involved many forms of tracing, along with pictures and coloring.

Once Ping Lian's fine motor skills had progressed to the point where he could functionally write, exhibiting control and grip abilities, we were able to accomplish many more tasks with him. We were even able to get him to start cutting. We started with cutting *on* a simple straight line. We eventually added tasks such as connecting "Dot to Dot" exercises. We alternated the dot to dot exercises by introducing connecting letter and numbers sequentially to form specific images and pictures. Upon completion, Ping Lian would also have to color the pictures. Ping Lian was learning! As a family we were all so happy for Ping Lian. Not only was he learning number and letter recognition, but he really enjoyed doing these activities very much. Ping Lian progressed learning the numbers 1-30 and learned all 26 letters of the English alphabet.

Our next step was to teach Ping Lian to trace pictures directly from a book. We permitted Ping Lian to trace directly over the pictures of his workbook. It didn't matter if the book became dirty or sloppy looking as long as he did his tracing. Once Ping Lian mastered the ability to trace a picture by drawing directly over the image itself, we introduced tracing paper. Ping Lian's interest perked. I began to look for books with more complicated images for Ping Lian to trace using very thin tracing paper. Ping Lian even started tracing his and my hands and feet without my guidance. As he progressed I introduced a basic stroke-by-stroke drawing guide book. Yet, Ping Lian remained focused on tracing instead of drawing independently. I decided to give him *thicker* tracing paper to make it more challenging for him to trace whole pictures. Ping Lian would trace what was clearly visible through the tracing paper, which was mostly just an outline. After he traced the outline, he had no choice but to draw in what the picture was lacking to reproduce the images. This lead Ping Lian to half trace and half draw. I kept hoping he would eventually grow out of tracing altogether and do some independent drawing.

I still continued to encourage him to draw by following me stroke-by-stroke via use of the drawing guide. Ping Lian finally began to show some effort and was eventually able to follow the guide as intended. At this point I searched and purchased various simple drawing guide books which taught the stroke-by-stroke approach. We started out with very simple drawings such as circles, squares, overall basic shapes and progressed to simple animal forms such as birds, cats, etc. Ping Lian was fascinated! He loved this. Next, we used a more complex drawing guide book to draw actual object such as buildings, etc. During this training process, another revelation occurred to me. I realised that I could use the tracing and drawing stroke-by-stroke to develop Ping Lian's imitation skills.

Although Ping Lian initially possessed poor fine motor skills; teaching him to imitate me drawing a line, was so much easier than asking him to imitate some other action like jumping, standing up or even sitting down. The command "Do this" seemed almost pointless when it came to gross motor imitation skills. Yet "Do this" or "Draw this" when a fine motor drawing task was expected, clearly had positive results. It was obvious that Ping Lian needed to have motivation in order to succeed. I began to pair the ABA imitation drills with the drawing. Instead of saying "do this" while jumping up and down, in order to get Ping Lian to "imitate" the jumping up and down behavior; I followed up the ABA drills with "draw this" to get him to draw a line. Each trial resulted in Ping Lian drawing another line so that by the time we completed the session, Ping Lian had imitated enough lines to have drawn a simple object. Sometimes a house, a house with a tree beside it, etc.

I would sometimes change the antecedent instruction from "draw this " to "follow Mummy" and eventually to "follow the book." My underlying objective however, remained the same: To get Ping Lian to use the simple drawing guide book on his own when no one would be beside him, or around to help him; and to decrease his tracing while increasing his independent drawing.

I incorporated drawing as part of the ABA drills in order to further motivate Ping Lian to be successful in the motor imitation and other instructional skill programs. By the end of each day, not only had we completed the ABA drills, but Ping Lian had also completed his drawing lessons!

I realized the importance of specificity when it came to Ping Lian. We made sure to have *specific* homework, a *specific place* to do his homework, and most importantly a *specific time*. These routines helped Ping Lian to understand what was expected of him and when. I even created a "Schedule Chart" for Ping Lian to use as a guide for his "Home Work". I would write down basic instructions, showing what he needed to do (i.e., tracing, drawing and/or coloring) with the page numbers for the assignments. Ping Lian would then place a tick mark on the page number that I had written on the Schedule Chart once he had completed the assignment and then get a reward (usually one piece of chocolate, as at that time, chocolate was his favorite). This procedure was used for all of his "Home Work" including writing, tracing, drawing, reading etc. This enabled me to monitor him and to help keep him focused and aware of what he needed to do throughout the day when I was not around. The Schedule Chart really helped and was one of the most effective methods that helped Ping Lian to remind himself of what he need to do.

As a matter of fact, upon sharing my use of the Schedule Chart with Ping Lian's music teacher in 2004, he chose to also implement the technique during Ping Lian's piano lessons. He began to write the page numbers that Ping Lian needed to practice for homework on the Schedule Chart. If Ping Lian was required to practice a particular page ten times, he would write the page numbers on the Schedule Chart and write numbers

1 to 10 below the assigned page numbers. After Ping Lian practiced one time, he would write a tick mark on it, and continue until he completed the assignment indicated by 10 tick marks. This was very helpful for me as well, because I no longer needed to spend so much time monitoring Ping Lian's music assignments.

Note: Even now (2011) Ping Lian continues to be successful using this method to complete his music assignments. He has however advanced to the point where he now writes the numbers himself and then makes a tick mark on each number every time he completes a practice. We have also replaced the use of the Schedule Chart with an exercise book.

It had been quite some time now (2000) that I had been teaching and *"brain washing"* Ping Lian to *"follow other people"*. Finally, one day while he was at church and again one day at school, I knew that he could *follow* other people, as I heard students complaining "Ping Lian is copying me"! At church Ping Lian imitated the general crowd's actions, standing when they stood, sitting when they sat, etc. At school he began to copy whatever the other children were writing or drawing. He even copied the exact colors a particular child had used. His peers often complained "Ping Lian keeps copying me"!"

So, the daily activities of tracing, coloring and "dot-to-dot" activities that Ping Lian has endured since he was five years old, coupled with the application of the principles " One stone kills many birds", and "something is better than nothing ", have lead to so many benefits. Little did I know that such activities would lead him to be an artist. At this time that was not at all my plan. I did not yet have a single clue that he would one day be an outstanding artist.

The turning points were one special day in mid 2002, and another day in 2003. I will always remember the images of that day and my thoughts so vividly.

THE ULTIMATE ICE-CREAM CONE MARCH 2002 – A TURNING POINT

Ping Lian came back home from an errand with his Daddy. I noticed his behavior was a little unusual. He shot into the house from the main door and ran very quickly straight up the stairs. I was a little curious and also worried about what he might be up to. I followed him and watched as I saw him run to his "homework time" table, pull out a piece of paper and start drawing; totally focused and full of energy. I watched as he started drawing the picture from his ice cream cone wrapper. I felt a little relieved to see he was not into any mischief. I proceeded to go down stairs to continue my unfinished work.

I recall that at that moment as I was walking down the stairs, I felt so good. "Ah, It is fascinating how my Ping Lian is progressing so well." It felt like another breakthrough. This was no doubt the first time I noticed Ping Lian drawing something independently, on his own initiative, without me or anyone for that matter encouraging him, sitting beside him or guiding him. It was also the first time drawing without reliance of the drawing guidebook or even tracing.

This was the very first time that Ping Lian drew *anything* that was not from the drawing guide book. On July 27, 2002, which was one or two weeks after the day he drew the ice cream cone wrapper, we took Ping Lian to the Forest Research Institute of Malaysia to a three day camp event. Ping Lian was eight years old. I remember that Ping Lian had been fascinated with a particular poster of the galaxy which was hanging on the Institute wall. Throughout the entire three day excursion, Ping Lian would constantly run to the poster and stare incessantly at it for long periods of time, until we would eventually coax him away. Min Seng and I would just stand beside Ping Lian quietly providing support and comfort, while wondering "What the heck is in his mind?"… "What is he looking at?" … and "What is it that is fascinating him?"….

Approximately a week later on August 4, 2002, Ping Lian drew the galaxy from memory. It was the first time I saw Ping Lian draw something without referring to a picture or anything. I was so happy. My heart spoke: "Wah! Thank you God! So fast, another time of huge progress and break through." I made sure to write down the date in my journal and vowed to get him to file that drawing for remembrance and as a record of his progress. Since then, Ping Lian had started to increasingly draw without visual subjects to refer to and has not stopped since! That "ultimate ice-cream cone" wrapper drawing was the beginning of Ping Lian's independent drawing history. He had finally outgrown tracing and was beginning to create drawings. He seemed almost obsessed with drawing and his love and passion are always apparent when he is drawing or painting.

Ping Lian's drawing "obsession" grew to the point that often time halfway through his other educational programs he would begin to draw on his work, his exercise book, his story book and even on his Schedule Chart. Actually he would draw anywhere and everywhere whenever he felt like it (but luckily only on paper and books, and not on the wall, etc). It's amusing to find myself having the need to stop Ping Lian from drawing after all the effort and time it has taken to motivate and encourage him to trace and draw. Even with his apparent obsession for drawing though, at this time I still had no clue that he was an aspiring outstanding artist. Life is so unpredictable.

When Ping Lian demonstrated the ability to survive in a mainstream school and started going to church, I was very happy with his progress. I actually stopped regularly recording about him in my Journal and my entries were far from consistent. By June 2001 my husbands financial situation had worsened. Upon finding an opportunity for a higher paying job, I resigned from my existing position. I however became even busier with work and seldom wrote down any details of Ping Lian progress or of my thoughts in my Journal. Sometimes months would pass before I recorded an entry. Thinking back, as

I write this book, I think "If I had known that Ping Lian would be such an outstanding artist, I would have regularly noted his progress in more detail and also have kept that ice-cream cone drawing."

JOURNAL ENTRY AUGUST 2002

> *Lately (since July) Ping Lian is very keen to draw, he draw freely, he started with star, moon and sun and he go on to seal and other animal….. Now he likes to draw everything and draw very well and even file up the drawing all by himself… I will develop him along this area.*

At that time "along this area" simply meant that I intended to develop his interest and skill in art as a hobby. I had no specific plan or course of action. I just knew I needed to continue to motivate his current interest. I continually searched for more complex drawing guide books to hopefully keep him motivated and to encourage him to sketch more complicated drawings.

Ping Lian always loved to trace the Statute of Liberty with the Eiffel Tower together on one page. Even once he stopped tracing, he continued to freely draw pictures of both structures depicted side by side on the same page. I began to notice that the manner in which my son drew was unique. There was something in his drawings that portrayed a strength and boldness. Hs drawings were full of energy and drafted with great passion, naturalness and spontaneity. I started to wonder what can and should I do with this passion for drawing. Once again I contemplated enrolling him in an art class. "Where will I find an art school or an art teacher who will accept Ping Lian?" I procrastinate as I have honestly already given up before trying. Instead I decided to teach him myself, while mindful of the fact that I had absolutely no educational background or skills in art.

As I continued to search for even more complicated and professional drawing guide books to help me teach him, I thought of the long journey Ping Lian has triumphed from poor fine motor skills to this point. I also however continued in my quest and concern to secure a livelihood for my son. *"Farm? nursery?, restaurant?"* - my mind still keeps searching and planning how and what would be the best way to make any of these a reality. All the while, as Min Seng and my domestic helper worked diligently to guide and train Ping Lian to cut grass… our Ping Lian was just getting more and more obsessed with drawing.

DRAWING AND FILING

Ping Lian's prolific obsession to draw often resulted with an array of drawings all over the house. He simply tossed his drawings everywhere. There were many pieces of A4 size drawings everywhere, some on the floor, some on the table, on shelves, etc. I took the opportunity to teach Ping Lian to file as part of his learning program. He needed to learn to file each of his drawings. I started by doing it and then did it with him hand over hand until he was able to do it by himself. As we went through this learning process, I continually said things to Ping Lian like:

"Ping Lian drawing is so beautiful. Mummy likes it. Ping Lian cannot simply throw the drawing all over the house". "Ping Lian drawing is so beautiful, cannot throw in the dustbin. It is wasted if throw in the dustbin". "Ping Lian cannot throw it on the floor, or Ida (my domestic helper) will throw it into the dustbin".

(Note: I usually use very simple English key words to teach Ping Lian on certain value of life, then I use the word he seem to understand to teach another "similar" situation. E.g. in this case he roughly know the meaning of waste; so I jus use the word "waste" to get him not to throw

his drawing. As initially whenever Ping Lian go to supermarket he will just take 4 or 5 packets of chip or as many as he like, I had been constantly telling him; "don't waste my money", so when he is at supermarket, he is only allow to buy one type of chip at a time, so he had to learn to make decision, to chose only one packet of chip each time. But definitely we had been through many struggle at the supermarket…but finally I "win"… and later whenever I said, don't waste my money, he will had no choice that put down all the chip on his hand and start making decision to chose only one. So he had learn the key words "waste" or "wasted" is not an acceptable behaviour but I am not exactly sure how much he really understand the meaning of waste).

I definitely did not want any of his wonderful drawings to end up in the garbage. Each of his drawings no matter how simple was a product of great passion. Later, it was obvious that Ping Lian had begun to take pride in his own drawing. He was also proud that he had the ability to file all of his drawings. In fact this was also one of the best ways toward helping to build his self esteem. There were many benefits in teaching Ping Lian a filing system for his artwork. New vocabulary and concepts were introduced daily. Ping Lian learned quickly from the obvious multitude of opportunities presented based upon the number of drawings he produced. He learned and practiced "fold, half, center, aim, press, finished, hole, file and keep" etc. In fact he learned an entire system of useful organizing skills. Sometimes when he would leave a drawing on the floor, I would purposely test him by taking the paper and aiming it at the dustbin while saying to him, "Can Mummy throw?" Ping Lian would rush over saying "file, file" and immediately take it and file it. This gave me additional opportunities to teach Ping Lian to take pride in what he does and to strengthen his self-esteem. I thank God for the wisdom he provided me to keep most of Ping Lian's initial drawings out of the dustbin. The fact that I have saved all of these, knowing now that my son is an artist is a wonderful feeling because I can share his journey with others.

Art has been an excellent vehicle for Ping Lian to learn and mature across all skills. Not only does he have a meaningful hobby that keeps

Chapter 7: Year 2002 – Our Dream: To Develop Ping Lian to Be An Artist   153

him functionally and happily occupied, but he has acquired calmness, joyfulness, an outlet for expression, pride and self-esteem and many other skills in the course of his day to day living.

DEC 2002- FAMILY CHRISTMAS HOLIDAY - ANOTHER IMPORTANT TURNING POINT

My concern regarding Ping Lian's hyperactivity and sometimes negative behavior limited my ability to take long breaks or vacations. It had been a very long time since I had spent a Christmas holiday with my sister and brothers family. In December 2002 for the Christmas holiday, all my sisters chose to "squeeze" at Kay Ing's (my 5th sister) house. We were four families, with many of Ping Lian's cousins and brothers and sisters in the same house for a full week. It is our tradition that once all of my sisters and brothers meet together, just about every day, we will sit at the dining table eating and talking from morning 9am till 3 or 4 pm. Only then would we take the children outdoors for activities. My brother in laws were always amazed at our ability to talk so much!

Cher and Sherlyn would play with their cousins in the house. Ping Lian did not know how to engage in play with his cousins, sisters or brothers. I suppose our Holiday times were very boring for him. This particular Holiday though was different. Ping Lian became fascinated with a magnetic drawing board that belonged to my sisters' child. He occupied himself with drawing on the magnetic board and would immediately pull and erase it and draw again. This was the first time he used a magnetic board to draw. His main drawing interest around this time was horses and carriages. I had noticed a difference in his drawings and started to become very impressed with the quality of his drawings. He drew for hours on the magnetic board and with a very fast speed. He began to draw much quicker, yet more beautiful and unique. So, while I was enjoying the time with my sisters, I still kept watching my son and wondering .. "What is in him???? ….. Siew Ing (my 6th sister) also noticed Ping Lian's unique drawing ability and obsessive nature. I remember that she mentioned several times "there must be something special in him". She said he must have a special talent in drawing and assured me that I needed to do something about it. I suddenly felt guilty about my procrastination in getting Ping Lian into an art class. I decided that I needed to take immediate action and do something with his drawing interest. Immediately after the Holiday, I would find an art teacher for Ping Lian to develop his talent.

In January of 2003, Ping Lian started attending art class. Mrs. Tan was a dedicated Christian who lived near my house and conducted art classes for children. After speaking to her about Ping Lian and also viewing some of his drawings, Mrs. Tan agreed to accept Ping Lian with one condition. She admittedly did not have any prior experience with autism and requested that I or my domestic helper sit in with the art class as shadow aids to Ping Lian. The request was more than welcome, as I viewed this as an opportunity for myself and Mylyn to learn some skills that we could implement for teaching and guiding Ping Lian in drawing at home as well. Ping Lian enjoyed going to Mrs. Tan's art class very much. Sometimes he would attend 3 times a week. Mrs. Tan was a very good teacher. She eventually admitted several other children with autism with an interest in drawing into her class.

At that time Chin Chin, who had been with us for several years decided to stop teaching Ping Lian as she needed to focus on her final year of courses. I was blessed to get a new domestic helper, Mylyn who was from the Philippines, a graduate in education and an ex- teacher. She had gone to the unemployment agency and although she clearly was offered *easier* employment options, after hearing about our autistic son, she chose to come to my family. Mylyn genuinely wanted to help Ping Lian. She enjoyed attending the art classes and seeing Ping Lian do so well in his art. Mylyn also began giving Ping Lian art classes at home based on what she learned while in the class. Ping Lian has been so blessed. Mylyn was also instrumental in his initial development of artistic skills. She was so good with Ping Lian and very passionate about his learning. After so many years of constantly drilling Ping Lian I was able to pull back. I was so very tired and was grateful for the break that presented itself by having Mylyn take over most of the teaching tasks in training Ping Lian, especially the ABA drills. I even sent Mylyn to seminars and conferences to learn more about autism and how to teach children with autism. Mylyn was the best domestic helper we ever had.

JANUARY 2003 - "HIPPO FAMILY II"
MARCH 2003 - I SET MY DREAM AND VISION FOR PING LIAN

By 2003, Ping Lian was showing interest in all kinds of subjects and would draw them beautifully. In the past, Ping Lian was fascinated by a Hippo picture from a book that I often used during "home work time". He used to trace the Hippo directly on the book page over and over again.

In Jan 2003, Ping Lian drew this beautiful hippo drawing (see 03410 Hippo Family II). These pictures heavily impacted my views on the future decisions I would make for my son. I was so impressed. I referred back to some of the pictures he had drawn earlier. There were a few drawings of "raining" pictures. The way Ping Lian drew to express rain looked so unique. There were also a few drawings of beautiful "outer space" and some horse sketches drawn with a similar style. Ping Lian still constantly draws horses and carriages. They appear to be his favorite subjects. I have no artistic background and have never been into art, so I did not know how good his drawings were or even if he really had a special talent. After all, as his mother, everything he drew was amazing. What I did know for sure, was that he always drew with a special energy. He showed a special manner when putting objects on paper with a unique stroke.

All this prompted me again as I asked myself: *"Is there really something in my son that is so special?" "Does he really have a talent in art?"* I continually studied his drawings looking for confirmation of a "talent". I even asked friends what they thought.

One day, I can't recall what drove me ....but I do specifically recall the moment it occurred:

It was like I suddenly awoke from a long sleep or stupor! An idea rushed over me. If I were to describe it from a Christian perspective – It would be called 'God sent wisdom'. It was a clear vision for me and it was God's plan and God's message. So was I now determined? Oh Yes! Yes! Yes! Yes!!! "My Ping Lian is going to be an Artist when he grows up!" I remember laughing at myself and thinking "What a fool I am." Why was I still searching and questioning my son's future vocation? Who will Ping Lian be? What job will he hold? Ping Lian has been showing me for quite some time now, what it is that he loves to do. Yet I have done nothing so far concerning his obvious desire? "Yes! Yes! Yes! It is so clear to me now. The message is so very clear! I do not need to open a Chinese Dim Sum restaurant. I do not need to worry and look for partners and investors for such a venture anymore. Nor do I need to find a safe place for Ping Lian to do gardening or cleaning. I do not need to look into the possibility of investing in a farm and relocating to the country side for Ping Lian to work as farmer. I do NOT ....., etc.

The answers were right before my eyes waiting for me to take action. I would stop searching for other "livelihood" options. I had suddenly realised that it was really not important to know whether Ping Lian had a special talent in art or not. What was important was that he was interested and he loved doing it.

Since Ping Lian had an obvious interest in art and was obsessive about drawing, I could get people to train him to be an Artist. I could get people to train him to be good in art. Why not focus on developing his skill and training him to be an Artist. Why not let art be his livelihood when he grows up? I can forget about jobs as a cleaner, a gardener, or even a server at a café. Art is perfect! Ping Lian does it on his own without any dependency on others at all. I was suddenly overjoyed and thanked God for showing His new plan to Ping Lian and me.

I had finally found Ping Lian's "possible talent", and we have a new Dream and a new Vision. Prior to this revelation, I believe that I didn't dare to accept this as Ping Lian's plan for his future. I dared not think ahead so ambitiously. After all an 'artist' would be a person of esteem to be revered. So, whenever thoughts of developing Ping Lian along this area (art) crossed my mind, I lacked the confidence to aim so high and subconsciously dismissed them. Having read many articles that said talent can be trained and should be nurtured, I was now ready to follow through. I began to re-apply the many principles by which I lived and worked all of my life. "Life is like going for an examination", "Never try, never know", "Something is better than nothing". As long as we try, Ping Lian will gain points. The only unknown is how good and how talented Ping Lian may turn out to be. How many points will he score? Regardless though, since my Ping Lian is an autistic boy, for his "exam" a score of 100% is not necessary. Any points he gains will result in a score that is "something" and better than "nothing.

After I managed to overcome my own mental block, I was filled with the excitement of "how" to now achieve this new and ambitious Dream for Ping Lian - "Yes!!! My Ping Lian will be an Artist one day". Now I am at the stage of deciding whether I should put all of my energy and limited finances toward this plan to develop Ping Lian's artistic skills. Confirmation came from one of the experts on autism that came to Malaysia from the United States to conduct a seminar. He said "… when they have interest in some area but are not particularly good at it, develop them to be good in those areas. When they are good in some particular area but have no interest in it, develop the interest". There was no more need for my hesitation. My thoughts had been confirmed and I now understood that I was not "crazy"!

JOURNAL ENTRY MARCH 2003:

I set a Vision to develop Ping Lian to be an Artist and some of my thoughts of "I'm A Dreamer".(details of I'M A Dreamer are explained later in chapter 9).

The following entry is the last two lines of March 2003 entry:

> **"I WANT TO DEVELOP PING LIAN TO BE AN ARTIST -
> I KNOW HE WILL BE AN ARTIST ONE DAY."**

I remember that at the time I made this entry I was thinking, it had been a long road to the progression of when Ping Lian was unable to hold a pencil to then being able to trace, write, and then obsessively draw independently with such passion. I am so happy and enthusiastic with my new plan.

At this young age, if I start to train and develop Ping Lian correctly there is no reason he would not be good. With this in mind I decided to put all my effort and energy to find out how to achieve this Dream and work toward it– Our Dream!! All my resources, including any additional surplus budget, focus, energy, effort and determination were invested in our Dream.

" Make Decisions AND Take Action NOW!!"

Chapter 7: Year 2002 – Our Dream: To Develop Ping Lian to Be An Artist

These are a few of Ping Lian's initial free hand drawings which led me to believe he may have a special talent and that I would nurture his love for art and develop him to be an Artist.

INITIAL WORK

"Raining & Rainbow"- Ping Lian created this drawing without any reference in 2002 at the age of 8.

INITIAL WORK

"Astronauts" - Ping Lian drew this with reference from a book in 2002 at the age of 8.

INITIAL WORK

03410 Hippo Family II, Painted in Jan 2003 at the age of 9.

Ping Lian drew this piece by referring to the book that I used for story-telling. He particularly likes this page of the book. Before Ping Lian drew this picture in Jan 2003, he had been tracing this picture directly on the book (many times). Later I encouraged him to trace using tracing paper (He traced this many times as well). After some time he then traced only half and drew the other half with the thicker tracing paper I provided. Once he was able to draw independently, he still also drew this many times. This particular piece is the most beautiful hippo among the other Hippo pieces (although each Hippo drawing refers to the one same page of the book).

CHAPTER 8

Ways and Means To Achieve Our Dream - Ping Lian Says "I Want To Be Artist"

After writing the following entry in my Journal **"I WANT TO DEVELOP PING LIAN TO BE AN ARTIST. I KNOW HE WILL BE AN ARTIST ONE DAY",** I started reading the book *"Think & Grow Rich"* again, but now with this new dream in mind. "*Turn desire into gold*"; "*create a definite plan for carrying out your desire, and again at once, whether you are ready or not, put this plan into action*"; "*there is no such reality as something for nothing*"! Each of these phrases delineated under the chapter "Desire to Perform the Impossible" moved and inspired me tremendously, as I read them again and again. I will never forget the author's description of how he transplanted his own burning desires to enable his son to hear although his son was born without any physical ears. I tried my best to apply my understanding of these principles, autosuggestions and the subconscious mind to my own desires for my son. I began contemplating that "**Ping Lian WILL BE AN ARTIST ONE DAY**" was not Ping Lian's Dream, but *my* Dream for Ping Lian. I must convert "My Dream" to become "Our Dream". Ping Lian must have his own desire to become an artist.

"*Wishing will not bring riches. But desiring riches with a state of mind that becomes an obsession, then planning definite ways and means to acquire riches, and backing those plans with persistence which does not recognize failure, will bring riches*".[19] Yes! This phrase is perfect for "Our Dream." "Riches" for Ping Lian here means - *"Ping Lian WILL BE AN ARTIST ONE DAY"*, and he will use art as a livelihood or to provide additional financial support for himself when he grows up.

TAKING ACTION TO ACHIEVE OUR DREAM

Yes, it was time for action, but I was still uncertain about how exactly to proceed. I knew nothing about art. Also, in my quest for guidance I still worried about people thinking I was "crazy" and the likelihood of receiving discouraging feedback. After all, aren't most "artists" starving? Even a typically developing artist encounters struggles when it comes to earning a living. My thoughts raced back to the positive stories of Temple Grandin[20] and Napoleon Hill's son and how they inspired me to bring Ping Lian to this point in his life. He had no affect and didn't know I existed. He is now a loving boy. He couldn't hold a pencil. He is now obsessed with drawing. This progress is undeniable. To develop an autistic boy to be an Artist and to aim for this to be his livelihood is a very ambitious Dream. Yet the long and tough journey would continue. In fact, any progress by Ping Lian, no matter how small has always brought me joy and renewed hope. Now, nothing will change my mind. I will take one step at a time and do my best again to achieve the conceivably "Impossible" dream.

I managed to get three more art teachers to guide Ping Lian within a

---

19 Think and Grow Rich – Napoleon Hill (1972).
20 Temple Grandin is the worlds most recognized adult with autism and a Professor of Animal Psychology at Colorado State University.

short period. By April 2003, Ping Lian was learning art from Sek Thim at his art studio once a week on a one to one basis. Sek Thim's art studio was not for children. It was typically used for exhibitions and group adult art classes. Upon first approaching the instructor, he urged me to come back when Ping Lian would be 17 years old. In my heart I cried out saying "Oh no! In 8 years time… too much time will have passed". I did not give up and told him that although Ping Lian is only 9 years old when it comes to drawing and painting, he behaves like an adult and he is calm (not hyperactive)…etc. I told him that I could not wait so long and I convinced him to meet Ping Lian before making a final decision. After recognizing my obstinacy, he eventually agreed to meet Ping Lian for one session to get to know him. After that one session, he continued working with Ping Lian once a week on a one to one basis. Sek Thim was so supportive of Ping Lian's talent and only charged me the same fee he charged for group sessions.

Ping Lian looked forward to going to Sek Thim's art classes and to the beautiful studio every Saturday. I am so grateful to him for accepting and teaching Ping Lian at his studio even though his studio was not meant for children.

That same month, Ping Lain joined My Favourite Art House (a children's art center in Malaysia) to learn art from Kwok Yeow once a week in a group setting. At the onset I remained with Ping Lian for the duration of the art classes as a shadow aide to assist him. However, Kwok Yeow was another exceptional teacher. He recognized and appreciated Ping Lian's passion for drawing. Kwok Yeow would often take Ping Lian to a separate corner of the room and coach Ping Lian separately on a one to one basis. He really enjoyed assisting and monitoring Ping Lian's overall progress. As a matter of fact, the first two years after we moved to Australia, whenever we returned to Malaysia, Kwok Yeow always made himself available to give Ping Lian a lesson. Ping Lian misses going to the art center. Within this studio setting Ping Lian was always inspired to draw and paint beautiful large pieces of art.

By July 2003, Ping Lian had acquired yet another art instructor. Yau Bee Ling[21] provided Ping Lian art instruction at least twice a week on a one to one basis. Sometimes she would come to our house and other times I would take Ping Lian to her house for lessons. The bond I developed with Bee Ling enabled me to share my dream for Ping Lian with her. She took my thoughts very seriously and was happy to help me make sure that Ping Lian would progress toward this vision. I requested her support in teaching him not just art, but also social and personal development skills as opportunities arose.

Bee Ling was very enthusiastic to help. She even went to the library to research and gain knowledge about autism before she started teaching Ping Lian. I then began to sort through some articles myself in order to give them to her. Actually, during this time of teaching Ping Lian, Bee Ling needed to reduce her hours teaching at the college. The lower pay that she received from me was secondary to her fulfilment watching Ping Lian progress and helping us to achieve Our Dream. Ping Lian has always enjoyed learning from Bee Ling and looked forward to her arrival. Bee Ling touched our hearts with the dedication, effort, care, love and warmth she had for Ping Lian. We developed a very special relationship in this process eventually leading to a very close friend and partner in Our Dream. Ping Lian's respect and love for her was obvious to me. I consider her a God sent "special Angel" to Ping Lian in his Artistic Journey.

Meanwhile my domestic helper continued taking Ping Lian to attend Mrs. Tan's art classes once a week. Ping Lian was so blessed. They were all very good teachers with little or no experience or background in autism, yet eager to allow me to guide them in this area. I shared my personal knowledge of autism as it pertained to my son and general research about educating individuals with autism. Some of the instructors eventually

---

21   Malaysian artist and college art teacher.

took the challenge of teaching art to other children with autism, as I often introduced them to other autistic children.

It was very important to me for each instructor to understand the seriousness and commitment with which I was entrusting them. I explained to each one of them individually that their task was to help Ping Lian toward becoming an artist. I contrasted Ping Lian as an individual with no "self-worth" versus Ping Lian as an "artist" full of pride. As I shared the nuances of the "dream" for Ping Lian, I could see the teachers felt nervous, pressured and "scared". However the advantages, such as the fact that Ping Lian loved to draw and also that he was "not bad" at drawing were strong points. Informing them that I was a patient woman, who was willing to wait five, ten, or even fifteen or twenty years if that's what it takes for Ping Lian to be an artist, relieved some of the pressure. After all, Ping Lian was still only 9 years old!

I will always remember, as a very young child how my mother would constantly tell us (my brothers and sisters), that "It is Okay if you do not have much money but you must have pride and self esteem. You must never be a 'useless' person, and should always remember to maintain your dignity."

My mother was sent to live with my father's family at a very young age. She may have been as young as three years old the day she was carried in a cane basket to my father's house, and "designated' as my father's future wife. When she was five they moved from China to Malaysia. She went through a tough life growing up without her mother. I have always remembered her words and her wisdom. Her influence taught me to pay much attention to my son regarding his future, his livelihood, his self esteem and dignity even though he is a boy with autism. My mother never attended school for even a day in her life, but she was indeed a very wise woman.

TOO MANY ART TEACHERS?

Many people have asked me the reason for employing more than one art teacher at a time. They have often suggested that this would only create confusion for Ping Lian. Funny, I have always responded "YES!" My intention is to "confuse" Ping Lian. Since my resources are limited in all aspects (time, finances and autism facility and services availability in Malaysia), I need to be very smart and attempt to capture all possible opportunities at the same time.

For instance, as ABA programs recommend: It is important to practice generalization. We need to teach Ping Lian to generalize whatever we have taught him as a table drill across to other settings and other people. For example any given instruction and command that Ping Lian may have mastered with myself or with Chin Chin, only results in a response to us. Whenever different people communicate with him, he has a problem understanding the same exact direction. So, as I guide the art teachers on how to communicate with Ping Lian and Ping Lian learns to take instruction from several art teachers at the same time, he is learning to generalize. Also, the fact that each teacher is in a different environment helps Ping Lian to generalize across settings as well. In short, the varied environments and the various instructors will create further learning opportunities for Ping Lian to learn, adapt and function effectively regardless of surrounding.

Another argument in support of the variability is to create change in routines. Rigidity and routines are characteristics that can stifle progress. I don't want Ping Lian to develop his talent based on any one person's specific skills or style in art. I want to empower him with the knowledge to develop his skill and style by making conscious decisions regarding his art and technique. Even if this happens due to "confusion" of what to do, it can only result in his own particular style. I am not knowledgeable about art but given my overall general knowledge of autism coupled with my understanding and expectations for my son, I believe this "confusion" may be the best route to success.

As I incorporate ABA into Ping Lian's art lessons, I proceed very carefully. Never think that this can be done blindly. Much care was taken to ensure that Ping Lian's interest in art would not be extinguished when paired with ABA drills. I had to be very cautious in being able to maintain his interest while still always "raising the bar" and pushing him toward more challenges. It was like a balancing act where you had to be careful not to "break the camel's back". Individuals with autism can be very idiosyncratic, and each individual may accept, receive or perceive the same stimuli or input very differently. I try to be very aware of the potential for rigidity that autistic people often rely on, but even with my heightened awareness I have made many mistakes along the way. As we progress and learn, I make constant adjustments in my approach and my communication with the art teachers. The "Do's and Don'ts" that I gave all instructors, were most important. For example; Ping Lian hates talking, or rather the verbal behavior communication ABA drills; so I advised the art teachers not to use art or his drawing as a tool for him to talk, as that may lead him to lose interest in drawing or in his art lessons. Also I advised the art teachers never to give Ping Lian negative comments about his drawings. Everything he draws/ paints is good and right and they should accept expression of his potential by allowing him to have his own way, style of drawing/painting through exploration. The common thread in the training techniques I developed for each art teacher was in their general role as instructors. Their role was primarily to guide Ping Lian in decision making through prompting and supervision, rather them telling Ping Lian how to draw. Specifics had more to do with helping Ping Lian to handle and accept changes in the environment as they taught and introduced him to use different medium; encouraged interest in different subjects, lead him and guided him to draw bigger sized works and infinitely how to get him to sit down for long sessions of serious painting and drawing. The underlying general skills learned would lead to teaching Ping Lian to make decisions and developing critical thinking skills.

God is so good!! The timing was just right. After so many years working with Ping Lian, it was time for Chin Chin to retire from his work. I realised at that point how busy Ping Lian had become. His days were filled with art lessons throughout the week, in addition to the art lessons received at home by Mylyn. He was attending the Kumon Mathematics program once a week, a "home school" program 3 - 4 times per week, and the Emmanuel Care Center supplementary program for special needs people twice a week! Ping Lian was indeed very busy and occupied every single day and most importantly, he was so happy. It was then that I realized that the plan to develop Ping Lian to become an Artist was "all-encompassing". He progressed so well in all aspects of his life (art, personal development, communication, vocabulary, independent skills, awareness of surrounding, behaviour, etc.) I did not realise or expect this.

PING LIAN SAYS " I WANT TO BE ARTIST"

As we continue along this journey I am searching for additional ways to efficiently achieve Our Dream. I came up with a "crazy" brain-washing idea. I would train Ping Lian to say "I want to be Artist". As most individuals on the autism spectrum have difficulties understanding, processing and using pro-nouns, Ping Lian was no different. In an attempt to simplify the sentence that I would train him to repeat, I purposely omitted the word "an". Including it would have no benefit to Ping Lian at this point. I wanted to keep the sentence "short and sweet", so it would be easier for Ping Lian to repeat and understand but meaningful.

I created an ABA drill in which I would ask Ping Lian "Who do you want to be when you grow up?" and the correct response from Ping Lian would be ***"I want to be artist"***. I would create constant situations where I would get Ping Lian to say " I want to be artist" and work toward getting him to enjoy and love saying it. My plan was to "brain wash" him. Yes, I said brainwash!. I wanted to get him to learn to say the phrase "I want to be Artist" and get him to believe it. I was hopeful that through this process I would be able to transplant and "program" my "dream" to eventually become Ping Lian's Dream. I am far from being an expert in any sense of the word in this area. I said to myself, "Who cares if it works or not? Never try never know!" Can anyone tell me a better way? Who can I ask? Where do I go? With no answers and no further guidance, I decided to make my own method and follow my instinct to "brainwash" my son. I felt that if I did not take action now, instead of continuing to search for answers in the research, that by the time I studied and became knowledgeable to an expert level about transplanting thoughts, etc. my Ping Lian would have lost much valuable time. So, I pretended to be an expert for Ping Lian to work on Our Dream. I proceeded privately (only in our house and only the immediate family members were aware) because I did not want to be perceived as weird or wrongly judged by others.

I also added the phrase "I want to be artist" into Ping Lian's motivational materials and his daily prayer. I even made a game with the phrase "I want to be artist" so that Ping Lian would learn it faster and say it spontaneously. I made him enjoy saying it by creating a zillion opportunities to play simple games that led him to say "I want to be artist". Sometimes I even gave him tangible rewards for saying it well or saying it spontaneously. Also whenever I praised him for artwork well done, I would always follow by asking him "Who do you want to be when you grow up?" to prompt his answer of "I want to be artist". I used gestures to symbolize a "winning spirit" such as what you might see on TV when athletes win a game. The gestures symbolise that I am "able", "clever", "powerful" and "victorious".

Afterward we would break out into a group of joyful " Ye!!!!!" to celebrate. This is how I "brain washed" him to love the joy of being accepted and recognized. Although many autistic people are often in their own world, I know that they can learn to appreciate acceptance and recognition, but I am not sure that they may actually need it. Anyway, although Ping Lian may not understand or even need acceptance and recognition, I could "brain wash" and influence him at this young age to enjoy and relate the goodness of acceptance and recognition.

Ping Lian eventually seemed to feel proud and exude pride whenever he said "I want to be artist". Although he didn't yet understand what the phrase meant, he knew he gave a good answer when asked "Who do you want to be when you grow up?" The joy and laughter he received from Mummy and his sisters was always so positive that he felt great. Sherlyn and Cher would always laugh happily because they felt it was so very "cute" the way their brother spoke these words.

As we progressed "I want to be artist" became part of our regular games and Ping Lian enjoyed and looked forward to it very much. This became a constant reminder for us all of Our Dream. I knew that "one day" Ping Lian would understand the true meaning of the words. I've since come to accept my crazy "brainwashing" ideas without concern about what others may think about my methods. In fact, I laugh at it myself whenever these past images come to my mind. Many times I ask myself how I could come up with such a series of "crazy" ideas. Looking beyond 2008 to the future, I felt that even if this would not prove to be successful, the many happy moments experienced during our "brain washing" games would make it all worthwhile anyway. The games provided hope and made the process of working toward achieving Our Dream a positive and joyful journey.

Note: As I was writing this chapter (2008), at this point I was so overcome with joy. I paused as my heart and mind only had one thought: "THANK YOU GOD"; "THANK YOU GOD";

Chapter 8

"THANK YOU GOD". I thanked God for giving me the wisdom to achieve and I thanked God for giving Ping Lian the special gift. "Thank You God for all the special happenings."

PING LIAN'S DREAM OR MUMMY'S DREAM

As I continued to nurture Ping Lian's talent en route toward the realisation of Our Dream I encountered many people who felt I was putting too much pressure on my young autistic son. So many lessons, so many teachers, "She's crazy!" I would hear people say. Many felt I was pushing my son too hard. Even acquaintances questioned my intentions. They felt that it was my dream and not my son's dream. "How do you know that is what Ping Lian will want for his life and his future?" Why are you rushing him into this when he is still so young?" "What if when he grows up he doesn't want to be in this Dream?" "Maybe he will be good at something else instead of art, or just prefer to do something else?" "What if he doesn't like what you arranged for him?" Although I did not allow such doubtful comments to alter my determination, I did take note not to overwhelm Ping Lian. I tried my best to make the entire journey a happy process for Ping Lian and not cause him pressure.

Yet, I was so determined and thought "SO WHAT!" It doesn't matter whose Dream it is. Ping Lian is autistic! I rationalized that he was living in his own world, with very low ability and no expression of feelings for his own family. He would not be able to set a dream for himself! I must set his Dream for him and guide him toward that Dream. In response to all those who commented that I should be patient and set a dream later when Ping Lian is older and has progressed further, I say: "Ha! It is easy to talk, but what will happen if that day never comes?" By then, it will be so much more difficult, if not impossible to train him or change him or "brain wash" him. The majority of research I came across in my readings while trying to educate myself about autism showed very grim portrayals of autistic adults.

No, I will not wait! I will "brainwash him" to love the "Dream" that I have set for him and influence him until it becomes his own Dream.

The task ahead now was to *transplant* my Dream to be Ping Lian's Dream, while getting him to acquire the necessary *desire* to *achieve* the Dream. The most important aspect will be that Ping Lian remains a happy boy.

(Note: Later true enough, Ping Lian's joyful attitudes are depicted in his painting, see the happy/ laughing horses; happy/ smiling fishes; happy/ joyful chicken; smiling sun; moon and sunflower with smiling faces; etc).

Life is about making choices. We must make decisions and make adjustments accordingly. This requires much wisdom as we need to be able to strike a balance to fit our own personal situations. The important thing is to actually *take action*. As parents, we are not perfect, not experts and not super women. We are however capable and must take ownership of a positive mental attitude and aim to do our very best in our own given situations. For me, my best meant "If everyone is happy and no one gets hurt" go for it.

PING LIAN'S HAPPY ANIMAL PAINTINGS:

04301 CHASING THE RAINBOW

A happy and relaxed horse (Painted at age 10).

There are many other happy, smiling paintings in this Gallery, including chicken and fishes!

05405 HAPPY FAMILY II
(A GROUP OF HAPPY AND JOYFUL CHICKENS)

05431 HAPPY FISHES

Painted in 2005 at age 11.

LIMITED RESOURCES

Moving forward with Our Dream was costly. Not only the time and effort needed to follow through, but the funds. I was spending a lot of money on the program fees and transportation to get Ping Lian from one place to another place for his various lessons. After paying all my fixed commitment fees and the daily household living expenses, I invested every additional cent I made at work toward Ping Lian's educational programs. As I have always done (even when Chin Chin was Ping Lian's instructor and for the ABA drills) I told his current teachers that if at the end of their scheduled instructional time, Ping Lian was still showing interest and still engaged in the lesson, they could continue on with him if they had the time and just record the additional hours they worked with him. So long as Ping Lian maintained interest and was able to cope with the additional lesson time I was willing to pay. However, as my budget fluctuated periodically, whenever it was necessary I informed his teachers of the maximum number of hours that I would be able to pay for any given month.

During these times I was blessed and based on my above good performance at work, I was receiving very good commissions. I felt lucky that the work came easy to me and I had a good boss who kept his promise in paying my rising commissions. At that time, I always joked that with the money I paid into Ping Lian's programming, I could actually take a holiday vacation overseas every month!

My boss knew very well that I loved taking overseas trips. One time he even challenged me by raising my sales goal and promised me an overseas trip as a reward for attaining the goal. I was so motivated and worked so hard and sure enough I won the trip! I have always loved to travel, buy myself nice clothes, relax, etc. But quite frankly, after working so hard daily to earn this money, such things were still not attainable for me. I would dream about it though, and also sometimes even wonder what my life would be like if I didn't have an autistic son. I couldn't take the trip! I eventually told my boss that I couldn't use the trip to enjoy myself. I requested that he convert the reward into cash so that I could enjoy it with my family. Although I used a portion for a local holiday trip with my family, some of the money I used to buy some things for my daughters Cher and Sherlyn that they had been longing for. At least half of the money, I again did indeed use for Ping Lian's instructional programs. I was satisfied with this as everyone was able to enjoy the reward.

My daughters are young. They tried to understand why all of my attention and resources went to their brother. They always seemed okay with my decisions but I know they felt it was unfair and I know that I often disappointed them. I was sorry about that but really wanted them to understand that whatever extra money I had was needed to invest in Ping Lian. Every single investment on him opens up doors and possibilities for his future. I often rejected Cher and Sherlyn's requests to buy "luxurious" goods. Due to my scarce finances, I considered much of the things they wanted as "luxuries". I always told them there are better ways to use money and that we needed to save the money for a "rainy day". However, it was so obvious that a "rainy day" came whenever an opportunity arose to contribute resources for Ping Lian's overall development. Seeing the disappointment in their faces has always caused me guilt and pain, but what choice did I have? I explained to my daughters that Ping Lian has been unlucky, but that they were lucky - normal, clever and smart. I wanted them to learn to be grateful for their lives and what they possess. I am not super woman. I had to set priorities as to what is best for the family as a whole in the long run. I tried to make them understand that it has to be a priority to help Ping Lian so that he would not have to rely heavily on them and be a "burden" to them in the future when they are all grown up and I am not around. As we are still very much "Chinese" thinking, our heritage dictates that it will become their responsibility to take care of Ping

Lian in the future and Ping Lian will be their " burden" (if assuming he still presents with severe autism and we do not talk about his art talent). So we need to work together as a family unit to make it "as easy" as possible in the future for all of us. We have no choice. These are the facts that we have to accept. We must adapt as a family. These are the lessons that I had to gradually instil in my young daughters. I was just trying to get them to understand the fact that their lives are different from other people's lives since this family has an autistic boy!

It has not been easy for Cher and Sherlyn. Life may seem to be unfair at times. On the surface, my decisions may appear to be unfair as well. In the long run my decisions will have a positive impact for us all. I constantly pray that later they can appreciate it. I hope my daughters can see, understand and accept this for now (2008).

After my husband passed away (2004), there were obvious times that my daughters seemed upset and angry that they had a brother with autism. I was now the sole bread winner of the family and had to take over the duties and responsibilities that their father had as well. I needed to handle everything at home and thus had even less time for all of my children. I had to be smarter in my decisions and alter my existing plans to strike a favorable balance within my resources, and across every aspect of our lives.

I know that I do not have to justify my decisions. After so many years of talking about this, I believe my girls have gotten bored and fed up with the "reduce the burden" story already. My intention has always been just to do my best in seeking their understanding and to replace any possible resentment with true understanding. My children each have very kind hearts and I expect that one day they will truly accept these facts along with the knowledge that I never did any of this at their expense. In fact, I am trying my best to practice so-called "fairness" in an "UnFair" situation. Sometimes I wonder, "What is fair? How can fair be defined in an unfair world"? How do you count or justify fairness? Who can give me a precise answer? No-one can! So I just continue using my own intuition, insightfulness and creativity and wisdom to practice what I think is best for everyone in our GIVEN SITUATIONS. I was constantly re-evaluating myself and making adjustments to the best of my ability for the benefit of our family as a whole. That is the best I can do when there are no choices. Acceptance is the key that leads to the attainment of happiness. That is why in most situations the most difficult part is to accept. Happiness does not come easily. Once we truly accept a situation we are on our way to conquering the fear and negative aspects surrounding that situation. Happiness is a choice! We cannot always control what happens to us, but we *can* control how we respond to what happens to us. I hope Cher and Sherlyn can accept that they will always have an autistic brother, and choose to respond positively to this situation in ways that will make them happy.

GALLERY 2003 - II 03701
THE VIOLIN - MUSIC OF LIFE PAINTED ON 28TH APRIL 2003, AT THE AGE OF 9

This was Cher's violin. It was broken by Ping Lian sometime ago and we ended up using it as a toy for Ping Lian's ABA drills.

Ping Lian and I had just come to learn about charcoal drawing. I was told by the teacher to get Ping Lian to practice charcoal drawing at home. One night just before going to bed, I was feeling guilty that I had not done any ABA drills with Ping Lian yet. I was very tired after a long day of work at the office but my guilt prompted me to at least get Ping Lian to draw instead of doing any ABA drills. As I was feeling exhausted, I simply grabbed the closest thing near me, which happened to be the violin and propped it up against my pillow for support, and gave him charcoal to draw.

I was amazed at the way he captured the violin on paper, and so I continued to put the violin in different positions for him to continue drawing. At that time even though I was new to art and not good in judging the quality of artwork, I just knew that this was a precious work of art. I had Ping Lian write down the date for me to remember that night. I felt proud and satisfied as it turned out to be a fruitful night. Even though we only spend very little time together we went to bed happy. Learning art is so good! Art is so good!

GALLERY 2003 -II 03301- THE KNIGHT PAINTED IN 2003 AT MY FAVOURITE ART HOUSE AT THE AGE OF 9

One day, I was too tired to attend a session as Ping Lian's teacher's aid. Ping Lian was on his own with the art teacher. Min Seng brought Ping Lian home from his art class and showed this art work to me. Wahl! I can't believe Ping Lian can paint such a beautiful and controlled art work. I remember thinking, the teacher must have helped him paint on certain parts....Ping Lian was still very new to charcoal...... In order to convince me that it is all done by Ping Lian without the help of teacher but only with teacher sitting beside him to prompt him on and off, the art teacher get Ping Lian to paint one more similar one in front of me. I believe it with my own eye. Another time surprise.

GALLERY 2003- 1

03211- SANTA CLAUS IS COMING TO TOWN
PAINTED IN 2003 AT MY FAVOURITE ART HOUSE AT THE AGE OF 9

I received a surprise phone call from Ping Lian's teacher. He said "You would love to drop by to see what Ping Lian has drawn today. You will not believe it…". If I am not mistaken, this was the first time Ping Lian used a combination of permanent markers with water color. Both his teacher and I were amazed with his ability.

Chapter 8

Ping Lian's worse had become his best. These art works and all of the progress Ping Lian has made to date in his behavior and overall personal development are proof that there can and should always be hope, regardless of the adversities that surface and the circumstances we may find ourselves in. There can always be a light at the end of the tunnel. Make it happen. Work with persistence, determination and perseverance. Focus and maintain a positive mental attitude; work hard and smart; work with faith and mold the spirit to resonate "YES I CAN…." Yes, I believe that even for a child with autism, these thoughts can be instilled. **With this, I Renewed Our Dream and Vision and in November 2003 I wrote it down in detail with my husband Min Seng. It is entitled " I'm A Dreamer".**

CHAPTER 9

Renewal of Our Dream and Vision To "I'm a Dreamer"

In September of 2003 I attended an Anthony Robbins seminar called **"Unleash The Power Within"**. He said "**There is Always room in your life for thinking bigger, pushing limits, Imagining the Impossible**". During the seminar we were asked to set a few of our personal goals. At that moment, I instinctively decided that Ping Lian's goals would be my goals. I wrote "Ping Lian will be an artist" as one of my personal goals. Robbins went on to get the group of attendees to imagine the joy of achieving our goals. He led us to visualize and feel the moment of our achievements. I actually visualized a scene where Ping Lian was an artist. It felt so victorious!

Anthony Robbins also says that **"good is not good enough....You need to be outstanding…and you need to have gratitude"**. Overall, I was extremely influenced by this seminar and it gave me the power to dare to dream with even more conviction. Ping Lian already proved that he loved painting. He thoroughly enjoyed his art classes, he was very good at it and he was still progressing and developing at an unbelievable pace. The realization that it was time once again to balance and make adjustments set in. The goal would no longer be to develop Ping Lian to be an "artist". Our Dream was renewed and the goal was **"to develop Ping Lian to become an "OUTSTANDING ARTIST"**. Robbins stressed the importance of writing down your goals. I left the seminar feeling so empowered and I set out to immediately put into action all that I had learned. The rest of Ping Lian's artistic journey was heavily impacted by the tenets of "Unleash the Power Within"

"I'M A DREAMER"

Touched by God and inspired by Anthony Robbins in November of 2003, with the support of Min Seng I proceeded to update my thoughts for "I'M A Dreamer". We wrote down that the goal was to develop Ping Lian to become an outstanding artist. I added that one day Ping Lian would be able to also contribute to society by helping other unfortunate special needs children through his art. I included my hopes that people would learn not to label autistic people or people with special needs as "disabled people". Min Seng and I agreed to work on this together as 'Our New Dream' and our new vision. The truth is that writing it all down (as prompted by Robbins) made us feel stronger. We were focused and action oriented to follow through.

Below is an edited version of our original "I'M A Dreamer". After Min Seng passed away, I began to fear that I alone would be unable to achieve what he and I outlined together as our goals. I changed some of the very detailed original plan and the adjusted version below is written as "I'M A Dreamer" – 2.

I'm A Dreamer...(2)

Written by Sarah SH Lee (Ping Lian Yeak's Mother)
@ Malaysia, November 2003 – edited after Ping Lian's father passed away

To develop Ping Lian Yeak to become an outstanding artist.

-Also to get him to contribute effectively to society by helping other more unfortunate special needs children.

Dream to realize the following.....

- Through Ping Lian, inspire and encourage parents with autistic children to come forward to share and develop their children's artistic potential into a means of livelihood, i.e. to develop their skill in art and to take up the challenge of using art as a means of livelihood when they grow up.

- Using art as a livelihood or to provide financial support for Ping Lian when he grows up, so that he will be independent without having to depend fully on his family.

- Apart from helping Ping Lian to be self-sufficient through art, he will one day be able to help or support other more unfortunate special needs people. This can be achieved by allocating a percentage of proceeds from the sale of his art works to help finance the needs of other special needs people/autistic people. (Any way he does not need to wait for that one day..... Total "funds raised" through Ping Lian's art works in aid of the special needs population for year 2004 already amounted to more than RM 119,000.00 ....DEC 2004)

- To inform the public of the talents of autistic people, thereby changing the general perception that "autistic people are disabled people". To promote that they are able to contribute to society in a different way even though they may have social and communication or whatever other weaknesses. This will also help the public to focus on the special skills of autistic people rather than on their limitations. And - Let us celebrate and focus on what autistic people can do (A- bility), not what they can't do (dis- ability) and do not label them as DISABLED

It is a fruitful journey of a Dream that can't be realized by Ping Lian and me only. I'm looking forward for passionate partners to walk with me in realising this Dream.

DO NOT LABEL AS DISABLED

I realised that moving forward by myself was also "not good enough". I wanted to move the general public with me. Google searches on art related to people with special needs or with disabilities were very offensive. I would come across terms like "autistic art" promotions for art exhibitions as "Art by disabled people". This always disheartened me. We are all people! My mother always use to say never be a "useless' person and always remember to maintain your pride and dignity. Where is the pride and dignity in these commonly used terms?

Many charities and organizations promote events as such "Disabled Art Exhibition" or "An art exhibition for disabled individuals". Not only is it offensive but it is a contradiction! On the one hand the individual organizations work hard to promote people with disabilities that have abilities (especially in art), yet on the other hand the marketing information, brochures, etc. promote the individuals as disabled people.

I do not like to label autistic people as Disabled people. 'Disabled' is a very negative word. What right do we have to call anyone "disabled"? Every human being has capabilities, the capacity to learn something and emotions. They are all human beings with feelings, needing respect and opportunities to develop self esteem. We must all be able to view the cup as half full as opposed to half empty. I'm sure many individuals who are referred to as "disabled" – whether they can express it or not, feel disrespected in having that label.

My thoughts go back to an incident one day when I was charged with picking up an adult with intellectual challenges from a special Olympics bowling game. I am not sure what I said to him during our conversation in my car, but I remember it must have been hurtful. He said "Aunty Sarah, I am a disabled people but I am not disabled". I was caught by surprise knowing that somehow I had offended him. Yet, I let him know that I was so proud of him for speaking up. Although his words were contradictory, I believe he was saying he did not want to be seen as disabled. From that day on, I have felt very strongly about educating others "not to label them as disabled". These sentiments are the rationalization for the following statement of "I'm A Dreamer" "Let us celebrate and focus on what autistic people can do, not what they can't do and do not label them as DISABLED".

I also later included this phrase in all of Ping Lian's summary (bio) write ups.

MAKING OUR DREAM PUBLIC

Immediately after attending the Anthony Robbins Seminar, my boss wanted me to share what I had learned from the seminar with my sales and customer support team. I encouraged them each to set their goals, not be afraid to make major changes in their way of thinking and to welcome paradigm shifts as they dare to Dream.

Although I had not planned on speaking about my personal agenda and my son, I found myself sharing this story with my co-workers at the meeting. "Ping Lian will be an Artist one day, regardless of who he is today." "Mark my words; he will definitely be an Artist. You all are my witnesses of *The Power of a Dream...*". "It does not matter who you are now, but it is who you want to be and who you become that matters, but you need to make a decision and take immediate action (Now!) to work toward achieving it....". I spoke about the importance of faith in our Dream and then continued on with my *business* motivational training.

I do not know why I suddenly shared details of Our Dream at the business meeting. I realized that I had just announced Our Dream for Ping Lian to become an artist publicly! There was now no turning back. These were private 'dreams' of which only God and my diary knew the details.

To date, I had shared this information only with my family (including my domestic helper Mylyn who is considered family) and Ping Lian's art teacher. Suddenly, at that moment I sensed it strongly - YES! Ping Lian would become an outstanding artist. It was like a little voice I heard inside me, and it is just too unique to describe. I was actually surprised with my own certainty about this.

"YOU CAN IF YOU THINK YOU CAN" & "YOU CAN BE WHATEVER YOU WANT TO BE"

If "what you think is what you get", then you attract what you think! A more positive message is *"You can if you think you can"*.

Many years ago immediately after graduating college I landed a job. After 3 months at my first place of employment I was performing badly. I felt so embarrassed about it that I decided to quit. One evening though, my manager asked me to stay back after work for a talk. He told me that he can see my potential in the job I was doing. He said that if I quit too soon, I will feel defeated and it will affect my future. He recommended that I be fair to myself, try harder and give myself more time to improve my performance. Then he pulls out one of his many motivational posters to share with me. The message delivered in that poster has been my guide ever since them.

<u>YOU CAN IF YOU THINK YOU CAN</u>

If you think you are beaten… you are!
If you think you dare not….you don't!
Success begins with your own will
It's all in your state of mind.

> Life's battles are not always won
> By those who are stronger and faster;
> And sooner or later, the person who wins
> Is the person who
> THINKS HE CAN

I purchased the same poster and hung it in my bed room. Today it still hangs in our home at Sydney. Needless to say; I took my managers advice and was eventually victoriously referred to as "an excellent performer, and one of the best at the company"! The rest of my life was obviously impacted by the life lesson of this message.

Years later I came across another motivational poster (by Donna Levine) which seemed to be an extension of the motivational poster "You Can if You Think You Can". It also, still hangs in our home in Sydney. I recall the stage in my life, when I read it every single morning at my office before starting my work day.

YOU CAN BE WHATEVER YOU WANT TO BE

> *There is inside you*
> *all of the potential to be whatever*
> *you want to be –*
> *all of the energy to do whatever you want to do.*
> *Imagine yourself as you would like to be,*
> *doing what you want to do.*
> *and each day, take one step towards your dream.*
> *And though at times it may seem too*
> *difficult to continue, hold on to your dream.*
> *One morning you will awake to find*
> *that you are the person you dreamed of –*

*doing what you wanted to do –
simply because you had the courage to believe in your potential
and hold on to your dream.*

My favorite line in this phrase is "One morning you will awake to find that you are the person you dreamed of". I tend to hang these motivational posters in our bathroom. It is the one place where I know my children will have to be still long enough to catch a glimpse. Reading it and being exposed to it daily may help to influence them and reinforce their thinking to remain positive in life, etc.

PING LIAN'S FIRST ART EXHIBITION

In December 2003 Ping Lian participated in "Different Strokes: Diversity through Art" at the National Art Gallery in Malaysia. It was an art exhibition sponsored by the Arab Women's Association. One of the major goals of the organization was for the exhibition to aim for ... "Change in society's perception of people with special needs in order that they are viewed as individuals with certain problems but also have strengths and talents. People with special needs have gifts that need to be acknowledged and celebrated. This exhibition deals with those whose talents lie in their artistic ability. The goal of the exhibition is to show the strength and talents of the exhibitors whose arts are to be judged on merits, not sympathy, and to show the world that they too can contribute to society."

This was the first time that Ping Lian participated in an art exhibition. Even more exciting, it was the first time that Ping Lian sold some artwork. Six pieces of Ping Lian's art were exhibited and all six were purchased. I was so encouraged by the expressions of the people as they viewed his artwork. This was also the first time that Ping Lian appeared in the newspaper. My family and all the people who have been involved in Ping Lian's life and his artistic journey were overjoyed. Our collaborative efforts were now bearing fruits. We clearly could see the light at the other end of the tunnel. I felt extremely validated. My "crazy" was paying off! I was catapulted to an extreme sense of encouragement toward bringing Ping Lian to that level of "outstanding".

PING-LIAN SPECIAL INTEREST AT YOUNG AGE: JOURNAL ENTRIES – WRITTEN ON FEB 2004 (JUST AFTER YEAK PASSED AWAY)

Ping Lian Yeak- Interest at young age:

> *Since very young age, maybe only 2 or 3 years old, even before he was assessed (at age 4), Ping Lian was very hyperactive. We needed to hold his hand tight whenever he went shopping with us. But whenever we passed by a book shop he would run into the book shop and rush to the adult section/ magazine section. (He never ran to the toy section or children's book section, at that time he still had no interest in toys or books. He still does not know how to read and he can't even sit down for a few minutes). At the book shop, he looks for magazines like 'Home' and 'Architectural Trends', 'Home & Living', or 'Sweet Home' or books of interior design, landscapes, gardens or similar in nature. He will take one magazine and sit down on the floor and go through it page by page, quietly and intensively. At these moments his hyperactivity is immediately gone. We (My family) always wonder what he is looking for and what he learns or understands from the book. We admire this and enjoy watching him. Because of this, we always*

buy a lot of these types of magazines and have them at home ……. for him to admire.

At some point I shared with my brother-in-law (Leong Chnong) the strange and unique characteristics of Ping Lian's behavior. All we knew was that Ping Lian was autistic. (We did not yet know anything about savants and islands of talent or splinter skills). Leong Chnong always reminded me that "May be there is something in him he is very good at. We do not understand and we do not see it because he can't tell us. Just keep an eye out and watch carefully". He also brought to my attention an article he read about the sudden appearance of musical skills in some autistic children. Min Seng and I were very careful to continually note Ping Lian's peculiarities in character. We thought maybe he has talent in interior design or architecture. However these trades as careers never entered my mind for Ping Lian because they would require excellent communication skills, which realistically Ping Lian did not possess. We never considered design and architecture related to art, especially not at this point in time when Ping Lian had such poor fine motor skills, and actually we had not yet seen his talent in art.

Another peculiarity in Ping Lian's character since a very young age was that whenever we took him to the lake side, he would run toward the edge of the lake and sit down with beautiful body posture like an adult. He would sit quietly, put both hands on his lap, and intensely admire the scenery. We were always so amaze by this action. Again, at these moments his hyperactivity and attention deficit disappeared automatically. He looked like a little adult sitting gracefully, admiring the beautiful landscape. We did not understand his behaviour, but it was always like a breath of fresh air watching him this way. We just enjoyed watching his cute, beautiful and unique behavior. Yet, once he was finished or had enough of this.... Ha! He gets up, starts running all over the place, and he is his usual self again. We had to quickly try to keep up with his pace by running after him to catch him and try to control his socially unacceptable hyperactive behavior in public!

04101 KUALA LUMPUR TWIN TOWERS I

When Ping Lian came home from art class, I was on the bed and not feeling well. He looked tired and exhausted. He lay down on top of me and immediately fell asleep. He felt slightly warm and I became concerned that he might be sick with a slight fever. After a short nap together, I got up and went downstairs. I saw this beautiful Twin Towers painting lying on the floor. I was again amazed at the quality in his work. When Ping Lian awoke, he was as active as usual with no signs of illness. I thought, no wonder he was so exhausted and tired. This was the first time Ping Lian drew and painted Kuala Lumpur Twin Towers and he also finished it all at once. The artwork was so detailed. These are the Kuala Lumpur Twin Towers through Ping Lian's eyes. Do you also see the car and the many motorcycles in the picture? Do you see the people riding on motorcycles passing by a traffic light? I am amaze with the way he captures the movement of this motor cycle with his pen. I am so happy and encouraged and I thank God for another time of amazement with this work.

04101 KUALA LUMPUR TWIN TOWERS I

Painted in April 2004 at the age of 10 (Painted two months after Ping Lian's Daddy passed away. This particular artwork specifically contributed to my focus on "I'm A Dreamer' again).

04102 KUALA LUMPUR TWIN TOWERS IV

Painted in Nov 2004 at the age of 11 Kuala Lumpur Twin Tower V (this original painting was donated to the church).

04102 KUALA LUMPUR TWIN TOWERS IV

There was a fund raising event for building the Cavalry Convention Centre, and at the "last minute", a friend from church suggested I get Ping Lian to draw a picture to be auctioned at the event. I always look at Ping Lian's artistic talent as a gift from God and I am grateful that he is so blessed, so definitely I said " YES!"

I told Ping Lian that he needed to draw a Twin Towers for the church and he needed to draw it very beautiful and finish it fast….. (I do not know how much of those directions he understood). The moment he started drawing, I knew it was going to be turn out to be an excellent piece of work. He showed great passion, focus and a special energy in the speed with which he proceeded to draw. I had to quickly tell myself that no matter how wonderful the experience and how beautiful the artwork turned out to be, I must be willing to part with it. This piece did not belong to me; it would belong to the church. Within two days, Ping Lian had finished 04102. It was exquisite. I had already committed to donate this wonderful and extraordinary work in advance and could not go back on my word. Typically I did not like to part with Ping Lian's work regardless of what price people would pay, but I had to also pursue the dream to help others through Ping Lian's art. I told Ping Lian that Mummy love this piece (04102) very much but this piece Mummy needs to let go and give it to the church. I tried to encourage him to draw another one, similar for me to keep. I believe Ping Lian understood how I felt. He is so good. He did it immediately and quickly finished another pieces of KL Twin Towers V (04133) "for Mummy". I still prefer the style of him drawing 04102 with a twisted line of Twin Towers but I kept my promise and donated the original one which I liked best!

I am so grateful to God and all the people in Ping Lian's journey who have supported him and guided us both. I feel so thankful to God. Yes! I thank God for Ping Lian's keen interest in art and I thank God for Ping Lian's talent in art. I also thank God for always sending the right and good people into our lives.

04133 KUALA LUMPUR TWIN TOWER V
Painted in Nov 2004 at the age of 11.

08501 FLOWERS - ACRYLIC ON CANVAS, PAINTED IN 2008

PART III
LIFE ALTERING CHANGES

CHAPTER 10
Daddy In Memory

"Daddy in Memory" was the most difficult chapter of this book for me to write. Many times I thought of giving up and totally omitting this chapter. However, I forced myself to continue since it is an important portrayal of so many incidents that affected our family's overall journey. The decision to include this chapter caused many delays in the final completion of the whole book. Subconsciously, whenever I started to write this chapter, I would find yet another excuse to avoid writing....In fact every draft written of this chapter was written in tears. I finally told myself that I must finish the book soon. I decided to face it and try my best to complete the chapter without any more excuses, regardless of my emotional state. My emotional state never did change. Through my tears I eventually and finally completed the chapter. To my surprise I cried more sadly.

Min Seng and I were progressing well in our careers, our investments and our finances. Yet, later the economy and shares market situation had put us in a very bad financial position. We sold almost all of our property, and what was left of our properties (bad investments) had become liabilities leaving us with huge financial burdens.

By the end of 2003, Min Seng's career and financial situation had come to a turning point. I had originally planned to resign from my position in 2004 or at least to work only part-time. However, in Feb 2004, while I was enjoying my holiday with my children in Singapore, I received a call from my brother. Min Seng had a sudden heart attack. He was gone???!!!! All this happened just a few days after the wonderful time I shared with Min Seng discussing how we were going to achieve "Our Dream" as detailed in "I'm A Dreamer". We had discussed how I would no longer work full time, how I would focus my time for Ping Lian and also have time to contribute to the autistic community at large. We discussed how Min Seng would take sole responsibility in providing for the family's financial needs, etc.

At some point I remember being so angry and disappointed with how life can turn out. I was so angry with God… for being so unfair to me (more than once!) *He* gave me an autistic son *and He* took Min Seng away just when life started to seem to be getting better for us. After so many years of hard work, this was a time when we were just beginning to see hope for Ping Lian. We were just starting to "dare" to have a big Dream for Ping Lian and for ourselves. So many years after finding out that our son was autistic, we were just finding a meaningful purpose in our lives. Yet, God had another plan…

PING LIAN DRAW DADDY, MUMMY & PING LIAN ON A NEW TABLE

We received the money of Ping Lian's art works that sold at the exhibition "Different Strokes: Diversity Through Art" Dec 2003. The amount was not much at all, but it was very meaningful to all of us. It was the first time Ping Lian participated in an art exhibition and also the first time we ever sold Ping Lian's original art works. We sold six pieces of original art works. We were so proud of Ping Lian's achievement. We decided to use this money to buy something meaningful for Ping Lian to remember this special occasion. After a few weeks of thinking, we decided to buy a table especially for him to use for his drawing as a reward.

We would always go shopping with Ping Lian and his younger sister Cher, but on this day (Feb 2004) we told Cher that we wanted to try to have Ping Lian understand that this is a special day and special occasion for him only. We decided that for this time, we would take only Ping Lian shopping. We wanted to make him feel special and we wanted to select a table for him for his drawing purposes to celebrate his first success.

After we purchased the table, we went for a long walk. It was such a very happy day. Min Seng was also in a very good mood. It seemed that all good things were finally coming to us now at the same time. We had been having financial problems for sometime now, but lately Min Seng had been working on a small project that yielded some financial rewards. Through this project he had developed some connections that led him to another new and bigger project. He was in the process of finalizing this new project which involved him as a consultant bringing huge financial opportunities. So, during our long walk Min Seng talked about how bright our future would soon be. I told Min Seng that with his new career turning around and with Ping Lian's artistic progress; very soon I would no longer need to work full time. Eventually, I would be able to work part time and also help Ping Lian while involving myself in charity work. Min Seng agreed this time. He said "OK, certainly" and we proceeded to set a target date of 2005 or 2006 when I would stop working totally. We even discussed what kind of charity I would get involved in and how to go about it. It was a very happy time together.

After purchasing the table for Ping Lian, we passed by Starbucks. Min Seng was in such a good mood and he suggested that we go in for a coffee. I love to go to Starbucks for coffee and it had been a long time since we had been there. I was definitely in the mood to stop but at the same time was already starting to feel guilty that we had come out for such a long time without Cher. Cher also loved going to Starbucks. I suggested to Min Seng that we come again next week with Cher instead. I did not realise that next week would never come. Every time I pass by that same Starbucks, I feel so saddened for not having gone in for coffee on that fine day with Min Seng.

Later that evening, Min Seng set up the table we had purchased for Ping Lian. He turned it upside down and suggested that Ping Lian draw Daddy, Mummy and Ping Lian *underneath* the new table top. This wooden table which was a reward for Ping Lian's successful first exhibition would be a very special table! Ping Lian enjoyed drawing us on the underneath of the tabletop so much! We even had him sign and date the work. This table now adorns our house in Sydney.

This was the first time Ping Lian drew on any type of object other than paper. Our whole family enjoyed watching him as he drew us underneath the table. This was such a happy and meaningful day for the entire family. It had been a long time since we were so relaxed and happy.

A "SPECIAL CALL"- MIN SENG IS GONE - FEBRUARY 2004

Just after the Chinese New Year celebration, both Sher Lyn and my niece (Yi Wen) wanted to go to "The Human Body Exhibition" in Singapore. Min Seng had been complaining that he was very tired and his stomach felt discomforted for several days now. He chose to stay home but he encouraged me to go with my sister (Siew Ing). Siew Ing suggested that instead of taking public transportation I should take this opportunity to learn to be independent in my driving. I had been driving for many years, but only for short distances and never out of state! I took her advice and mustered up the courage to go for my first attempt at long distance driving. In fact, I have always feared long distance driving. I had never driven a long distance in my entire life before. This would be the first time! I was feeling proud and happy.

We had a good time with my sister for several days. On the last day of our visit to Singapore we attended the "Human Body Exhibition". At the

Exhibition Hall, initially Ping Lian was very well behaved and remained calm. He was actually very brave. The preserved dead bodies were frightful to me, but not to Ping Lian. However, half-way through the exhibition, Ping Lian suddenly began to behave very strangely. He appeared to be in agony and great fear. He started getting a little hyper and his emotions became very unstable. I had sensed that something was not right, but when I asked him if he felt scared or if he saw anything scary he was not able to answer me. Ping Pian just kept pointing to one direction in great fear and worry saying "there … there…". I did not understand what he wanted to say, nor what had caused his demeanor to change so suddenly. I cannot understand Ping Lian's severely limited verbal communication attempts, but I always know when something is wrong by his unstable behavior. At this point I am sure that something is not right with him and so I start to wonder if he saw something that may have scared him. Ping Lian's behavior worried me and since I could not figure out what triggered him I quickly took him out of the exhibition hall and waited outside for my sister and my other children. For whatever reason, while waiting outside for a while, Ping Lian did calm down.

After the exhibition, we proceeded to go to Johor Bahru to my fifth sisters' (Kay Ing) house which is just across the border of Singapore. The moment we crossed the immigration border… my phone rang. My domestic helper (Mylyn) called… she was crying! She said "Sir is collapsed on the floor in the bed room". Simultaneously, my sister's phone also rang… It was my brother! He said that it appeared as though Min Seng was already gone for sometime. I was told that late into the evening, Min Seng had not come down for dinner at all. So my mother-in-law went upstairs to check on him she found him collapsed on the floor. My poor mother in law, she is 79 years old. I cannot imagine how she managed to witness all of this and then make it downstairs to ask Mylyn for help.

I was in disbelief that this could happen to Min Seng. It was too sudden. I was not prepared. I immediately felt so sad and sorry for Min Seng and for our family. I felt sorry for myself, Cher, Sherlyn, Ping Lian and also for my mother in-law. We lost a husband, father, and son. Cher and Sherlyn also could not believe it and they started crying. As for Ping Lian, it was as if nothing happened. I tried to tell him that "Daddy had gone for long sleep; Ping Lian had no more Daddy; and Daddy is gone." I continued with "Daddy is going to be put in the soil" at the 'last resting place' and "Daddy cannot come back anymore, Ping Lian had no more Daddy". Since Ping Lian did not know what die or death meant, he did not seem to understand (at all) what I was talking about. I had not taught Ping Lian the word die. I never even used the word "die" before because I did not like words such as die or graveyard. Instead I chose the words "long sleep" to speak about death and "long resting place" to replace graveyard. Such terms are typical in the Chinese culture for describing death. Still, Ping Lian seemed unaffected by my words. My heart was so broken. I had no idea how much Ping Lian understood but I knew then that I must tell him and try to make him understand that his "Daddy" was gone. There were times that it did seem obvious that Ping Lian was wondering why Cher and Sherlyn were crying so sadly. He would approach them, get close to them and many times get very close showing his care and concern for them.

Through my sadness, I remember the tremendous fear that overcame me. The burden of my now sole responsibility to raise three children (10, 12 and 16 years old) plus have full responsibility to take care of my old mother in law (age 79) who also lived with us. I asked myself *"How am I going to face and manage all this?" "What will my future be like?" "How am I going to take care for my autistic son by myself...?"* I started to feel sorry for my self. I was so scared and found myself on the edge of collapsing emotionally. Yet, almost simultaneously I also told myself that for now, "I can't collapse." "I can not feel sad for now, nor can I think of the future now…it is too much to cope with!" In order to proceed and make sense of my life I convinced myself that since this has happened and there is no way I can reverse it, there is no point in feeling sad. "I will face it".

I would think about the future at a later time, face it and take it slowly - one day at a time. At that moment, I felt that I needed to lock away my emotions of sadness and to lock my mind from thinking about the future. I can't think of "how" and "what"… I can't think about our life without Min Seng, or imagine Ping Lian's life without Daddy. At this moment I had to be strong. I had to be very clear of what I needed to do next. I thought…

"I must be strong, so my children and my mother in-law know that they still can depend on me. Also these are to be our last moments with Min Seng, and so we need to have good moments with him for the last time. Now is not the time to feel sad and to worry about the future. If by chance, Min Seng still can know and hear what is going on and if he knows that I am strong, he then can leave us in peace".

I am not sure what I did to my mind, but I do know that I decided to switch off part of my thinking and my emotions. I convinced myself to stand tall and be calm no matter what. To my surprise, I did suddenly become very calm. I was consumed with a level of "calmness" that brought with it a realisation of how powerful our minds can be.

Later my sister arranged for us to take a bus home to Kuala Lumpur. During the bus ride I constantly repeated myself, trying to get Ping Lian to understand that he had "no more daddy" and to explain his Daddy's death. On the bus, when everyone fell asleep, I became very emotional. I started to think of Min Seng, and again wondered what my future would hold and how was I to cope with all of this responsibility by myself? I couldn't remain "switched" off any longer and just started to cry. I was so sad and so scared of the future. I also had feelings of being upset with Min Seng for not taking care of his health. We had urged him several times over the past few days to see a doctor as he was consistently complaining of discomfort for the past two weeks. He just brushed it off, insisting that he just needed more rest.

Note: I believe that all parents have an obligation to be responsible to their bodies; if not for their own sake, then for their children's sake. Most children with severe autism have no friends. Their family members are their friends. Ping Lian not only lost his Daddy – He lost his friend!

The moment I reached home, I knew I had plenty of decisions to make. I began by again attempting to shut off and cast away my emotions. I was very calm, with a very clear mind. I gave myself strength in this manner to a point I could not believe was possible. *"We must have good last moments with Min Seng for the next two days. There is no time and no room for feeling sad."*

As the Chinese traditional ceremony dictates, Ming Seng would be viewed for three days and two nights at the funeral parlor so that his friends and relatives could see him for the last time. Ping Lian would not understand this and so I decided that he would stay at home with my domestic helper. In order for him and his father to be together for the last moment, we brought Ping Lian to the funeral parlor in the evening of the second night, which was the night before the actual burial.. When Ping Lian came, even though he saw his Daddy in the coffin, and I explained to him many, many times, in many different ways, and in very simple language about "Daddy passed away", Ping Lian still could not be bothered. He still did not know or realise what was going on.

Being in this new place was exciting to Ping Lian. He was filled with curiosity and just wandered around, exploring and playing on his own the whole night. He looked so happy and even laughed often as if nothing had happened. He was probably wondering why so many people had come by

Chapter 10: Daddy In Memory

and were being served some light food and drinks. He probably thought we were having a party. For Ping Lian there was no sadness, as a matter of fact he seemed to be so happy with people, food, and drinks around. He was still very unaware about the eternal departure of his Daddy. My heart was breaking with the realisation that Ping Lian did not understand that he had lost his Daddy forever. I began to wonder *"What is in his mind?", "How much does he care and love his daddy?"*

Ping Lian began to actually show us affection several years prior to this incident. For some time now thoughts of "how much does Ping Lian love us" had been crossing my mind. I would wonder if he loved us in the same way that a typical child loves his parents – like Cher & Sherlyn love us. Whenever I had gone away on a brief vacation or during a holiday for a few days, upon returning home I knew that Cher and Sherlyn had missed me. Their actions, their words and their behavior were clear indications letting me know that I was missed. I was never quite sure if Ping Lian missed me when I was away from home. I would always ask for feedback regarding Ping Lian upon my return from those brief trips. I would ask about his behavior during my absence, but the answer was always that Ping Lian did not mention Mummy nor look for Mummy. I think for Ping Lian apparently it did not matter if I was around or not, as long as his needs were being taken care of and he was still surrounded by other loving family members. It was the same when Min Seng or my mother in law went away. My mother in law especially would get extremely disappointed that Ping Lian did not seem to miss her whenever she was away. Actually, even the numerous occasions that I had to replace and hire a new domestic helper, Ping Lian did not show any emotional response to the changes. When I took Ping Lian to the airport with me and explained to him that our domestic worker was leaving us forever, this did not seem to matter to him. So long as he had a new domestic helper taking care of him at home already, it just didn't seem to matter!

Seeing Ping Lian without any emotional response to his Daddy lying in a coffin was very difficult. His nonchalant attitude during that entire evening lead me to question his emotions. I thought, even *"if Ping Lian understands the meaning of 'death' or if he understands the meaning of "'Daddy is gone forever', how is his mind functioning?"* "How does he feel about the loss of his Daddy?"

I wondered if it really mattered to Ping Lian if his Daddy was alive or was gone forever???!! Did he feel sadness about his Daddy being gone forever?...did it matter at all to him if his Daddy was alive or gone forever??... or was he really indifferent as long as his needs were being taken care of???!!! …Did he love his Daddy and how much did he love his Daddy? Is this is the kind of boy who I need to take care of for the rest of my life? A son who shows no affect or caring response in our absence so long as he is cared for by others? Who is he?... And who would he be? Would he ever reciprocate our love for him?

At that time I still did not have any answers to all my questions and I prayed to have answers immediately. I thought Min Seng's passing would provide answers to these questions. I was in so much pain. It felt as if my heart was bleeding!!! There are no words to describe my feelings at that moment. I wanted to give up and also to ignore my son's actions. I needed to just accept whatever and whoever he was. .. but I couldn't.

Ping Lian must know and understand that Daddy is gone forever. What he actually thinks and feels about his Daddy being alive or gone remains another issue. I needed to make Ping Lian understand that his Daddy was not going to be with us after tomorrow. Today would be the last day he can still see Daddy. Many times I took Ping Lian alongside the coffin to get him to look at his Daddy and told him Daddy is "long sleep" and we will be putting him in the soil tomorrow…etc etc. That entire evening my heart continued to bleed as I fruitlessly continued explaining this to Ping Lian.

On a few brief occasions a puzzled look came over Ping Lian's face as he watched his sisters crying. On and off he would approach and get near

Cher and Sherlyn by leaning his body on them. It seemed to be his way of showing love and concern for them when he saw them crying. On his own initiative, he finally then started to approach the coffin, on and off and look at his Daddy.

Again my mind started racing with a million more unanswered questions and anticipated predicaments. I asked myself… *"How am I going to cope through life by myself and handle a child like him alone?"* I felt sorry for myself and I felt sorry for my son with autism who at this young age of 10 had lost the care and love of his Daddy. *"He already has no friends… Daddy is very important in his life…Daddy is his only male friend. Ping Lian is not only loosing a Daddy, but in fact is also losing his only special friend."*

We did not have an opportunity to talk with Min Seng before he passed away. I have heard people say that within certain hours after a person passes away, their spirit can still hear us. I hoped that Min Seng could hear what we had to say. Cher and Sherlyn gathered beside the coffin and took turns talking to their father. We got Ping Lian to join us regardless of how much he would understand. One by one we asked Min Seng for forgiveness if ever we had offended him, and also told him that we forgave him if ever he (Daddy) had offended us. We told Min Seng that we loved him very much and that we commit to him that we will behave, we will take care of each other and we will take good care of Ping Lian and Ah Mah (grandmother). We ask him to go in peace. I do not know if Ping Lian understood any of this but I guided him to repeat each saying, when it was his turn to speak to Daddy. I also had Ping Lian commit to Daddy that he would be a "clever boy" and a "good boy" from now on.

Min Seng was an only son. My mother in law had been living with us since I gave birth to Sherlyn. Thus, I also told Min Seng not to worry. I would take good care of all the children and that I would also continue living with his mother. I committed to continue taking good care of her, and I asked him to go in peace.

On the second day of the funeral parlor viewing, Ping Lian appeared to understand a little more of what was happening. I guess that as Ping Lian sees the closing of the ceremony as the coffin is being closed that he must be wondering "why men are sealing his Daddy in the box?" This point of the ceremony represented the last moment we would share with Min Seng and would be our final good bye.

After all of the necessary decision making for the funeral was over and as the final closing of Min Seng's burial ceremony approached I suddenly felt that the "switch" which I mentally pulled to switch off my emotions was no longer functioning. I was once again at a point of emotional collapse and I burst out crying.

The hearse transported Min Seng's body to Sitiawan for the burial. The journey by car from Kuala Lumpur to Sitiawan took approximately three and a half hours. In the front seat of the hearse there was only one passenger seat. In my quest to continue to try to make sure that Ping Lian understood his Daddy's death, I sat Ping Lian on my lap in the front seat. I hoped that travelling with Daddy in the "box" for the next 3 or 4 hours, Ping Lian might come to realise what was happening or hopefully understand Daddy's death better. I did not use the word coffin with Ping Lian. He had already been exposed to so many new situations and words just over night, so I tried to keep it as simple as possible for him. When referring to the coffin I used the word "box". Having Ping Lian ride with me was still yet another attempt on my part to extend his time with his Daddy and for Min Seng to be with Ping Lian for the last time. I remember thinking "Daddy is gone forever, Ping Lian you must understand this before Daddy is buried!" I was unable to control my emotions and kept crying. Between the tears I used simple language to explain Daddy's death. I needed to get an emotional response from Ping Lian.

I noticed Ping Lian looking over to the back – The box where Daddy was inside! I noticed a certain expression, possibly one of confusion. His eyes

Chapter 10: Daddy In Memory

and facial expression were different. I guess he must have been wondering why Mummy kept crying and why Daddy, such a big man was closed inside the big box?.. And that this time he cannot see Daddy anymore. Many times I asked him "Where is Daddy?" and he would point toward the box at the back and say, "there"... Seeing all this happening, I believe that Ping Lian started to sense something was not right. Throughout the hearse ride I continued to explain to Ping Lian what happened to Daddy and how our life would be without Daddy.

I asked Ping Lian "Where is daddy?", and Ping Lian pointed "There". Then I would tell him "Yes! Daddy is inside the box and Ping Lian has no more Daddy already". I continued on saying that " Daddy going for ' long sleep' and Daddy together with the box going to be put in the soil, at the 'last resting place' and Daddy will not come back any more, he is gone forever:" I would pause and again emphasize "Ping Lian have no more Daddy already". I pause again "No more daddy already. Mummy very sad"... I was still worried that my attempts at explaining were not good enough and he would not understand so I repeated again and again and again! "No more Daddy" meant - *"Daddy go for long sleep, so Daddy will be put in the soil, so Daddy cannot go shopping with Ping Lian already.... no more Daddy to go to beach together already..."* etc, etc." " *Cher is sad, Sherlyn is sad, AhMah is sad, Mummy is sad, we all have no more Daddy already... Daddy going for 'long sleep' and Daddy going to be put in the soil". "Next time, we cannot see Daddy already"*. I continued talking while I was crying and all the while thinking "I hope he can grasp and understand some of this."

Due to his autism Ping Lian has extremely limited speech and limited social skills. I don't pretend to know or to understand how his brain and his emotions function but I am concerned that he may forget about Min Seng now that "Daddy" will not exist in his life. I do not know if he will remember and miss his Daddy or love his Daddy once his life does not have Daddy in it anymore. I do not want him to totally forget about his

Daddy so I showed him to point to his heart and say that "next time Ping Lian cannot see Daddy already but Daddy will live inside Ping Lian heart forever…". Also I showed Ping Lian to point to his head and say "Daddy also live inside Ping Lian brain". We were running out of time. Three hours pass very quickly and I did not have much time left to talk to him. I tried my best and continued *"Mummy do not have Daddy already; Mummy is very sad, so no one help Mummy already; Ping Lian must be a clever boy and Ping Lian must be a good boy.. OK?!!"*

For the first few weeks after Daddy passed away, Ping Lian did indeed, on and off ask me "Where is Daddy?" We visited Daddy's grave two months after the burial ceremony. I think Ping Lian finally understood that Daddy was gone forever.

VISIT DADDY'S GRAVE

Two months after Min Seng passed away was "Ching Ming Day"[22]. On Ching Ming families visit their ancestors, relatives' or their loved one graves to do grave sweeping and to pay respect. Since my childhood I had never missed visiting my grandparents and later on my parents and in-laws graves on Chin Ming. Our family would get together and go from one grave to the next until we had paid respects to all of our deceased parents and grand parents. Even in our adulthood, after working and raising our own immediate families we never failed to keep this tradition. No matter how busy we were, we would take leave to come back to our home town, Sitiawan for Chin Ming.

22　*Ching Ming Festival* is one of the 24 segments in Chinese calendar. It normally falls on the 4th or 5th of April because it's depended on the Cold Food Day (105 days after previous year's winter solstice). In the old days, Ching Ming was celebrated 3 days after the Cold Food Day but Cold Food Day was shorted to one day and then abandoned. So nowadays, Ching Ming and Cold Food Day fall on the same day although no one celebrate Cold Food Day any more. Ching Ming is also known as "Remembrance of Ancestors Day" or 'Grave Sweeping Day'.

Chapter 10: Daddy In Memory

Throughout my life I continued the (Chin Ming) practice out of obedience to the family traditions. I now however have a deeper understanding that the purpose is to ensure that we and our children do not forget about our ancestors (even if we have never met our grandparents, etc. in our lifetime). Chin Ming is a reminder of our family tree, our roots and our heritage. Never before had Ping Lian been to Sitiawan for Ching Ming. This time would be different. Due to his autism and lack of understanding regarding "death" I had never involved Ping Lian in this tradition. This time would be special. I decided that Ping Lian would come along with us to visit his Daddy's grave.

The day before Ching Ming, in my anticipation of visiting my husband at the gravesite, I told my son "Ping Lian we are going to 'see' Daddy tomorrow morning". Ping Lian still had very bad communication and language skills and was unable to cope with excessive vocabulary. He would not know the meaning of the words "pay respect" or "visit". In my attempt to keep the language simple, I said... *"Ping Lian, we are going to 'see' Daddy tomorrow morning."*

As a form of respect to the elders, Chin Ming tradition dictates that we must first pay our respects to Ping Lian's grandfather by stopping at his grave before proceeding to Ping Lian's father's grave. Again, because of Ping Lian's autism I usually only communicate to him what I believe may be relevant and understood by him. In fact, I would often unwittingly exclude Ping Lian from our family's daily verbal interactions by overlooking his presence, especially when I was busy or pre-occupied. I did not mention to Ping Lian that we would visit his grandfather's grave first before we can go to his Daddy's grave. Ping Lian's grandfather had passed away before Ping Lian was born, and so visiting his grandfather's grave would have no significance for him. He also definitely did not understand the concept of family tree or roots yet. I did however inform only my daughters about visiting grand father's grave first. Ping Lian often seems like a trained and obedient "puppet" to me. At times I would reflect upon how unbelievable it is to me, that my once very hyperactive son with attention deficit disorder, no feeling for others, no sense of danger, and living in his own world could be so obedient (like a puppet). Under normal circumstances, he usually just follows and goes along with me. He would obediently follow whatever I have arranged for him.

While at Grandfather's grave Ping Lian was very unhappy, upset and emotional. He kept pointing in the distance and complaining " there, there…go there, go there …". At first I wondered why Ping Lian was not behaving; not being "obedient". I did not realise that he actually recognised his Daddy's grave and that he was eager to go to "see" his Daddy. I was unable to keep Ping Lian calm and after a while I was so sure that what he wanted was to go to visit his Daddy. I knew that I had forgotten to explain to him that we will only visit his Daddy's grave after visiting "GrandpaI"!

As Ping Lian stood in front of his Daddy's grave he appeared so happy. The rest of us, Cher, Sherlyn and myself took turns talking to Daddy. I got Ping Lian to talk to Daddy by having him repeat what I said on his own behalf and then we placed the flowers on the grave. When it was time for my other family members (brothers, sisters, brother and sister-in-law, nieces and nephews) to pay their respects to Min Seng they stood in front of the grave. At this point Ping Lian walked to the side and squatted down beside the grave. He began scraping at the cement, trying to open the cement that covered Daddy underneath and saying "open, open…. ". He was very persistent, insisting in his way that we must open the cement. I had never expected this behavior from Ping Lian. Suddenly I realised that I may have made a huge mistake. My autistic son has "literally" translated my message that we were "going to see Daddy"! Ping Lian now expected to actually see his Daddy under the soil. I believe that he thought we could open the grave to see Daddy. I knew then that my Ping Lian still did not really understand death. I realised I made a big mistake and was careless in my communication with my autistic son.

I reminded Ping Lian that *"Daddy go for "long sleep" under the cement"; "We have no more Daddy already"; "We cannot open the cement."; "We cannot*

Chapter 10: Daddy In Memory

see Daddy anymore."; "Daddy is now living inside Ping Lian's heart and inside Ping Lian's brain"; "Ping Lian can only 'see' Daddy in the heart and in the brain." While I am talking to him I also pointing toward his heart and head... Many times, I tried to stop him from using his hands to scrape the cement but he was so determined. Cher, Sherlyn, my sister and my brother all also tried to talk to Ping Lian and to prevent him from scraping the cement. They too were pained watching him hurting and cutting his own skin as he scraped the soil and cement with his hands. He continually scraped saying "open"; "open"; "open". He often looked back at me as if to say "help me"... but I could not help him. He started to cry as he scraped at the cement and called out "open".

Eventually, Ping Lian gave up his fruitless attempts at scraping the cement. He then began biting his shirt, jumping up and down, kicking his Daddy's grave and the neighbor's grave while still crying "open.. open... open..." I again began to wonder how much of what was happening did Ping Lian truly understand. Did anything that I had told him have an effect on his mind? Seeing him behave like this, eager to see his Daddy, and with the expression of asking for help when no one can help him...I was so sad and my heart was breaking. Unable to hold back my tears any longer they streamed down my face rapidly. All the family members at this Chin Ming were in tears.

It had been a very long time since Ping Lian had displayed such severe tantrum behavior. He was now usually very obedient, always following my instructions and happy with whatever I gave or provided him. I have very seldom seen him cry or throw a big tantrum like this in recent years. At this moment no one was able to control him. This was the first time Ping Lian cried after his Daddy's death. I guess Ping Lian was now missing his Daddy after not seeing him for so long. Much later, as we walked to the car and I held onto Ping Lian's hand, he was now calm but extremely sad with tears rolling down his face. I guess this was the day that Ping Lian came to realise and accept that his Daddy was gone forever and that he would not see or hug his Daddy ever again.

My poor Ping Lian, autistic with limited communication skills and limited understanding about death wanted to open the grave to see his Daddy. It was so hard to reflect back to this scene again. I feel guilty and sorry for my mis-use of the word "see" (Daddy). I have always felt responsible for Ping Lian's tantrum behaviour on that day, but I am also thankful for my mistake. It showed me that Ping Lian was eager to see "Daddy" and that he did not really live in his own world. His actions indicated that he did love and care about his father and that his father's existence mattered!

After returning from Sitiawan, Cher noticed on several occasions that Ping Lian was spending much time lying under his wooden art table looking at the drawing he had made. We guessed that he must be missing his Daddy.

PING LIAN DRAWS - DADDY IN MEMORY

After Min Seng passed away, when Ping Lian went for his first art lesson, I told the art teacher that I wanted Ping Lian to draw Daddy. I wanted to see how Ping Lian would draw Daddy from his memory. I also hoped for Ping Lian to draw his Daddy before he would forget what his Daddy was like. So on that day, Ping Lian drew Daddy from his memory. When he finished, the art teacher asked him "What else do you want to draw?" and he added a smaller figure at the bottom of the picture. Later when we asked him "Who is this small person?" Ping Lian responded "Mummy". However sometimes he also responds "Ping Lian" to this same question; so to this day I still do not know who exactly that smaller person represents to him. The art teacher also informed me as we were walking away that Ping Lian had just written the word "crying" on his work. As we walked back to Ping Lian we saw him erasing on his paper. He was erasing the word, but if you look closely at his picture you can still clearly see the word "crying".

04201 DADDY IN MEMORY

Painted a few days after Ping Lian's daddy passed away.

"BRAIN WASHING" - "PING LIAN WILL BE A MAN"

I was raised in a conservative Chinese family. My childhood was influenced by a belief system that emphasized that "the man is head and leader of the family". Such belief systems are similarly portrayed in old/traditional Chinese dramas on television – "a family needs a Man". The Man represents a special person in the family; having a special place in the family as one who protects the family, and has specific roles regarding strength and certain jobs that are mainly done by the Man of the house. Although a very small example "carrying heavy bags" was one such example in our household.

With Min Seng leaving us, I started to question myself about "Who will represent the Man in our home?". " Who will represent our family in the future?" "Could that be Ping Lian?" ;"Can he be one?". My strong Chinese traditional thinking had led me to worry about myself as an aged parent in the future. It has always been my belief that when we as parents grow old, our children will take care of us (just as Min Seng and I took care of his mother.)

I have nine sisters and brothers. My own father passed away when I was 12 years old due to a sudden stroke. My eldest brother is number two in the family, and he immediately took over as head of the family. But Ping Lian is the only boy at home. ….and he is so young and he has autism! Oh! No! He can't be the Man of the Family! He is not one! He is autistic! Definitely without doubt, I will have to be the person to take over as head of the family. I asked myself again and again, can Ping Lian still be the "Man" of the family in the future or would he just be a burden to the family??!!

Going to the shopping complex as a family was a typical weekend outing for Ping Lian, my daughters, my husband and myself. Shopping and walking together at the shopping complex was like a routine weekend leisure activity for our family. After Min Seng passed away, my first

Chapter 10: Daddy In Memory 227

"shopping and walking" trip to the complex was just Ping Lian and myself. We went to the same old shopping complex, took the same lift, used the same elevator, went into the same shops, but the people involved were different. Now it was only Ping Lian and I. Min Seng was not with us. Cher and Sherlyn also did not come along because they felt that without Daddy the mood was different and shopping together would not be fun or the same anymore. The truth is, walking at the shopping complex is not a leisure activity anymore, it is now part of a duty, it is a job. I had to make the purchases now, so this was the time.

I decided to use these "weekend" trips as opportunities to teach Ping Lian to accept some of these responsibilities toward being the "man" of the family. I wanted to make sure that Ping Lian understood that Daddy was gone forever. From now on our daily activities would not have Daddy involved. I wanted Ping Lian to understand life without Daddy would be different and for him to start picking up some good behaviors about how to take care of himself and Mummy. These would be "life lessons" toward maturation without Daddy and Mummy always having to take care of him.

New opportunities arose for teaching Ping Lian additional and new vocabulary. On the way to the complex, while in the car, I told Ping Lian; *"Ping Lian Daddy had go for 'long sleep' already, so Ping Lian have no more Daddy already, so no more Daddy go shopping with us anymore"*. I continue *"From now on, Ping Lian only go shopping with Mummy Ok!"* I pause and say *again "So Ping Lian must be good boy and clever boy Ok!"*

I was surprised by Ping Lian's sudden and immediate tantrum response. He made some defiant vocalizations, began biting his shirt and kicking the car. It had been a very, very long time since Ping Lian kicked the car! This was his way of showing his sadness, and unwillingness to comply and accept change. Seeing him respond in this manner saddened me further. I felt sorry and sad for him. I do not really know how much he understood, but I knew from his response that it upset him. However, his reaction gave me a glimmer of happiness to think that he understood something of what I had said. So I decided to test him by again repeating the same statements a few times and…Yes! He responded the same negative way each time. Funny isn't it?... That a mother can be happy to see that her child tantrums in response to a statement. I like to see the cup as half full, not half empty. The tantrum is half full – because it shows me that my son understands. He may not be happy with the changes, but he is aware that they exist. This can be a great feeling.

Holding onto Ping Lian by the hand and walking at the shopping complex for the first time after Min Seng had passed was so very different. I did not expect that it would be so difficult to continue on with this routine activity. The experience aroused many different emotions in me and I was consumed with sadness and fear. I was once again unable to control my sadness and the tears began rolling down my face. I couldn't help myself and I couldn't control my emotions. My tears just kept dropping….each time I kept attempting to control myself, yet another tear flowed. I tried to convince myself that… *"It is just shopping, it's no big deal, why am I so emotional and why so sad?"* I do not know how to describe the emotions I experienced at that time. Even then I did not fully understand the extent of my sadness. I thought *"Maybe I feel so helpless and alone, maybe I feel sad and sorry for Ping Lian…maybe I miss Min Seng,,… maybe I miss my family going out shopping together, … maybe I feel that my family is no longer complete without Min Seng.* "*Maybe I know that from now on life will be different,…maybe I could foresee the challenges ahead of me,…. maybe I feel the burden of loneliness handling Ping Lian …I AM SO CONFUSED!"*…I was overwhelmed by all of these thoughts all at once.

The thought of having to care for Ping Lian on my own for the rest of my life without Min Seng in my life "terrified" me. I asked myself, "How?"… "What will happen when I am old?" … "What if one day Cher and Sherlyn go overseas to study or get married far away, or chose to settle

Chapter 10: Daddy In Memory

down overseas?"… "*What happens when I am old and weak and I still need to face the challenge of taking care of Ping Lian alone, by myself??!!"* … *"Will I cope? "„, "How??"* … *"When I am old who is going to take care of me with my back pains and hand pains?".* I have always suffered from back pains and hand pain problems (later diagnosed as Carpal Tunnel Syndrome). Whenever an extra hand was needed for carrying bags, it was always Min Seng and my daughters who helped. In my chaotic state of mind, I also began to think about my fear of darkness. Since I was a young child my sisters and brothers would always accompany and accommodate me to make me feel safe in darkness and dark times as well. Min Seng was also always very patient, supportive and accommodating of my weakness in this area. He would always help me through this unexplained fear. He never complained and always accompanied me whenever I needed him during such times. *"What would I do now?"* … *"Who will keep me company and be patient with me. Can my Ping Lian have such patience?*

These thoughts continued to consume me. *"Will Ping Lian be my burden for the rest of my life alone?"* My mother in law had three daughters and Min Seng was her only son. Min Seng's mother had been living with us for the past seventeen years. Together, Min Seng and I were able to take very good care of her. Min Seng is now gone and my mother-in-law is 79 years old. She expressed to me that she wanted to continue living with me, and I happily took over the full responsibility of caring for her. However, at the time I thought *"She is so lucky, but when I grow old like her, what will happen to me?".* Knowing full well, that I also had to take care of Ping Lian, I felt myself becoming increasingly emotionally unstable as these thoughts dominated my mind.

Driven by fear I knew I had to take control of this situation and turn it around. Ping Lian *cannot* be a burden to me for the rest of his life! It cannot be one way traffic with regard to care and love. The care and love must be reciprocated. I need Ping Lian to be able to care for me somehow, someway when I grow old. I pondered the simple tasks. *"Can Ping Lian represent the "Man" in the family, can he be my good helper?"… "Can Ping Lian do some of the simple tasks that Min Seng did, like carry heavy things and carry the shopping bags, etc.??!!"… "Is it possible that when he grows up and when I grow old, that he will be a companion to me?".*

It suddenly hit me very hard. An eye-opening revelation of *"No way! I am not willing to accept the fact that my autistic child will just be a burden to me and the rest of our family! I will demand a two-way street of care and love! My Ping Lian will also be a contributor to the family.* I rationalized to myself that Ping Lian although autistic can still represent the "Man" in the family in certain modified ways. I have created modifications and adaptations for Ping Lian throughout his entire life up until now, so why should this be any different? This is when I decided to begin applying the principle "something is better than nothing".

I was overjoyed. Yes! My Ping Lian will be my good helper, and learn to do some of the jobs that Min Seng did. I have always heard people say "you get what you expect". I will change this self-fulfilling prophecy to benefit us all. At this point I made a decision to "brain wash" and train Ping Lian just like I trained him in art. I would "brain wash" Ping Lian to be a "Man" of the family. I began thinking that it is time to start applying the subconscious and autosuggestion techniques again.

I took the opportunity to begin this "Man training" immediately upon entering the shopping complex. It was time to start teaching Ping Lian that he has his own role to play in this family from now on… not only *"Mummy take care of Ping Lian, but also Ping Lian take care of Mummy!"* So, as we walked in the shopping complex, I held on to Ping Lian's hand. I reminded him that *"Ping Lian have no more Daddy already, so Ping Lian need to be a clever boy from now on".* *"Ping Lian is no more a small boy already, and Ping Lian is a big boy now".* I told him that *"big boy need to help Mummy".* *"Ping Lian have no more Daddy already, so no one help Mummy, so Ping Lian will be Mummy's good helper OK!"*. As I repeatedly spoke those words, I was becoming extremely emotional. With tears streaming down my face and a cracking in my voice I continued *"Mummy has back and hand pain, so Mummy cannot carry heavy bag, so now no more Daddy already, no one help Mummy to carry the bag, so Ping Lian will need to help Mummy to carry the bag OK?!!* " He seemed to understand. I repeated these phrases on and off several times. It seems that I was not only telling Ping Lian this, but I was also attempting to reassure myself that this is how it would be.

My mother was a "housewife". When my father passed away, she was left with six children who were still attending schools and university. Immediately after my father passed away, my mother expected us all to "be more clever, more obedient, more mature, more understanding and more hard working". It seems we were expected to grow up quickly and immediately. I asked myself now, "Can I also expect this from my 10 years old autistic child. My answer was so certain. YES! I need that. I do not want to be so sorry for myself. I would have love, support and contributions from my son too."

While at the shopping complex, I was so desperate that I needed to know at that moment if my Son would be a "Man". I immediately stopped in a corner, held on to both of Ping Lian's hands, looked into his eyes, and I said to him *"Ping Lian is no more small boy already, and Ping Lian is a big boy now"*. I paused and continued to ask *"Big boy grow up will become a Man. When Ping Lian grows up and becomes Man and Mummy so old like Ah Mah, can Ping Lian take care of Mummy?"* So funny, Ping Lian answered Yes! I was so happy. I wasn't sure if he knew what he was answering, but it was the answer I was hoping for, "Yes!" It could be that my body language influenced him to answer "yes". It could be that the ABA drills we previously used by asking questions with certain embedded prompts influenced his answer. It could be "who cares!"…He said "Yes" and for that moment I was so happy with his answer. I still would have plenty of time to train him and "brain wash" him toward understanding. This is only the first session of my discovery toward this new hope.

Ping Lian seemed to understand me. He was now behaving obediently during our shopping session, and it was very easy to be with him. The mood of the trip shifted to being a pleasant one. He behaved like my assistant. He seemed to understand his responsibility as a big boy without Daddy. I was very surprised with what seemed an almost instantaneous change in behavior and demeanor on his part. I thanked God!

Ping Lian was now my good helper during this shopping trip. He tried his best to help me carry the shopping bags (one in each hand) with his two little hands. (During this time, my hand and back pains were not that severe and I could have managed to carry the bags myself if I absolutely had to. I just wanted to " hit while the iron was hot", and make him carry the bags as a start to his training. As he carried one large bag in each hand I witnessed pride in his face. As he walked in front of me, the bags appeared too long for his short body and I felt proud yet still quite sad. I was happy that he really seemed to understand that he was helping me, but sad to think that at such a young age I needed him to take on some of Mind Seng's small responsibilities. I thought… "Such a small body, carrying such a big and heavy bag, it seems to be a little too much for him." Yet, I was eager to train him to be a " Man." One of the bags was quite large, and I felt too long and dangerous for Ping Lian to carry onto the up escalator. I offered to take the bags from him just for a short while. *"Ping Lian, the bag is too big, let Mummy take the bag for a while"*, but he refused my help. So I let it be and I monitored him from the back thinking that in future *"He will be a "Man"*, and *"He will always help Mummy."*

From that day on I began the following training with Ping Lian… *"When Ping Lian grows up becomes Man, and Mummy grows old like Ah Mah, Ping Lian take care of Mummy or Mummy take care of Ping Lian?"* To my surprise Ping Lian answered "Ping Lian take care of Mummy". I still do

Chapter 10: Daddy In Memory

not know if he simply chose any answer or if he really knew what he was saying. In any case I proceeded with the aim of teaching him to understand that when he grows up and Mummy is so old like his grandmother, Mummy also needs Ping Lian to take care of Mummy. I told him that now Mummy takes care of Ping Lian, but when Mummy grows old like his grandmother, I wanted Ping Lian to take care of Mummy.. I paired these words with specific body movements to depict positive and powerful body gestures representing that when he grows up he will be an Able Man, able to help and take care of Mummy, not just Mummy take care of Ping Lian. I do not know what he was able to understand but it seemed to have an effect. Any way, it did not matter to me. I always teach concepts that I know he does not understand, and believe that with repetition of simple language and training toward that goal, one day he will understand! I have noticed that since Ping Lian's father passed away, Ping Lian has definitely become more understanding, stable and mature. So as of the year 2004 I would routinely ask the following question for Ping Lian to choose a response:

"When Ping Lian grows up become a Man, and when Mummy grows old like Ah Mah, Ping Lian will take care of Mummy? or Mummy take care of Ping Lian?" I would prompt Him to select "Ping Lian take care of mummy". If Ping Lian answered "Mummy take care of Ping Lian", I would pretend to cry and I would mumble *"When Mummy so old like Ah Mah, so who will take care of Mummy, uh! uh! Uh!"* When Ping Lian would see me behaving in such a sad manner, he would usually become anxious and then say "Ping Lian take care of Mummy". Then I would show my joyful face and hug him and say *"Yes! Ping Lian take care of Mummy."* Initially, I doubt that he understood but my objective was to know that Ping Lian would love me and take care of me. Ping Lian had seen Mummy and Daddy take care of Ah Mah. I wanted him to also need to take care of Mummy in certain ways. I also did not want to believe that my Ping Lian would just be a burden for the rest of my life. I wanted to make sure that he understood

that he was expected to take care of me too. I didn't really worry any longer at this point whether or not this goal was actually "achievable". Getting him to say all this at least gave me hope and allowed me to continue my life with positive expectations. With Min Seng gone, I needed this hope, desperately.

2006, 2007 AND 2008 – AMAZING AND UNBELIEVABLE PROGRESS

Ping Lian had become a very good helper, especially when it came to carrying things for me. In the year 2006, when we moved to Sydney, Australia I was experiencing more severe back problems. When the containers with our belongings arrived from Malaysia, Ping Lian not only helped me to unpack our things but also helped in handling many of the heavy boxes. I was pleasantly surprised and couldn't really believe how involved he was. He showed initiative and wanted to take charge and be responsible. He actually enjoyed helping me, and even expressed that he did not want me to do some of the things I was attempting to do as he wanted to do it himself. Some of the boxes were really too heavy for him to handle but Ping Lian enjoyed being treated as a "Man" at home. Later, with the help of Sherlyn and Cher we would be able to unpack all of our boxes. Even at the airport, he refused to let Sherlyn or Cher carry the bags. He fought with them to pull the luggage out from the baggage claim area belt when it finally arrived. Although the bags were too big for him to handle, he still fought to remove them himself. Now when I travel with Ping Lian, I just need to stand beside him and relax, and monitor him pulling the luggage out from the belt and then we carry it on to the trolley together. Ping Lian was always ready and available to help me. For the heavy boxes I told Ping Lian to wait for Sherlyn to help, but many times Ping Lian did

Chapter 10: Daddy In Memory

not wait.....he preferred to do it himself. Could be he knew that he was the "Man" in the house. He appeared eager and responsible. I remember thinking that without Ping Lian; I would not have gotten all of this done so fast! ... Yes! My Ping Lian in some way had become the "Man" at home. Upon watching Ping Lian get all of this done, I felt so happy and so proud. I felt I loved him so much and I loved him even more. I started to wonder again how much did he know about love, and how much did he love me? So I asked him *"Ping Lian, do you love Mummy?"* His answer was certain, *"Yes!"*. I then asked him *"How much do you love Mummy?"*. So funny, he answered firmly *"one dollar"*. I screamed out loud *"Ha!? Only one dollar?!"* and I continued loudly *"Oh! No! Only worth one dollar??? Ha! Ha! Ha!"* I laughed happily.

In my heart I said *"My beautiful, lovely and cute Ping Lian. You are really mummy good and fantastic helper, I am happy with your one dollar love. Your one dollar love is so precious to me. I think Mummy now can't live without you around. I love you so much. You are so wonderful big boy but still small "Man"!"*

Sherlyn, Cher and I also enjoyed seeing Ping Lian take pride in taking over many of the small jobs at home, especially those jobs which were usually done by Daddy. Ping Lian actually tried using the pliar, a screw driver and some tape to make an outdoor repair. Even when he couldn't fix it, he would not allow Sherlyn to take over. He wanted to do it himself. Eventually Sherlyn or myself would have to take over... but we are happy that at least in Ping Lian's mind he may think that he is a big boy doing a "Mans" job. Despite his autism he had taken responsibility and initiative as a "Man" of the house. We were so happy and so proud of his progress.

In 2007 when I needed to go to the USA for an art exhibition Ping Lian again proved to be a really good helper. On departure day, I told Ping Lian that he will have to help me and that he was in charge of all the bags. He seemed to stand tall and powerful with pride. He was enthusiastic and showed initiative to carry all of the luggage into the car. In fact, I had expected to assist him, but without me knowing, he had already carried most of the bags and placed them in the car. Luckily I still had time to stop him from carrying the biggest and heaviest boxes into the car. Throughout the entire trip, whenever my sister and my brother in law were not around, he behaved like a "gentleman" and was my very good helper in handling all my bags.

At present (2008), Ping Lian is a very fantastic helper at home. He is very happy to help around the house and he is a hard working boy at home. He will do any job we ask him to do, including helping with the laundry, the dishes, meal time preparation and vacuuming (although he still needs much assistance when vacuuming) etc. Ping Lian does these chores happily and never complains. Since living in Sydney, we no longer have a domestic helper with us. Cher and Sherlyn were very used to being served by the domestic helpers in Malaysia. Ping Lian became very happy to help and he actually enjoyed serving his sisters. At time Ping Lian was so fast and efficient in serving us. We felt so good and also really enjoyed watching his cute way of serving us. Once I even heard Cher and Sherlyn laughing and commenting that Ping Lian was sometimes so much better than a domestic helper we had in Malaysia. Can you believe that a boy initially living in his own world, with no sense of danger, and no feeling for others; hyperactive and unable to carry out one simple direction (it took so long to train him just to be able to carry out one step simple directions), can now do all of this? I thank God for all these changes and the progress that my Son has made. Our new life in Sydney left me with no time for socialization. I was tied down with day to day activities and extremely busy with Ping Lian's Artistic Journey. Sherlyn and Cherlyn had grown up and often had their own agendas and schedules. They were usually off doing their own thing with their friends. Going out with just Ping Lian had become the norm. Ping Lian was now not only a helper to me, but also as a companion. He was always around for me and happy to go with me anywhere. Without Ping

Lian I think I would be very lonely. Also if ever I fear darkness, and dare not be alone somewhere, I know Ping Lian will be around to accompany me with patience and no complaints, like his Daddy.

Note: Nowadays (2008) I still continue to teach him….and remind him "Ping Lian has no Daddy already. Ping Lian is no more small boy. Ping Lian is big boy now. Big boy needs to be more clever, obedient and hard working, and big boy grows up to be a Man like Daddy. Man will be Mummy's good helper and Man will take care of Mummy." In fact Ping Lian had been performing very well not only as Mummy's good helper but also Mummy's good company. I had forgotten for how long, whenever I felt uncomfortable going out anywhere in the dark alone, how Ping Lian was always more than happy to come with me to give me company. It's amazing that though he has autism, and is rigid at times; so far every time I have ever said "Hey, Ping Lian can you please give mummy company to go xyz place", Ping Lian will immediately let go whatever he is doing (even drawing or painting) and enthusiastically go with me. Isn't this amazing, who said autistic people are not flexible…. That make me think though they seem to be rigid, but at time or at certain circumstances, with training or constant "brain wash" we are able to break their rigidity to certain level to make them chose and happy to be flexible. Definitely for sure every time he did that, I always praised him as Mummy's good helper. I often was very animated, giving him joyful hugs and saying things like … "Thanks so much for company. Mummy, mummy need you so much". Hearing that always made him happy. I know that he knew his contribution was very much appreciated and he felt full of pride.

EXTRACT FROM PING LIAN'S JOUNAL: PING LIAN AT 10 YEAR 5 MONTHS

March 2004

- Teaching Ping Lian Monday to Sunday for the passed few years.. but he did not get it. Very frustrated. I almost give up; luckily I did not give up totally. Lately, he suddenly got it. Life for Ping Lian also suddenly become so different once he get to understand the concept of Monday to Sunday. He now understands what is next to expect. After he understand Monday to Sunday, he also come to know the meaning of today, yesterday, and tomorrow. After Ping

Lian grasped the concept of Monday to Sunday, communication with him also become so much easier. Also after he understand the concept of Monday to Sunday and Today, tomorrow and Yesterday, Ping Lian suddenly has become much more mature and life for him suddenly become more meaningful… and he another time upgrade his awareness of surroundings and what is happening as he know what is next (future) and what is passed.

- Ping Lian stopped taking Ritalin.

Note: I had been attempting to teach Ping Lian about Monday to Sunday and the concepts of Today, Yesterday and Tomorrow for many years with all kinds of methods and techniques that I had learned from friends or experts. I tried intensive "table drills" and even a variety of charts that I specially made for teaching these concepts. Ping Lian did not get it, no matter what I did or how intensively I tried. So I am very frustrated and I "give up", and put the program aside. Instead, I would try again by introducing the concept, on and off naturally…especially when I was driving, waiting for traffic lights or stuck in a traffic jam. I would ask him to recite Monday to Friday, … and then prompt him to repeat after me like Today is Tuesday, so, Yesterday is Monday, tomorrow will be Wednesday, etc. I recall how after attempting this repeatedly each time we waited for a traffic light to change, Ping Lian would be so fed up.

DEPEND ON GOD AND HAVE FAITH IN GOD

My relatives and many friends were amazed that I was able to attain so sudden a calmness in dealing with Min Seng's sudden death. I was even the one who made all of the funeral arrangements and necessary related decisions. They praised me for being so strong. They did not know that it was my "shut-down" emotionally, automatic response for what I felt was a "no choice" situation. I had to be strong for my children and for my mother-in-law as I was now the head of the family. I couldn't afford to lose control or direction. My family's future, my autistic son's future, the outcome of all of the challenges that lay ahead….depended upon me.

The fact is that during this period of grief, I did indeed achieve a state of calmness, clear mind, strong and decisive will at a level that I had never reached before. A level that I did not know was attainable for me. Still, no one knew that although I appeared strong; inside part of me was also filled with much anger and fear that I tended to supress. I was SO angry about how cruel and unfair a life I had been dealt. I think at times I was also angry with God.

I would often ask *"God, how am I going to achieve my Dream.* At this stage of my life I was very bitter. I felt that in this world, the most important people are my family. The rest is not my business. *"Who cares!! I had been kind and had a very generous heart. I cared so much but God did NOT care and did NOT help me. He was so unfair to me. For my goodness and kindness He not only gave me an autistic son but He also took away Min Seng! It is not fair to Ping Lian either. Min Seng was still young. It was too early for him to go. It was not fair to Min Seng either. God took away Min Seng and left me alone, so how am I going to achieve all the Dreams of 'I'm A Dreamer' without Min Seng? How can I do it by my self, a widow??!! No way!!*

My husband's death was so sudden and unforeseen. I now viewed life as extremely fragile and began to live in fear of mortality, thinking that something bad would happen at any given moment. *"If I am also gone, who will take care of my children?...* "*Who is going to take care of Ping Lian????"* ... *"Oh! How are my two girls going to take care of him?"* I am a very imaginative person, but I dared not think nor imagine further....I was so scared!!!

My mother-in-law, 79 and with osteoporosis was on heart medication. I wondered how strong she could be having witnessed her son die. I jus couldn't imagine life if she also left me. Life was so miserable living under this constant fear of what might be.

My mother in law had been living with me for more than 17 years. She never did express her pain over the loss of her son, but I could see it clearly in her face. My constant assurances to her of my commitment to continue to live with her and to take care of her could only bring a little relief to her. She would usually wake before I did. Every morning I experienced a sense of relief upon seeing her first thing in the morning. Whenever I did happen to wake first, if I did not see her I would rush to her room to check on her. I would feel relief immediately upon seeing her move. Any movement by her relieved my fear that she would not wake up. Even when Sher Lyn went out, if she was not home by 10.30 pm I started feeling worried that something bad might happen to her.

Frankly, as I think back, I do not know how I was able to mentally and physically survive all of the misery experienced during this time in my life. I know now that if I did not have God to depend on it would have been impossible. Here I was an adult with three children, one autistic child and an aged mother- in- law depending on *ME*. Although my brain told me that I was able to take on these responsibilities, a part of me felt like I was just a little girl myself, in need of protection and shelter. In fact not long ago, Min Seng said to *me "Even though you are smart, mature, capable and independent in the office, in your job and career, when it comes to our home, a certain part of you has not grown up. You have three children already, but are sometimes still like a child, like a little girl."* (One of the reasons he spoke to me of this was about my fear of the dark. I have always been scared to be alone and scared of darkness. When darkness would fall, I would not like to be alone at home or to go out alone. If ever I was alone, I would feel very uncomfortable). Min Seng continued to say to me.. *"I wonder if this part of you will ever grow up when you are old…."*. *"If one day I am not around, I do not know how you will get through it…"*

I thought, yes, may be those parts of the child in me, did not have an opportunity to mature or may be I just chose not to grow up. I loved to be pampered. Ever since my childhood I was pampered by my mother. I even slept with my mother and my youngest brother (three persons in one bed) in the same room until I was ten years old. My father slept in another room by himself. I was always surrounded by so many brothers and sisters (ten of us all together). Later, when I left home to study in the city, with no more mother, brothers or sisters around me, I immediately got to know Min Seng. He was seven years older than me. I was then pampered by him! At work, on company trips I had kind colleagues who understood and accommodated me, happy to keep me company. After that, my mother-in law also always pampered me as well in many ways. I guess I never really felt the need to "grow up." The past few years of raising an autistic child and handling financial challenges together with the loss of my husband, forced me to grow up, a lot!

For quite some time after Min Seng's funeral, I only felt comfortable if other people (my sisters, brothers, close friends or relative) were with me. I still needed adult company. The moment they left me, I began to feel very uncomfortable. I felt alone. Still, I knew that everyone had their own lives to return to. At the beginning, many friends, relatives, my brothers and sisters surrounded me but after one week I was "alone". Sherlyn, Cher, Ping Lian and my mother-in-law's company was not enough. I knew I would be forced to start facing my new life on my own.

After the burial ceremony, my children and I stayed at Sitiawan at my brother's house for almost a week. Some of my brothers and sisters also took leave to be with me. My mother-in-law stayed home (at Kuala Lumpur) and was taken care of by my sister-in-law and my domestic helper. After one week, surrounded by my brothers and sisters, it was time to go home to face the reality of my new life without Min Seng. It would be the same house, the same furniture but everything would be different.

When we reached home, I immediately felt that "home" was so different. I can't describe it except to say that it was as if I was feeling an "invisible pressure". The moment my sister-in-law saw me home she began preparing to leave and return to her own house. I was so scared of being by myself and "alone" (even though I had my mother-in-law, my domestic helper, and my children). I asked my sister-in-law not to leave. I explained to her that I am not used to this different "New Home" now. I was very scared and still needed her company. She stayed for an extra night.

My boss had told me that I could take as much time as I needed before going back to work. However, after a few days staying home, and with all the children back in school, I decided to go back to work. Once back at work, I was unable to focus on my job as before, so I began to work half days instead. One day, upon driving home and reaching the front gate of my house, I instinctively kept going. I suddenly did not feel like going into the house and I drove off again. I drove around with no direction and no where to go. I finally ended up at my eldest sister's house. By the end of the day I knew I still needed to go home. I had to force myself to go home. The strange thing was that, when I *was* at home, I did not feel like going out. Especially at night. Even with my brother's offers to come over and pick me up to go out, I refused. I wondered what was wrong with me. When I would come back home from being outside, I didn't want to go in and would often drive off, knowing the children were already home and they needed me. This went on for several weeks. Life at that time was just so miserable.

Every area of the house reminded me of Min Seng! I would "see" him everywhere – sitting at the dining table, out in the garden chair, etc. I started shifting furniture to change my visual memories. I moved the location and position of the garden chair. It helped a little bit, but not much. I started to sense that I was getting into trouble and that something was not right with me. I kept reminding myself that every one at home needed me. I was the leader of the family now. I had to be available, all responsibility of the family was now on my shoulders, mine alone! With all of this pressure I was still so aware that I was undergoing tremendous change and stress and that I could not let it get out of control, or let it control me. I felt the need to rely on my 'stronger personality'. I am a person who is strong and capable, and yet I am a person who sometimes exhibits a weaker, child-like personality that seeks pampering and shelter. I have always felt as though I have a dual-personality. My strengths appear through a strong-willed woman with a clear mind to handle everything that may come my way. My weaknesses, sometimes dormant, show up every now and then as a pampered little girl, who needs help and is scared to be alone.

As each and every corner of the house kept reminding me of Min Seng and of his death, I felt that my overall fears were growing and growing. I cried every night after my children all went to sleep. I knew that in order for me to rescue myself I needed a change of environment. I pondered the thought of moving to a new house and starting a new life. I mentioned this to my older sister and coincidently her neighbours had just moved out and the house was available for lease. We agreed that the move would be a step in a positive direction and immediately began the preparations. Psychologically, it was the best thing for me knowing I would have both my brother in-law and my sister and my nieces and nephew closer to me. I would not be "alone". I decided to move immediately and I thanked God for such a "coincidence".

Both Cher and Sherlyn wanted to stay in our old house. They did not want to move from the house that has (for them) so many memories of Daddy. Yet, I knew very well that in order for me to continue to stand tall, we could not live in those memories. I explained to them that this house kept reminding me of Daddy's death. I needed to get out of this house and soon. We needed a new house, where we could start a new life and still have many beautiful memories of Daddy. Of course I couldn't share with them all of the problems I was having coping and I could not let them see the weaker part of my personality. I did not want them to feel insecure. Without their blessing, I went ahead and finalized the decision to move. I knew in the long run that it would be the best decision for all of us. The actual moving day made me sad because both of my daughters were still very unhappy to move. They were very upset and angry with me; They may have felt that I was mean in not respecting or considering their feelings and also that I was not respecting their Daddy. I'm sure they did not understand that I had no choice if they wanted a strong Mummy who would be able to continue to support the family. When we moved to the new house I also hid all photos and materials related to Min Seng's death. I only displayed those photos that provided happy times and sweet memories.

Since the year 2000 I had started attending church regularly. After attending church for a while, I had come to realize that all this while I walked my life on my own (without God in my life) and I was so glad that I got to know God. With God, I could depend on His power, his provisions, etc. I had lived with this belief system for several years and now I felt forced to question God's power or at least my ability to depend on him. Min Seng 's death could not have come at a worse time. God had disappointed me and I felt angry with God. But It took me quite a while to realize that God is a mighty God ....and that this was the time that I needed God the most. I needed His strength and most of all his protection.

I recall one evening when my brother came with a group of friends to visit me. They all knew about my "uncomfortable feelings" when friends or relatives leave me, especially at night. Just before they left, at the door step, one of my brother's friends turned to me and said, *"Sarah, We may go home and leave you, we may not be present all the time for you but God's presence is always here. He is always there for you. You are not "alone"....You can depend on God ... let God be with you."*

His statements struck me like a bolt of lightning. Oh! Yes! Suddenly I found reconciliation and realized that this is the time I need God. I need Him to give me strength and protection. I gave in to my emotional struggles and decided to continue depending on God again. After making that decision I felt so relieved. I now had a place to lean for comfort, assurance, guidance and protection. I later committed myself and my family unto Him once again.. *"Let Him lead us, guide us and protect us."*

My focus when praying became very much on protection. Every morning when I awoke, I thanked God that I was alive and had a beautiful day ahead of me. I thanked God for my children, that they were okay and for my mother-in-law waking up and staying healthy. Without God I don't think I could have continued my life in peace. Without God I don't think I could have gained the strength needed for my self and for my family. I attest to the words of many of my friends when they encouraged me "Why just depend on yourself, why don't you also depend on God's power and his love?". Yes! I feel that it is so good to get to know God and to depend on God again to be loved and to love. I depend on God for protection, for guidance, wisdom, strength, blessing etc etc.

Now in 2008, if you ask me how I survived the last few years with so many challenges in my life, I say *"Frankly without God, I do not know how I would have endured and survived through the last few years"*. During the last few years, my love for God has grown much stronger each day and my Faith in God flourishes. If you ask me about God, I would say, *"God is so real to me. Many times I experienced God's grace and God has been favorable in our Special Journey with Ping Lian. Many times we experienced God's lead. Many times we experienced a "Special Happening" and often those "Special Happenings" always come with obvious indications to me that "God's hand is at work"*. Also many times as I personally experienced these " Special Happenings", I felt shock and amazement realising that God has even taken care of minute details in our Special Journey with Ping Lian. My Faith grows stronger and stronger as we (my daughters and I) walk with Ping Lian in his Artistic Journey. We experience "God's hand at work" regularly. For those people who may call these simply "coincidences",... it is "amazing that we have experienced so many unbelievable 'coincidences' in the past six years of Ping Lian's Artistic Journey. I believe that indeed it is God who has created these 'coincidences'.

I am thankful that I am no longer in doubt or angry with God. My decision to come back to God and depend on him, has led me toward continued progress and fulfilment toward Ping Lian's Artistic Journey. Ping Lian's life has been totally changed for the better along this Special Journey. Our lives have been changed and uplifted as we walk with Ping Lian. My daughters and I never expected that this could be our future. We thank God for his grace in all these blessings. I will continue my prayers for Ping Lian's miracle healing and continued "Special Happenings"!

PING LIAN'S FIRST EXHIBITION: DIFFERENT STROKES:DIVERSITY THROUGH ART DEC. 2003

This was the last photo taken of Ping Lian and his Daddy together. (Min Seng, Ping Lian, Sarah & Cher)

FAMILY PHOTO TAKEN IN DEC 2004

"No more Daddy already"
Ping Lian, Sarah SH Lee, Sherlyn, Cherlyn and Ping Lian's grandmother (Hong Kiew Ling).

PING LIAN AT THE ART MARKET – NATIONAL ART GALLERY, ART BAZAAR – SEPTEMBER 2004

PING LIAN AT HOME IN SYDNEY, PAINTING 14003 NEW YORK CITY – MARCH 2014

CHAPTER 11
The Joy of Achieving/ Realizing a Dream

Upon my graduation from the university and my welcome into the work force, I was fortunate to have an employer who believed that the "Sky is your limit" and "Where there's a will, there's a way". I was constantly attending personal development seminars, like the "National Achiever Congress" which gave me the opportunity to hear many well known international public speakers and personal development authors. Motivational phrases were always emphasized at such seminars. My own motivation grew as I practiced what I was learning throughout my career. There is no doubt that these teachings led me to apply these positive outlooks and principles to "train the talent" in my autistic son. I adopted the "never try, never know attitude" and embarked upon developing my son's interests and talent. I did not expect that my son would progress so fast in his art, and that together we would actually achieve some of our "Dream" in such a short period. Ping Lian was now a testament to "there is no limit to one's abilities". The motivational phrase would now be the "Sky is the limit"!

THE ENTIRE WORLD IS "RED COLOR":

I remember when I first started to try and teach Ping Lian colors. It was so ***frustrating!*** I tried teaching blue by introducing a blue sky. When he learned blue, I introduced other objects that were also blue. I thought he had it! But as soon as I introduced other colors, his answer to *everything* was blue! Every time I pointed to an object and asked him "what color is it?" he would answer, "Blue color". I had to start again and only introduce two colors at one time. I then taught him the color red – or so I thought. Now it seemed, for Ping Lian the whole world was "red color". Even the previously learned blue sky was now "red color". No matter what I pointed to, when I asked him "what color is it?" he would respond "red color". I tried using only colored pencils to teach the different colors, but still, "red color"! I was extremely frustrated. He just didn't get it. The entire world was "red color"! Actually, *I* didn't get it. He could repeat the colors, red, blue, green, etc. Anyway, I gave up my tactics and again decided to focus on different teaching techniques. I eventually colored 3 different colors on 3 different pieces of paper. I drilled him on "colors" every day, and every day I got the same response "red color". I just couldn't believe that such a simple drill, after months of intensive training would go unlearned. In my frustration I complained about this to the speech therapist. She finally advised me that perhaps Ping Lian was not ready and to put the color drills aside for a while and come back to them at a later time. For my own sanity, I took her advice. However the stubborn part of me did not really let this go. I started introducing color to Ping Lian throughout situations in his daily living. For instance, when he had to put on his shoes, I would point to them and ask "what color" etc.; his laces, his socks, etc. I did not keep a record of this, so I am unsure how long I actually spent trying to teach Ping Lian to identify colors. I do know it was well over a year! At some later point, I began the drills again and he GOT IT! I introduced three colors at one time. He was ready; he quickly progressed to five colors at a time. Finally, the world was no longer just "red color".

It's so ironic to think that there was a time when learning colors was so extremely difficult for Ping Lian, and knowing now that he is a genius with colors! I recall my fears when the art teacher informed me she would be teaching about the concept of mixing primary colors. I was so concerned thinking he would "mess up" and the world would become "red color" once again. I observed as the teacher taught some of the higher functioning students with autism the theory and practice of mixing two colors to get a third color. They appeared to have the ability to memorize facts like "red and blue makes purple". How will Ping Lian learn all of this, I thought. This will take him years! Surprise! Surprise! Ping Lian did not need to memorize any of this, as the neurotypically developing or higher functioning students did. There was no theory or practice; he just seemed to know it instinctively or perhaps intuitively. I remember an art teacher once saying that "Ping Lian is a genius with color". He just starts mixing and seems to know what the colors will turn out to be.

It always puzzled me when Ping Lian would insist on having two separate pails of water (one small and one larger) available while he was painting. I later came to realize that depending on what color he was using, he dipped his brushes in a specific pail of water so as not to " contaminate" the water with the wrong colour group.

PING LIAN DREW MANY BEAUTIFUL ART WORKS AT AGE 10

In April 2004 to my surprise Ping Lian painted beautiful "04101 Kuala Lumpur Twin Towers I". He painted this just a few days before his solo art show. This was the first time Ping Lian drew and painted the Kuala Lumpur Twin Towers. We were surprised with the beautiful results and decided to make some prints to be able to share his beautiful work. This was the first piece of artwork that Ping Lian had created which I made a print of. The print was available for sale at the event that night. The Art work image and details of the story are mentioned in chapter 9. Many of Ping Lian's original art works as well as the "04101 Kuala Lumpur Twin Towers I" print were sold. "04101 Kuala Lumpur Twin Towers" was the first and only print I had made at that time.

In June 2004 Ping Lian painted beautiful "04105 Ubudiah Mosque I". This was once again just a few days before the art submission for the exhibition of "Different Stroke: Diversity Through Art", June 2004. It was a surprise to both myself and the art teacher that Ping Lian had painted such a beautiful art piece. He always kept me very busy, rushing at the last minute to send art works to be photographed when he completed a beautiful work, always just a few days before an exhibition dead line.

Please refer to www.pinglian.com and click on the Gallery for more beautiful art works created by Ping Lian. I would like to share some of the special paintings with you here:

Chapter 11: The Joy of Achieving/Realizing a Dream

04111 SWIMMING POOL – PAINTED IN 2004 AT AGE 10 - CHRISTMAS- SANTA CLAUS & SWIMMING POOL

Sometime in December of 2004 we noticed that Ping Lian would often remove his shorts (he wore shorts in the house), stand on a chair or sometimes even on the table and look at himself in the mirror. He would usually pull his under pants tight to his body, turn himself around, focus and appear to be admiring the lower part of his body. Then he would put his shorts back on. Cher use to complain and say that something must be wrong with Ping Lian and that he was "obscene". After noticing and observing him do this several times, I finally asked him what he was doing. However, every time he then quickly put his shorts back on and ran away. I was concerned and wondered if my Ping Lian was growing up and starting to show interest in his own body. Yet, I was really worried, thinking it was too soon, he was too young for such an interest.

Days later we noticed that Ping Lian was sketching many different Santa Claus wearing a Santa hat, but also wearing swimming trunks. We then realised that Ping Lian had been looking at his body to be able to sketch Santa in trunks! Several weeks earlier I had taken Ping Lian to see a Santa Claus presentation at the shopping complex. I guess that inspired him to draw Santa in the first place, but the swimming trunks were definitely his own creativity. It was so cute of him to imagine Santa without Santa clothes, but instead wearing swimming trunks and a Santa hat. We all kind of felt bad for misunderstanding his actions. My poor boy, always being misunderstood due to his lack of verbal abilities. He was actually not being *obscene* or interested in his own body. He was actually examining in detail how his body was shaped so he could draw it

GALLERY 2004 I – 04111
SWIMMING POOL 37X 54CM, INK ON PAPER,
DRAWN IN 2004 AT AGE 10

Ping Lian wanted to draw a swimming pool. He drew this by referring to a swimming pool photo. He drew this picture with a lot of energy. Can you see the many special animals and people in the swimming pool?
Definitely there are people swimming in the pool.
How many hippos do you see? Do you see the big fish?
Do you see a Santa Claus' face in the swimming pool? My family did not notice the Santa face in the pool until December 2004 when Ping Lian drew many pieces of Santa Claus wearing swimming trunks; then only did we actually see Santa Claus' happy face in the swimming pool.

Later on Sherlyn discovered something more. A few days after Ping Lian drew Santa in swimming trunks, Sherlyn shouted so loud and said "Ma! I see a Santa face in this picture….". She noticed the Santa face in the "04111 Swimming Pool" picture. We all gathered around the picture to see. The more we examined the picture, the more hidden things we discovered in it. This artwork (04111 Swimming Pool) had actually been hanging in the hallway of our house for quite a while, but we never noticed the Santa face in the swimming pool until much later after seeing Ping Lian's other drawing of Santa in swimming trunks.

We were so proud and excited about Ping Lian's imagination. Not only could he draw, but he was creating "puzzles" in his pictures too. After that day, we began to always search within his artwork for other hidden items.

Actually in the artwork 04111 Swimming Pool, if you search, you will also see a Hippopotamus and a big fish (possibly a whale or dolphin) in the pool. I remember having such mixed emotions about this particular artwork (04111 Swimming Pool) when it did not sell at the 2004 art exhibition. It was modestly priced at only RM 450 (approximately $140 US Dollars) but no one bought it. All of Ping Lian's art works with color sold out that day. We even had to take orders for prints of some of his sold works. However, this black and white drawing "04111 Swimming Pool" seemed not to be appreciated like his other works. Initially I was disappointed and wondered why such a special and beautiful piece was not appreciated. I thought perhaps my art judgement was partial. Of course, afterward I was so happy that no one purchased it and that we still possessed it because this is the work through which we later noticed Ping Lian's imaginative creativity of hidden forms. It is indeed a beautiful and valuable piece and I now know *why* it did not sell at the 2004 art exhibition. *"God is so good."* It was meant for us to keep this piece so that we would discover Ping Lian's hidden talents.

Ping Lian's artworks were later described by art curator Dr. Rosa C. Martinez as follows:

"I see his art as images of communication. They are visual interpretations symbolizing thoughts and imaginations. His paintings tend to encompass hidden aspects or forms, not initially seen or noticed upon first view. His use of color and his creation of intricate lines result in images within images that often appear unlimited…."

This particular artwork is still hanging in our main hall. Whenever we have visitors, especially with children, I always get them to see what they can find in the swimming pool.

"MIRACLE GIFT" AND "MIRACLE HAPPENING" 04105 UBUDIAH MOSQUE I

When Ping Lian painted "04105 Ubudiah Mosque I", I was yet again so very amazed by him. Ping Lian was only 10 years old. Initially this art work "04105 Ubudiah Mosque I" was sold for RM450. I am so sad that I "need" to sell that work. But God is so good. He had His own plan for Ping Lian and the art work. The art work was finally "Walked Home"…and later it auctioned for RM100,000.00 (estimated US$ 30,000.00)

See details of this story below . ….

"04105 Ubudiah Mosque I" was drawn in May 2004. It is one of the first few pieces that Ping Lian drew on larger paper (A2 size). It was also the first time that Ping Lian drew using permanent markers and water color together to draw a building in A2 size. I gave him larger paper wondering

Chapter 11: The Joy of Achieving/Realizing a Dream   257

how he would do and hoping he could deal with this particular change. Obviously, he did just fine. So this particular drawing has very sentimental value to me.

The actual Ubudiah Mosque was built in 1917, officially declared open by Sultan Abdul Jalil Karamtullah Shah, successor to Sultan Idris. It has the reputation of being the most beautiful mosque in Malaysia. Ping Lian drew it by referring to a photograph.

In June of 2004 there was to be another art exhibition at the National Art Gallery (for people with disabilities). It was "Different Strokes: Diversity through Art 2". Ping Lian had done very well at the first exhibition so I was very eager to have him participate again. Although, I did not intend to sell "Ubudiah Mosque I", it was a condition of the exhibition that all art works submitted for the exhibition must be available for sales. I clearly wanted to be able to share this beautiful work, while creating visibility of my son's talent. Understanding that Ping Lian could more than likely draw the mosque again… I reluctantly decided to let go of this artwork and make it available for sale. The organizer of the event set a price of only RM450. I asked "Isn't this price too low for such a beautiful and quality painting?" I was told that it was the highest priced art work in the exhibition. I rationalized that since Ping Lian is a new artist, a child, an unknown, and with a disability that a price of RM 450… is probably already considered as a big favor for Ping Lian. I was also told that the other artist works were priced between RM 200 and RM 350, so the price of RM 450 set for Ping Lian's work definitely shows "appreciation" of his talent. I was sad to let the piece go. Ping Lian had just completed it a few days before the dead line for the submission of the artworks, and in fact, I hadn't even had the opportunity to send this art work to the photo shop for a professional photograph to be taken as I had done with his other pieces.

On opening day of the exhibition, "Ubudiah Mosque I" received so much attention! It was sold quickly, and bought by an important guest, a

VIP. Many people stood in front of the art work posing for photos with Ping Lian, including the VIP buyer. Several of my friends had told me that they actually intended to buy the piece, but that the yellow dot (which represents SOLD) was posted on the artwork so quickly, they didn't even have an opportunity to make the purchase. Ping Lian had a total of five pieces exhibited in the show. Within a few hours, they had all sold.

Two months later, one morning as I was driving on my way to an appointment I received a phone call. It was a friend who called to inform me that Ping Lian's painting "Ubudiah Mosque I" art work was featured in the newspaper. It said " The painting by a 10- year-old autistic child will be on sale at the inaugural KL Arts Market this Saturday". I was very puzzled as I understood that this artwork was sold on opening day at the initial exhibition. I was also unaware that any artworks not sold at the initial exhibition ""Different Stroke: Diversity through Art 2" would be made available for sale again on another date.

I couldn't wait. Without hesitation, I pulled my car aside and I called the Gallery. I spoke to the person in charge to find out what happened to "Ubudiah Mosque I". The person confirmed that Ubudiah Mosque was indeed available for sale the upcoming weekend. I reminded her that it was sold on the first day of the exhibition to the VIP. I was told that it was not sold. I just wanted to make sure there was no mistake made…so that I would know what to do next. Once again I asked for confirmation that the VIP did not buy Ubudiah Mosque I. I stressed that I saw the 'yellow dot' placed on the artwork immediately after the opening of the show. "Are you absolutely sure?" I asked again. She assured me and said that all of the art work that was purchased by the VIP had already been sent to his office, he had settled all of his payments and the artwork was not included in those purchases.

I still don't know exactly what happened but in any case I was confused but completely overjoyed. I put down the phone and started to think,

" How can I get this art work back?" I immediately called my brother and explained the situation. I told him that I wanted the art work back immediately before it would go on sale Saturday!" My brother said " Just tell them that I bought it and take it home". "It belongs to you!" Without wasting another second I called the person in charge of the exhibition again and asked once more...."So "Ubudiah Mosque I" is available for sale now?" She said Yes, so I informed her that I had a buyer and asked for her permission to go over and pick it up immediately. I did not want to wait. I would feel good once I had picked it up, gotten it home safely and hung it in my living room hall. I am amazed and happy that this art work had come back to us in such a miraculous way. I don't know what happened with the original sold status of "Ubudiah Mosque I". I just know that God had his own plan and I did not want to lose this artwork again. I cancelled my appointment and immediately drove to the gallery, picked up the drawing and took it home.

OH! I always describe "Ubudiah Mosque I" as a miracle piece that "Walked Home"! Some of my friends, who had actually attended the exhibition, always asked me "How come this art work is still at your home?"... and I always responded it *"Walked Home", long story …. In essence, God had given a miracle gift to Ping Lian and God has created many Miracles for us."*

The "Walking home" of this art work now also gave me an opportunity to have it professionally photographed. I hung "Ubudiah Mosque I" on our living room wall. I admire it every day and appreciate God's plan every time I see it. I knew that in no time, this art work would be worth a lot of money. I told Cher about my thoughts, and said it may be worth RM 10,000 to RM 20, 000 one day soon. Although I really felt it was worth so much more, I couldn't believe my own thoughts and didn't dare say those numbers out loud to Cher. I decided to keep this piece as part of our personal collection. I told Cher "*Ubudiah Mosque I walked home, so even if we get an offer of RM 20,000.00, we cannot sell it! Regardless of the offer or how much we may need the money, we will not sell it!"* Even more beautiful than the artwork itself was the story behind it.

"UBUDIAH MOSQUE I"
Auctioned for RM 100,000.00, 100% of the proceeds were donated.

04105 Ubudiah Mosque I (Painted when Ping Lian was 10 years old.)

At age 11 - Ping Lian's work, "Ubudiah Mosque I" was donated to Riding for the Disabled Association, Malaysia charity auction. It sold for MYR 100,000.00 on 20th Nov 2004.

Ping Lian"s artistic skills continued to progress at a rapid pace. His drawings and paintings were beautiful beyond my belief. He continually surprised me with his creativity, his rate of progress and his personal development. His ability to create such beautiful works time after time within such a short period was mind boggling. I am so very grateful for Ping Lian's personal and artistic growth. I am grateful to God. I am grateful to Ping Lian's teachers. I am grateful that we got to know Dr. Treffert, etc., etc... I began to feel that it was time to use Ping Lian's artwork to bless others who were less fortunate. I made a promise to Sandra Coopers who oversees event management for Riding for the Disabled Association of Malaysia (RDA),[23] that I would donate five of Ping Lian's original art works for their 2004 Charity Dinner Grand Auction. We would select one of the best pieces for the Grand Auction and the remaining four pieces were to be part of the silent auction. I had chosen to donate the original "04102 KL Twin Towers II" art work for the grand auction. The organizers were very happy with that selection.

The morning that I was to deliver the five donated works, I was upstairs in my room getting dressed and ready to go out. As I was sitting in front of the mirror of my dressing table combing my hair, many thoughts rushed through my mind about Ping Lian's artistic journey and about donating his artwork. Thoughts about my Dream, Our Dream, etc. just rushed through my mind all at once. Suddenly, I had this feeling that I was supposed to let go of "Ubudiah Mosque I" for the grand Auction.

I finally made the decision to use "Ubudiah Mosque I" to replace "04102 Kuala Lumpur Twin Tower II" (which I had promised earlier) for the grand auction. "Ubudiah Mosque I" was not one of the five artworks I had originally planned to donate, but I knew it would make a difference for the proceeds to the charity if I donated this one instead. It hurt me to think of letting this piece that had *walked home*, go, but I also had thought that maybe that was why it did return to us after all. I was thinking that donating this piece from

---

23 The Royal Selangor Polo Club has for many years been the mother branch for *Riding for the Disabled Association Malaysia*. Our six branches report back to the main committee during the year. This main branch heads up the major fund-raising projects which supports all six branches.

our best personal collection might raise RM20, 000 or higher for the RDA. However, then I started thinking about "Us". What about my family? Not only do I have an emotional attachment to this art work, but maybe I should keep it to help my family financially. I can use the funds when I sell it for my children's education. It's only been a few months since Min Seng passed away and very soon we will have used up, all of the insurance money. My children are still very young, our future is insecure. How will I support my three children all alone? Maybe I should wait until our financial situation is better. Then I thought, these financial concerns will be a problem for the few years or for many years yet to come. I rationalized that if I kept all the "best" pieces for myself, how could we make a difference in other people's lives. If I wait for tomorrow, tomorrow may never come. Ping Lian is so blessed now. He may be considered so much more fortunate than many other kids with autism. His "worse" (initial fine motor skills problem) has become his "best" (drawing ability). What if "Ubudiah Mosque I" did not "walk home"? I wouldn't even have the art work to consider to "donate" it or "keep" it. Under the 'strange' circumstances with which we were blessed to still have this artwork in our possession, we would now bless others. I revisited "I'm A Dreamer" in my head and instantly knew that I wanted to contribute it. It is the best opportunity now for Ping Lian to bless others who may be more unfortunate. There is no need to wait for a next time. Thoughts of the motivational phrases raced through my mind as well. "If I want to do it, I will do My Best, do it Fast and do it Now". So, without waiting for next time, and without informing my daughter Cher (whom I had just instructed a few days earlier NEVER to sell); or asking others for a second opinion… I went downstairs, took the picture down from the wall and put it in my car.

During the entire ride to the exhibition location I wondered if I was doing the right thing. At this point my dilemma was not about separating myself from this amazing artwork. It was about whether or not others would see the beauty and value of it as I did. *"Would they appreciate the quality*

Chapter 11: The Joy of Achieving/Realizing a Dream   263

of Ping Lian's art? Would it be viewed as precious? Would the outcome be as I have actually envisioned it? ... an artwork that will raise a good sum of money to help the charity and make a difference in the lives of others...or.... should I wait until Ping Lian becomes more recognized as an artist? Perhaps when he becomes more famous the artwork will have the ability to raise more money for charity, etc." I didn't want to "waste" the artwork. I envisioned the worst case scenario as a possible auction *price of RM 10,000.00 or below, thinking if that happened I would buy it back myself! Meanwhile I will pray to God that it auction at a minimum of RM 20,000.00. Suddenly, I thought, wait a minute – if it's worth RM 20,000 and I am generous enough as a widow trying to make ends meet, to donate it to charity, then perhaps some wealthy person will be generous enough to overbid as a donation for the cause! I daydreamed about the work auctioning for RM 50,000.00!!! I immediately asked God to please help and make sure that I was making the right decision to let go of "Ubudiah Mosque I" to help make a difference in the lives of others who were less fortunate. This was the first time I ever prayed to God about asking for the price/ value of Ping Lian's art work. I had never prayed to God to bless Ping Lian's art work regarding price or prayed for certain specific values. In fact, no one with a rational mind at that time at (Nov 2004) would think that Ping Lian's art could sell for so much money. He had just turned 11years old! It would have been inconceivable to think that his art work could be auctioned for such a high price (even for charity), so immediately. I asked myself, "Am I crazy?" How did such thoughts enter my mind? However, in all honesty, I continued to pray to God "Please help me to make sure that I do the right thing. Make sure Ubudiah Mosque I auctions for RM 20, 000 or more. RM 50,000 would be best".* Praying over and over again, before I knew it, I had arrived at the RDA center. The person in charge was overjoyed to see that I was donating our personal collection piece, "Ubudiah Mosque I". I simply told her that I changed my mind and decided to donate Ping Lian's best art work instead of the one we originally listed. I did not share with her my original hesitation and periods of uncertainty regarding this decision. Who knew it would actually auction for RM100,000.00?

In 2003 I wrote "I'm A Dreamer" ... "One day *we can together start to bless more unfortunate people. Apart from helping Ping Lian to be self-sufficient through art, he will one day be able to help or support other more unfortunate special needs people. This can be achieved by allocating a percentage of proceeds from the sale of his art to help finance the needs of others special needs people/autistic people.*"

Recalling this, on that morning, at the RDA, I challenged myself to make today that 'one day'. Today I would learn to be more giving and take today as that opportunity to make a difference in the lives of others...And so I finally managed to give away one of my son's best works.

When Cher realized that the art work I mentioned just a few days ago which was so precious and was not to be sold was no longer hanging on our wall and that I "gave it away" she was very sad. She was extremely unhappy with my decision and especially with the fact that I did not speak with her about it beforehand. There were many, many times that I refused to make purchases for Cher and Sherlyn of things they wanted to buy. I would always explain to them that our finances were low and we had a limited budget. I explained the need to save money for their education and life necessities, etc. They were exhausted at hearing the same story again and again about "we do not have Daddy already, etc. They would eventually succumb to my decisions but this time when Cher realized that I donated an art work that was worth RM 20, 000 without even discussing it, she was livid. Cher is a sentimental person. She did also love the art work so much and she cherished the details of how the art work "walked home". She started complaining " ...when I want to buy new clothes and shoes, you said I should save money! You said 'NO MONEY' and now you give away art worth may be more than RM 20,000…etc ..etc". In her anger, she actually expressed to me many of the same concerns I was debating before making my final decision. She worried that her brother's art would not be

Chapter 11: The Joy of Achieving/Realizing a Dream 265

appreciated by others and that I had just wasted it by giving it away as if it was worthless. I found myself explaining in detail to my daughter about my '*worst case scenario*' plan and how we could make a difference for other special needs people. I explained to her how blessed her brother actually was that we needed to take this opportunity to express our own gratitude and to bless others.

Yes! God is good! My prayers had been answered. I asked that "Ubudiah Mosque I" sell for a minimum of RM 20,000 but I prayed for RM 50,000. Wow!!! I was so happy! I knew that I had made the right decision with God's help. The result of the bidding at the auction was nothing short of a "miracle". The auctioneer started with a bid of RM10,000.00, but someone rushed onto the stage and announced that an anonymous person had just bid RM 100,000.00 (For Malaysian RM100,000.00 that is an awful lot of money. Approximately $30,000.00 US Dollars). So many people were stunned and amazed. I was so thrilled with my decision and with these results. It was another validation for me of "never try, never know…". Cher, Sherlyn and their friends who were volunteer workers at the event stood with their mouths open. They were completely shocked at what they just heard announced. They could not believe it. Later, that night, Cher came to me and told me she now understood and that I had made a good decision. God is good indeed!

That night, we had also contributed four other pieces of Ping Lian's paintings for the Silent Auction. '04906 Selling Rambutan and Durian' were bid at RM 1,500. '04116 Sultan Abdul Samad Building IV' was bid for RM 1,700. '04321 Grand Prix 2004' was bid for RM 3,000. '04310 Polo Match I' was bid for RM 3,000. A huge effort was put in by the organizing committee for this event and RDA Malaysia raised a total of RM 205,300.00 from this event.

My inspiration for having written "I'm A Dreamer" came from an article I once read about a Taiwanese special needs lady. She held an exhibition of her work and donated all the proceeds (approximately $100,000.00) from the sales to a special needs center. From that point on I had been inspired with this secret dream of mine, that one day Ping Lian's art would become more valuable... And that when I become financially stable, I would like to do the same. I would like to use Ping Lian's art work to raise funds of RM100,000.00 in one exhibition for a deserving special needs center. Little did I realize that there was no need to wait for that *One Day* when Ping Lian would be grown up, or when we achieved financial stability. I just had to be ready to let go. I let go of one piece of his best original work and God had his own plan. It happened so fast. Ping Lian had now for the first time donated his art work for charity. We raised in excess of RM 100,000.00 and Ping Lian wasn't even *famous* yet! Now I know why people always say it is good to have a Dream and we must always have faith and trust in God. The total amount of funds raised through Ping Lian's art in one evening for RDA was RM 109,200.00. In fact as of the December 2004 (Ping Lian had just turned 11 years old), the total funds raised through Ping Lian's art work in aid of special needs people amounted to more than RM 119,000.00.

God works in a very special way, doesn't he? The next day after the auction as I sat in front of my dressing table again...my mind started to wander. I played back what had happened, from my decision making, to letting go, to the results of the actual auction and to the 'miraculous' happenings time after time in Ping Lian's Artistic Journey. I suddenly felt that maybe God had a Special Plan for me and Ping Lian. I did not know what the Special Plan might be, but I suddenly felt so "scared". I was still struggling with the death of my husband, with my life with my children, with Ping Lian and with my financial situation. I feared that I may not be ready or might not be good enough to handle that Special Plan He may have for me. I became extremely anxious and so I called my friend for help. She said "Sarah do not be scared. If God chose you, He knows that you are able to handle it and He will assist you. He will be with you.. and He will send people to assist you too … you do not need to worry!!…" I suddenly felt at ease believing that, yes indeed, if God had a Special Plan for me, he would show me the way. I will continue to just take one day at a time, and happily move forward with my family following Our Dream and the goals we had set earlier for Ping Lian.

Note: Later I will reveal the many, many times that I know God sent us 'angels' to help Ping Lian.

MIRACLES OF GOD

Ping Lian's talent is a gift from God and a miracle healing. The fact that his art work can auction for RM 100, 000.00 with no pre plan, no promotions, and no special arrangements has to be a miracle. At such a young age, a new artist, unknown, never heard of by others, his artworks for auction exhibited competitively with other well established artist works – a success! The other artworks were bigger, they were better framed and better presented on high quality easels and specially made stands. Having no experience in this area, I was not prepared and didn't even have an easel for Ping Lian's work. Actually, at the last minute, having no other choice, the organizer displayed Ping Lian's art work for the auction on a chair on the stage. It auctioned for RM 100,000.00! This is unbelievable isn't it? Sometimes I still wonder "How can that happen? It was so fast, so soon! I have no doubts about the quality of my son's artwork. It is definitely brilliant and stunning, but still the results were unbelievable. There is no other answer to me other than "God's hand is at work".

Eventually I started receiving many congratulatory SMS messages from people on my phone. My outdated limited mobile phone was unable to store so many messages so I started to delete messages as I read them to make room for any new ones. After a few days of doing this, I suddenly realised that these were very meaningful and beautiful messages and I shouldn't just delete them. I then started the practice of copying down the messages before deleting them from my phone. Below are a few selections from some of the last messages I received:

* Some of the SMS Ping Lian's Mum had received on; "Ubudiah Mosque I" sold for RM100,000.00:

- Heartiest congratulations on the sale of Ping Lian's artworks. It is wonderful that he can make such a difference in other people's lives too. Best wishes. - From Nicola Kuok
- Well done Ping Lian! For someone his age, this is remarkable. - From Lee Yen
- Congratulation! U are an extraordinary person. Your commitment 2 him not only makes a difference 2 his life but the lives of many, many others. Please get present 2 the greatness you are. - From DR Fauziah (Ping Lian's dentist)
- Congratulation. Ping Lian has contributed so much to society. - From Hani
- I am in awe for what is God able to do through a mom of an autistic child. I 'm also speechless 4 what God has shown that Ping Lian can do. WOW! N Yahoo. - From pastor Serena Phang

THE MONTHLY ART MARKET

In 2004, when Ping Lian was only 10 year old, once a month, I took him to participate at the Art Market at the compound of The National Art Gallery of Malaysia. This art market at the National Art Gallery was a new event in Malaysia.

Ping Lian loved going to the Art Market. Getting him to participate in the art market was one good preparation in training him to be able to draw and maintain focus and concentration in a busy and active environment. It also proved to be an excellent social atmosphere as it provided many opportunities for Ping Lian to relate to people and "survive" in a very public environment.

Participating in the art market presented me with many hardships. In addition to the added work, it was extremely hot as it was an outdoor market and we had to set up under the cover of a simple tent. My regular employment as a senior manager was in an office with air conditioning. Our house also had air conditioning. At first, staying outside, in a tent like this was pretty unbearable for me. However, after a while, the more I saw Ping Lian progress and enjoy himself at the art market, I knew it was worth bearing. After a while, seeing how people were so inspired by Ping Lian, I too began to enjoy participating in the art market!

Watching Ping Lian enjoy himself and all our customers being so supportive enjoying watching him draw and paint was so encouraging. Later on I even tried to get Ping Lian to draw people/ portraits at the art market. Ping Lian's young age and his awkward yet cute behavior when dealing with people attracted many people to view him drawing. He was always very happy and he enjoyed having a crowd watch him as he painted. Please refer to chapter 4's FIGURE for the type of people/ portraits he drew.

Since the quality of Ping Lian's painting or drawings of people was not consistent and was often affected by his mood, I gave the people options that regardless of the quality of his drawing, they could just pay any token of their appreciation to Ping Lian if they chose to keep the drawing. If they did not want the drawing they did not have to pay anything. Ping Lian was gifted in drawing whatever he felt like drawing, and getting him to draw people was not one of his best endeavors. The real objective was to get him to interact with other people, so whether or not they wanted to purchase the portraits I appreciated the time and patience they gave my son as an opportunity for him to increase social interactions. In any case, everyone showed the artist respect! Surprisingly, everyone loved his interpretations of them and always took home the drawings. The two years that Ping Lian spent drawing people at the art market was a blessing. He learned so much and developed appropriate communication skills, in addition to respect for others.

Many teaching opportunities arose from the art market. I found myself stressing "Do's and Don'ts" to teach Ping Lian what was appropriate and what was not acceptable. Many people would find humor in Ping Lian's limited communication and social skills. His awkward, idiosyncratic "autistic" behaviors were often amusing. Many times as he was drawing a portrait, he wanted to draw the person's leg, but he could not see it because the one leg was blocked by the table. Instead of getting up to get a better view, he put his head under the table and table cloth and continued to draw the person's leg from underneath the table. Another time, as he was drawing a young girl, I started talking to the girl's mother. The girl's younger brother was eating some chips and Ping Lian stopped drawing and helped himself to some of the brother's chips. I knew that I needed to take some steps to teach him right from wrong and respect for other people's things. Given the occurrence of such behaviors, it always surprised me that people would still line up for Ping Lian to draw them!

I had originally taught Ping Lian terms like "our people" which meant his immediate family, relatives and our very close friends; and "other people" which meant strangers. I used these terms when teaching him about appropriate behaviors (like asking or taking food). I wanted him to be able to differentiate what would be appropriate and okay to do with family and friends but not okay to do amongst strangers. To Ping Lian however, I believe whenever he saw me happily engaged in conversation with someone, he thought they were friends and in his mind what clicked was "our people"!

I was successful in teaching Ping Lian to respect others time. Originally when Ping Lian started drawing his "serious drawings" (not the portraits at the market), either myself, his teacher or the maid would sit beside him until he was finished. If no one was at his side, or if we left his side, he would often walk away. The day he was drawing the little girl I spoke of at the art market, he did just that. Sometimes when I needed to serve or speak to another customer, Ping Lian would get up and walk away while in the middle of drawing someone. The customer would just sit there unsure of what to do next. So I took this opportunity to teach Ping Lian to respect people's time. I told him "do not waste other people time." I told Ping Lian that Mummy was not free to sit beside him, and the girls Mom and brother were all waiting for Ping Lian to finish drawing the girl. I told Ping Lian that it was too hot, that the girls Mom still needed to do shopping, etc. I repeatedly used these types of sentences for quite some time. Later on, whenever Ping Lian drew someone half way, or got up before he completed a person's portrait, I simply needed to say to him "Don't waste other peoples time…" He would quickly return and continue to finished his drawing, even without me sitting beside him. It turned out to be a perfect and effective way to teach Ping Lian to appreciate and respect the time of others. At the same time it taught him to independently complete his task and without me sitting beside him.

Note: By 2006 Ping Lian had become so independent in doing his art work. If I sat beside him while he was drawing or painting one of his 'serious works' he would say "Mummy go away"!

In general Ping Lian was always well behaved at the art market. He was always happy to help me setup and also pack up when it was time to leave. At first this was very hard work for me, because as much as Ping Lian wanted to be helpful, it was a very big chore. He didn't really know how to help, but I involved him with the initial set up and he liked to take charge and felt in control when he was at the art market. There was a time period though when Ping Lian began suddenly throwing severe temper tantrums. It took me a long time to realize why he was having tantrums at the art market.

At some point prior I had thought it would be great to involve Sherlyn and Cher to help with some ideas at the art market and also to become more involved in their brothers' Artistic Journey. However, I later realized this was the problem. Whenever Cher and Sherlyn came to help in the art market, Ping Lian would have a big tantrum. In retrospect, I believe that Ping Lian enjoyed "running" things and setting up at the art market by himself. It was something he loved to do and loved to learn from me. He did not want any restrictions on these tasks that he enjoyed and considered himself capable of now doing independently. Ping Lian did NOT want to share this with his sisters! He was especially sensitive and would become upset whenever Cher or Sherlyn corrected him or told him what to do at the art market. Any instructions on what he should "Do" or should "Not Do" with regard to his behaviour were annoying to him. At home such corrections from his sisters did not upset him at all. At home, he was usually perfectly okay with his sisters telling him "Do's" and "Don'ts". By the same token, I would imagine Cher and Sherlyn were *more* overly concerned about their brothers actions in the general public than they would be if he were at home with family. Yet, surprisingly Ping Lian was always happy and totally obedient with me teaching him and instructing him what to do and not to do at the market. I found myself instructing my daughters to ignore Ping Lian's behavior and not to teach him or correct him at the market. They also had to stop performing any of his job duties and responsibilities at the market. In my attempt to bring the family closer by sharing the art market experience; I had created havoc. The girls now felt unappreciated since they were restricted in the manner in which they could assist their brother, and Ping Lian's tantrum behaviors increased. Watching Ping Lian tantrum was very difficult for my daughters. They always felt saddened and disappointed. Everyone was becoming increasingly frustrated. Eventually I came to the decision that Cher and Sherlyn should not come to the art market after all. Ping Lian was still learning about the art market and he obviously did not want help from his sisters. The negatives outweighed the positives. This was also a very emotional time of our journey for me, because many people, including my relatives assumed that my daughters did not support Ping Lian and that they were resentful of my time with him. They would note Ping Lian working hard at the market, but no sisters to help, and yet there I was sometime's reaching out to friends for some assistance. The truth is, for whatever reason – Ping Lian did not mind if a friend or relative helped us. He never displayed a tantrum, if a friend or relative gave us a hand. The problem was definitely with his sisters. I believe he was so proud of himself, that he wanted his sisters to see that he could perform the art market tasks (just like the man of the house). For those who assumed that my daughters were resentful; I let you know now that, that was never the case. It was my decision for Cher and Sherlyn to stop coming to the art market, but I never took the time, nor did I possess the energy to explain our reality. I could not worry about this. I had to focus on what was best for my family and continue surging forward.

Ping Lian's tantrums at the art market consisted of him biting his shirt and jumping. Many times he would also take the boxes where he kept his drawing pencils and oil pastels, walk to the middle of several rows of art stores and throw the box high up toward the sky. Every time he did this, the many other artists and booth workers would look at me "special"! I always translated those looks to mean "What kind of mother pushes her son to come to an art market and work so hard, in this hot weather, and cause him to throw tantrums?" I wondered how many onlookers also thought that a boy like him (Ping Lian) should be kept at home rather than go out in public embarrassing himself and his mother? Little did such people know, that for Ping Lian going to the art market was a huge treat! Ping Lian loved and enjoyed participating at the art market. The only times he actually tantrummed at the market involved times that I did not allow him to do more work, and the times his sisters were present and actively assisting with the market related tasks or correcting him. I knew that it would be best for Ping Lian to learn, by allowing him these opportunities in a real setting. *How* people looked at me, or *what* people thought were really secondary issues. I continued doing what I thought was right for Ping Lian. I allowed him to have his public tantrums at the art market and I used those opportunities as best I could to be teachable moments. Through this, Ping Lian learned to deal with stressful situations more appropriately as he learned to adapt to changing situations. It was always much easier to teach Ping Lian something efficiently when he was in an environment that he enjoyed. As a matter of fact, Ping Lian loved going to the art market so much, that other times I would actually threaten him by saying "If you do not behave well, you will not go to the art market anymore." This often helped him to behave better.

Ping Lian loved his personal collection of art pencils and oil pastels. I tried several different approaches to teach him *not* to throw his pencils. I needed to teach him a more appropriate way to let me know that he was not happy. So, whenever he would walk to the middle aisles in the art market store and throw his pencils high up into the sky, I decided I would walk out to him and demand that he pick them up immediately! If he did not pick them up, I would not help him to pick them up and I will leave the pencils on the ground until I convince him to pick them all up. However, every so often, a well-meaning, kind passer-by would start to

Chapter 11: The Joy of Achieving/Realizing a Dream

pick up the pencils for him. I found myself telling them "No, thank you, it's okay. I would tell Ping Lian that if he didn't pick up the pencils, I would give them away! I would then proceed to pretend to give away the pencils that were remaining in his pencil box. At times, I even told him that if he did not pick them up, other people will pick them up and take them away, leaving Ping Lian with "no more pencil." It would take forever with constant repetitions of talking, teaching, pretending and threatening not to bring him back to the market before he would finally pick them up. After a while, throwing his pencils in the air became a predictable occurrence. It became a habit for him and some days he did this two or three times while at the art market. I eventually became so frustrated and began to lose my patience with Ping Lian. I was tired of wasting my breath and my energy trying to rationalize with Ping Lian by having these long discussions. I was also very worried that passersby might trip on the pencils and fall. I had to use a different approach. Instead, once Ping Lian threw his pencils in the air, I would take the remaining pencils and throw those in the air too! I explained to him that, throwing his pencils meant he did not want or like his pencils, so Mummy will help him to throw the rest of them away too. I proceeded to throw his remaining pencils, slowly and one by one. Crazy?? I know that most people, who were passing by and watching, were thinking just that...."She's crazy!" To them it must have looked like Ping Lian and I (mother and child) were having a tantrum together. In any case the strategy known as "reverse effect" turned out to be very effective. Shortly afterward, whenever Ping Lian would see me going to throw the balance of pencils... he quickly would say "No, no" and quickly picked up every single pencil from the ground all by himself. He also behaved well for the rest of the day. This continued for months until Ping Lian finally stopped having such tantrums. Actually, I taught Ping Lian to use his *shirt* whenever he needed an outlet to express his unhappiness. Of course we all want to see expressions of happiness, and those usually come easily expressed with a smile, or hugs or laughter. However, just as important are the needs to be able to express sadness, anxious, anger or unhappiness. Ping Lian desperately needed an outlet to be able to express these emotions. Tantruming was not the answer. Given his limited communication abilities I needed to teach him a more socially appropriate means to express his negative feelings. I told him that when he is not happy or anxious he could " squeeze " his shirt. This served as a perfect replacement action for Ping Lian when he was upset. It was convenient and instantly available for squeezing anytime he needed it. Secondary positives to this were the facts that squeezing his shirt caused overall less destruction of any other objects and this behavior was also less noticeable by other people. It was less embarrassing and it helped Ping Lian to achieve his objective of expressing negative feelings. After several months, Ping Lian no longer displayed tantrums to express unhappiness and he appears always happy. Still today (2009), at the art market he is an excellent boy.

I always took a camping cushion with us to the art market for Ping Lian to sit on the floor while he drew. He was still very small and the cushion was so soft and comfortable. He fit right into it. We spent long hours at the art market and whenever he was tired, he would sleep on the cushion. I was always pleased whenever he napped there because it made the long day shorter for him and when he awoke he was again eager to participate. I often received encouragement and positive comments from people who acknowledged the hard work I put into guiding and training Ping Lian. However, I probably received just as many negative comments from people who believed that I was "exploiting" my son. I was "pushing him too early", I was "pushing him too hard!" he was "too young", etc. Even my own relatives were feeling sorry for Ping Lian. They thought he was too young to be put to work like this and referred to his working at the art market as "pitiful." Although I did try to explain that regardless of how it looked, Ping Lian enjoyed the art market. He was motivated and I always made the experience enjoyable for him. True, it wasn't a pretty picture to see such a young boy asleep on a cushion at a "work" site in such hot weather, but it was part of the process. Ping Lian actually slept fine there on that cushion. He was not uncomfortable, nor was he overworked, nor was he unhappy!

Remember, there was a time, that Ping Lian was hyperactive and didn't need much sleep. Now he gets all the sleep a young boy's body should require. It was important to me for Ping Lian to remain at the art market until closing time. He needed to learn that everything also needed to be packed up and stored away appropriately. I averted the negative comments of relatives and others and proceeded to train my son to paint outdoors and to learn to be independent in this environment that he loved. The term "exploit" is a very negative and very strong word. I would rather my son was "exploited" by me with my good intentions toward teaching him independence, responsibility, social skills, and appropriate communication, than to let him be "exploited" by autism. I am a mother first and nothing I do for Ping Lian is at the expense of his happiness or his well being.

In 2007 Ping Lian was invited by Dr. Darold Treffert to participate in the Windows of Genius art exhibition in the United States (Wisconsin). I did not know that he would be given the opportunity to paint live in front of the massive audiences that attended the exhibition each day. However, his art market "training" really paid off. Ping Lian was a "show off"! He was so well behaved and while he painted he kept looking for the TV coverage and media crews. He absolutely enjoyed all of the media attention and I know he was full of self-esteem and pride as he continued painting for the audiences.

To date, I continue to take Ping Lian to the art market. Even though since 2009 he has his own permanent gallery in Malaysia and has grown to the status of a "prominent" artist, I continue taking him because regardless of his progress the art market helps to provide the best natural environment and opportunities for Ping Lian to continue to progress emotionally and socially. It is the best job training ground to integrate him into society step by step.

When I look at the cheerful and colorful paintings that Ping Lian has created, I know he is so happy. Looking at his smiling and happy horses, his happy chicken, happy sun, happy dog etc., (www.pinglian.com) I know that I did not "push him too early", or "work him too hard." He is so talented and so happy!

2004 – PING LIAN IS "A SAVANT"

With an autistic boy and my dedication to train his talent, I never had much time to do other things of interest like reading or even watching television. I had actually become very narrowly focused in my day to day life with the plans for Ping Lian's future. I didn't know much about what was going on in the world outside of my immediate surroundings. At times I would sit and join my mother-in-law or children, but usually only for 30 or 60 minutes watching Chinese drama programs. On occasion I would catch a documentary of interest to improve my own personal development (mental power and attitude) or to improve my overall knowledge with the thought of helping Ping Lian in the journey I was paving for him.

Prior to 2001, I would often go home from work during my lunch time, to work with Ping Lian on his reading. After changing jobs in 2001, my new office was too far from home so I no longer went home to Ping Lian during my lunch hours. It was probably the best thing for me at the time anyway. I found that it was my only *leisure* time. I could relax with co-workers and a good meal. However, once Ping Lian's obsession and talent in drawing surfaced, I again became very busy utilizing my lunch break to work toward the new goals and Dream I had set for him. Just about every single day I would eat a quick meal within 15 minutes and devote the remaining lunch time to searching the internet to learn more about art in relation to autism. In fact, my friends and colleagues consistently told me not to work so hard. They would ask where I got all of my energy from and how come I wasn't tired. My energy was always renewed whenever I discovered something new. I would anticipate new discoveries while web surfing and learning something new was the best body battery charger! I didn't consider this part of my life as 'work' because I was not under pressure. As a matter of fact, it felt leisurely! Of course, I tried my best to maintain good health and always made sure I took supplements and vitamins. This made me ponder that, possibly when one lives with purpose and aim, their energy will automatically be generated from within. Mostly, I believe that having a positive mental attitude is what gave me strength.

I spent many hours, days, weeks and months researching the topic of art and autism on the internet. Through a Google search, I learned so much more about the talents of savants or "islands of genius" in some individuals with autism. Finally, one day I came across a website; www.savantsyndrome.com. and it was here that I learned of Savant Syndrome and Dr. Darold Treffert's[24] work. I was so amazed and inspired by the many stories from the Savant profiles. I read each and every profile and some even repeatedly. I hoped that one day Ping Lian could be one of them. Through Dr. Treffert's website I also learned about the sudden appearance of musical genius (which is what my brother-in-law Leong Chong had mentioned to me several times). Since Ping Lian was very young, Leong Chong always said "There may be something good in Ping Lian. Something we do not

---

24 Dr.Darold Treffert, a renowned American psychiatrist, is also an internationally known researcher who has been studying the Savant Syndrome for the last 45 years. He is also the author of "Extraordinary People: Understanding the Savant Syndrome" and has over 50 publications on professional journals to his name. Dr. Treffert has appeared in many TV shows; TODAY, Oprah, Larry King, Discovery and several others. Dr.Treffert is also in the "BEST DOCTORs in AMERICA " by peer selection since 1979. He was a consultant to the Award Winning movie Rain Man. Dr Treffert maintains a website savant syndrome at www.savantsyndrome.com (reprinted from - Who is Darold A. Treffert. MD: www.daroldtreffert.com)

understand or know about. You should keep an eye out for it." After learning about savant syndrome, I became even more motivated and confident about achieving Our Dream. This was the first time I really knew it was not just a daydream. I was so encouraged that I contacted Dr. Treffert and told him all about Ping Lian! In my letter to him I included many photos of Ping Lian's art works. From then on, Dr Treffert constantly encouraged me and provided guidance toward further developing Ping Lian"s artistic skills. Dr. Treffert has been very supportive and still continues to advise and encourage us today.

On September 10, 2004 I received my first e-mail from Dr Treffert! It was so wonderful. He acknowledged Ping Lian as a savant and I was so elated. Below is an excerpt from that e-mail:

> " … Ping's art is really very amazing. I would certainly put him into the category of 'savants' and his progress is evident through his works. "Training the talent" is the proper course to follow with him and more good things will follow both with respect to his art and his overall development…… I really like your son's art. I think he has a good road ahead for himself with his art talent. ….. Gradually in the U.S. there is more emphasis on A-bilities, rather than dis-abilities and "dreams" such as yours hopefully will be realized more and more often even in the short term…… Thank you for sharing these remarkable materials and I will keep you and your son in mind as resources, leads, and facilities are brought to my attention. ………"

This email was so impactful to me in my effort in develop Ping Lian's talent further. On September 17, 2004 I received another e-mail from Dr. Treffert with further encouragement:

" ... I am pleased to see your son's work is getting the recognition it deserves. His works, along with your dedication toward focusing on A-bilities, will serve as an inspiration to many parents, teachers and others... ..... Please keep me posted on your son's progress and I am glad to have this distant contact and to learn another nation will come to know more about, and appreciate, persons with savant syndrome. They are national treasures wherever they are located."

Later, I purchased Dr Treffert's book, *"Extraordinary People: Understanding Savant Syndrome"* and became so informed about savant syndrome. The most striking information was that *"... Musical interest in children, whether they are of normal intelligence or are mentally handicapped, is universal. Musical ability is common. Musical genius is frequent. Not so with artistic talent.......while child musicians were not uncommon, the child artist was a 'rara avis'[25]... "* Upon learning that my son's talent was a rarity, I came to appreciate Ping Lian's talent even more and worked even harder and smarter with regard to "investing" in training and nurturing of Ping Lian's artistic talent.

In December 2004, I received another very encouraging response from Dr. Treffert upon he receive a batch of Ping Lian's artwork in print from me:

"...Thank you so much. The prints are magnificent. We went through them one by one this evening and each one is a treasure. Such remarkable talent... We love the colors....and the black and whites as well."

"... I am very impressed with these prints. They are remarkable

---

[25] Darold A. Treffert, M.D. - Extraordinary People: Understanding Savant Syndrome (Lincoln, NE: iUniverse Inc, 1989) p.108.

in their own right, and show how Ping Lian's a-bility towers over whatever dis-ability he might have.... And while the talent is inborn, it flourishes in the sunshine of his mother and families love, just like sunshine brings forth the beauty of the planet around us..."

My reply to Dr Treffert:

" .....For the sake of Ping Lian & my other children's future, I will resign from my existing full time job (at the moment I am a senior manager in sales & marketing for telecommunication services company) & I venture into Real Estate as a Real Estate Negotiator (my brother's company). I believe this job provides me with flexibility to be involved in Ping Lian's art activities & provide better opportunities to earn more money for my children's education."

"......By next year, I will have freedom of planning my time, so I do wish that if there is an opportunity, I hope that Ping Lian will have a chances to exhibit his works overseas (any country), based on your & Dr. Becker's advise. Better still, if the travelling can be sponsored by corporation, so that I do not need to "eat" into my other children's already limited education budget.(Hope this dream can come through by 2005. When you meet Dr Becker, would you share/ discuss this plan with him pls?)...."

At that time, I never thought that this "Dream" to have Ping Lian exhibit in USA would come to fruition so soon! Ping Lian had his first exhibition in New York, USA in January 2006. Also little did I know that I would also be uprooting our lives in May 2006 to live in Sydney, Australia. Life is so amazing.

Chapter 11: The Joy of Achieving/Realizing a Dream

Ping Lian was included on the Savant Syndrome Profile at the age 11. In December 2004, Sherlyn had completed creating Ping Lian's website. In Jan 2005, when Ping Lian was only eleven years old he was profiled and listed as a savant on the Savant Syndrome website https://www.wisconsinmedicalsociety.org/professional/savant-syndrome/profiles-and-videos/

At that time, less than 15 savants were listed on the Savant profile. This acknowledgement of Ping Lian's talents meant so much to me and Ping Lian. It was such a privilege and testament of my belief in my son and his talents. It has always been the one most influential validation for me regarding the path and experiences I have created for life with my son. My dream, our dream, for Ping Lian to be an Artist had become a realization. I would continue to "push" my son to achieve even greater heights.

15502 GARDEN - (OIL ON CANVAS, 2015.)
This painting hangs proudly in Ping Lian's home.

EXTRACT FROM WEBSITE SAVANT SYNDROME PROFILE:

Ping Lian Yeak: A Remarkable artist[1]
By Darold Treffert, MD

I was delighted to learn about Ping Lian through the worldwide savant syndrome Web site which brought his remarkable work, and his dedicated family, to my attention. Ping Lian's artwork stands on its own demonstrating a remarkable artistic ability in an 11 year old boy. His drawings are colorful, cheerful and impressive. Those drawings take on an added significance, however, when one sees that such a-bility co-exists with a dis-ability as described by his mother and teachers. Savant Syndrome is a rare condition in which remarkable skills and abilities — islands of genius — are seen in striking contrast to limitations from a variety of circumstances such as autism or other developmental disabilities. Such artistic prowess as Ping Lian demonstrates, in addition to providing us with beautiful art, serves as a source of satisfaction, development and growth for him, helping eventually to minimize whatever limitations might spring from his disabilities. Standing behind and beside each of the savants I have worked with as well, however, is a dedicated, patient, loving, determined and perpetually optimistic family which appreciates the special gift within their child, and wish to share it more widely with world. Thus we all become, then, the beneficiaries of that special giftedness, and that determination and optimism, while the artist himself continues to grow and flourish.

(The preceding paragraph was originally written for Ping Lian's Web site.)

Learn more about the extraordinary Ping Lian at http://www.pinglian.com.

For more information, please contact:
Darold A. Treffert, M.D.
St. Agnes Hospital, Fond du Lac, Wisconsin
Clinical Professor, Department of Psychiatry
University of Wisconsin Medical School, Madison
Personal Web site: http://www.daroldtreffert.com
e-mail: savants@charter.net "

---

[1] www.savantsyndrome.com Wisconsin Medical Society

On that morning when I read Ping Lian's information was included in the Savant Syndrome's website, I was overcome with a joy I had not experienced in a very long time. The powerful words like "Remarkable", "extraordinary", etc Dr. Treffert used to describe my son is very encouraging. I couldn't believe what my autistic son had achieved! He WAS AN ARTIST! I quickly played through in my mind all of those tracing drills and creations of inspirational materials. Yes, we did it! We turned Ping Lian's worst into his best! The " Impossible" became the "Possible". He was now a living testimony of embracing the 'Spirit of Determination" and the "Power of the Dream" and " Power of the Love". I kept asking myself "Am I right?? Am I right? Is he one of them??. ..but this is when I knew and I was sure that I was no longer "dreaming". Ping Lian and I worked very hard and our results were truly amazing and wonderful. I patted myself on the back. I was right… "never try never know". I patted myself once more, thinking it is good to "Dare to Dream" and maybe even to be viewed as "crazy". My daughters were so excited. They too couldn't believe this was happening. What a great feeling! I didn't even need to wait 5, 10 or even 15 years for this achievement of my son's. I was so pound of Ping Lian!! At this moment I was very proud of my entire family. I will always feel grateful to the powerful writing of Napoleon Hill. His insights gave me the inspiration I needed to move forward with my son and my daughters as a family while embarking upon this artistic journey.

UPDATE 2008:

> Jan 2008 Dr Treffert commented about Ping Lian again "….. Ping Lian's artwork stands on its own demonstrating a remarkable artistic ability. His artworks take on an added significance when one sees such ABILITY CO-EXIST with DIS – ABILITY. He is a natural artist whose work draws immediate attention, and appreciation. His works are a spark of joy and flame, talent and enthusiasm….."

Dr. Treffert is such a wonderful person. Without his constant encouragement and guidance, Ping Lian may not have progressed to such heights so quickly. The information I learned from his savant syndrome website gave me the additional knowledge I needed to wisely continue in my quest to empower my son.

Ping Lian continually progressed at great speeds in his art. He was so inspired to paint. In his initial artistic journey, he would usually draw first, and then paint on the drawing. I recall an instance in 2004, when he just took his brush and painted without first using the pen to draw. As this was never his style before, I was fascinated watching him. He controlled the brush so well. I knew then that I no longer needed to worry about him. The possibility of him losing his artistic ability (as has been reported in some cases in the literature) at some stage of his life was not a big concern to me anymore.

Motivation and perseverance are the important keys I want to be noted as the pillars of Ping Lian's success. I strongly relied on "The law of attraction", the "subconscious mind" or as I have used it "brain washing" and the effect of "positive energy". Ping Lian's current accomplishments with regard to his overall personal development (not just his artistic development) are a direct result of these applications. The theories and principles which guided my work with my son in his daily life were crucial to the positive outcomes achieved. The "Dream" that I had set for Ping Lian many years ago when he was still a very young child were sustained by these inspirations. And above all, I thank God for the gift of Ping Lian and thank God for continuously granting me the wisdom of how to guide and lead Ping Lian's gift toward becoming a functional reality.

Ping Lian's story is a testimony to the fact that there is always hope regardless of the adversity encountered. There can always be light at the end of the tunnel. Always "Dare to Dream, set Goals, dare to Change and take Immediate Action to Make it happen." Work with persistence, with determination and perseverance. Focus on maintaining a positive mental attitude, work hard and smart, work with faith and mould your spirit to resonate "YES I CAN…." Yes, even for a child with autism, these thoughts can be instilled. I know because I have lived it with Ping Lian!

Ping Lian's story is also a testimony that at times, a person's "worse" can become a person's "best". I share this story, Ping Lian's story not just to share his talents, but to share "how" those talents were made possible amidst the struggles and tribulations of the alternative which appeared to be that there was… "No hope"!

UPDATE 2009:
EXTRACT OF MY EMAILS TO YVONNE REGARDING PING LIAN'S PROGRESS

> 23 June 2009- "… Ping Lian is so wonderful… after my hand surgery, I still can't do much yet but Ping Lian is very eager to go back to the art market on weekends. Seeing him so eager, I have agreed to go back one week earlier than planned. Ping Lian promised he will do more work/ take more responsibility at the art market.

He is even more capable then I expected. Without much help from me, he was able to pack and unpack all the art market stuff into the car for going to and for returning from the art market. Also I had two sets of art prints for display at the market, one for Saturday at Paddington Market (I go with Ping Lian) and another set for The Rocks Market that Sherlyn will handle. I labeled them as set 1 and set 2. I told him pack set 2 for Mummy. He did it and even tried to make sure he did the right thing by asking " set 2? set2? set 2?"... as one of the set I did not label clearly on the plastic... I am so glad to see him doing all this...and so excited and happy with his progress..."

Another incident, one day, at the market,... He noticed the sky start turning dark and cloudy. So....before the rain start, he reminded me to get ready to put the plastic on to the non water proof umbrella. For me, this is one of his great progress...I am so pleased.

15-June 2009..."... he is also very good and cooperative in the hospital for dental work (fillings). Ping Lian was excellent during the whole process without going through the general anaesthesia. Initially we were quite worried and had planned to get him to do it under general anaesthesia, but I changed my mind and requested the dentist complete the filling without general anaesthesia. I " brain wash" him before we went to the hospital. I am so happy that we (I, Ping Lian and the hospital staff) were willing to take a chance. I feel Ping Lian has progressed to another level.

Seeing Ping Lian doing so well... for the past few days/ weeks, I believe that art has provided him with wonderful opportunities to learn, grow and be happy. I am happy to let him be in the art market for a longer period of time for training him in terms of his personal development area ...I hope one day, in the near future I can start training him to serve customers... For now, I have taken him to two markets for experiencing and learning to cope with different environments. He Saturday, I took him to Paddington Market, and Sunday I took him to The Rocks Market. And he enjoys both markets. He is adapting well and he is flexible to the variations of the two markets regarding totallly different environment and different setting.

FYI; this email I will save as my Journal Entry. I do not write Journal in Ping Lian book about his progress anymore... now adays, the many emails I send to you or Rosa have become my Journal record."

After experiencing the unexpected again and again, I now realized the truth in what my friends would tell me "Sarah Lee! God has His own plan and his own way for you!" Yes, I now understand.

CHAPTER 12
"*Come Here!*"...
Rooster

2005 was the year of the Rooster.[26] Caroline & Gillie from The Association of British Woman In Malaysia (ABWM) had organized an exhibition of Ping Lian's works. They approached me several times suggesting that I get Ping Lian to draw a Rooster to print some Chinese New Year cards to be sold at the exhibition. However I was tired; so tired. The thought of trying to get Ping Lian to create a drawing of something in which he showed no interest would require a lot of effort on my part. Ping Lian always draws and paints whatever he wants. It was less than a year since my husband passed away and I was still coping with my loss and the stress of supporting my family. Getting Ping Lian to draw a Rooster, finding a printer to make the cards and the expenses this would involve were not at all tasks that I wanted to take on at this point. I decided I would not waste my time trying to get Ping Lian to create a rooster painting. My response to Caroline and Gillie was "No!" However Caroline did not give up on the idea. She was very persistent and continually brought it up.

One afternoon, I was upstairs in my room busily working on an important project. In the distance I heard Ping Lian speaking to someone from the garden. "Come here!!", "Come here!! I did not hear anyone reply

---

26 Chinese New Year - 2005 Year of the Rooster; The Chinese calendar is based on solar and lunar cycles and thus the new year falls on a different day of the Western solar calendar each year. Each year is designated by one of 12 animals in the Chinese calendar.

to him and again I heard Ping Lian continuously saying "Come here!", "Come here!" First I was excited, because Ping Lian very seldomly initiated any speech. He usually only spoke when I prompted him to say something or when he wanted something (usually food). Secondly, I was worried about who he was talking to. I quickly ran to peer out of the window, but I saw no one there. As I rushed down the stairs to go to the garden I also wondered "Who would ignore such a persistent call to 'come here' by a young boy with autism?" When I reached the garden I was speechless. Ping Lian was alone in the garden. There was no one else in my garden. There was no one else in my neighbors' garden. There was only a rooster wandering about. Ping Lian was talking to a rooster! He was holding out a handful of leaves through my neighbors' fence and was calling "Come, here!", "Come here" to the rooster. Even as I approached Ping Lian, he continued pushing his hand through different parts of the wire fence that separated the gardens and trying to get the rooster to "come here" to eat the leaves. The rooster was however, obviously not interested in the leaves or Ping Lian.

I went and got some rice and told Ping Lian to give the rice to the Rooster. We tried together to get the roosters attention. I was just so happy that Ping Lian had initiated some communication. Never before had Ping Lian initiated an effort to communicate with someone so persistently. True, it wasn't a person but it was still communication! Ping Lian was talking to a rooster! I was elated.

The next morning I received a voice message on my mobile phone from Caroline. She said that if Ping Lian painted a Rooster she would help to make arrangements to get the Chinese New Year Greeting cards printed and that Gillie would pay for all the printing costs. What a "coincidence"! I was stunned. I wondered if the rooster incident the day before was really a "coincidence" or if God was showing me His plan for Ping Lian. I quickly called Caroline and said "Yes"! I shared the story of what happened in the garden with the rooster and excitedly we both decided to move forward on this project immediately!

Soon after, I obtained the neighbors' rooster. I decided we would use this rooster that Ping Lian was so interested in, as a model. Surprisingly, this rooster was very "obliging" serving as a model for Ping Lian to practice drawing. The progression of events appeared unbelievable and remarkable.

Initially I dared not hold the rooster, and got my neighbor to help me and hold the rooster. Later on, as she felt tired and had back pain from holding the rooster, I had no choice but to take over and hold the rooster myself. This was the first time in my life I ever held a rooster. I was worried that it would run away and so when I caught it, I held it rather tightly with two hands. I soon felt though how cooperative the rooster was. I eventually only had to hold the rooster as if positioning him supportively. If he wanted to run away, he could easily have gotten away. To my surprise, the Rooster not only stayed while Ping Lian drew, but it stayed in the same position. As I held the rooster, it stood still for long enough periods, maintaining a "pose" that allowed Ping Lian to complete several drawing sessions. He practiced drawing the rooster for several days. The rooster had been very patient with us for those few days. I was growing tired of holding the rooster and wondered if the rooster was growing tired too. This rooster was amazing! I wondered how all of this could be happening. As my neighbor witnessed all of this, she was equally amazed and she commented, " Sarah Lee, God is at work Now!!". I enjoyed the fun of these events and I was very curious about what else the rooster could do, but I still didn't take my neighbors' comment too seriously. My faith with God was not yet strong during this time. I actually wondered to myself, "What is she talking about?"

During this process, Ping Lian drew many sketches of the neighbors' Rooster. Over the next few days, The Rooster had become so cooperative, that I started moving it around into different positions for Ping Lian to draw. After each drawing, Ping Lian would hold the rooster and play with it. He would hold the rooster closely appearing to visually take in every facet of the roosters' features. He was so happy. I eventually also got Ping Lian to use acrylics to paint the Rooster. This of course took longer periods for Ping Lian to complete than the simple drawings and sketches. Apparently a rooster can maintain the same position, with no movement for long periods of time. It was so unbelievable how obedient and patient this rooster was, which allowed Ping Lian to complete the acrylic painting. The roosters behavior was so peculiar that we actually took many photos and videos of the painting sessions. We had so much fun during this time. The end result of Ping Lian initially calling "Come here" was a beautiful stunning Rooster titled "05401 Come Here Rooster". At that time, we did not know that all these experiences would lead/may be had inspired Ping Lian to paint a beautiful and stunning painting of "05402 Prosperous Year I (Rooster)".

PING LIAN DRAWING/PAINTING AND PLAYING WITH THE NEIGHBORS' ROOSTER

05401 -COME HERE ROOSTER – 41X 57CM ACRYLIC ON PAPER - PAINTED IN 2005 AT AGE 11

Additional paintings and sketches created by Ping Lian during these few days with the neighbors rooster, can be viewed at www.pinglian.com
Gallery 2005 II -"My Neighbor's Rooster" series.

On January 10, 2005, Ping Lian's 80 year old grandmother (Ah Mah) who had lived with us under the same roof for the past seventeen years, fell down and having suffered severe brain damage passed away. Just eleven months after Min Seng's sudden death, we were now on our way back to Sitiawan for another funeral. We all are very sad to deal with another sudden death in our family and so we remained in Sitiawan for one week.

Ping Lian was scheduled to have an art exhibition on January14, 2005 just before the Chinese New Year. We had to postpone the exhibition until the following month due to his grand-mothers death. It was rescheduled for February 25, 2005, which was to be after the Chinese New Year. We had originally selected "05401 Come here Rooster" to be the print image used on the New Year cards. However, the colors in this painting were so dark, that we felt they were not really for a cheerful New Year card. So, upon returning from Ah Mah's funeral, I continued to get Ping Lian to paint another rooster for the New Year cards. Not knowing what to expect, in my personal opinion, he had painted the most beautiful rooster and we named it - "05402 Prosperous Year I (Rooster)".

"05402 Prosperous Year I" turned out to be a stunning art work. This painting had become another important turning point in Ping Lian's Artistic Journey leading to many other events and opportunities. The painting received so much attention. In general people were fascinated with the quality of this picture that was painted by an eleven year old boy. I couldn't believe it myself as I had originally watched Ping Lian while he created each stroke with his paintbrush briskly resulting in this beautiful Rooster. The experience Ping Lian gained from drawing, painting and playing with our neighbors' rooster contributed to the skill and creativity with which he created such a beautiful painting as "05402 Prosperous Year I (Rooster)".

The circumstances we experienced as additional "special happenings" in Ping Lian's Artistic Journey coupled with the quality of the art work he painted "05402 Prosperous Year I (Rooster)" made it impossible for me to doubt my neighbors' initial comment. Definitely, I now agreed " YES!…God is at work!" Frankly, all these so called "coincidences" and unique special happenings have lead to so many great outcomes. One after another, each incident made me take her comment more seriously and made me trust in God more and more. I wholeheartedly believed these were circumstances created by God! Yes! Gods Hand was at work all along, since the beginning of this journey!!

05402 PROSPEROUS YEAR I (ROOSTER) - ACRYLIC ON PAPER - PAINTED IN 2005 AT AGE 11.

THE STORY OF " 05402 PROSPEROUS YEAR I "

"05402 Prosperous Year I" was the first picture Ping Lian painted after his grandmother's funeral. He was very emotional as he created this painting. Ping Lian was usually very calm as he painted. Yet, when painting this piece he was very unsettled. Half way through the painting, he kept getting up and jumping and biting his shirt. Interestingly, he started by painting the Rooster head first and it was so beautiful. In view of his apparent unstable emotional state, I became very concerned that he would ruin the painting if he continued. I continually tried to encourage Ping Lian to stop painting, telling him that he could finish the painting later. However he did not listen to me and he kept painting. He was so insistent that I decided to leave him alone. I believe the passion with which he created this wonderful artwork reflects his emotional state at the time of his grandmothers death.

Look at the beautiful big rooster protecting the little chick. Could it be that the big rooster represented Ah MAh and the small chick represented little Ping Lian? Only Ping Lian knows the answer to that question. I remain patient, awaiting that one day when Ping Lian can tell me. I have never stopped praying that this may *one day* become a reality.

" MOMENTS OF SADNESS ABOUT PING LIAN'S ACHIEVEMENT" – FEB 2005

Although I was very happy about all that Ping Lian had attained up to this point, I was also experiencing a sadness with regard to his achievements. I had entered what I referred to in my journal as "Moments of sadness about Ping Lian's achievement". I was now asking myself, So, "What is Next? Where? How?"

Below is an extract of one of my e-mail correspondences with Dr Treffert:

> From: Sarah Lee <sarahshlee888@yahoo.com>
> To: Darold Treffert MD <daroldt@dotnet.com>
> Sent: Tuesday, January 25, 2005 3:51:09 AM
> Subject: Ping Lian Website & new painting
>
> Dear Dr Treffert,
>
> Thank you for your email. I feel encouraged and warm when reading your mail and occasionally I share your mail with my daughter too..........
> I have good news to share: Ping Lian had just painted a fantastic fine piece, strong and vibrant Roster, (Acrylic on paper, no drawing, immediately paint with the brush and he could control the brush so well. He paint it so fast and so spontaneously). I name it "Prosperous Year". Based on Chinese calendar, this year is a Rooster year, we get him to draw and paint rooster for the past few weeks, without knowing that he can come out with this fantastic piece.
> It is always my concern that whether Ping Lian special and spontaneous strokes will stay on or not (especially after knowing Nadia[27] story), but with this special painting he portray, I am really encouraged and feel certain that he is on his way moving steadily and rapidly into the next level. Based on this piece of work, I can see that he had another breakthrough in his art ability. It is

---

27 Nadia was an autistic savant artist who after gaining communicative speech yet also experiencing the loss of her mother later in childhood, apparently lost her artistic talent. In the 1977 book by British psychologist Lorna Selfe. The author suggests a trade-off between language and artistic skills: that as language skills are refined, special artistic skills may disappear.

difficult to believe that this work is done by 11 year old boy. (So fortunate that I am around to watch him paint this piece). I am so pleased and also feel such a relief. I guess that, always using pen or pencil to draw may possibility lead to rigidity, but I think once he is so skilful/artistic with the brush, I guess rigidity is very much more difficult to set in......"

God Bless You
Sarah SH Lee

PING LIAN SAY "I MISS DADDY, I MISS AH MAH"

In 2004, Ping Lian lost his father due to a sudden heart attack. It wasn't until well after the funeral was over that Ping Lian came to the realisation that his father was gone forever. Sadly, less than a year later in 2005 just four weeks before Chinese New Year, Ping Lian's grandmother "Ah Mah" also died. I remember Ping Lian's behaviour at his grandmother's funeral. He was extremely hyperactive throughout the entire funeral. I could tell though, just moments before the actual burial that this time Ping Lian knew what to expect. He knew that once Ah Mah was buried, he would not see his Ah Mah anymore..... just like he couldn't see his Daddy anymore. He became so hyper that I could not control him. He did not want Ah Mah to be buried.

Sometime after his grandmother passed away, Ping Lian began to be rapidly maturing. During our traditional Chinese New Year celebration Ping Lian came to me and said "I miss Daddy, I miss Ah Ma". This was the first time he had celebrated Chinese New Year without his Daddy and his grandmother. This was also the first time Ping Lian ever said that he missed someone in his life. Although he learned this the hard way, I was so happy that he understood the feeling of "miss" and was able to communicate it.

It was an evening in February 2005 and our entire families were gathered at Siew Ing's house in Sitiawan celebrating the New Year. I was enjoying myself with my brothers and sisters. All of the children were playing cards upstairs. Ping Lian was just walking around alone. He suddenly came over to me and repeatedly said "Daddy, daddy". For some reason my first thoughts were that he could see a vision of his Daddy. I finally responded, "Do you see daddy?" He just kept saying "Daddy" and whenever I would again ask him "Do you see Daddy" he would run away, but then return again saying "Daddy, Daddy". I thought to myself, maybe Min Seng has come back during this special occasion too be with Ping Lian. I even asked Ping Lian "Where do you see Daddy?" I think I was just so desperate that I wanted to believe this to be the case. Anyway, Ping Lian just grew increasingly upset with my responses. He must have been thinking, that I had told him " Daddy long sleep. No more Daddy already, cannot go shopping with Daddy already" and now here I was asking him, "Do you see Daddy?"

The next day, this started all over again and I still asked Ping Lian "Where is daddy?" I finally came to my senses and realised that he did not see his Daddy but that he was missing his Daddy. I felt so bad. My Ping Lian must have been thinking "My mother is always smart, but how come this time she is so stupid? She doesn't understand me… How can I still see my Daddy?" These thoughts were most likely frustrating Ping Lian causing him to run away from me each time I thoughtlessly responded "Do you see Daddy?…Where is Daddy?". This inability to understand my son when he makes communicative attempts is the one most ever present frustrating element in our lives. I don't always know what he intends or what is on his mind and often have to guess. I felt guilty and ignorant as I quickly hugged him. "It's okay OK, I know Ping Lian miss Daddy. No more Daddy already, no more Daddy celebrate Chinese New Year with Ping Lian already. Daddy is inside Ping Lian heart (I point to his heart).

Daddy is inside Ping Lian brain (I point to his head). Uncle Pak Ling and Uncle Leong Chong celebrate New Year with Ping Lian. OK!"

A day later, while still at Sitiawan, I was driving somewhere and I sensed that something was wrong with my car. I drove straight to a mechanic to have it checked. I was now feeling overwhelmingly irritated. Every Chinese New Year, I return to my home town of Sitiawan to be with all my other nine brothers and sisters for a long holiday break. This is the first year we celebrate Chinese New Year without Ping Lian's daddy. I hate long distance driving and this was the first time in my life I needed to take this three hour drive myself. We were supposed to be leaving to Kuala Lumpur tomorrow for the drive home! Ping Lian has school the day after that!. I have to get back home! I have to fix the car! These were NOT things I ever had to take care of before. These were NOT my jobs. With each thought I became increasingly frustrated and the barriers I had created in my mind to keep from falling apart were quickly breaking down. I was frustrated, sad, and very angry.

While waiting for the mechanic to inspect the car I sat in a corner of the repair shop with a very long face. A few times Ping Lian came over and asked "Where is Daddy?" I told him "Daddy, long sleep. No more daddy already!" and he walked away. While waiting Ping Lian was either waiting at the other corner, sitting beside me or walking around in the repair shop. Every few minutes he would return to me "Where is Ah Mah?"and once more I would respond, "Ah Mah also long sleep, no more Ah Mah already". Why did he keep asking me this? I was now in such a bad mood and running out of patience.

The Chinese New Year holiday had always been exactly the same for Ping Lian his entire life. Every year it was the same exact routine and it never changed, until now. This was the first year he celebrated New Year's without both Daddy and Ah Mah. I know that it was very hard for him. Usually I spent most of the time with my sisters and brothers and Ping

Lian would be with Daddy most of the time. His Dad always took him "out" to visit specific places in Sitiawan. It has been a full week already of Ping Lian asking for his Dad! Sometimes he would just come over to me and simply say "Daddy" or "Ah Mah".

In his own way, Ping Lian also asked about going "out" to the places Daddy would normally take him. I found myself telling Ping Lian "No more Daddy already, so Uncle Pak Ling will take you there Ok?!" I didn't want to take Ping Lian to these places myself because it was such a wonderful time and memory for Ping Lian of experiences with his Dad. Instead, my brother Uncle Pak Ling could replace his Daddy. I wanted Ping Lian's memories and experiences of our traditional Chinese New Year celebration to remain special. Going "out" during these times would also help Ping Lian to understand that "No more Daddy...", but Uncle Pak Ling can take him out.

This time Ping Lian put his face very close to mine, " Where is daddy? Where is Ah Mah?" I started to wonder again if he really understood death? I thought he did but was now doubting it; again! Trying very hard to keep my composure, I patiently said "Ah Mah long sleep, Daddy long sleep. Chinese New Year celebration, no more Ah Mah and no more Daddy already!" This time, he did not walk away. He sat beside me. I continued "No more Daddy drive car already, so Mummy have to drive car back to Kuala Lumpur. See! Now car spoil already!" As he paid close attention to me, he seemed to understand. The worry, the frustration and the sadness must have shown on my long face. Ping Lian knew that I was upset and sad. He was engaged and looking at me so closely. From this point on he continued to wait for the car to be repaired with a surprising patience. His behaviour was not typical for him when in a new setting. He was not his usual curious self. Normally, he would be walking all around checking, touching and looking at things. I wondered if he really understood my anger and frustration, and decided not to add the stress of my having to look after him there. I continued "So! No more Daddy already! So no more

Daddy drive car go to Sitiawan for Chinese New Year. When Ping Lian grow up, can Ping Lian drive car take Mummy to Sitiawan for Chinese New Year?" Ping Lian answered firmly "Yes!" and he walked away again. I did really wish this could happen "one day".

Seconds later, Ping Lian returned to my side. This time he sat down on my lap and placed both of his hands around my neck... "I miss Daddy, I miss Ah Mah." This was the first time Ping Lian ever expressed such a feeling spontaneously. It was the first time in his entire life that he said "I Miss.......". I hugged him so tightly and said " Yes, I miss them too" and tears started rolling down my cheeks.

Ping Lian remained on my lap until the car had been repaired. For most people simple words like "I miss" are taken for granted. Finally, after so many years my son expressed a true emotion on his own. This was a very, very extraordinarily special moment for me and my Ping Lian.

FOLLOWING IS A VERY BRIEF CHRONOLOGICAL ACCOUNT OF PING LIAN'S JOURNEY THROUGH 2006:

PING LIAN PARTICIPATES IN MORE EXHIBITIONS IN MALAYSIA

September 2004 - Ping Lian drew many artworks of the University Malaya Faculty Building. These works were all exhibited at the University Malaysia Pesta Pendidikan Kokurikulum for a two day show. Ping Lian attracted lot of attention from the university students in attendance. They were amazed by his talent. They enjoyed watching Ping Lian as he painted and drew. They appeared to be most amazed with his energy level as he painted exuding such happiness which also showed in his works. The University later purchased most of the artwork that depicted their faculty building.

Also in 2004, after sharing "I'm A Dreamer" with the owner of the Villa Lotus he sponsored and hosted an exhibition for Ping Lian, along with two other special needs boys. The exhibition was titled "Through My Eyes". A percentage of the proceeds of the exhibition was used to conduct an art workshop for people with autism and other special needs. The exhibition attracted much media coverage bringing awareness of the abilities in special needs people to the forefront.

HEART CLUB

Some time in 2004, after sharing " I'm A Dreamer" with Pam from the Calvary Church in Malaysia she introduced me to Karen. Our discussions eventually led to the establishment of a new club called the HeArt Club and the HeArt Club Plus in Jan 2005. We were actively involved with a Christmas Card project in December 2004 which was to kick off a fundraiser for the start of the new programs. All of the children who participated in the Christmas card project were children with disabilities. By the end of the month 24 children had joined HeArt Club with their parents involved in HeArt Club Plus, and in December 2004 the cards created by these kids had raised a good sum of money from the pilot project sales of the Christmas cards that featured their artwork.

HeArt Club is a club for Children age 7 to 18 with special needs and learning difficulties and an extended ministry of Calvary Life Ministries (CLM). The general goal of HeArt Club was to provide opportunities for special needs children to experience different types of creative activities (drawing, music, crafts, acting, and dancing). The objective was to try to reveal strengths and talents to restore self-esteem, teach self-expression, communication skills and independence. They provided an atmosphere of fun and support for family and care-givers. HeArt Club Plus was run simultanously with HeArt Club, with one providing parent self-help groups while the other provided fun and learning activities for people with special needs. This enabled the parents of the special needs children to get together, while knowing their children were being taken care of. One of HeArt Clubs long-term goals was to build a home for people with special needs in Calvaryland, a social compassionate ministry of Calvary Church in Sungai Pelek, Malaysia. The home would facilitate training in income-generating skills and independent living. It was very rewarding and also humbling to see that so many of my acquaintances were able to get their children involved in art and later successfully sell the cards of their child's artwork.

PING LIAN'S FIRST SOLO ART EXHIBITION AND UPDATE

Feb. 3, 2005 - The Star, Star Metro Newspaper Featured many pages about Ping Lian, titled "Stroke of Genius from an 11 yr old Autistic Child". Ping Lian was fascinated with the tiny little flowers on the Star reporters dress. He kept saying "draw flower" and getting so close to her. His closeness was so inappropriate that I had to encourage him to paint a flower from one of our flower books. Inspired by her dress, Ping Lian painted a beautiful flower, just by using brush with acrylic. See painting *"05501 Flowers I"*.

Later New Straits Times also published an article about Ping Lian. Additionally the program, *Eve's Diary* (TV8 - Malaysia) featured Ping Lian and his solo exhibition at ABWM House. At that exhibition, HSBC Malaysia bought some of Ping Lian's original art works. Also at the exhibition, the manager of Renkitt Benkersar offered 10,000.00 RM to buy one of Ping Lian's A2 size original art works of " 04102 Twin Towers II" that he painted at the age ten. It was the highest priced art work Ping Lian sold at that art exhibition. In fact, this is the art work that was supposed to be used for the grand auction at the RDA Charity Dinner Grand Auction in Nov 2004 but that I replaced with "04105 Ubudiah Mosque I". When Renkitt Benersar offered to buy this painting, she did not know about the story behind this art work. "Coincidence?" ….Or God's hand at work again!

Feb. 25, 2005 - Through Caroline and others, The Association of British Woman In Malaysia, sponsored a solo art exhibition for Ping Lian at ABWM House. We received a tremendous amount of interest about the exhibition. Many people loved the "05402 Prosperous Year I" painting and the responses were very positive. There were many offers made to buy the original… but because of the "coincidences" or God's plan behind the creation of this artwork I would not sell it regardless of the price. The exhibition and "05401 Prosperous Year I" art work attracted many reporters and art collectors.

Since Ping Lian's first exhibition, he has sold over 70 original pieces of artworks to corporations and individuals. Also through this solo exhibition and The Star newspaper, I met a kind businessman who loves art, and appreciates Ping Lian's talent. Through him I was introduced to two of his friends (all three who have requested to remain anonymous) that also appreciate Ping Lian's talents. Together, they offered to support Ping Lian. Later they jointly supported me in terms of finances to help my family start our new lives in Australia. My family is very grateful to them. They have helped contribute to change Ping Lian's life and indirectly helped to change my family life. Whenever I said thank you to Caroline and Gillie, they would modestly respond that they did not do much and simply offered a little help. Little did they know that it was their persistence, their "little help" that had somewhat of a multiplier effect causing a chain reaction of life changing opportunities for Ping Lian. I will always regard them both as the people who set off the beautiful and amazing works of "05402 Prosperous Year I". Without their encouragement, it could be possible that we may never have seen such a beautiful rooster painting created. Their initiative and effort in organising the art exhibition for Ping Lian led to the initial recognition of Malaysias eleven year old talented boy. As Dr Treffert commented previously, *Ping Lian's paintings......" ... are national treasures wherever they are located...".* Without this exhibition and The Star publication and the "05402 Prosperous Year I" art work, I may never have gotten to know the businessmen, who helped us financially to start off our life in Sydney, etc. I am eternally grateful to them all.

Sept 2005 - Mr. Jung from Korean Broadcasting came to Kuala Lumpur to film Ping Lian as part of their 60-minutes *Savant Syndrome* documentary which also featured Kim Peek[28] (real Rain Man) and Kodi Lee.

Jan 2006 – We made it to New York!

---

28 Kim Peek was the inspiration for screen writer Barry Morrow's 1988 Oscar-winning movie *Rain Man*.

PART IV
PINGLIAN ENTERS A NEW PHASE OF LIFE

"WINDOWS OF GENIUS: ARTWORKS OF THE PRODIGIOUS SAVANT"

Art exhibition in Wisconsin, USA, 2007 - from left Sarah, Ping Lian, Dr. Rosa Martinez & Dr. Darold Treffert.

CHAPTER 13
My Journey – USA and Dream To Go To Disney Land

Through Dr. Darold Treffert I was introduced to Dr. Laurence Becker from Texas, USA, and through Dr Becker I was introduced to Dr. Rosa C. Martinez, New York, USA. They soon became special people in Ping Lian's Artistic Journey. Both Dr. Becker and Dr. Rosa were amazed by and loved Ping Lian artworks. Together they collaborated to arrange an art exhibition in the United States for Ping Lian along with several other internationally acclaimed artists. The exhibition was entitled " Don't 'dis' the Ability" and featured works by Richard Wawro (Scotland), Christophe Pillault (France) and Dr. Temple Grandin (USA). The year was now 2006 and Ping Lian was only twelve years old.

Ping Lian's introduction into the art world in the United States was a direct result of the collaboration between Treffert, Becker and Martinez. So much was happening for Ping Lian now in the United States! Dr. Treffert had been advising and guiding me via e-mail for the past two years already. Dr. Treffert served as a consultant and mentor to me. He advised me, guided me, led me and encouraged so much of what came to be Ping Lian's Artistic Journey. He played a very crucial role in the reasons that Ping Lian was doing so well and progressing so quickly, in a short period of time. Dr. Rosa C. Martinez or Dr. Rosa as we have come to call her, is a special " Angel" that God sent to me and Ping Lian. Dr. Becker was also a tremendous influence in our lives. He constantly guided me and sent information to keep me updated. I am very thankful to him for bringing this wonderful lady, Dr. Rosa into our lives.

Together, the consistent informal contacts that I received from these three specialists constantly staying in touch with me were a pillar of strength, support and encouragement to help me move on. They gave me moral and emotional support, provided information and knowledge and I can honestly say that I don't believe we would have accomplished so much for Ping Lian without their input.

"BIG PAPER", "SERIOUS ART WORK"

After Ping Lian was able to draw freely, he usually drew randomly everyday either sketching on small paper or in his sketch book. He did not paint or draw "serious paintings" all the time. "Serious art works" or "serious painting" meant that Ping Lian was to use the bigger pieces of paper to draw specific subjects. I would simply call Ping Lian and say draw on "big paper". Ping Lian had a big drawing table which was used for only such works. When he was going to draw "serious art works", he would draw on the "big paper" (A2 or A1), that was placed on his art table. He drew a little each day on the big paper until he eventually completed his picture.

Sometimes he would start a picture on the big paper, and days would pass before he would go back to that particular artwork to draw some more or to complete it. Ping Lian would independently draw something that fascinated him or caught his interest. If Ping Lian showed initiative by starting a new drawing on the 'big paper' at the art table, that meant he already had a subject in mind to paint. Sometimes I would suggest for him to paint a "serious art work" of specific subject, which usually required a

Chapter 13: My Journey – USA and Dream To Go To Disney Land

lot of encouragement from me to him about the particular subject. I always used simple terms to communicate with him about drawing a "serious artwork". Ping Lian learned that whenever I said "draw on big paper" that meant he was not to randomly draw anything on the paper. If anything fascinated him and he wanted to randomly draw it, he would actually take one of his smaller sized (A4 or A3) sketch books and lay it on top of his "serious art work" so that he could still draw randomly when he felt like it.

Ping Lian would usually complete one "serious art work", and then only move on to another one. However sometime in the middle of 2009, Ping Lian decided he could paint as many serious paintings at the same time as wanted. He began to start painting two pieces of "big paper" at the same time. If he did not complete one serious drawing, but suddenly became interested in another subject, he would pull up another piece of big paper to start a new "serious art work". So on his big table, he now had two pieces of " big paper" side by side and he would draw on each intermittently.

The big paper for "serious art work" always remained on the big art table until Ping Lian completed the entire drawing/painting. Once he completed the drawing, he would place it at the "complete artworks plastic bag". A completed artwork sometimes took Ping Lian anywhere from one week to two months. It always depended upon his mood on any given day and how much time he spent on it daily. Ping Lian would not usually start another "serious art work" until finishing the one he had started. However, there were times that he started a painting on "big paper" and then apparently after some time he chose not to complete it. I created a "not complete plastic bag" for Ping Lian to keep his unfinished (uninterested) work in. Ping Lian has many half drawn artworks in this bag. I don't know the reason he chooses not to complete them, but I moved them to the "not complete ..." plastic bag. Creating a " not complete plastic bag" allowed Ping Lian to have the flexibility to put away the half drawn art works that he had at current time lost interest in continuing. It gave him the capability to move on to another new piece of "big paper". This was perfect for Ping Lian because sometimes he would continue to draw the same subject matter but other times he would start to draw something completely new.

Ping Lian usually draws and paints subjects that he is currently interested. His passion for each subject changes from time to time. It is not easy to influence him on what subjects to paint, unless at that time, his mood is on that particular subject. Otherwise it takes much encouragement to motivate him to by creating situations and providing incentives.

Most drawings on the " big paper" generally took Ping Lian a long time to complete. Once he began to watercolor the drawing he was very fast. He would simply dip and clean his brushes and know exactly what colors he wanted to use. He usually completed the entire water color painting in one session.

PING LIAN'S ARTISTIC JOURNEY IN THE USA

Ever since Ping Lian was able to trace, his initial favorite subjects were sunflowers, hippos, horses, the Statue of Liberty and Eiffel Tower. In order to fade him from tracing, I providedg Ping Lian with a thicker stock of tracing paper. He then began "drawing" (although still half traced and half drawn freehand). At this stage, he still loved to "draw" the Statue of liberty and the Eiffel Tower. He would "draw" them again and again, next to each other and on the same sheet of paper. He had a special interest in these two architectural structures and I often wondered why he would always depict them together, without yet knowing that his first overseas exhibition would be in New York.

Note: Ping Lian continued to half trace and half draw for quite some time. It took Ping Lian quite a long time to totally stop tracing and to draw freely. It did not happen until after we hid all of the tracing paper and any paper that was thin enough for him to use to trace.

Upon our return from visiting Australia in May 2005, Ping Lian was very motivated. He worked very hard producing many beautiful artworks in preparation for his New York exhibition in January 2006. He was so motivated to go to see Statute Of Liberty, that I used "going to visit the Statute Of Liberty" as a reward to motivate him to paint "serious art works" and draw on " big paper". I told him that the Statute of Liberty was in New York. I constantly asked him "Do you want to see Statute of liberty?" and he would reply "Yes!". I explained to him that he had an exhibition in New York....and if he did a good and beautiful painting/ drawing on "big paper", I would take him to sit on an airplane to go to New York. When he goes to New York for exhibition, then he can see the Statue of Liberty.

At the time Ping Lian did not know where New York was, but he just wanted to see the Statue of Liberty. He learned to relate New York to the Statue of Liberty. Ping Lian began to produce some beautiful paintings. He was so motivated to draw on " big paper" because he wanted to see Statue of Liberty which he has enjoyed tracing and drawing since he was very young. Whenever I noticed his "big paper" lying on the table for a few days untouched, I just needed to say… "Ping Lian want to go New York?"… and he would very quickly run to the table and start drawing again.

I believe that Ping Lian worked very hard drawing during this particular year (2005) because he was so motivated to go to see the Statute of Liberty. Having just recently returned from Australia it was easy for me to use sit in the plane in my description to him for going to New York. He was so cute during these times. Often times whenever I prompted him to go paint on "big paper" he often responded "Finish painting can go New York!" Although he did not know where New York was, he knew he could see the Statue of Liberty there!

GETTING TO NEW YORK

Ping Lian's USA exhibition was initially prompted when a Courier company expressed interest in supporting Ping Lian. That led me to discuss a plan and dream to have Ping Lian's artworks exhibited in the United States while he was still a child. I prayed for Ping Lian to be able to have his artwork shown anywhere in the US. I never thought his first opportunity would be in the amazing city of New York! This was definitely an extravagant blessing from God. It all happened when Dr Becker brought the subject up to Dr. Rosa. She was very impressed with Ping Lian's artwork and said she would be happy to explore the possibilities of making arrangements to have an exhibition for Ping Lian in New York. Shortly thereafter, she announced that we were to have an exhibition in New York during January 2006 at Henry Greg Gallery. The exhibition was titled "Don't 'dis' the Ability!"

Now what I needed was for the courier company to sponsor Ping Lian by funding the shipping of the framed artworks from Malaysia to the USA for the art exhibition. This initial courier company had suggested that I explore the options of Ping Lian having an art exhibition in the USA and said there should not be a problem for them to support Ping Lian in this way. However, maybe it just all happened to quickly for them. As I did not have a budget to incur this type of expense, I kept contacting this courier company who had actually sparked a US exhibition in my mind. The response was always "It won't be a problem" ; however I was never informed as to how I should proceed and no action was ever taken. As the exhibition date was only a few months away, I continued seeking out the *right person* to speak with in charge of *sponsorship* at the courier company hoping to get some direction. However, I still only got "It shouldn't be a problem" as a response. It was now October 2006 and I still hadn't heard back from the courier company. I was starting to worry about how I would get the framed artwork to New York. I started contacting many various transport and courier companies seeking sponsorship for Ping Lian. The responses were not positive. Now I was starting to panic! The exhibition is already scheduled for January 4, 2006 and I'm running out of time. One day I suddenly remembered a customer that had previously purchased some of Ping Lian's artwork. She loved and appreciated his art AND she worked for DHL Express! I immediately called her explaining my dilemma and asked if she could put me in touch with the person in charge at DHL. She directed me to write an email to her and said she would forward it to the right person. That person was Charles Brewer the DHL Country Manager in Malaysia. I was so touched and surprised by his immediate response. YES! DHL would sponsor Ping Lian by shipping the framed artworks from Malaysia to New York! We packed two huge wooden crates of framed art. Although Charles was later transferred to USA, Florida he continues to support Ping Lian from Florida. I'm very happy and very thankful to Charles for everything he has done and especially for how quickly he allowed this to happen.

Now that we had a set date for the exhibition, and a way to get all of the artworks there I needed to get the family to New York as well. With the help of Omar and Lynda, I wrote a proposal to Malaysia Airlines requesting sponsorship for the air travel. We were so blessed! Malaysia Airlines also said YES! Malaysia Airlines sponsored our tickets to New York! Ping Lian and the family would be able to go to New York to attend Ping Lian's first art exhibition in New York in person.

GOD- SENT ANGELS FOR PING LIAN

While working with Dr. Rosa, Dr. Becker and Dr. Treffert on getting ready for the art exhibition, I was again so touched by their support in helping Ping Lian and organizing the exhibition. This was a time in my life that I so strongly felt my Faith in God and I described them each as "God-Sent Angels."

Below is part of the email I sent to all three Doctors:

September 23, 2005 - Dear All, Whenever Ping Lian do well or achieve certain height, I always feel grateful. Definitely first I feel grateful to God and my daughters for their support and sacrifices made. Then my mind will flow to you all and my heart will feel touched again and again and many times I drop my tear. I am touched by a few of my friends from Malaysia, and you all (Dr. Treffert, Dr. Becker and Dr. Rosa) who assist, support, encourage and inspire me and Ping Lian. I always think that you all are God sent "Angels" to change Ping Lian's life, where by my life change too (a lot of hard work and sacrifice - but luckily I am happy). "YOU ARE SPECIAL"! I would say that all the good things happening and still to happen in Ping Lian's life will not be possible if without all of you - " Angels ". "...also my friends here in Malaysia Lynda and Omar; Catherine; Caroline; Gille; etc. "Thanks for all that you have done and continue to do for Ping Lian!"

Dr. Rosa was very helpful in assisting me in preparation for the art exhibition and our arrival to New York. In addition to making recommendations for the selection of art to be exhibited; organizing and curating the exhibition, she even helped us get accommodations in New York. She was able to obtain a sponsor in the USA for a hotel stay at the Marriott!

Another email:

October 15, 2005 – Dear Dr. Rosa " ....Thank you for what you do; A lot of hard work, is not easy and time consuming. I had put in so much hard works and time for Ping Lian; is because he is so talented and he is my SON. So, It is also my duty & responsibility too. So I need to sacrifice a lot and do a lot for him. BUT Dr. Rosa you are not Ping Lian's Mummy or family, and you have not even met Ping Lian yet. You are so Special and Super. I really do not know how to describe my feelings for what you do for him. I have run short of vocabulary and phrases to describe. I can only say, I feel so touched and I appreciate so much what you do ...."

PING LIAN'S ARTWORK STORY:

This was the first time that Ping Lian had worked on such a big canvas. Surprisingly he enjoyed it. I am so touched by a several people that have come into our lives and I describe them as "Angels sent by God to assist me and Ping Lian". These people have contributed to Ping Lian's achievements and have given me support and encouragement to go on with my "Dream". They are so special to Ping Lian and me but I had never described them as Angels. One day I suddenly felt that they are Angels sent by God and I shared this with my friend, Catherine. Just a few days later Ping Lian painted "05309 Ocean of Houses II". I saw an Angel in the ocean. Was this another *coincidence*? Or was God's hand at work? Did Ping Lian know what an angel is? I saw nothing but *miracles* occurring in my son's artistic journey.

05309 OCEAN OF HORSES II
Painted in 2005- 76x101cm Acrylic on canvas

In this picture, do you also see two romantic couples hugging? Do you see a deer in the painting? Do you see a boat? Human faces? Allow your imagination to tell you what else you see.

05008 US CAPITOL BUILDING I- PAINTED IN 2005

"05008 US Capitol Building I" was originally done by Ping Lian in black and white. That is how Ping Lian wanted it. One day, due to a breakdown in our communication to each other, Ping Lian misinterpreted something I said and he thought that I wanted him to color the art work, so when I was out with my friend for lunch, he painted the art work 05008. Upon my return, my domestic helper informed me that Ping Lian carried the art work to my sisters' house (two doors away). She said he was looking for me and he was crying. When he couldn't find me, he returned with the drawing, set up the art table and proceeded to paint over the black and white artwork. She said he sporadically ran up and down the stairs looking for me and crying out "Mummy" while completing this watercolor.

I returned from lunch to find Ping Lian having a tantrum. He was crying loudly. He had almost finished painting the picture. I tried to talk to him to understand him but I didn't really understand what he wanted or why he was so upset. We had not had such a poor communication breakdown in a long time. Once I received the feedback from my domestic helper, the reason for Ping Lian's behaviour became clearer to me. He intended for this drawing to be a black and white completed work. I think that he did not *want* to color this art work, but something I must have said or done at some point led him to think that I wanted him to paint it. Ping Lian was looking for me because my car was in the driveway. He did not realize that I was not home. I believe he was looking for me to tell me he did not want to color this art work. Believing that this was the cause for Ping Lian's tantrum, I proceeded to tell him…. "… is OK, very beautiful colour, the picture still very beautiful, Mummy like it. Finish painting this picture.." Ping Lian picked up the paint brush, and with a few more simple strokes on the sky said " Finished". I was stunned that while still sad and crying, Ping Lian *finished* and so beautifully. The black and white painting was one of the original artworks that Dr. Rosa had recommended be exhibited in New York. However, it was now a watercolor. I had to inform her of what happened! Her response was so calming.... "*....so long as 05008 BW Capitol Building is available! It is the most amazing black and white art I have ever seen in my life, anywhere. I am drawn to every single fine line of this piece. The detail is amazing!*"

Although I was saddened that Ping Lian colored his beautiful black and white "05008 US Capitol Building I", and now there was no original, I felt lucky I had previously already taken the original for a photo session before it was painted. So, fortunately, we do have an excellent US Capitol black and white in print.

05008 B&W
US CAPITOL BUILDING I

05008
US CAPITOL BUILDING I

06019 US CAPITOL BUILDING V -
PAINTED IN 2006

It took a while for me to appreciate the new color version of "05008 US Capitol Building I", probably because I knew of Ping Lian's initial intention to keep it black and white. Still, even colored, it is a masterpiece. I later asked Ping Lian to draw one more US Capitol building for mummy in black and white, and he did. He painted "05011 Capitol Building II" and "06019 US Capitol Building V".

"DON'T 'DIS' THE ABILITY" ART EXHIBITION

On January 9th, 2006, we arrived at LaGuardia airport in New York! This was our first time overseas to the USA and our first meeting with Dr. Rosa C. Martinez. Her husband (Michael) had booked a limousine to pick us up from the airport. It was also our first time in a limousine. Sherlyn, Cher, Ping Lian, my nephew Daowen and I walked out to see a sign that read "YEAK" being held up high. We were all so happy and excited. We are so grateful to Mr. Michael Martinez for his efforts and his kind heart for us.

We kept telling Ping Lian, "Hooray!! We are in New York now!" as we proceeded to the limo. "We are in New York! We will see the Statue of Liberty!"

This was always Ping Lian's dream – to see the Statute of Liberty. I was overcome with joy that His Dream would very soon come true. Thoughts of how this could be happening raced quickly through my mind.... "New York at such young age. This is real...My son is an artist...This is proof..... Oh! Our Dream for Ping Lian to be an Artist has come true...... He is 12 years old and an artist in New York! ....Oh...!"

With the support of Malaysia Airlines, DHL and The Children's Charitable Foundation[29] we had made it to the United States of America!

---

29 Founded in the year 2003, the Children's Charitable Foundation was started by Mark Morand, the Executive Director of the foundation.

Chapter 13: My Journey – USA and Dream To Go To Disney Land 325

I never dreamed this would all happen so fast. In 2002, Ping Lian was still tracing. In 2003 I set a vision (My Dream) for Ping Lian to hopefully be an Artist in five, ten or even fifteen years. It is only 2006, he is twelve years old and he has an art exhibition in New York. We just couldn't believe it!!...but here we were sitting in a limousine, driving from the air port to the New York City! Ping Lian's excitement was crazy! He touched everything in the limo. He kept playing with the windows and couldn't stay still! There were no words to describe the Joy and thankfulness we felt for our God sent special "Angels" that made this "miracle" happen.

We are very thankful to Dr. Rosa together with the Children's Charitable Foundation who sponsored our stay at the Marriott Hotel. I admire Dr. Rosa's passion, energy, spirit and the heart she has for my family. Since then, she has become someone very special in Ping Lian's Artistic Journey and a special person in my life too.

Dr. Rosa was taking care of Ping Lian's art work and curating exhibitions for his art in New York. She always provided me with information, advice and encouragement. Actually, it was Dr. Rosa who encouraged me to write this book and share Ping Lian's story. She said his story will inspire many! Her dedication and passion are reflected below:

November 16, 2008

Dear Dr Rosa -"I am touched by your effort and concern... I know you are very busy, especially with economy situation like this....You make me love you more and more and grateful to you more and more. You are really so special to Ping Lian. Sometimes I think how come on earth we can meet good people like you? Even though you are so far away, I feel like giving you a hug now. Frankly without your help, guidance, support and encouragement all this while, I or Ping Lian would not go this far..."

Reply from Dr. Rosa:

"..... When I began the first Jewish School for kids with autism in 1998, I learned a word "bashert"[30]. This means destiny. Ping Lian's "journey" is my "bashert"..."

The passion with which Dr. Rosa and Dr. Laurence Becker together with the owner of Henry Gregg Gallery[31] (Andre) collaborated to put on the "Don't 'dis' the ability" exhibition was evident. They were each so emotionally invested in the mission of creating awareness of the abilities of individuals on the spectrum.

The discussions I had with Andre were always additionally inspiring. I learned so much from him and his words regarding Ping Lian were so encouraging. Andre made me feel extremely confident in knowing that this was just the beginning of fulfilment regarding My Dream for Ping Lian. I will never forget the wonderful and long discussions that I had with him. One particular evening he spent several hours talking, guiding, encouraging and motivating me as he spoke of Ping Lian's "exceptional" talents. That evening's discussion held a special place in my heart for Andre, and also hugely influenced the direction and strategies that I later took in moving forward in Ping Lian's Artistic Journey.

This New York exhibition had indirectly changed so much of Ping Lian's and my life. Both, from the experiences gained and the lessons learn from Andre, Dr Becker and Dr. Rosa. Upon returning to Sydney from New York, I focused on what could be next for Ping Lian. How should I upgrade his Dream? How should I set a New Dream and New Hopes for Ping Lian?

---

30   Bashert. Bashert (or Beshert), (Yiddish: באַשערט), is a Yiddish word that means "destiny".
31   The Henry Gregg Gallery is an art gallery owned by Henry M. Reed in the heart of Dumbo which is in Brooklyn, New York.

COOPER UNION, NEW YORK EXHIBITION

"Don't 'dis' the ability" was an art exhibition tour. The original exhibition included four artists on the autism spectrum. The exhibition was held at the Henry Gregg Gallery from January 11th – February 4th, 2006. The exhibition was then moved to Cooper Union[32], also in New York. My family and I were not able to stay in New York for the next exhibition. Dr. Rosa enlisted the help of her family to move the show. Her husband, her mother-in-law, her sister in-law, her nieces and her daughters all helped to move the show to this new location. Knowing full well how much work this actually entails, because I have done it myself for my son; when I read her e-mail telling me it was done, I was so touched. Tears streamed down my face. There were many times I had to carefully wrap, transport, carry and hang many of these artworks that were wood framed and with heavy glass. This was by no means an easy task. It required not only strength, but also love and care. I have done it for my son, because he is my son. I am his mother and I would do anything it takes to succeed with him. Yet, this was something that Dr. Rosa and her wonderful family took on. I was so touched by their passion.

NEW YORK 2006

While in New York Cher, Sherlyn and Daowen spent much time sightseeing, shopping and just walking around the City. Ping Lian and I of course spent most of our time at the gallery. Ping Lian has always enjoyed walking around with his sisters. I actually worried for a while about Ping Lian feeling left

---

32 Founded by inventor, industrialist and philanthropist Peter Cooper in 1859, The Cooper Union for the Advancement of Science and Art offers education in art, architecture and engineering, as well as courses in the humanities and social sciences.

out and unhappy that he could not join them daily in their walks while in New York. My main concern was that he would start thinking that being an artist or drawing is not good, because he cannot go out with his sisters but must instead stay at the gallery. Remember, people with autism often have drastic or extreme perceptions of what is happening. Luckily, none of these issues arose and there was no need for my concerns in this area. Ping Lian enjoyed going to the gallery. He actually preferred it, than to going walking with his sisters and cousin. His behaviour once again amazed me. It showed me how much he really loved his art and drawing. Going out with his sisters at this point was secondary. Going out was always the most potent motivator and reinforcer for him in the days when he was being given table drills and rewarded for a job well done.

As a matter of fact, normally when we are at home and even during the holiday celebrations at my sister's house, Ping Lian would always show disappointment when he was not included to "go out" with his sisters. Cher and Sherlyn would plan to go out with their cousin whom they did not see very often. If Ping Lian was not invited to join them he would start "Go, go, go!" to let us know that he wanted to go with them. Sometimes he would just follow them out and take a seat in the car. The disappointment on his face whenever he was asked to stay behind, or get out of the car was pretty heartbreaking. His sisters did need to be able to have sometimes without him. He was not easy to watch and they also needed their occasional freedoms to have worry free fun. Although they often included Ping in, it was not and could not be always.

Back in New York, one morning I left the hotel earlier than usual with Ping Lian intending to go to a cafe that was very near the gallery to have some breakfast. Ping Lian insisted we go to the Gallery. It was too early and the Gallery wasn't even open yet. We had not yet eaten any breakfast but Ping Lian insisted on waiting outside the gallery. It took me quite some time to manage to convince him that there was no point waiting outside of

Chapter 13: My Journey – USA and Dream To Go To Disney Land

the gallery and that we must eat breakfast first then come back to the gallery. I must say, I was very impressed with his spirit. Wow! He would even forego "food" to get to the Gallery! Food has always been a primary reinforcer for him. Going Out and Food have always been his greatest pleasures....now it's "going to the Gallery"! On most days, Ping Lian usually planted himself right in the middle of the gallery floor and would start drawing the minute we arrived. I am not very sure why he loved going to the gallery so much. Perhaps he feels that the gallery is a place where he belongs, or where he feels proud and accepted. Perhaps the gallery is simply a place that he sees as the most conducive environment for drawing. What I do know for sure, is that he loved being there!

"06102 KUALA LUMPUR TWIN TOWERS"
Ping Lian painted this while in New York in 2006.

During the exhibition Ping Lian was very inspired to draw. He drew some of the most beautiful pictures while lounging at the gallery or at the Marriott hotel. Below is one of the works that he produced. He was also very excited when he finally visited the Statute of Liberty. Ping Lian drew many drawings of the Statue of Liberty while we were in New York, and he continued to draw even more when we returned to Sydney.

06020 STATUE OF LIBERTY   06024 STATUE OF LIBERTY

While in New York, Focus Productions from UK filmed Ping Lian at his exhibition in the Henry Gregg Gallery for a documentary. The program was to be a one hour documentary titled "*Painting the Mind*", for Channel 4. It also aired on Four Corners, ABC TV Australia in April 2007, and in

Chapter 13: My Journey – USA and Dream To Go To Disney Land

Scandinavia. Painting The Mind examined the origins of art and creativity in the brain. The film featured two artists who became passionate painters following a stroke, and it also featured " the extraordinary child savant artist Ping Lian and the amazing memory artist Franco Magnani."

Due to the tight schedule of the Focus Production film crew they needed to film Ping Lian immediately. We had only been in NY one night, having arrived late in the evening and we were all very concerned that Ping Lian would be too tired, or in a bad mood so soon after a twenty hour flight from Malaysia to NY. We were also concerned Ping Lian may even have jet lag and throw a tantrum when asked to paint for filming. To all of our surprise, Ping Lian was very cooperative as well as motivated to draw for the film crew. He actually painted from morning through evening so that Focus Productions crew members could film him. Even after we returned from dinner, the film crew outwardly expressed their amazement that Ping Lian still wanted to continue drawing! I saw Ping Lian really start to enjoy all of this attention. He seemed to understand that he was being appreciated. He seemed to understand that he was important!

The Focus Production film crew visited the Henry Gregg Gallery the day prior to our arrival and viewed all of Ping Lian's art works being exhibited. The next evening, when we arrived in New York they returned to the Gallery and I showed them a few more of Ping Lian's artworks that I had hand carried from Malaysia. A film crew member said "Your son's art work is amazing, I am sure you will not have come to New York only once, …you are going to be here again soon." Boy was I happy. Such encouraging words. Just minutes later, I had already begun pondering "How will that happen?" " Would it be possible? We had just arrived a day ago, and here I was already trying to figure out the "How's and When's and Why's, etc. Of another exhibition for Ping Lian here in New York! The confidence I was given was so strong and so empowering. I wondered….this art show has involved so many people and it has taken so much effort, energy and time on the part of others (not just myself) to arrange. Soon we must return to the USA for another exhibition, but who will organize it? Even if someone does arrange it, the financial limitations will not allow us to come to New York again or to ship the artworks here again.

My questions were soon answered.... as it appeared to me that God had his own plan. A few days before we were to fly back to Malaysia, Dr. Rosa said that she would be happy to store the art works with her here in New York and continue to exhibit and share Ping Lian's talent and story in the United States. DHL's support included transporting the artwork from Malaysia to New York and back from New York to Malaysia. However understanding that returning to New York if the opportunity presented itself again in the near future would not be a viable option for me and Ping Lian, I decided not to ship the art works back and instead to give them a life here in New York. Dr. Rosa is a wonderful lady and we later came to realize that she was not an ordinary "Angel" that God sent to Ping Lian, but one of the "Special Angels" God send to Ping Lian. Ping Lian has been so blessed.

Note: During our brief stay here in New York in 2006, we came to know each other very well. As she (Dr Rosa) learned more about Ping Lian and his story, later she recommended I write a book about his journey to share with the world. She said it was a very "unique" story, yet a very inspiring one that should be shared for the benefit of others.

As time passed Dr. Rosa remained very involved in Ping Lian's Artistic Journey. Through her support, Ping Lian has been featured in various exhibitions throughout the United States, and he has also been profiled in numerous publications, text books and radio….. And now, you are reading "our book". Isn't it amazing?

STORY OF PING LIAN'S DRAWING AND HIS DREAM TO GO TO DISNEYLAND

In 2006, upon returning from the United States to Malaysia, I had to focus on our upcoming move to Australia. Several months after our New York exhibition trip, we uprooted to Sydney, Australia in May 2006. The details are chronicled in the next chapter. Soon after our arrival to Sydney, Ping Lian kept asking me to take him to Disneyland, Sea World and Dreamworld. He refers to the Sea World and Dreamworld Theme Park that are located in the Australia, Gold Coast. His desire to go these placesare depicted in some of his s paintings. Although Ping Lian had always enjoyed drawing pictures of Disneyland characters, especially the characters in Toy Story Buzz Light-year, Woody….now he was requesting "Go Disneyland" on a regular basis. I think the two almost back to back plane trips (Australia and then USA) that we had just taken clicked the thought in his head and now he wanted to go to Disneyland! Possibly the resulting trip to see the Statue of Liberty based on his artwork gave him a more complex understanding of expectations. He may have made the connection that his hard work can pay off. Perhaps he learned that he can have a dream and it can come true. Perhaps he had set a goal to work hard in order to get to Disneyland and see the characters. I still never know exactly what my son is thinking or feeling, but I do know that he has learned some very valuable lessons in his adventures overseas and that he continues to work hard for such great rewards.

Oct 2006 written to Dr. Rosa:

"……… Ping Lian had drawn and painted many beautiful pictures in 2005 because he was motivated to go to New York for an exhibition. Because I used visit Statue Of Liberty as a reward

> to motivate him to paint 'serious' art works" on 'big paper'. Amazingly he is so motivated to draw and paint because he wanted to see Statute of Liberty so much, which he always loved to trace and draw since he was young. He is so happy that he finally had the chance to see it. He still continues to draw many beautiful Statute of Liberty pictures even after we come back from New York."

For the next few months, Ping Lian was continually asking 'Do drawing can go Disneyland??? ". Whenever he did a painting and one of us (Cher, Sherlyn or I) said it was good or beautiful, he quickly asked "Go Disneyland???" He was so cute!

Even whenever I asked him to go draw on a "big paper", he quickly added "Do drawing can go Disneyland???". I guess I taught him well! Unfortunately, the reality was I could not afford to take him to Disneyland or anyplace overseas even though he created an amazing artwork! I began to reply " Ok, you do good panting or drawing we can go Disneyland, but not now! One Day! OK?" At times he was obviously not happy with my answer. I'm sure he was expecting my answer to be "OK yes! Let's go now". Each time I looked at his disappointed face, I felt sorry and I usually added a few extra little words of hope, like, "One Day! Definitely!" Sometimes he would just run off and put his completed art work in the correct place.

It appeared as if Ping Lian was becoming increasingly disappointed every time I responded "One day"; "Not now", etc. His facial expression and his body language indicated to me that he was not so happy any more. I sensed he may be starting to wonder "Why not now? Is my art work not good enough?" I did not know for sure if my son could think in this complex way, but I did not want him to ever feel that his work was not good. I decided, that whether he understood or not I would take the time to explain to him the reasons we could not go now. I talked to him about

Chapter 13: My Journey – USA and Dream To Go To Disney Land

money, costs and our financial situation. "I do not have enough money to take you to Disneyland. We can sell this beautiful drawing to buy air tickets for you to go to Disneyland. For now we cannot sell and we do not have money for the plane."

Deep inside I knew that one day I would definitely be taking him to Disneyland. Many times I had actually intended to teach him to write down his dream – "Go to Disneyland - One day!" ...but as I was always busy with something, I procrastinated on this thought and never did get him to write it. In any case I had a very strong feeling that the day would be soon. I didn't know how or when, but there was a specific moment of a particular day that when I said "Yes! We will go Disneyland, One Day; just wait for that One Day! OK!" that I felt it was no longer a dream. The words flowed from my mouth as a truth soon to be a reality. Next moment I immediately asked myself "How could it be?". We hadn't even settled down in Sydney yet and we have such a limited budget. I felt that I must be going crazy with desperation. A few months later in September I found myself also thanking God for what seemed to be a gift to *sense* things. Yes! Ping Lian's Dream to go Disneyland came true in September 2007.

The comments by the film crew from Focus Productions that we would be returning to the United States came true! Once more, so fast so unbelievable! At the start of February 2007 I was contacted by Dr. Treffert to inform me he was arranging an art exhibition for September of 2007. *"Windows of Genius: Artworks of the Prodigious Savant"* was to be held at the Windhover Center for the Arts in Wisconsin, USA. I immediately told Dr Treffert that I would do my best to come for the exhibition. I always wanted to actually meet him and for him to meet Ping Lian. Dr. Treffert explained that the exhibition would "provides a very rare opportunity to see paintings, drawings, sculptures and other art forms of various prodigious savants displayed in a single show." We were honored that Ping Lian's artwork would be a part of the Prodigious Savant Art exhibition.

April 16, 2007 to Dr. Treffert:

"…. Thank you for your email. I will try my best to come to Wisconsin for the exhibition. I always wanted to meet you, so this art exhibition will be the best opportunity.

… I am in the process of finishing the first three chapters of Ping Lian's book. Many times while I am writing, I keep on crying. I train myself to be strong and to be happy, but frankly I had been locking part of my feelings and my emotions for many years. I seldom cry. But while writing about initial part of life of Ping Lian and the time his Daddy passed away, my tears just keep dropping and sometimes I really cry up. I wonder how I got through those times. If you ask me now, I would say I am not strong enough to go through all this. I guess due to I need to go backward (re-visit) my emotions in order to write down what happened in the past. I feel……emotional and vulnerable. May be that is the reason I am so sad. Also with my writing I am feeling so sad again …I feel so sorry for Ping Lian at that time - I just feel that he is such a poor boy. Writing and thinking back on how difficult those times were, has led me to think of your support, so I would like to share with you the following:

Do you know why I always say Thank you to you, very grateful to you and feel so much of your support? The time when I just get to know you, that is the time my husband just pass away. I am at the angry stage, I feel very unfair and also I am wondering how I go on with "I Am a Dreamer" without my husband's support.. I am also very worry for Ping Lian had no father to support. Too much to describe state of my mind at that time…. But one thing I know is that I must be strong to maintain a happy family and develop and nurture Ping Lian's talents. How good and how strong can I

Chapter 13: My Journey – USA and Dream To Go To Disney Land

be? I am not sure. I am scared that I am not strong enough. I just know that I need to train my mind to lock away certain negative thoughts....

At that time Ping Lian's artistic skills progressed at a very fast speed and I just learned about 'savant'. I am happy but I also have fear. Fear that Ping Lian may lose his talents, like what I had read about savants losing their skills. I am so grateful that you were always there to provide me info, advice, knowledge, encouragement and praise. You always praised me, saying I was strong, and that made me think that I was. You were always willing to read my long emails and always responded to it fast. The way you responded....... comforted me a lot and encouraged me greatly at that phase of my life. I remember I told my daughter that, Dr Treffert is so good, he reply my email so fast and is always so motivating, informative and full of impact. My daughter was also amazed. We were thinking that a person of your position, to give us such kind attention makes us feel honoured...it makes me feel significant. Also this make us feel more confident and makes me have more confidence in Ping Lian's works too. I do not know if you understand what I mean to say, but in short, your overall support to us during those times was very special..

I tell myself that Ping Lian and I must meet this wonderful man one day to say thank you to him personally. But I always wondered when!! And happy that you have now provided that opportunity by hosting the exhibition. I am so happy. I also think if God had sent you to give me and Ping Lian support at the worse period of my life, then I'm sure God will arrange us to meet. God had already created so many "coincidences" for Ping Lian, so such a good opportunity, we sure would not miss it.....

Also thanks to you for bringing Dr. Becker, followed by

Dr. Rosa into Ping Lian's and my life. I am looking forward to see you...

April 17, 2007 – Dr. Treffert replied:

Dear Sarah Lee,

I am glad my comments and support were of some help during your difficult times. The good news is that "time is a pretty good therapist too". I have been continually impressed, and renewed, by the resiliency of the human spirit in the midst of turmoil, and you are a good example of that resiliency, rebound and determination. And Ping Lian, and the rest of your family, are its beneficiaries.

Once again, Malaysia Airlines extended their support to my family by sponsoring the air tickets to fly from Sydney to New York (to meet with Dr. Rosa) and then later from NYC to Wisconsin enabling Ping Lian to attend the "Windows of Genius: Artwork of Prodigious Savant" exhibition. Ping Lian was also blessed to have the support of Shell Malaysia to sponsor him for the trip expenses to USA for this exhibition. I will forever be so grateful to these organizations for their generous support of Ping Lian...

Shell Malaysia used Ping Lian's art works for their 2007 Calendar and also bought one of Ping Lian's original art work. At the beginning of 2007, The Management Team of Shell Malaysia had made arrangements to meet me and Ping Lian. At the meeting they asked "What can we do to support Ping Lian?" At that time I did not have a response, I was unsure how they could help in Ping Lian's journey. However, many weeks later when the opportunity to go to Wisconsin, USA for an exhibition came up, the answer was clear. I approached Shell and explained to them that Ping

Lian has been given this opportunity to meet Dr. Treffert in person and to participate in this wonderful exhibition "Windows of Genius". Without any delay, Shell responded, "Yes"!

As I was making all the necessary arrangements for our trip to the USA for the exhibition, I still had no intention of taking Ping Lian to the Disneyland as I thought it was too costly. I didn't want to use the money I had budgeted and reserved for my daughters' education. However, one morning I completely changed my mind. I figured we already had air tickets to the United States; we could spend a few more days and go to Disneyland. I would only have to pay for the tour cost and the additional domestic flight. Ping Lian worked so hard to be an "outstanding artist" and he deserved this trip. We would make his dream come true and visit Disneyland.

I managed to get a very reasonably priced tour that started from Chinatown in New York (with four persons sharing the same room), and included a seven day East Coast Tour (The Statute of Liberty, the Capitol Building in Washington, D. C, Niagara Falls, etc.); and a 7 Day Package, at Orlando, Florida. The total cost for 4 people for two packages was approximately US$ 4,000. The total included accommodations, transportation and entry to the Disneyland theme parks.

Ping Lian's favorite buildings were the Kuala Lumpur Twin Towers (Malaysia); The Sydney Opera House and Harbour Bridge (Australia); the Eiffel Tower (France) and the Statue of Liberty and US Capitol Building in the United States. He had drawn several pieces of the US Capitol Building from pictures he saw in books and postcards. He had not seen the actual building yet. He also loved waterfalls and the water fountains, big or small, indoor or outdoor. Ever since he was a very young child and before he could even draw, he was always mesmerized watching water flow from a fountain. I knew he would love seeing Niagara Falls as well as the US Capitol Building. I thought of this as not only a deserving wonderful leisure trip, but also as an "Educational Tour". It could be a learning experience through which Ping Lian's skill of painting architectural structures and landscapes from around the world could further develop.

    I was thrilled when my third sister (Swee Eng) and my brother in-law (Hiang Kian) said they would be willing to travel with us to the USA. They would be so helpful to me in caring for Ping Lian. Frankly, at this stage I was still 'scared' to travel alone with Ping Lian. I reflected back for a moment to that day in September of 2006 when Ping Lian held his painting in front of me and said "Do drawing go Disneyland", and I once again thanked God for my realizing the "Power of the Dream" and God's hand at work again. I also thanked Malaysia Airlines and Shell Malaysia for indirectly contributing to help Ping Lian's Dream come true to visit Disneyland and for making such a difference in his life.

Note: I would like to especially say thank you to Tan Sri Dr. Mohamed Murni, who is the Chairman of Malaysia Airlines, and his team of staff for appreciating Ping Lian's talent and for their continuous support of him.

    I also would like to thank all of the support provided to Ping Lian for the Wisconsin exhibition by DHL (US) and Crown Relocations (New York).

    Our trip was absolutely amazing! The exhibition was fantastic! Ping Lian gained so much attention from the attending guests and from the local media. He also attained additional international media from this unbelievable event. *EBS was there to film Ping Lian for a documentary titled "Uncovering the Secret of Childhood". The program* featured an interview with Ping Lian during the *"Windows of Genius: Artworks of the Prodigious Savant"* art exhibition at Wisconsin USA with Dr. Darold Treffert. Also there, was a reporter from a German publication who published an interview and wrote a story about Ping Lian.

    While attending the exhibition I had long discussions with Dr. Treffert and Dr. Rosa, whenever we had such opportunities... The encouragement and support for Ping Lian seemed as phenomenal as the course of events. Even the staff and management at the Windhover Center for the Arts, where the exhibition was held were incredibly supportive. Ping Lian and I both learned so much from this exhibition and the trip in general. I knew that my son was an "Outstanding Artist." Ping Lian was not only a savant[33], he was a prodigious savant![34]. Based on this new found information I set out to consider an even more challenging Dream for my prodigious son. December 31, 2007 was when I drafted the New Dream.

---

33   "Savant Syndrome is a rare but remarkable condition in which persons with developmental disabilities, including but not limited to autistic disorder, have some spectacular "islands of genius" that stand in marked, jarring contrast to overall limitations. Skills most often exist in art, music, calendar calculating, lightning calculating and mechanical or spatial abilities. Whatever the special skill, it is always associated with massive memory; a memory exceedingly deep but very narrow within the area of the special skill." (Treffert, 2006).

34   A *prodigious savant* is someone whose skill level would qualify him or her as a 'prodigy,' or exceptional talent, even in the absence of a cognitive disability. "Savant skills occur on a spectrum of ability ranging from *splinter skills* (such as memorizing license plates, sports trivia, birthdays etc.) to *talented* (skills such as music or art that are quite conspicuous over against overall limitations) to *prodigious* (skills so remarkable that they would be termed at a 'prodigy' or 'genius' level if present in a non-disabled person). The prodigious savant represents a very high threshold group and there are probably less than 100 such known persons living worldwide at the present time. All the above is discussed in more detail on the savant syndrome web site at www.savantsyndrome.com and in *Extraordinary People: Understanding Savant Syndrome* (Treffert, 2006).

"WINDOWS OF GENIUS: ARTWORKS OF THE PRODIGIOUS SAVANT"

07001 US CAPITOL BUILDING VI

Ping Lian painted this art work on the opening night of *"Windows of Genius: Artworks of Prodigious Savant"* art exhibition. He painted from memory without referring to any photos. Ping Lian loved seeing the actual US Capitol Building during our visit to Washington DC.

July 7, 2007 was the official opening of the *"Windows of Genius: Artworks of the Prodigious Savant"* art exhibition at Wisconsin USA. *Ping Lian painted 07001 US Capitol Building VI and Flowers in front of a live audience. He was so proud of himself and thoroughly enjoyed the attention of the media crews and the local reporters taking photos of him as he painted.*

DRAWINGS DISNEY LAND CHARACTERS - 2007

PAINTING AIRPLANE WITH MS PAINT

As I constantly was talking to Ping Lian about Malaysia Airlines, reminding him that Malaysia Airlines likes his drawings and that is why they gave him air tickets to go to see New York, the Statue of Liberty and Disneyland he developed an interest to occasionally draw a picture of the aircraft. Sometimes Ping Lian enjoyed playing around with the computer program Microsoft Paintbrush. One night, on July 30th, 2008 Ping Lian very busy on the computer for a very long time. He became upset when his sister called him to get off of the computer. As I approached him to see what he was doing I was amazed to see what he had created. Using the paint program he painted a Malaysia Airlines plane. The detail was amazing and most exciting to me was that he did this of his own initiative. Ping Lian had been using the computer paint program for the past two years, but never before did he create anything so completely detailed. He usually only paint very simple pictures, like Road Signs. I began wondering, what other talents my son might have. I remembered that some years earlier Ping Lian had created some beautifully detailed figures of 5 cartoon characters with Play-doh. As I started to feel guilty about not nurturing this possible talent, I quickly put the question of "What other talent might my son possess?"... out of my mind. Anyway, I tell myself that I am not a super woman! I had no more time to nurture his other talent.

MORE HAPPENINGS IN THE USA

Later with the support of Dr. Rosa Martinez, and Dr. Laurence A. Becker, Ping Lian continued having art shows in the USA. These included several very prominent venues such as The United Nations World Autism Awareness Inaugural Exhibition in 2008, The prestigious Salmagundi Art Club and even Carnegie Hall in 2010 and 2011 respectively. Also, in 2008, Dr. Martinez submitted a nomination for Ping Lian to the Australian 2008 National Disability Awards. Ping Lian was selected as the finalist for the Young Community Contribution Award.

Below is an excerpt of the biography written about Ping Lian:

> " …..Ping Lian's works were also recently featured at The United Nations in recognition of the inaugural World Autism Awareness Day (WAAD) April 2, 2008. His artwork aided to expand public understanding of the diversity of people with disability or on the autism spectrum while educating the world about the abilities and opportunities to encourage advancement beyond individual challenges. He has encouraged people with disabilities to succeed beyond their perceived limitations…… Ping Lian's contribution as a participating artist was an extension of the message to 'Train the Talent' and to foster independence."

UPDATE 2015

In 2010 and 2011, Ping Lian was featured in a few books that were published in the USA – to name a few below:
'Islands of Genius' by Dr. Darold Treffert, "Artism: The Art of Autism" and also one chapter of the book "Adventures in Autism" by the master

Chapter 13: My Journey – USA and Dream To Go To Disney Land

of motivation, Peter A. LaPorta (USA). One of my biggest surprises was, Ping Lian's story is featured in one chapter at 'Real Reading 3 – An English textbook published by PEARSON Longman. In this chapter, his story is used for reading purposes, teaching vocabulary skills, and building comprehension. More amazingly, Ping Lian's chapter was featured in the "Born Special Unit" that also featured a picture of young Mozart, and photos of John McEnroe and Shirley Temple.

Also in 2011 Ping Lian was featured in the book by EBS published in Korea, titled 'Knowledge', which also included the Real Rain Man (Kim Peek), Albert Einstein, Abraham Lincoln, Warren Edward Buffett, William H. Gate, Michael Schumacher etc

I cant' believe all this has happened in Ping Lian's life to this point. Many of my friends ask how he can be in so many books at such a young age and how can he get to be featured in the same book as such prominent and famous individuals. I do not know how to answer them. The feeling is "Can this be real?" I have a hard time believing it all myself, but it is truly real… and I am keeping many copies of these books. I can't explain all these good happenings, except to understand that they are truly "blessings" that have occurred so fast and so soon…. so I can only explain by giving credit to God, and saying that God's hand is at work and He has made it happen!! With God all thing are possible!! I am very grateful.

In 2014, Dr. Rosa curated a two month long art exhibition of Ping Lian's Architectural Landscapes artworks at Port Authority, New York City. She coined his work as "Architectural Impressions". The term very accurately describes Ping Lian's artworks. In 2016 Ping Lian's art made it into the New York Chelsea Art District art scene!

We are now in 2016, so expect more details about Ping Lian Yeak and his future Artistic Journey on his website, while anticipating the second book in his amazing journey.

CHAPTER 14
My Journey – Uprooted To Sydney, Australia

Min Seng had always planned and hoped to one day move back to Australia. He even purchased a good winter feather blanket which he kept for many years in the cabinet, waiting for the day we might move back again. After he passed away in Feb 2004, I never had that thought anymore and I doubted that I would ever make that move. As a widow with three children, including one autistic boy it seemed an impossible hardship. The thought of uprooting my family to a strange new place, to start all over again terrified me. Here in Malaysia I have so many friends and relatives. I am the second youngest of all of my sisters and brothers. My life is so used to always being surrounded by my many elder brothers and sisters, and in-laws. I would definitely miss my family so much. I had a good well-established career and business contacts. After Min Seng's passing, I no longer considered the move to Australia part of our life plan. With so much to handle, including limited finances, I continued busily with my day to day life coping with my daughters Cher and Sherlyn, my son Ping Lian AND his art journey. All our finances from now on into the future would be my sole responsibility. Thus, the thought of moving to Australia was most likely, the last thing on my mind. Sometime in March 2005 though, after my mother-in-law passed away, several occasions arose where everyday discussions with different people prompted me to seriously start thinking about the move again. The more I thought about it, the more I convinced myself that a move to Australia would be the best thing for my kids. In May 2015, I finally made the decision to move to Sydney. Today, when I think back upon these time, I amaze myself. What a daring and brave life changing Decision and Action I took, and without much hesitation. I think I can only give credit to God again for his New Good Plan for me and my family. He has lead me and given me the wisdom and strength to *"Make a Fast Decision"*, and to *"Take Action Immediately"* to move to Sydney.

We moved to Sydney, Australia in May of 2006. We were to start a new life here without any friends or relatives. In the past I had visited Sydney twice. In the year 2000 I went to Sydney for three days and in the year May 2005, I went for seven days for the holidays and also to survey the locations in preparation for deciding which part of Australia we might like to move back to. After moving to Sydney, I had made some friends at the local Church. With their support and the grace of God we adapted fairly smoothly to our new location. I still look back at this enormous undertaking of my decision to uproot my family and the fact that I actually did it! I am amazed with my own adventurous spirit.

"WHAT IS NEXT" – "WHERE AND HOW"

Email to Dr. Treffert:

February 2, 2005

Dear Dr. Treffert

Chapter 14: My Journey – Uprooted To Sydney, Australia

Thank you so much of your care & concern. Me, my daughters and my family (I have 9 brothers and sisters) are definitely very proud of Ping Lian's progress both in term of his personal development and his abilities in art.

Ping Lian is also definitely very proud of himself and his art work. His ability in art has given him so much of confidence and self esteem. Also we are very grateful to the support from the community centers and the church here. They focus so much on his abilities and not on disability. Ping Lian enjoys when people admire and praise his art work. He does understand this. The past few months he has improved so much not only in terms of art but also other aspects of his life. He has started having his own preferences and has started requesting more often what he wants. He requested to buy his favorite CD and asked me to buy it for him (as a reward for doing a good job). So much progress to list down. He is even getting more mature and helps me a lot since he lost his grandmother.

The morning I saw his profile included on the Savant Profile at your Savant Syndrome website, I felt overjoyed. When I first opened the site, he was still asleep, beside me. It is his achievement; we do all this together for him. I would like to share this achievement with him as like with my daughters (I am a person who is always thinking very fast and very far. So many thoughts coming in to my mind at that moment). I would like to reward him. I would like to explain to him that morning what was happening and to share with him my joy. I would like to tell him that the world now can view and appreciate his art and his story through Savant Syndrome website and his own website. I would like to tell him who Dr. Treffert is, as I had told my daughters about you and how your support and care for him. I also would like to tell him about

Dr. Treffert's passion in talented people….and so on…. But he does not even understand what is a website at this stage……Also at this stage, he does not understand what is the implication of having his own website and his profile listed in the Savant Profile. So at this moment, suddenly I feel the sadness set in immediately as I was also enjoying his progress and achievements. (This type of mixed feeling occurs in many others occasion in the past). In my heart I said "poor boy, I feel so sorry that, you do not know what is happening at this moment". "You are such a brilliant boy in art, people are enjoying and appreciating your art work so much, do you know that?" … " The other day, The Star and News Strait Times reporters came by. They like your art works so much. They are writing about you. Do you understand what it is all about? How do you feel about that?" Every time he appears on the news paper, I always share with him, and tell him that he is so good in drawing that he is in the news paper. He does seem happy and look contented. At the same time I also have feelings of "So, after all these achievement… What is Next..???t" ……… The questions in my mind go on and on and my tears also start dropping. I like to share so much with him, he is such a wonderful and loveable boy, he is so cute…….If you meet him, you will be sure to like him too, …he likes to hug and be close to people who care for him… and he can read the body language of others very well……..

I do focus very much on his abilities but I do understand that he has his own limitations. But like all mothers, we always hope to have more for our children. We try our best to get him to think, to learn and to understand like normal people. (At times I feel that he is even more willing to work harder than the normal kids). But my expectation and hope for Ping Lian to understand more "complex" feelings and values still seems to be very "far" and seems to be not reachable... or I am doubtful if it can ever be reached... As he grows more mature, he will have his own thoughts and ideas; but with his limited verbal language, it is going to be hard for him.

My daily prayer is "Ping Lian will think, talk and behave like other normal kids ". My husband had written a prayer note for my daughter; Cher to pray for her brother quite some time ago (may be two or three years ago). He wrote:

Talk To God

*Lord, my brother Ping Lian has lived
without understanding as normal children do.
He has tried very hard to learn and
speak every day for long hours.
Now, what is become of him?
He must have you. Come help him.
Break your vow of silence.
Heal him, Lord.*

Having said all of the above, there is no need to worry for me. I am OK. The sense of sadness just stays for a short moment. I get it out of me very fast after I express it. It is ok that I cry over it, but I know there is no point that I cry over it for long. Once I cry over it, I put that sadness aside; I divert my energy to think about what's the best way for him to understand the implications of having art work on the website and to appreciate his own achievement. Also I am getting him prepared, so when he grows up, he understands that he can support his own livelihood through selling of his art works on the website. I also know that my energy should focus more on giving him therapy on communication, which I had neglected so much since my husband passed away (almost one year now). Many times these types of sad moments trigger me to set new plans for him. Anyway as the mother of an autistic child, we all do have a lot of moments of "So, what is next?", "What is his future?" I am also concerned of who will look after him one day when I am gone?!!! Where, How and Who will be with him?!! How will his "art career" be? Who will be his manager and his guardian?!! With the lack of knowledge, understanding, resources, and support systems here with regard to autism, where is Ping Lian's life leading...... Anyway do not worry for me. These are just my thoughts and although they set off fears, I have already learned to live day by day. I take one day at a time. I also have learned to switch my focus to appreciate the good things, the good happenings. I try to always be happy with what I have now and to look forward for the better times to come. I believe " Happiness is a choice, be contented but not complacent, and always work and look forward for better times to come"

Even though Ping Lian has two sisters to depend on, Sherlyn is always thinking of studying in Australia ...... I always wonder should Sherlyn have the opportunity to study overseas (Provided my financial situation allows that);,Would she come back after studying. I do have doubts on that. (Three of my brother's children, all chose to live in Australia after completing their degree programs at the university in Australia. I am really concerned whether or not my daughters would stay with Ping Lian in Malaysia when I am gone one day?!! Sometimes I find that it is not fair for me to constrain my daughters' freedom of their choice where to study based on their brother sake. They have both already forgone so *much of my time, attention, and my financial allocation (as most of my additional financial dollars are always allocated toward the cost of Ping Lian's development.)*

I personally believe that I have the duty, to start thinking "WHAT is NEXT" and to explore the "WHERE and HOW" of continuing to develop Ping Lian's potential in terms of a future in art and greater personal development. Now without my husband around, everything is so different, especially the finances. Anyway with Ping Lian so talented in art, I could not sit and do nothing. I feel that I have even more responsibility to study and EXPLORE!!.

………

Thank You So much for reading this long email.

God Bless You
Sarah SH Lee

PLAN TO MOVE TO AUSTRALIA

In September 2003, I attended an Anthony Robbins seminar "Unleash The Power Within". I learned "Don't ask HOW, just ask WHAT"! Figure out *what* you want and then follow up by imagining the joy you will experience once you achieve your selected goal. "HOW" will come later. If you want it so much you will find out HOW later. The goal I set then was for Ping Lian to be an artist. I applied this "technique" in training and nuturing Ping Lian to be an artist….After the February 2005 Ping Lian ABWM Art Exhibition, upon reviewing the goal I set in 2003, I was happy and satisfied.

I have always hoped to be able to support Sherlyn to be able to study at Australia University. In Sept 2004 I attended another presentation of "Unleash The Power Within" and this time I had set a goal to be able to send Sherlyn to study in Australia. However time was passing very quickly. In 2005 I revisited this goal knowing that in 2006 Sherlyn should be going into her first year of University studies. I did not see the solution on "HOW". I couldn't afford to send her to study in Australia. The cost of living in Sydney was so high, especially when compared to living in Malaysia. Three Ringgits in Malaysia are only worth around one dollar in Australia! Where would I get the money for Sherlyn's education and support her cost of living in Australia when I put every cent into educating my autistic son?

After the ABWM exhibition, I somehow became involved in various conversations where certain people mentioned the possibility of Ping Lian going overseas to study. That is what initially prompted me to start thinking about finally moving back to Australia. Min Seng always wanted to but because he was an only son, it was his responsibility to take care of his mother in Malaysia. Ping Lian loved South Bank in Brisbane, Australia. Cher was born in Brisbane; Min Seng always told Cher that one day she would be back to Australia. On the other hand, I was not so eager like Min Seng, as I was often emotionally "child like" regarding my need to be surrounded and supported by my brothers and sisters. Also, one of my brother's who previously lived in Brisbane, had also moved back to work in Malaysia. They were all in Malaysia.

Prompted by all of this "What is Next, Where and How" I eventually felt so strongly that I must seriously be open minded and consider the possibility of moving back to Australia. Anyway that was always Min Seng's plan. Min Seng and I always had such sweet memories of our first living in Brisbane many years ago and sweet memories of our visit to Australia with Ping Lian in the year 2000. We were at Brisbane for approximately four weeks. We took so many pictures of Ping Lian as he played by the water almost every day at South Bank, Brisbane. On occasion whenever the family would sit and look at old photographs, Ping Lian would say "South

Bank, South Bank" whenever he viewed those photos. I start thinking "What If....?"

...If Sherlyn studied in Australia and happened to choose *not* to come back to Malaysia after her studies, or if Cher would also one day study there and choose to stay on at Australia...What would become of my poor Ping Lian? The thought of just Ping Lian and I, all alone in Kuala Lumpur, Malaysia - no husband, no Daddy, and no sisters was the worst thing I could have ever imagined. What would happen when I was too old to care for Ping Lian? What would happen when I pass away? I knew that due to his autism, Ping Lian would require support until he himself was old.

In fear of losing my daughters to Australia I decided it made perfect sense to move Now!! Move now, while Ping Lian was still young. I had no right to hold limits to where my daughters might decide to study and to live as adults upon their graduation. Moving now would also allow me to have my daughters with me a little longer. The educational programs available for people with autism are also more advanced there and that would open more educational opportunities for Ping Lian. One immediate advantage would be the confusion for Ping Lian with spoken language. In Malaysia there are three major languages used (Bahasa Malaysia, Mandarin and English), not to mention the various Chinese dialects spoken. In Australia, Ping Lian could basically just be expected to focus on learning one language, English!

I can work in Australia and Sherlyn could live at home while attending the University. There would be no additional cost of paying for her to dorm there and also since her sister Cher was born there, she would one day most likely also attend the University in Australia. Once I made all these considerations I immediately took action. I booked our flights and in May 2005 Cher, Ping Lian and I flew to Australia to check what City would be best for us to live in. Min Seng had stated that if we ever move back to Australia, we would not move to Brisbane again. Partly influenced by his thoughts about this, I only considered Sydney and Melbourne, but was still indecisive.

After our short visit to Australia, Sydney was the decision. Ping Lian has always loved to draw the Sydney Opera House. We would start our preparations for this big move, after our trip to New York. Although, I can now say that this was definitely the right decision for my family, it was also the most hectic time of my life. With no husband and still trying to juggle Ping Lian's needs on a daily basis, feeling all by myself.....I decided to move to Sydney! ...To start my life there with no existing friends and no relatives!!.....While at the same time getting prepared for Ping Lian's exhibition in New York! Many times I think back to this time in my life and wonder, "How did I survive all this turmoil? These are the reasons I believe God was walking with me and strengthened me with the support of many family members, friends, relatives and organisations. Many years ago I bought a poster for Min Seng that said "Take Each Day One Day at a Time". The poster hung in his office until after his death and has been hanging in the bathroom of our house in Sydney ever since. These words helped guide me through these most difficult times....

Take Each Day One At a Time

One day at a time- this is enough.
Do not look back and grieve over the past,
for it is gone, and do not be troubled
about the future, for it had not yet come.
Live in the present, and make it so beautiful
that it will be worth remembering.

~ ~ Ida Scoot Taylor ~ ~

Chapter 14: My Journey – Uprooted To Sydney, Australia

In my opinion, "Do not be troubled about the future" did not mean that I should not plan for the future. It meant still "have a *plan*" for the future! But do not get troubled by it. These words gave me the wisdom to be able to strike a balance between my long term plans and my daily reality.

With autism in our lives, there were so many things that were not within my control. There were many things that I was not able to change, but also things that I believed I could. I had to find that balance, find those things that I *could* change, and I constantly prayed to God for the wisdom to know the difference.

THE YEAR OF THE DOG

05412 MY DOG III
Painted in 2005 at age 11.

2006 was The Year of The Dog. Upon returning from our trip to Australia I was approached about having Ping Lian draw a Dog series for Australia Westpac Banks 2006 Chinese New Year calendar. This time was not as easy for Ping Lian. When he drew the Rooster, his first works were marvellous. However, to paint the dog required much practice in comparison. Ping Lian painted many dog pictures, but they were not impressive. I remember thinking of giving up, and almost telling Ping Lian to stop painting the dog subject.

Once I believed that he would not be able to paint a dog good enough to use on the Westpac Bank calendars, I resolved to let him continue drawing dogs just as an excellent opportunity to train his patience. However, Ping Lian eventually produced many beautiful paintings of "Dog." My special favorites are " 05410 My Dog I", "05411 My Dog II", "05412 My Dog III" and 05420 My Dog IV.

More art work images can be viewed on www.pinglian.com Gallery 2005 III

UPROOTING OUR FAMILY
'My emotions' about uprooting my family to Sydney.

After making my final decision to move, I realized how sweet the plan was, but how difficult the move would really be. Not only would I not have my husband and my mother-in-law, but soon I would also not even have a domestic helper when I move to Sydney. I had some serious lifestyle adapting to do in addition to working on the new education plans for my children. I was actually in "emotional turmoil." Not until, I started to pack our possessions did the impact of my decision to move really hit me. I do believe I was actually on the verge of depression.

Every morning I awoke with the intention to start sorting and packing. I had to decide what to take to Sydney and what I would leave behind. However, each morning I found myself staring at my living room blindly, not really seeing or looking at anything in particular. I was feeling overwhelmed and felt empty. I would find any excuse to allow myself to get distracted and do something else instead of packing. As the days passed, each day I said the same thing to myself "I will start organizing for the move today?" but each day was the same. I stared at my walls for weeks before I actually snapped out of this procrastination mode. My decisions were tough ones. Some of the belongings were possessions from a very young age. Since I did not know the size of the house we would be moving to, and I knew costs would be high; I dared not intend to bring too many possessions. Being the sentimental person that I am, parting with some of my old things was very difficult for me. Even the simplest things (my shells, stones, cane baskets, collection of books, CD's, DVD's, gift from friends, etc.) were of extreme sentimental value to me. I had to let go of most of them.

Finally, as I found myself running out of time, with no other alternative I eventually began the heart breaking process. So now, here I was at the last minute, with my severe back pain recurring trying to sort out all that my husband and I had accumulated for the past 20 years.

Still, I know we were so blessed with the support we received from Crown Relocations (Malaysia). Not only did they sponsor the move, but they helped us pack all of our belongings and Ping Lian's art works that were to go from Malaysia to Sydney. During the final packing process, Ronan Kelly, the Regional Managing Director of Malaysia and the Philippines, Crown Worldwide Group, personally came to my house in Malaysia to put his special care and attention to make sure that everything we wanted was packed and prepared for shipping safely. He came to ensure that our relocation to Sydney would be as smooth and easy as possible! Crown Relocations sponsorship included the insurance coverage for our contents and for Ping Lian's art works. Due to my back pains getting worse, I was unable to physically and mentally exert the energy needed to establish the content values needed for insurance purposes of our possessions and art work. Although Crown relocation staff were kindly reminding me daily that I needed to complete the insurance schedule, I had already pushed myself to an unhealthy level of stress. I was thinking about how Min Seng left us so suddenly, and I feared that I might also end up leaving my children that way. Well aware of my own physical limitations; I informed

Crown Relocation staff not to worry about the insurance. My children needed their mother and my body was more valuable than anything in all of our packed containers. Ronan was so kind and he cared so much about Ping Lian and his art work. He sat down in my living room and assisted me in getting the Insurance Forms completed. I was so touched by his kindess. A few months after settling in Sydney, he came over to our house to visit. Ronan Kelly is another individual whom I regard as a God sent special Angel. He will always be very special to us and to Ping Lian.

e-mail to Ronan

" ... my family will always remember that you and your company contributed greatly in our Special Journey with Ping Lian.... Moving was one of our toughest times after my husband and mother in-law passed away... and your personal care, support, and attention during our move meant so much to us and was such a comfort in our difficult time...".

It was now April 2006, just one month before our departure date and I had still not received or confirmed an actual address of where we would live. My house hunting was via internet and telephone with various real estate agents. However, now that it was getting near the nitty gritty, I realized that no one actually wanted to rent a house over the phone or internet. I started getting anxious. It had been approximately three months that I had been communicating and negotiating with realtors in this manner. The truth was, I had to be present to close any deal. I had to view the property and then file the rental application. Unfortunately, I did not have any relatives or friends in Sydney at the time that could help me with this and submit an application for me. I began preparing for the worse, thinking we may have to initially stay in a motel or some other type of

Chapter 14: My Journey – Uprooted To Sydney, Australia   363

short term accommodation upon arrival, and continue my house search after we arrive in Sydney. I would arrive with a 10 year old autistic son, a 13 year old daughter, no car and limited funds. A hotel would surely be costly! This was not going to work! Even the cost of a cheap motel or short-term accommodation would be costly and definitely too expensive for me. I became anxious and stressed, as I worried about using up my extremely limited funds for lodging instead of their budgeted extended use. God is good! Just a few weeks before our scheduled departure date, at one of our farewell parties, I met Ping Lian's kindergarten principle. When she heard about the difficulties I was encountering regarding my move to Sydney; including no friends or relatives there, no realtor cooperation to rent a house long distance; she called upon her Aunty Kim. Aunty Kim lived in Sydney! What a small beautiful world. She actually lived near the suburb we were planning to live in! Sherlyn was already attending Sydney University for the past three months and living at the Malaysia Care Hostel. Sherlyn, also very new to Sydney was also just starting to settle down. Kim got together with Sherlyn and helped us to obtain a home we could rent prior to our arrival. Kim even picked us up from the airport and continued helping us for many days. The first few days, she drove us around. She helped Cher to get registered at the nearby school in Chatswood and even helped me when I went shopping for my appliances. Kim helped us to make it over the hills of the most difficult parts of starting off our new lives at Sydney. No words can express my gratefulness to her for her kindness, efforts and support. She alleviated all of the fears and anxieties I was feeling concerning "uprooting" to and "arriving" at Sydney. Kim was truly a phenomenal woman and a phenomenal *friend*. She was full of assurances and her encouragement was so comforting for me and my children. I wondered how many people even had an aunt who could be so wonderful and so helpful. She's not even "my" aunt! Isn't it amazing how in our Journey, we can meet such wonderful people? I thank God for "Aunty Kim"; as I thank Him for all of the other timely yet miraculous occurrences in this journey. Meanwhile, Caroline had also called upon a friend of hers at Sydney and asked her to send some basic necessities to us for use when we first arrive. Another Malaysian friend called upon his friend, Pastor Tay to come over to visit us to check if we were in need of anything. We travelled to Sydney as "strangers", but God made sure we arrived with friends. They all made sure that we had whatever necessities we would need (like kitchen appliances, chairs, a table, a mattress and blankets, etc.) until our belongings arrive, so that we would not need to spend money unnecessarily. Also, we moved to Sydney I made a new friend. This new friend referred me to a friend of hers living near me in Sydney. Upon contacting this new aquaintance we got together and he helped me when I went shopping for a car. There were so many unbelievable last minute incidents. Just too many to just be coincidences! I believe these occurrences would not have happened without "God's hand at work". Our journey with Ping Lian is unique and very blessed.

    I have been called "daring" and "adventurous" by many of my friends. They have said it takes so much courage to do some of the things that I have done by seemingly "throwing caution to the wind". I do know that once I make up my mind about something, I just go for it. I think of myself more as "stubborn" than courageous. The bottom line is that I am always optimistic. I believe problems are temporary and that if you go for the short term pain, you will get long term gain.

OUR ARRIVAL IN SYDNEY ON 7TH MAY 2006

With all that I had to do, not until just before leaving our house to go to the airport, did I realize that Ping Lian did not have a new shirt to wear. Most of his shirts were torn from him biting on them whenever he becomes anxious. Even the new shirts that I had recently bought for him for the purpose of going to Sydney were already torn. Although I was teaching Ping Lian to squeeze his shirt instead of biting it, this is how he let out his frustrations whenever he had a tantrum. Typically, after wearing any shirt for more than a few hours, you will see holes in it, either on the collar, the sleeve, or at the bottom corner of the tail of the shirt.

To date, Ping Lian had made much progress and his behavior had improved drastically, but travelling was still not easy for him (or for us!) Going on flights with him was always so stressful, frustrating and upsetting for me and his sisters. By the age of ten, although his tantrum behavior had decreased, there were still times that his mood dictated serious misbehavior. It was also often predicatable by the actions of his sisters. Ping Lian was always more sensitive to any "criticism" he received from his sisters. Whenever Cher and Sherlyn would correct Ping Lian by telling him what to do, or what not to do, he would usually become very easily upset and throw a tantrum, especially in a public place. So on our flight to Sydney; I had to constantly remind Cher not to correct Ping Lian's behavior. Recalling some past travelling experiences while on airplanes with Ping Lian, this time I strictly instructed Cher "Don't try to teach Ping Lian what to do when we're just about to board the plane or when we are on the plane." "Don't try to teach him anything!" I remember the time (in the pass few flight experienced) when Ping Lian took off his shoes and threw them toward the passengers seated in the rows in front of him because his sisters were "correcting" him. He was so fast and unpredictable that I didn't have a chance to stop him. To make matters worse, he did it several times! Interestingly, after several hours of peaceful flight, though Cher had fallen sound asleep and thus stopped correcting Ping Lian hours ago, for what seemed to be "no reason" he suddenly took off his shoes and threw them toward the front seats. He would then remain seated quietly. I do believe that this was his way of letting us know he wanted some attention. I had to keep apologizing to the passengers in front of us. "He's autistic" I would explain. Most people were understanding but there was once a passenger who became so upset, that the aircraft crew spoke to me and even changed our seats. I was so worried that we would get banned from ever boarding a plane again.

I explained to Ping Lian that we were moving to Sydney and constantly reminded him to behave well and be a good boy in the airplane. I told him I would take him to Sydney to see Sydney Opera House for being a good boy. I wanted him to commit to being a "good boy" on the plane but I also threatened him. I told him that if he threw his shoes in the airplane again, he could never sit on an airplane anymore, we could not move to Sydney and he could not see Sydney Opera House anymore. Also, just for the sake of trying to make sure that we could have a good flight and to avoid the anticipated stress of our long flight, including the possibility of severe consequences we may need to face if Ping Lian misbehaved on the plane,…. this time Cher decided to treat Ping Lian like a VIP! Whatever he might do, she would not correct him. Everything he did said or requested, we would just say "OK." Even if I needed to "lie" to him, I decided I would lie and then deal with the reality later. After all, everything didn't need to turn into an educational lesson for Ping Lian. At this point we just wanted to continue our journey peacefully without any more drama. As long as Ping Lian would not have a tantrum during flight, what would be the harm in relaxing and enjoying the flight? As it turned out, our trip was "uneventful". There were no tantrums and no shoes thrown! For the first time ever, Ping Lian behaved excellent for the duration of the flight. I want to mention here, that after this flight Ping Lian has had many flights and each has been a blessing. He had totally broken the "behavior pattern" of throwing shoes on a plane flight. His behavior change has been a major breakthrough. He is a happy traveller and a very good helper, all the time helping to take good care of all our bags and luggage.

We arrived in Sydney on May 7th, 2006 to start our new lives at our new place. We are so happy and proud of him.

PING LIAN LOVE TO DRAW SYDNEY OPERA HOUSE, HARBOUR BRIDGE AND ANIMALS

Back in Kuala Lumpur, when Crown Relocation staff were packing away all of Ping Lian's art materials into the container, he kept requesting to take them out. I explained to him many times that we were moving to Sydney and Crown Relocations was helping us to ship our belongings and his art materials to Sydney. However, I don't know how much he understood of what was going on. I do know that for the first few weeks that we were in Sydney, he missed all his drawing materials.

When the Crown Relocations shipment of all our belongings arrived to our new house, Ping Lian was so happy when he saw all of his art materials and his art works. He was overjoyed!

I guess that he must have thought I gave all of his art materials and artwork away. Upon seeing them, he couldn't wait to start drawing and painting even though the house was still in a big mess with boxes every where. During this time Ping Lian obsessed with drawing the Sydney Opera House, the Harbour Bridge and animals. He forgot about the Malaysian Twin Tower buildings he previously obsessed over and for the next few months, he only drew the Sydney Opera House, the Harbour Bridge and various animals that he had seen during his last two trips during the holidays to the zoo in Australia. That is the reason why we have so many beautiful Sydney art works painted by Ping Lian at age of 12. He prolifically painted these just after we arrived at Sydney.

ARTWORKS PAINTED IN 2006, JUST AFTER WE MOVED TO SYDNEY:

06003 SYDNEY OPERA HOUSE-NIGHT SCENE

06001 SYDNEY OPERA HOUSE I

06006 SYDNEY HARBOR, OPERA HOUSE

06002 SYDNEY HARBOUR BRIDGE AND HARBOUR BRIDGE AND CITY CENTRE II OPERA HOUSE V

Chapter 14: My Journey – Uprooted To Sydney, Australia

STORY OF PING LIAN DRAWING "06401 AUSTRALIA ZOO- CROCODILES STORY"

I would like to share the email below I wrote to my friends in Sept 2006 about Ping Lian and the beautiful crocodile art works – 06401 Australia Zoo- Crocodiles Story

"... We moved to Sydney from Malaysia in May 2006. The environment here is very conducive for Ping Lian to draw. Sydney may possibly remind Ping Lian of our visit to the Australia Zoo in the year 2000 and to the Taronga Zoo in the year 2005. Ping Lian was then obsessed with drawing animals. After drawing most of the animal pictures, Ping Lian referred to them as either "Australia Zoo" or "Toronga Zoo." Some of the serious animal art pieces he drew were giraffes, koalas, kangaroos, deer, lion and crocodiles. You may visit www.pinglian.com and click on "Gallery 2006- Australia" to view some of these animal pictures.

06401 CROCODILES STORY
Ping Lian said "Draw crocodile","Big Paper" – August 2006 Painted at the age of 12.

I am so impressed by the form and the energy Ping Lian put into drawing the "Crocodiles Story". In fact, initially I was wondering why, of all animals he chose to draw the crocodile. Anyway, regardless of my thoughts, I do not interfere with what Ping Lian chooses to draw. Surprisingly, the picture turned out to be a beautiful and unique piece of art work. Ping Lian drew crocodiles with different expressions.

My children, my husband and I all love to watch Steve Irwin's documentary show. I recall that many years ago, when we were all still in Malaysia, when my husband was still alive, how we looked forward to Steve's documentary show. We tried not to ever miss his show. In the year 2000, we set out to the Australia Zoo just to be able to see his live performance. After that we felt so proud that we had an opportunity to see him in person and see his performances with crocodiles live! At that time Ping Lian was still quite hyperactive, but he also watched the entire performance. Also, at that time the extent of Ping Lian's drawing ability had not yet emerged. (Ping Lian only started drawing independently around mid 2002, at the age of 8). We kept many pieces of the Australia Zoo catalog, and later my husband had cut up Steve pictures from the catalogue and arranged them in our "Visit Australia Zoo Photo Album". (From the year 2000 Ping Lian would constantly look at this photo album and still continues to do so, to this day.)

One day (in August 2006) Ping Lian tells me that "Draw crocodile" and say "Big Paper".

I was thinking "What can he come up with drawing a crocodile and how can a crocodile picture be a beautiful serious art work?" I assumed that most likely he will just want to scribble/sketch here and there. So I asked him to use the A2 size paper. Because the bigger size paper is costly. "Big Paper" like A1 size paper costs around $8 per piece or more, and I use Malaysian money which actually costs me approximately RM24 per piece. I only give Ping Lian big good quality paper when he is ready to do serious artworks. He use a lot of paper for simple random sketches, and I can't afford to give him the better quality bigger paper all the time. In Sydney, we keep many different sizes and grades of paper at home. He can access himself to average quality A2 size paper, but he must ask me to access the "big paper"(larger than A2.) In Malaysia he was able to access all sizes and all quality of paper by himself. As a matter of fact, he often used the very good quality big size paper just to scribble. After moving to Sydney, I had no choice but to be more budget conscious. (The currency in Malaysia is worth approximately one third of the currency in Sydney.) So, Ping Lian is not allowed to just take the "Big Paper" by himself. He must ask me for it.

After a while of "bargaining", Ping Lian still persisted that he wanted the "Big Paper" to draw crocodile and kept asking "Big Paper", "Big Paper" and trying to get the paper himself. Due to my eagerness to save money and my doubts about the artistic quality of a crocodile picture, I finally managed to convince Ping Lian to save money, and use the small A2 size paper for drawing crocodiles. In all honesty it is not my son's artistic ability that I doubted but the subject (crocodiles!). Finally, Ping Lian settled on the smaller A2 sized paper.

The moment Ping Lian started the drawing, I was impressed by the way he focused and the energy he put into drawing the crocodiles. He was so intense and especially focused and energized. At that moment I immediately knew that, he was serious and not just casually scribbling. I then quickly offered to change to a bigger sized paper, but it was too late. He was so involved and focused, that I was unable to get him to switch the paper to the larger sized one.

Ping Lian took a few days to complete the whole picture. I noticed that Ping Lian opened the "Australia Zoo Photo Album" many times while working on his drawing of the "Crocodiles Story".

He drew more than 15 crocodiles with different expressions on the one paper. There are two people in the picture. Ping Lian still had limited communication and limited social skills. When I asked Ping Lian "Who are these two people in the picture?" he replied "boy and girl". He later pointed to the pictures of Steve Irwin and Bindi in our "Visit Australia Zoo's Photo Album".

I feel so guilty about it….I underestimated Ping Lian and the impact that the Crocodiles show had on him. I underestimated our visit to the Zoo in year 2000; I underestimated the "subject" of crocodiles! – I guess our visit to the Australia Zoo in year 2000, the "Visit Australia Zoo Photo Album" that we created after our visit, and also the Crocodiles show influenced the way that Ping Lian looks at crocodiles. The result is his creation of this very special piece of crocodile art work.

It seems I still don't really understand Ping Lian and his potential! I have learned a valuable lesson from my son. "I should not doubt his chosen subject, nor underestimate him. No one knows what may come from within Ping Lian's creative mind."

I showed the picture to a friend and we both felt that we needed to show this picture to Steve Irwin."Who in this world will love crocodiles more than Steve Irwin?". We both agreed that he loves crocodiles the most. We must show it to him and he could be the person that would appreciate this art work most". Ping Lian captured the expressions of more than 15 crocodiles in A2 size.

We agreed to send a print of this picture to Mr. Irwin to share this art work with him and let him know that he had inspired an autistic boy to draw beautiful crocodiles.

I have been busy looking for a job and procrastinated, saying to myself that I will do it next week, and then again next week….. Until that one afternoon my daughter told me the "bad news". Steven Irwin had passed away. I can't believe it and I am so sad.

In fact, I intended to let Steve Irwin know that he not only inspired my 12 year old boy, Ping Lian to draw crocodiles but also love to draw animals..... But it is just too late..... I should have done it earlier... I feel so sorry that I did not send the "Crocodiles Story" picture to him earlier.

Later on I came to realize that in the "Australia Zoo- Crocodiles Story" picture, there are many numbers on the crocodile body. I had not initially noticed that on the crocodiles Ping Lian drew, he had written numbers from 1 to 10.

Ping Lian still constantly draws Australia Zoo and Toronga Zoo.

PAINTING THE MIND DOCUMENTARY & HAPPINESS IS A CHOICE

April 25, 2007 e-mail to Pastor Anne

"... Hi! You would not believe that God had blessed Ping Lian in such an extraordinarily special way. I did not plan to watch TV on Monday night (I was working on Ping Lian's Book), but Ping Lian wanted me to do something about his pen's ink. He had asked many times since last year, I had say later many times, this time something happen (long story...), I feel really guilty and also "angry". So I decided to put my writing of Book aside, get up and do it for him immediately. I decided to watch TV while doing it. I turned to Channel ABC, 4 Corners and the documentary "Paining the Mind" was on! This was the film taken with Ping Lian in New York last year. I had not seen it yet. I always wondered what happened with that filming and when it would be shown in the US and UK. I did not realize that it was showing in Sydney. I can't believe it; here it was in front of me. It is the first time I watched it...."

Ping Lian wanted me to fill the ink for his marker pen. I asked Cher or Sherlyn to help, but none of them did anything. Ping Lian had an entire box of pens that had no ink. I was full of inspiration and busy writing my book after dinner. Ping Lian was still insistent that I must fill his ink pen. At this point, Sherlyn was not home and Cher was watching TV. I asked Cher to do it for Ping Lian., but she refused to do it immediately despite my explanation of inspiration to continue my writing without distractions. Ping Lian continued insisting and I yelled out "later!" With his face showing such extreme disappointment and Cher, still stubbornly watching her TV, I became so upset. I stopped what I was doing and angrily began to fill Ping Lian's ink pen. I felt I was wasting valuable time (as filling the ink is time consuming). I decided to watch the TV while filling the pen. Unbelievably, what I saw as soon as I flipped to a channel, was my son. A documentary that he had been filmed in started to air at that very moment. I saw Ping Lian on the TV screen. It was New York 2006, and I screamed so very loud to call Cher to come see Ping Lian on the TV. ... and we both so happy... and Cher so happy and cute and said, "Mom you should thank me for not helping you and Ping, or you would not have put on the TV and you would not have seen this., God wanted you to see the TV…" Yes! She is right, and I would not even know if the filming they did of Ping Lian in New York was used for the documentary or not. (I did not receive any information from the film company after they filmed Ping Lian in NY and was not informed if they would include the footage in the final documentary.) More amazingly, I never expected it would air in Sydney as I was told the documentary would air in the US and UK.

I was again astonished by God's work in our journey. At this point, even Cher believed that we were being *led* in this journey of Ping Lian's. God had arranged it and he was even laying out the minor details in our paths. To this day, I am still very much influenced by this "coincidence". The fact that Ping Lian was on TV and being featured in a documentary was secondary to the emotions I experienced knowing God sat me in front of that TV at that particular moment. I realised that, Yes! God is very real in our lives! We constantly experience God in our lives and His hand at work. My faith had been elevated to another level.

MAY OF 2007 (SHARE EXCERPT OF AN EMAIL SENT TO THE MANY PEOPLE WHO SUPPORTED US):

> "……. May2007 is my first anniversary of arrival here in Sydney! Moving here was not easy and it was actually very scary. I will always be grateful to you for your contributions which helped make it all easier for me and for my family. Thank you for your help, support and advice…"

I will always remember that, as a widow, living in a new place, there has been so much for me to cope with. It was a tough and hectic move which took a lot out of me. There is so much for me to learn and to familiarize myself with here in Sydney. Sometimes I feel so alone. I have been so heavily invested in my son's Journey, that I feel as if I have drained my own life. Yet, I know that my son's life…is my life. There are moments when I *worry* about my financial burdens. I *worry* about providing for my three children adequately, I *worry* about being a mother and a father, I *worry* about finding a new job here, I *worry* about making a career here, I *worry* about adapting to this new lifestyle, I *worry* about Ping Lian's education here, I worry about ME! My Future and my own personal life, etc. I *worry* about all this while ALL THE TIME taking care of my autistic son. These were not easy times, and when I think back on these times I honestly don't know how I survived and managed to maintain a positive mental attitude, most of the time.

Ping Lian as a "genius" autistic artist required a lot of my time and attention to nurture his genius. Starting a new business is never easy. Since I am not an artist myself and my background is not in art, it is much more difficult for me to help Ping Lian to build an art business and create a career and future in art for him. I needed to spend so much time researching, studying and learning about this myself. Thus, my life in Sydney had actually become even more hectic than it was in Malaysia. I find that I never have time for myself. No time for just me. These are the thoughts that lead to my feeling alone. I never felt lonely because there was no time in my lifestyle to contemplate loneliness. However, I definitely felt alone. When I regain focus to "take life one day at a time" ; I manage to maintain my happy personality and optimism about life. I believe that happiness is a conscious choice, so I always take the opportunity to create happiness and fun in everything I do. I strive to keep this journey as joyful as possible. My life has become more meaningful through this Special Journey. My family's lives have been enriched by the many organizations, new people, new friends and new experiences we have encountered while on this journey. We have supporters in Sydney, Malaysia and the USA, who constantly provide encouragement. They support and believe in Ping Lian's Journey. They really care for him and his future.

JUNE 2008 (SHARE EXCERPT OF AN EMAIL SENT TO RONAN):

"....Thank you for all you do. I am once again touched by you and your company. In fact the moment I received your call, without knowing the outcome, I already felt warm as I feel that you care and so we are not alone with Ping Lian's special Artistic Journey. I am grateful that you are walking with us in this Special Journey. Frankly if it were not because of Ping Lian's Special

Journey I would not go through the hardship of starting all over again at Sydney (as for me, I was comfortable with my Senior Manager career in Malaysia before involving myself to create this Artistic Journey for my son). Yet, I am happy and grateful to God for providing this opportunity... .... Thanks again for being our special partner, for continuously walking with us in this Special Journey. I definitely will not disappoint you and your company.

I stopped working part time since 2007. I have been "working full time for Ping Lian", getting more involved with his Artistic Journey and involved in his art works, and writing a book about his journey. My hope is that once this book has been published, someone will approach me to make a movie about Ping Lian's story. I have seen many movies about autism or a person with autism. They are always inspiring and that is my intention and motivation for sharing my son's life and our family's life. This journey required, still requires, and always will require patience, dedication and research. It requires constant nurturing to get Ping Lian to reach "there"; wherever "there" may prove to be. That is why I am always busy and the money does not come in so soon.

My land lord finally said he is willing to lease back the house to me but with a higher rental amount. I will let you know if we need to move again. Rentals in Sydney have been going up in a "crazy way"..... My children and I are not in the capacity to move and to deal with a new place and new environment again. We have had too much change and disruption in our lives for the past few years. I think we have reached our maximum limit of it, and I don't think we can cope with anymore changes now...."

Note: Since this time my land lord has come to understand our Journey with Ping Lian and he has become supportive.

PING LIAN AT SYDNEY ART MARKET

Ping Lian and I had not participated in the art market for quite some time since before moving to Sydney, as there was just too much to get done in preparation for our move. Even once we arrived to our new home in Sydney settling down was a long and uncertain process. It was all really very overwhelming and there was always "something else" to get done. My expectations seemed endless, never, ever, finishing.

I was constantly telling myself that I needed to take Ping Lian back to the art market soon to continue his training, but I always procrastinated. It took me about a year to take that first step to participate and get involved at the art market at Sydney. The first art market Ping Lian participated in at Sydney was Kirribilli Art Market. I need to said "thank you" to Bronwyn, the manager in charge of the art market for motivating me to take this first step in Sydney. Her appreciation of Ping Lian's art work and talent moved me from procrastination to *taking action*. I was pleased to see that Ping Lian still enjoyed participating after such a long period. Eventually, I took him to several different art markets in Sydney to expand his training and learning opportunities. We went to the art market at Manly, Paddington and later The Rocks Markets. Ping Lian enjoyed them all and he was able to adapt to each new environment quite easily. I became so tired and Ping Lian had learned to be "flexible" at the different markets, so I eventually started to take him only to The Rocks Markets every Saturday and Sunday. Ping Lian appeared to enjoy going to the art market even more than before. He was now much more aware and full of pride as he set up for display and also packed up when closing. It took quite a few years for Ping Lian to reach this level, where he could hang his own work independently. At the Rocks Market we only display prints of his artwork (limited and unlimited) so I do not need to be too concerned regarding the handling of the art. They are high quality 24" canvas prints for display only, with the purpose of providing Ping Lian the opportunities to learn to hang them and to listen to instructions. This is "job training" for Ping Lian. For sales at the stall, we make available additional signed prints. Through these experiences, Ping Lian has become more and more aware of his surroundings. He now derives such joy from the many praises received for his art. Throughout these many years of training, Ping Lian has also become able to excuse himself to go to the bathroom and return to his stall independently. He no longer needs to be accompanied by me. He is slowly integrating into society and looks forward to going to the Rocks Market, rain or shine. Often time, I hear him singing in his verbal stimulatory style and I feel his happiness. The art markets have been one of the most important places for Ping Lian to learn independent life skills and the ability to adapt to changes with flexibility.

Note: The owner of Argyle Gallery at The Rocks appreciates Ping Lian's talent very much. In 2015, Ping Lian's original artworks and Limited Edition canvas prints were proudly hung at the gallery and made available for sale. Ping Lian loves Sydney Opera House and he loves to paint and draw it. He has painted a series of Sydney Opera House (with and without the Harbour Bridge) from different angles and from morning scenes to night scenes. He painted the colourful Sydney Opera House, inspired by events like Vivid Night festival and New Year's Eve fireworks etc. Some of these are available at the Sydney Opera House's gift shop on postcards and paper prints, to share Ping Lian's story.

PING LIAN AND MUSIC (PIANO)

During 2005 and 2006 while we were still living in Malaysia, Ping Lian showed an interest in piano playing. I sent him for classes and he would play casually on the piano and seemed to really enjoy it a lot. However, once we moved to Sydney, I was unable to support him in this venture. I had to prioritize the use of my limited funds and control our expenses. In 2008 I decided to expose Ping Lian to music again. His piano instructor Phoebe, would come to our house and give Ping Lian basic piano instruction at a special reduced rate. Ping Lian enjoyed these lessons very much. On April 24, 2008 I wrote some words and asked Phoebe to add music to the lyrics to sing it with Ping Lian. She did get to introduce and sing with Ping Lian, but soon after, she returned to her homeland of Hong Kong for a job opportunity. So we did not continue this song. The words were very simple English so that Ping Lian would be able to understand the meaning.

Ping Lian's Song:

I am Yeak Ping Lian.
I am 14 years old.
Father God, thank you for helping me and heal me;
so i can speak well and understand things well.
I want to have good communication skills.
Father God, thank you for helping me to be an outstanding Artist.
Mummy says, i also need to work harder to be a clever boy
and to be a great Artist;
I want to have good social skills;
so i can be like Daddy and James.*

*James is my nephew who was living with us at that time.

I AM NOT "SUPER WOMAN" - GUILT? REGRETS?
2007-2008 (sharing some of my innermost feelings while in Sydney)

> "...I need to use art as a livelihood to provide financial support for Ping Lian when he grows up, so that he will be independent without having to depend fully on his family......"

The above statement is part of what I wrote in "I'M A Dreamer", for my son back in 2003.

I believed that the younger I could start his training, the better his chances for success. I revolved my every move and every decision around my autistic son. I have no guilt and I have no regrets concerning the way these decisions have impacted the lives of every member of our family.

Often I would hear criticisms from friends, family and even mere acquaintances and strangers. The most hurtful and most general criticisms were that I 'spend too much time with Ping Lian.' That I am '…always talking about Ping Lian. What about her daughters? She seems to forget about them. It is not fair, etc."

I actually put my feelings about this down on paper long ago. It was actually an email reply to a friend that I never sent or shared with anyone. I would like to take this opportunity to share it now: (below written sometime in 2007/2008)

> "…..Thank you for your concern. My two girls are wonderful now! I am happy. I do understand their difficult situations. It is hard for both of them to face and deal with so much change in their lives in such a short period. But for now, so far so good. I see many positive changes.
>
> Especially Cher, who has gone back to church, after she had stopped going for a few years. I see that her faith in God has grown. She is happy with her school as all subjects are in English. She was hopeless in Bahasa Malaysia. The other day her school required her to work for one week at a selected site in preparation for "job training". I was so happy to learn that she chose to work in Ping Lian's school. This was her own initiative. She actually chose to go Ping Lian's school and she was happy about it. This really surprised me because I thought she had

enough Autism experiences at home to decide not to have any additional encounters with autistic people in general.

Sherlyn is also smart and has always done well in her studies. When we first arrived in Sydney, she drowned herself in computer games day and night (she didn't even come out from her room to join us for dinner), but I am so happy that she did eventually snap out of that. Sherlyn loves cooking. She takes after her Daddy in this respect. She often cooks for the family and now more often spends quality time with her family, and has started to again actively participate in most of our family activities. She has also started sharing more with us about what is happening in her life now. Many of Sherlyn's good friends are in Melbourne. She misses them so much. She misses her friends and her life with them in Kuala Lumpur. In fact at first, Sherlyn preferred to move to Melbourne as she didn't know a single person or have a single friend at Sydney. Later Sherlyn did feel that Sydney was a nice place to stay. I am happy to see that both Sherlyn and Cher have healthfully adjusted. They are happy now, as they have settled down and made more good friends.

I know it has not been easy for my daughters. Cher and Sherlyn have never received enough of my attention. I am not a super woman. I had to prioritize what would be best for my family as a whole. Whatever I do for Ping Lian, is not just for Ping Lian. My entire family eventually will benefit from what I do for Ping Lian now. My general goal is always to make sure that Ping Lian will be as less of a "burden" as possible to all of us in the future when he is grown up (then I need to "Act NOW" before it is too late). I personally feel that if we have an autistic member at home, thus we are an "autistic family"! We are a family unit, and so we will need to try our very best to live and support each other all the way in our futures. I have no choice and they have no choice either. The fact is that we all need to learn to accept, adapt and find happiness within whatever we have been given. I have done my best to gradually instill these beliefs in my daughter's since they were very young.

Most importantly, all I can do is to try my best to make the process "as easy" for every one as possible and to get them to understand the fact that their life is different from other peoples lives. If you live with someone with autism, the facts are undeniable! My husband, my daughters and I are all affected. This will not change; we are all affected for life. But we can change our thoughts and how we take it. We need to work together toward shaping a better future for Our Family. So, whatever I have done, and whatever I will continue to do....is preparing for the future .....is not just for Ping Lian but for the good of everyone in our "autistic family"!

Regardless of Ping Lian's current talent, it remains to be extremely important to get Ping Lian to reach his highest potential across all aspects of living life. My thoughts and actions have always been based on this motivating factor "independence". If the siblings of an autistic boy can understand this, then their journey of living with an autistic brother may be more meaningful. I have worked very hard to have my daughter's understand this. They are aware of the general objective and have been exposed to this way of thinking gradually since they were young. The reality is sooner or later they need to face the lifelong problems of autism. I know they did not fully understand when they were young, but as they are reaching adulthood I know they have a clearer understanding. It is of course a long arduous journey, but....... I believe my two girls have become more aware of the realities of autism and their level of acceptance is growing everyday.

Above all else, I know they both love their brother very much. Last year I overheard my daughters quarrelling with one another. Sherlyn was very angry as I overheard her tell her sister " .... I'm telling you... next time when I have a house, I will not let you stay in my house! I will only have a room for Ping Lian.". Wow! She was really mad at her sister but I was so happy. She was so cute! I was thrilled to hear that even in her most angry and emotional state of mind, she was still thinking of her autistic brother. I had always prayed and expected that when the time comes that my girls are old enough to have their own house,(if at worse case Ping Lian would be unable to live independently), that his sisters would both keep a room for Ping Lian. Ping Lian could stay in both of their homes and they could share the responsibility of taking care of their brother. (more ideally though, I always Dream, one day, as we train Ping Lian to be independent, and Cher and Sherlyn will still live at Sydney, and we will become financially able to build a Town House with 3 unit, Ping Lian live in the middle and hope both the sisters are happy to live at his left and right as his neighbour).

Some parents say that they treat all of their children equally, including their autistic child. My belief is that life is never fair. I have an autistic son and it is not fair. Therefore, I cannot practice "real fairness" in my home. I cannot be "fair" to my family. I tell my children that "Life is not fair..." Ping Lian is not lucky like you, as he cannot learn things as you and other children do. He cannot understand things like you and other children do, and he can not talk like you do. Worse of all, he does not have friends like you, etc.. I tell my children that Ping Lian will get more attention and more of my time and have more privileges *at home, while constantly assuring them that that doesn't mean I love them less. These early lessons regarding our lifestyles and the fact that we are "different" have served me well in trying my best to keep my family healthy and happy. Yes, this involves some pressure at an early age, but I believe it has taught his sisters compassion, tolerance, nurturance, empathy and strength to accept the realities of our lives and our inherent futures.*

I have two wonderful daughters. They are healthy, beautiful, caring, smart and have very big hearts. I pray for my two girls daily. My prayer is simple – I ask God to protect, lead and guide them, help them be kind and loving, be happy …."

Sometime in the year 2009, Cher invited Ping Lian to go with her to her school party. She even took him to the after party supper with her friends. She wasn't concerned about others accepting her brother. She included her brother knowing full well that by taking him with her, she would be sacrificing some of her own freedom and enjoyment as she would need to care for Ping Lian attentively.

Not long ago, during the Chinese New Year (Feb 2010), when we were visiting in Malaysia, Cher told me that she was going for a one day trip to Malacca with friends and she wanted to take Ping Lian with her. I was so touched by her that day. I actually asked her… "Are you sure? You know you will have less freedom to have fun with your friends. It may be troublesome with Ping Lian around; you know you have to make sure he is with you at all times? What about your friends? Are they okay with Ping Lian being around all the time?" … but she said "It's Okay." She just needed to get Ping Lian to promise to be obedient and to follow her closely. She said her group of friends are okay with Ping Lian coming along and if someone is not okay, she would convince them. Cher has such a big heart for her brother. At her age it would not be unreasonable to expect that she would want to enjoy time with her friends and not include her brother. Actually, Cher had not even seen these particular friends of hers for almost a year. I think about the "early" life lessons I tried to instill in my daughters, and I know they learned them well. Cher was including her brother out of love not necessity.

ADDED NOTE AND UPDATED STORY:
(Written in 2010)

While trying to educate my daughters about the responsibilities of an "autism family", I knew very well that in order to practice so called "fairness"(my own meaning of fairness, especially as related to my daughter's future) I needed to do my part too. I am trying my very best to help Ping Lian grow up to be as independent as possible......to be an asset and not a liability; regardless of who's home he may be in, in the future. As with most families in Malaysia, my children too grew up with a stay-in domestic helper from overseas. They appreciate the "relaxed" lifestyle of having a full-time live-in maid who fully takes care of the house chores and serves them. I have thus, often wondered if I can develop Ping Lian to be like, or at least as good as our domestic helper in Malaysia. As I see the way Ping Lian progresses, I feel more positive toward him becoming an asset At Home. He loved doing housework and always took pride helping at home. He enjoyed every opportunity to serve his sisters. He would help by making and bringing them drinks. He prepared and served them fruit after dinner, etc. His sisters definitely enjoyed the pampering service they received from Ping Lian. At our dinners or family gatherings, he enjoyed staying around to clear the table and would take away the plates quickly once you had finished your meal. He was as good as any waiter in a restaurant. He was fantastic and we always laughed and enjoyed watching him because he did this with so much pride. So, it seemed logical to think that Ping Lian could contribute within 'a household' as a "special house maid/domestic helper" is not bad too and hope that he is well come "At Home". 'A household' means "At Home", as I am still not sure one day when I am old and gone, which "Home" he will be staying in. My motivation and the long term objectives are always the same...To make sure Ping Lian is not a burden to others, including my daughters. I do not want my daughters to feel or to be tied down by him. However, the reality is that I do not know how or where my daughters may choose to live in the future. All I can ensure is that I am imparting in my children a "value system". A value system to be able to strike a balance when making choices in their life for their future. They will of course have the freedom to choose what is best for them while at the same time take their brothers needs into consideration. My hopes are that this value system and positive education that I have shared with them as a reality and truth, will bring more wisdom to their future decision making.

ADDED NOTE AND UPDATED STORY:
(Written in Nov 2012)

Although I knew I couldn't afford a house in Sydney and the limited monies I had would soon be expended into a monthly high rental fee, I still dared to make the move to Sydney! We would "live our lives" one day at a time. Although we would be unable to control the cost of having a roof over our heads, we could control our daily expenses and what we spend on food and leisure items. Before moving, I discussed these financial constraints with my daughters and presented another possible "worse case scenario" with them. It was important to me that they understood we would be living on a "budget" upon our move to Sydney. I even explained to them that if I would be unable to return to a high income career job as I had in

Kuala Lumpur and if and when we used all of our funds, that I may need their help to contribute to the family to help out with the rental in order to continue to live at Sydney. I was so glad and proud of my daughters, who at that time only 14 and 18 years old both agreed to work while they studied in order to help contribute. Sherlyn also said that upon her graduation in 3 to 4 years' time, she could earn more to help support the house rental. This made me feel secure in a temporary plan for survival from 2006 until Sherlyn would graduate. In fact, it prompted me thinking again that with my capabilities and experience I would return to the work force after living in Sydney for a short period. I should definitely be able to earn a comparable salary to what I was making at Kuala Lumpur. Given my own confidence and attitude in my ability and experience, I felt I could be an asset to many companies. I have always had a passion to work as a real estate agent, and I felt certain that I could do well in this area.

The truth is that many of my friends and relatives advised me not to choose Sydney as a place to relocate. They advised me to consider another state, but I still decided there would be no other place and proceeded with my choice to move to Sydney. Later on I realized that life was not going as planned. Ping Lian and his Artistic Journey demanded so much of my attention. The first few years at Sydney, I didn't even have an opportunity to think about employment for myself. My earning power was actually devastatingly effected in comparison to what it was in Kuala Lumpur. However, in the face of all the special happenings that seemed to present themselves throughout our journey, I decided to commit 100% to Ping Lian's Artistic Journey and to abandon my own career and passion. I believe this was the path God laid for me.

Yet, there was another unforeseen change! Upon Sherlyn's completion of her first degree, she decided to continue with a post graduate course of study to be a doctor. She would need to study another 4 years. Any parent would of course be so proud. I was extremely proud of her, but

Chapter 14: My Journey – Uprooted To Sydney, Australia

also knew that this was not as we planned. Our funds from Malaysia were diminishing. Between the little income I made; the little income Sherlyn made from her part time job; the monthly house rental; Sherlyn's university fees and the general family expenses....I had no more budget! I was now unable to depend on Sherlyn having income from a full time job. Our initial plan to "survive" in Sydney by supporting each other was falling apart. Although Sherlyn considered sacrificing her medical career, we did not let that happen. Sherlyn is now in her third year of study and she will have completed her medical degree in 2013. As for me, ...my last resort was to sell my little house in Malaysia to extend our funds until Sherlyn would graduate. At times I feel insecure knowing that I no longer have a house for my old age. I tell myself not to worry and to take it one step at a time because Ping Lian's art journey and my daughters' education were priorities that I needed to support. As long as we could "survive". I constantly reminded myself that there was nothing to worry about as long as I did the right thing and worked Hard and Smart,. I also believed that God would also surely provide.

Although my initial decision to move to Sydney was based on improved opportunities for the sake of my children.....I have fallen in love with Sydney! I am so happy here in such a beautiful and unique city. I love living here and I feel so blessed having made this decision. My sacrifice paid off. Our 'sacrifice" has bring goodness and unforeseen reward. Though it was extremely tough the first few years, I can now say that we have "survived" happily for 6 years plus. A few days ago while having a discussion with my daughters, they seem to be even more supportive with me, Ping Lian and his Artistic Journey. They both make me feel so "secure" and I feel all has been worth it – even selling my house in Malaysia. At one point we were discussing the undertaking of a possible "New Plan" that I was considering for Ping Lian. When presenting the "worse case scenario" of this New Plan.... I was so happy that they both remained supportive and still offered to commit and contribute. This would require them to delay their own "leisure plans" by one or two years. I was so touched and I said "…so if thing don't work out well with this New Plan, are you both willing to commit to help?" And I jokingly added "…at worse case scenario you won't mind to continue to "suffer" with me (as they would be required to contribute financially to the family and The Plan) etc?…..". To my surprise, they both laughed and jokingly and happily said…" What is " suffer?".. "We are already use to it." There views were that "Living in this family we already need to 'suffer' and we already plan and prepare to "suffer"…. What is that the additional "suffering" we may need to endure?…What we can do is "live for less"… less freedom, less money, more commitment and more responsibility"

Most of my daughters friends are from well to do families, with plenty of financial support from the family for a luxurious life style, holiday vacations, leisure plans and "freedom." In comparison, my girls "suffer". Since a very young age; they can't do this, can't buy that, can't go here or there, etc. After speaking with my daughters, I am proud of their spirit and amazed of their continued supportive attitudes. However, this time, I do not want to involve them to the point of tying them down too much and I start to rethink this New Plan. Maybe I am not ready to take on this New Plan. I am also emotionally and physically tired. I decide to abandon The Plan for now and let God lead.

Though I did not proceed with The New Plan, I am so happy and feel so good about my daughters' responses. I have come to realise that they have grown to be so mature, and such big hearted ladies. Although I cannot be sure of what will happen in the future, for now I am pleased with their spirit to "sacrifice". Lately they have become more and more involved with Ping Lian's day to day life. Sherlyn and Cher even take Ping Lian with them when they do their lady shopping, without me! Ping Lian always feels so good and happy when he is being pampered by just his own sisters without his mommy. Ping Lian happily and patiently waits for his sisters when they are shopping (as lady shopping can take hours!). My daughters say that he is happy to go on the train with them, walk with them, go from shop to shop, wait for them and then carry their bags. This also makes my daughters feel so good as they realize that Ping Lian also wants to be with them, and not just Mommy. I honestly believe that Ping Lian just wanted to be with his sisters and feel accepted by them. More recently, on several occasions, Sherlyn took Ping Lian to join her during her weekend nights out for dinner with her friends. I am also very pleased to see Cher with her own initiative getting very involved with Ping Lian's life. She takes Ping Lian to the beach for swimming (just the two of them), to the zoo, to cut his hair, teaches him how to style his hair (she said Ping Lian is so handsome, she needs to teach him how to style his hair so that he looks like a normal teenager with a beautiful and modern hair style). She has even taken Ping Lian to buy facial care products to teach Ping Lian how to care and maintain his handsome face. When she cooks, she gets Ping Lian involved and teaches him to cook and bake cake. She takes Ping Lian to and from the Studio Artes (a Center for adults with disabilities). Cher has even made offers to fully take on the responsibility of caring and watching over Ping Lian in order to enable me to go overseas for a few days of holiday. I am so proud of all this progress. Ping Lian's character, gratitude and love for his sisters continues to grow and his behavior has become more and more stable. As Ping Lian's sisters strive to keep him involved by helping him to experience "typical" teenage experiences out of their love and appreciation of him and not out of obligation, Ping Lian continues to grow emotionally and socially. I recall how "once upon a time" I vowed to teach my son Ping Lian to be grateful! I still do not know how much of that he understands but I do know, that my persistence has been paying off. I have started to experience the fruit slowly coming out… Yes! Never try never know… worth the effort and try!!!!

I WOULD LIKE TO SHARE THIS BEAUTIFUL E-MAIL SENT TO ME BY A FRIEND WHEN WE WERE IN SYDNEY:

" …. Hi Sarah,

Indeed it is so wonderful to know that you have been so blessed with such tenacity, faith and talents to turn what appears humanly to be tragic circumstances in your life and the life of your family into one of such great testimony of what God can do to turn negatives into positives and possiblities!! We are priveleged to have come into your life and to witness the goodness of God working in a very real way in what we witness and what you have been sharing with us thus far.

It is nothing short of miraculous in seeing how so many prominent and gifted people have been brought into your path to help you and Ping Lian and to give you the full support in so many ways. Thank you for keeping us posted and to continue to amaze us with the way God continues to bless you. I trust that you know and acknowledge that this can only come from the hands and heart of God……….."

Excerpt of my reply:

"... Thank you for such a beautiful, spiritual and motivating reply. It is just so good, I just love it, I enjoy reading it and I read many times……In fact I am so blessed that I keep a Journal for Ping Lian many years ago. At that time, I did not know he would be an artist. Some parents always asked me why I record so many details. I tell them that I just want to keep some special incident

Chapter 14: My Journey – Uprooted To Sydney, Australia

as a record, and jokingly I add- "Who know's, one day Ping Lian may become an important person. This Journal will be very important for me." At that time I did wonder -WHO CAN HE BE?

In fact many times I also asked myself the same question, "What am I writing so much for??!!" ...but there was always a voice inside me saying, "He may be 'Someone' just in case." (Could it be that even at that time, God already started giving me wisdom and leading me to an answer?") Although I wasn't even attending church then. I returned to church in the year 2000. Keeping this Journal about Ping Lian has made writing his book much easier.

Family photo – At Sydney Harbour Bridge 75year anniversary - Bridge Walk 18 March 2007 (Sherlyn, Sarah Lee, Ping Lian and Cher).

I would like to one day write a detailed account of all the incidents and situations that I believe God lead me and my family and Ping Lian through. While writing his book, as I reflect upon all of the hurdles that we had to overcome as a family, I am so humbled. I know that God sent us "Angels" to support us. There are so many people that we came to know in a special way and at a special time. My autistic, poor motor skills son had developed to the point where his art was auctioned at a charity event for RM100,000.00! How can this not be considered miraculous!"

MARCH 2009 AT SYDNEY HOUSE - HAPPY PAINTING

Ping Lian painting and his sister Cher Lyn standing behind him providing good support. Ping Lian feels so content, being appreciated, loved and supported by his sister.

Photos by Diane MacDonald

MORE RECENT PAINTINGS:

11010 SYDNEY HARBOUR BRIDGE
Painted in 2011 (Size: A2)

10001 SYDNEY
Painted in 2011 at age 16 (Size: 66x102cm)

11005 SYDNEY OPERA HOUSE, HARBOUR BRIDGE & LUNAR PARK
Painted in 2012 (Size: 65x100cm)

12003 SYDNEY OPERA HOUSE
Painted in 2012 (Size: 52x75cm)

11303 HORSES

Painted in 2011 at "The Rocks Pop-Up Project" (Size 76x101cm)

12301 HORSES - PAINTED IN 2012 (A2 SIZE)

PING LIAN, HIS MOM, SARAH AND SISTER CHERLYN

Photos by Diane MacDonald

CHAPTER 15

My Journey – Malaysia & New Upgraded Dream

My initial goals and Dream for Ping Lian to become an 'outstanding artist' came to fruition so quickly. I never expected the results would be realized so precisely and so soon. He is already an "outstanding artist".

On December 31st, 2007 I upgraded my Dream for Ping Lian. It was New Year's Eve and I set a new, more challenging Dream for my fourteen-year old son. Here I was again, thinking "Am I crazy?" and then "Who cares?" If there is No Dream, then there is No Hope. I prayed that I would still have the support of God's sent angels, as well as his continued guidance for my Dream was so ambitious. Yet I knew it was achievable and not unrealistic. I proceeded with adding this new dream to Ping Lian's daily prayers that he would "work hard" to achieve his "New Dream".

Every New Year's Eve, I reflect on my life and make my new year's resolutions. As I admire the fireworks, that is the time I tell God of my new goals and my new resolutions. I repeatedly state my prayer to God to help me to achieve my goals until the fire works stop. As is my style, 'always one stone kill many birds' 🐦 ... not just one bird... that is not enough. My resolutions are layered into two categories. I have my simple basic resolutions: (to be a better mother, to be more patient with my children, etc) and I have my sophisticated crazy resolutions: (to reach the goals of my Dream for Ping Lian, etc.)

The New Dream includes for Ping Lian to have his own gallery one day. Hopefully in Malaysia! Isn't that a realistic goal? After all he has been creating beautiful paintings of his homeland since he was ten years old! Also, my research has led me to understand that there are not many "genius" child artists in the world. It would be a wonderful contribution to society to show Ping Lian's beautiful paintings of Malaysia at his very own gallery, for people to appreciate.

EXHIBITION "MY JOURNEY..." 2008 IN MALAYSIA

In Jan. 2008 The Art Commune in Malaysia showcased Ping Lian's talent in a grand way. He was to have a solo art exhibition titled "My Journey ..." at Kuala Lumpur. In collaboration with Yvonne Hon (co- founder of The Art Commune), we created the first book catalog of Ping Lian's artworks *("My Journey ... ")*. In addition to his artwork it included many touching and beautiful comments about Ping Lian that I and Dr. Rosa Martinez had collected from around the world. The solo exhibition was a huge success with many newspapers and magazines covering Ping Lian's art work and his story.

In the process of planning this exhibition, Yvonne and I considered making it a charitable event. After several brain storming sessions and discussions, we decided not to make this exhibition a charity event. We wanted to portray the Artist "Ping Lian Yeak" as an artist not a 'disabled artist'. We wanted to project to the public that this exhibition was by a *real artist*. When people would come to view his artwork, I wanted to know that they were genuinely appreciating and purchasing his art because they loved his work, and not solely for the purpose of making a charitable contribution. I would like to see that Ping Lian's support was not based on sympathy. As I feel that Ping

Lian has been very blessed, whenever he had an art exhibition in Malaysia in the past, I always donated a percentage of the proceeds for charity. We have also donated numerous original art works at various exhibitions. This is all part of our general goal in "I'm A Dreamer". Was Ping Lian's current level of success and "celebrity" due to his ties with charity? .... or was his "artistic talent" really being recognized? This was truly to be Ping Lian's Journey and frankly, Yvonne and I were both very eager to see the outcome.

I was not denying the fact that Ping Lian had autism. I cannot deny or hide his autism. As a matter of fact I have learned to be grateful for his autism. Ping Lian, initially with very poor fine motor skills had become an outstanding artist. I will always be grateful. Yvonne put a lot of effort into this exhibition and had contacted a lot of media. It was a perfect opportunity to spread autism awareness. It also provided opportunities to inspire hope about the "abilities" which has always been my personal mission. My son was an example of "look at what he *can* do, not what he *can't* do!"

The exhibition "My Journey" was a huge success. It attracted many visitors and art collectors. Many original art works and prints were sold. Numerous articles were published about the event in magazines and newspaper from Malaysia, including a magazine from Singapore. Many people offered to buy some of Ping Lian's original works which were on exhibit, but not for sale. These special pieces are reserved as "artist's collection" pieces. I explained that some of these were only available for sale as prints, because they were painted when Ping Lian was very young and were being kept for his long term plan – to exhibit his child hood works. I was surprised when several purchasers (obviously high end collectors) initially told me that they do not buy prints. However, they later did indeed buy a Ping Lian original work (that was available for sale) and some prints of the "unavailable" original works.

Secretly, I hoped to someday exhibit these childhood paintings in Ping Lian's own gallery. Most of his original works were thus exhibited just for display, and mostly I sold only limited edition and unlimited edition prints of Ping Lian's artworks.

I also shared with whomever I could the book written by Dr Darold Treffert which I mentioned in a previous chapter. I always carried it with me to exhibitions to make people aware about savants. The part that stated ... *"among savants, musical genius as the special ability is quite common, but phenomenal art ability is rare";* was especially compelling to me.

My New Dream for Ping Lian has led me to think differently now that I am more knowledgeable about my son's challenges and his strengths. I gather that young savant children who create quality art work are very rare in this world, so even my son's limited edition prints should be preserved. My intention has become to sell some of them slowly and in stages (control release), so that hopefully Ping Lian's stunning childhood artworks can still be around when he is thirty, forty or even 50 years old. Doesn't it sound exciting to think that when Ping Lian is elderly and has an art exhibition, we can still have some of the works he painted when he was between ten and sixteen years old available for show and for purchase? Also, although I tend to plan for the best, I do not forget that there is also always the possibility for the worse to happen. I have also thought about the possibility of Ping Lian losing his artistic ability when he grows older, and so this makes me want to hold on to his earlier work even more. Preserving his original and limited edition works for future availability may be a way to assist in Ping Lian's future livelihood. My original plan to "Use art as a livelihood or to provide financial support for Ping Lian when he grows up ..." – It all fits, doesn't it? I have convinced myself that it is a good plan. Should Ping Lian lose his artistic skills in the future, he may still have the possibility of generating income and may not need to become 100% dependent on his sisters or others for financial assistance.

Due to this reasoning, I am very reluctant to sell many of Ping Lian's early original works. I may sell many of his original adult works because adulthood has a greater lifespan. Childhood lasts five to seven years, but adulthood may exceed beyond thirty years.

Yvonne and her family worked so hard to create Ping Lian's first ever catalog of his artworks. The printing was sponsored by GP- Girard-Perregaux through FJ Benjamin Luxury Timepieces Sdn Bhd. This exhibition and all that occurred because of it was another turning point in Ping Lian's life. It further validated and encouraged me to continue with my New Dream for Ping Lian. Our efforts and sacrifices were being rewarded. Ping Lian was worth all of it. The attention and appreciation that the public showed for his artwork was so amazingly uplifting.

After organizing the "My Journey" art exhibition for Ping Lian in Malaysia January 2008, Ping Lian and I stayed on in Malaysia for a few weeks, and spent a lot of time with Yvonne. After learning a little bit at a time of Ping Lian's story from me and watching him work, viewing his creations, gaining insight about the stories behind his artworks Yvonne had grown to love Ping Lian.

Once Yvonne said in her email in 2008 that "My heart is with Ping Lian.... I will follow what God guide and lead me.... And I am really not too bothered about all those things like credit or credit mention... I also don't wish any glorification, we just move with the flow - God guides..."

It's really amazing how God works his miracles. Although Yvonne and I originally both lived in Malaysia, I did not know her when I lived there. Yvonne originally met Ping Lian through one of the art bazaars that Ping Lian had participated in before we moved to Sydney. She was impressed by Ping Lian's talent and later was looking for Ping Lian, hoping to hold a solo art exhibition to show case his talent. She did not realize that we had relocated. Later, through a common friend, she found us. After "My Journey...." art exhibition in Malaysia, Ping Lian's relationship with Yvonne had grown tremendously. He later called her "Aunty Yvonne" given my constant reminders to Ping Lian of everything she had done for him. I know that Ping Lian eventually realized that Aunty Yvonne loved him very much. Ping Lian had become very grateful to Yvonne. Ping Lian loves to be at his exhibitions and you can tell that he loves when his talent is appreciated. Aunty Yvonne became very influential in Ping Lian's life, including the ability to tell him what subjects to paint. Sometimes it seemed if I said "Aunty Yvonne wants you to paint a "___" ; that was even more effective than Mummy making the request.

2008 UPDATES OF "MY JOURNEY…." EXHIBITION AND IMPACT

One of the magazine editors came to Ping Lian's 2008 My Journey –solo exhibition with her son Scott. Afterward we got together a couple of times for dinner followed by a Durian session for the night. Although I definitely sympathized with her as she complained about her teen-age son and his lack of drive and commitment, it made me feel so proud of Ping Lian's personal progress and his motivation. Hoping to share Ping Lian's story to inspire Scott to understand the benefits of hard work, patience and perseverance; I decided to tell them about an incident which I had never shared with anyone before. I told them about the anxiety and difficult times we experienced with Ping Lian on airplanes at the beginning of his Artistic Journey. In detail, I told Scott about all the times that Ping Lian threw his shoes at people; I told him about how anxious and frustrated we were about Ping Lian's temper tantrums while we travelled to New York, to Sydney and back to Kuala Lumpur etc. I explained how Ping Lian use to do this without any warning and how I was unable to control or stop him. "Ping Lian's sister's and I had to be very patient and we had to be creative in trying to find out what triggered these tantrums in Ping Lian. Imagine, the anxiety we felt wondering what consequences we may have to face from the people he threw shoes at. I ended up sharing many of Ping Lian's "tantrum" stories with Scott and his Mom, including the times that Ping Lian for no obvious reasons would bang his head on the walls, pull all of the books down from the book shelf, use a fork to hurt himself half- way through enjoying a meal at a restaurant, etc. Fortunately, these were all tantrum like behaviors that ceased to occur by 2007. Prior to 2007, Ping Lian would display a variety of these misbehaviors without an obvious trigger.

The bottom line was that we also needed to have humor. Without finding humor in some of the things that Ping Lian did, we would be totally stressed for life! Most importantly, you have to be able to laugh. (Even though laughter was usually after the fact, when recounting personal stories.). As you can see, Ping Lian is now a wonderful boy. He always behaves now on airplanes, at the galleries, at home and in restaurants. This was the first time I had actually shared so much about Ping Lian's negative escapades regarding his misbehaviour when travelling on an airplane, with anyone. On that day I realized how important it was for others to know all this about Ping Lian. Seeing Ping Lian now, Scott and his mother were mesmerized by all the details of his misbehaviour in contrast to the loving, calm and obliging character they witnessed before them now. Overall they were so amazed, especially Scott, with Ping Lian's stories and his developing progress that we talked all night. That evening at around 12 midnight, just as I was about to get into bed, I received the following most beautiful messages on my mobile phone:

26 August 11:54 (message from Scott's mother mobile phone): Scott said that he wanted to study hard so that he can earn a lot of money to help Ping Lian to open his art gallery all over the world.

26 August 11:59 (From Sarah)
So good. Tell him, thank you. We wait for that day.

27 August 12:07 (From Scott)
Hi! Aunty Sarah! It's my pleasure. I will do my best to help.

27 August 12:07 (From Sarah)
Nice to hear that. Thank you.

27 August 12:05 (From Scott's mom)
I want to thank Ping Lian because he influenced Scott so much

It was a wonderful feeling to realize that Ping Lian's story could motivate and inspire another boy.

"PING LIAN @ THE ART COMMUNE"- PING LIAN'S PERMANENT GALLERY IN MALAYSIA

In August 2009, Yvonne initiated *"Ping Lian @ The Art Commune"*. It was a permanent gallery for Ping Lian. It was initiated and dedicated specifically for featuring a permanent showcase of Ping Lian's works in Malaysia as Ping Lian was about to turn 16 years old. The most beautiful part was that she and her entire family worked together to do this for Ping Lian in Malaysia while we were (now) all living in Sydney, Australia. Her mission was to create visibility of Ping Lian's art and to share his story to inspire others. I recall Dr. Treffert's words of wisdom *"Thus we all become, then the beneficiaries of that special giftedness, and that determination and optimism, while the artist himself continues to grow and flourish".*

"How could this happen? Ping Lian is just going to be sixteen.!"

In 2008, Yvonne Hon, described Ping Lian's solo exhibition "My Journey…"

"This is not just an exhibition of remarkable artworks but it is about the sharing of possibilities, it is hope, it is about aspirations, struggles and victories. It covers mother, child, and talent, recognition and autism awareness"

The exhibition "My Journey" was supposed to be for only two months, but because of its popularity it was extended another month. I later received yet another e-mail from Yvonne informing me that they were extending it again, an additional month. Later the best and the most surprising message I received from Yvonne said *"Sarah… We, The Art Commune finally decided to open a permanent Gallery dedicated for Ping Lian only…."* I screamed as I was overwhelmed with happiness. What! Ping Lian's New Upgrade Dream was coming true so fast, so soon.

It was always my Dream to have a permanent art gallery for Ping Lian in Malaysia, but I never thought that this could happen so soon. The arrangement was such that the gallery would be managed and supported by The Art Commune. Ping Lian only needed to paint more pictures for hanging in the gallery, and I only needed to prepare Ping Lian's art related works like the prints for sale in his permanent gallery. As I am always so busy with Ping Lian's daily life routines, I loved this arrangement! *Coincidentally*, on a Sunday morning, soon after having discussed the opening of Ping Lian's permanent gallery with Yvonne, I received another wonderful email from the Senior Country Officer of J.P. Morgan Chase – Mr. Clement Chew. Part of the e-mail said " …. *Ping Lian is extremely gifted - and it will be nice to help him showcase that there is no limit to one's abilities. His talent has the potential to touch many people in different corners of the world….".* I read this email just before going to Sunday Church service and while sitting in the church, I could not contain my tears. I just did not expect all these wonderful developments so soon. I thought about all these wonderful people who were so supportive of my son. They were neither my relatives nor my friends. They were not initially even acquaintances. How did they come into our journey? Our paths crossed through the art work of my son. They are God sent Angels to Ping Lian. How else can I explain all of this? These are "miracles"! At that moment, while still sitting in church, I decided that Ping Lian and I would donate one more of Ping Lian's original art works to an autism organization the day of his official gallery opening at Kuala Lumpur. On 15th August 2009, Ping Lian at the young age of only fifteen was honored with the opening and Inauguration of his own Permanent Gallery of Works at The Art Commune of Malaysia. *"Ping Lian @ The Art Commune"* featured a permanent showcase of Ping Lian's works in Malaysia, established by The Art Commune of Malaysia and supported by JPMorgan Chase Foundation (for grant 2009) in collaboration with ABWM *(Association Of British Women In Malaysia).*

At the inauguration Ping Lian donated 100% of the proceeds from the sale of an original artwork to the United Voice and PR4a (Parents' Resource for Autism), two organizations dedicated to serve people with special needs including autism. During the official opening of Ping Lian's gallery, Ping Lian was filmed over the course of three days, by Mediacorp Pte Ltd for Channel News Asia (CNA), Singapore. They were filming for a documentary program about Asian prodigies, which was to be a series called "Asia's Wonder Kids" documenting the stories of young people who have exceptional talent in different areas. The program would aire in Singapore on October 28th, 2009. It was a regional program that would be shown in most capital cities of Asia.

I couldn't get over it. Fifteen years old and already with his own permanent art gallery! "Ping Lian @ the Art Commune"! What an amazing accomplishment. On opening day he had more than 45 artwork prints, including canvas prints and more than 40 original art works painted between the ages of ten to fifteen hanging at the Gallery. In total there were more than 100 Ping Lian Yeak artworks on exhibit.

My family and I are very thankful to the various parties that made this happen. We thank The Art Commune initiative for setting up this gallery. We especially thank Yvonne and her family who worked so hard and went the extra miles to set up such an impressive gallery. We also thank J.P. Morgan Chase Foundation; ABWM, MPSJ (Selangor – Municipality of Subang Jaya) and once again Malaysia Airlines for their continuous support and sponsoring our air tickets to fly back to Malaysia for the official opening.

Following are some comments published by our supporters. They are extracts from Ping Lian's catalogue book (2009) - "Savant Art" Note Book[35], produced by The Art Commune.

> "The artworks of prodigious savant, Ping Lian are now being showcased in his personal Gallery, made possible with the support of J.P. Morgan Chase Foundation & ABWM-Association of British Woman in Malaysia.
>
> "Ping Lian @The Art Commune" is not only about great art by this young savant who has exhibited throughout New York City, Kuala Lumpur, Sydney, Brisbane, London and Germany. It is about a sharing of possibilities, recognizing a journey, it is the aspirations and the struggles and the victories… It is our hope that with this sharing, comes a world of possibilities in hope, of growth and of colours in the unexpected, an exalting new light, a new understanding for artist and audience.

---

35   *"Savant Art" Note Book - A book created which included* Ping Lian Yeak's art work images, some information about Ping Lian, media and public comments about Ping Lian, together with many empty pages for use as note book. The "Savant Art" Note Book was given away as a gift souvenir on the official opening day of the *"Ping Lian @The Art Commune"* gallery.

The Art Commune is happy to have initiated this project and to take on the active role of implementation. Together we hope to reach out with Ping Lian through his art as he journeys on... Discerning collectors are already aware of the distinction and value of his art that is gaining international recognition with each passing day".

YVONNE HON, BOB LEONG A. K. AND BILLY LEONG MUN CHEON

FOUNDING MEMBERS-THE ART COMMUNE, MALAYSIA

"Let us pay tribute to the courage of children with autism and their families" Ban Ki-Moon, United Nations Secretary - General

"We are delighted to be presented with this special opportunity to work with Ping Lian. Ping Lian is blessed with an exceptional gift. Through his art, Ping Lian has touched the lives of many people around the world. His work inspires hope and reminds us of the extraordinary heights a child can reach with a family's love and dedication. Ping Lian's widely exhibited works convey a powerful message that the special skills of autistic children can be harnessed and developed to their full potential.

J.P. Morgan is delighted to partner the Association of British Women in Malaysia in support of Ping Lian's art.

Each year, the J.P. Morgan Chase Foundation is involved with thousands of not-for-profit organisations around the world. Frequently we focus on children and assist in allowing them to reach their potential through education. Our Foundation actively promotes arts and culture as a means of celebrating diversity, enriching our society and promoting self-expression. Our goal is simple - to be the catalyst for meaningful and positive change in the communities we operate in.

Chapter 15: My Journey – Malaysia & New Upgraded Dream

J.P. Morgan is pleased to be part of an effort to showcase Ping Lian's art so that it can be enjoyed and appreciated by more people. Finally, we hope we can make a contribution to Ping Lian's love for drawing and his journey as an artist."

CLEMENT CHEW, SENIOR COUNTRY OFFICER, J.P. MORGAN CHASE

"The members of the ABWM first met Ping Lian when he was 11 years old. We were so impressed by his talent and achievements that a few of our then committee members began to promote his work – holding exhibitions at the ABWM house, selling his works, including cards made from his paintings – a favorite with our members was his wonderful rooster, which he created for the Chinese New Year. Ping Lian visited the ABWM house on several occasions and met many of members – he captured our hearts and we were delighted when he was finally offered the opportunity to go to Australia. Sarah, Ping Lian's dedicated mother kept our members informed of his progress. And we are all obviously delighted, Ping Lian is now able to maintain a permanent showcase here in Kuala Lumpur. ABWM is happy to be part of this collaboration with The Art Commune & JP Morgan Chase Foundation. The ABWM is a long standing association whose aim is to support our members, those members volunteer with several Malaysian charities and raise significant funds to help the less fortunate. It is therefore, a privilege for us all when one of our protégés has been able to succeed in his given talent and with that, offer hope and inspiration for all other autistic people. Congratulations…"

TRACY DALE, CHARIMAN(2009), ABWM KUALA LUMPUR, MALAYSIA

PING LIAN IS SO HAPPY AND PROUD WITH HIS GALLERY

During the days prior to the opening of the gallery, Ping Lian was very busy with newspaper and magazine reporters. He was very excited and proud of himself. He posed beautifully again and again for pictures. He was patient and extremely cooperative during the photo sessions. On several occasions he even showed his good manners holding the photographers hands to take photos with them. Several of the reporters even commented about how "friendly" Ping Lian was.

The morning of the opening, I suddenly decided that Ping Lian should give a brief speech at his gallery Inauguration. I worked with him and prompted him on what to say and I wrote down his speech on a piece of paper. Once we finalized what he should say, I made him copy the speech by himself into his "Savant Art" Note Book. After that I prompted him, until he read it alone again and again. He was actually very enthusiastic while practicing reading his speech.

Also, that morning, the Singapore Media Corp Documentary crew came to film Ping Lian at my sister's house as he was getting ready for the big event. Ping Lian loved this. At the Inauguration and official opening, Ping Lian was happily walking up and down, throughout the gallery. He helped himself to the snacks and then painted live for the guests. When he gave his short speech I was so proud. He read the words from his notebook happily and gracefully, saying "Thank you…" to many people. This was not a scheduled item on the program. Mostly everyone was caught by surprise at Ping Lian's initiative, confidence and enthusiasm. … especially those people who had met him many years ago, either at the art market, or another venue. I would imagine that Ping Lian's general attitude and progress must have appeared unbelievable to most.

Ping Lian's speech:

"Thank you for coming to Ping Lian's gallery.
I want to thank you Mummy, Sherlyn, Cher and Aunty Yvonne, Uncle Bob and Clement.
Thank you The Art Commune, JP Morgan Chase Foundation, Malaysia Airlines, ABWM, Dr Rosa, Dr Treffert, Dr Becker and all the people who have help me.
I like my gallery... thank you for like Ping Lian art works and thank you for support"

Ping Lian's pride was evident that afternoon. He was proud of his gallery and he was proud of himself. We had never quite seen him exude such self esteem before. We could see his confidence from his body language, his actions and his facial expressions. He was feeling at the top! He knew very well that he was the star of the show. He loved the spot light and thoroughly enjoyed being the center of attention. Ping Lian loves attention and praise. He may not always show it, or respond to someone who compliments him, but I know my Ping Lian enjoys it and that he feels good when people praise him and acknowledge him. He understood that the gallery was dedicated to him, with all of his artwork gracefully hanging on the walls. I can read him and read his body language quite well. Sher Lyn and I could see the difference in his eyes. We both agreed that Ping Lian had never shown such emotion with his body language as he did that day. When I asked Ping Lian "Who's gallery is this?" He responded firmly and proudly "Ping Lian's gallery".

Ping Lian also surprised me when it was my turn to give a speech. He helped me by holding the paper for me as I read. As I held the microphone in one hand, and embraced Ping Lian with the other, he held the paper for me to read my speech from because there was no podium to lay the paper on. He stood calmly and supportively by my side until I completed my entire speech. This was not rehearsed at home. Little did I know, there would be no podium. I was so proud of Ping Lian's spontaneity. He had definitely grown into my "good helper". The desperate expectations that I had expressed for my son in Chapter 10- "Daddy in Memory" had come true in so many ways. These moments were all milestones of great achievement by my autistic son.

Below is part of the speech I gave at Ping Lian's Gallery Opening:

"...Finally... I would like to share with you a little background about Ping Lian's gallery–
Even though I am living in Sydney, in my mind I always tell myself that 'One Day' I would like to open a gallery for Ping Lian in Malaysia and I also ask how can it happen. I have time and budget constraints. Then I think, Ok! based on Ping Lian's outstanding art works, it will happen. I do not know How??... Maybe we have to wait till 'One Day' when we do well. And in my mind I thought, that 'One Day' will come but I hope I did not need to wait till I am too old. After Yvonne organized Ping Lian's solo art exhibition, "My Journey......" in Jan 2008, One day Yvonne said..... We would like to open a gallery for Ping Lian. I was amazed and said...
How did you know that it was always my Dream for Ping Lian to have a gallery in Malaysia.?
Oh! This one day has come so fast... God has his own way... The Art Commune was there for Ping Lian... for a permanent showcase of his works in Malaysia. I was even more touched and amazed when I visited the gallery. So much hard work has been put into this. I can't believe that Ping Lian can have such a beautiful gallery at the age of 15. I believe Yvonne has put her heart and soul into Ping Lian's gallery... and I know she loves

Chapter 15: My Journey – Malaysia & New Upgraded Dream   419

PING LIAN'S MOM, PING LIAN AND SHERLYN (AUGUST 2009)

Ping Lian and his talent... Ping Lian is so blessed to have Yvonne. Ping Lian also knows Yvonne is some one very special to him. For example: when I ask Ping Lian to draw the Twin Towers... ... nothing happens... but when I ask Ping Lian "Do you want to go back to Malaysia?" And if I say Aunty Yvonne wants you to paint Malaysia... I see an immediate positive response. This has lead to so many Malaysia beautiful art works on the wall now. Yvonne, no words are enough to describe how grateful we are. To make it simple... I just want to say... thank you and I love you so much... and Ping Lian loves you so much!"

To end our speech, Ping Lian also said: *"I love you Aunty Yvonne!"*

EXCERPT FROM MY WRITINGS: "ABOUT PING LIAN YEAK - HIS JOURNEY AND GALLERY..." (WRITTEN BY SARAH SH LEE, AUGUST 2009)

"...Daring to Dream, setting Goals, daring to Change and taking Immediate Action is important for Ping Lian and us...."

"...Ping Lian's story is also a testimony that at times, a person's "worse" can become a person's "best" ...."

"....There can always be light at the end of the tunnel. Working with persistence, determination and perseverance, we can make it happen. Focus and maintain a positive mental attitude, work hard and smart, work with faith and mould the spirit to resonate "YES I CAN...." Yes, even to a child with autism, these thoughts can be instilled. I know because I have lived it with Ping Lian! ..."

".... I thank God for this "miracle gift" and the many "miracles happening. I also thank God for the special favors he has granted to Ping Lian's Artistic Journey. ... What Ping Lian has achieved thus far would not have been possible without the support, advice and encouragement of many special individuals and organizations. All have contributed to change Ping Lian's life and also have indirectly set a course for changes in our family life.... I would like to take this opportunity to say a word of special thanks to all the people and organizations involved in contributing and being part of Ping Lian's journey in life. I regard them as God- sent- angels..."

"..The memory of Ping Lian's father and his grandmother are also strength for our family. I believe they both smile upon us from heaven, as they witness the progress Ping Lian is making and the positive changes in our lives..."

"I thank The Art Commune for the establishment of Ping

Chapter 15: My Journey – Malaysia & New Upgraded Dream

Lian @ The Art Commune, featuring a permanent showcase of his works in MALAYSIA. This is his permanent gallery and a wonderful reality for him at such a young age. Also, big thanks to JPMorgan Chase Foundation and ABWM (Association of British Women in Malaysia) for their support of Ping Lian's Gallery. Ping Lian's permanent gallery provides an outlet for many to see his talent and his personal growth yet serves the general purpose of perhaps opening many minds regarding the capabilities and the "ability" in "dis"ability! Most importantly such opportunities showcase the strength of believing and having faith as a path to such wonderful outcomes through hope, aspiration, struggle and victory...."

Art has played a very special role in Ping Lian's journey throughout life. Art has helped Ping Lian by providing him with an appropriate means of leisure activity, increased focus, increased social opportunities, advanced job training and overall personal development. Ping Lian communicates through his art. Ping Lian is proud to be an artist. He also loves to be respected and appreciated".

IT DOES NOT MATTER WHO YOU ARE NOW,
IT IS WHO YOU WANT TO BE AND WHO YOU
BECOME THAT MATTERS...
MAKE DECISIONS AND TAKE ACTION NOW!

"The above is a quotation that I wrote many years ago in an effort to motivate myself and my company's sales teams. At that time, I did not know that this quotation would later on play a very important part in inspiring me to develop and set goals for Ping Lian in his Artistic Journey and his personal development".

Ping Lian's life is a testimonial to this quotation. Even though Ping Lian does not understand it; I have applied it time and again, and I also impart this motivational thought and spirit onto Ping Lian".

"....I believe through "Ping Lian @ The Art Commune" and through Ping Lian's art exhibitions, Ping Lian is provided with an outlet to express the thought that "...Although I have autism and have social and communication skill limitations, I am an outstanding Artist....Please do not label me as Disabled."

"Ping Lian is a happy boy, we are happy with all that Ping Lian has achieved thus far.... but we still have a long way to go to achieve the "Ultimate Level".... we continue to live by the above quote one level at a time...... and look forward to additional progress and change in the future."

Note: In September 2014 "Ping Lian @ The art Commune" was relocated to "Ping Lian Art Gallery @ The Settlement Hotel", at Malaysia's Historic City, Melaka. In 2014, Billy Leong, Yvonne's brother in law, and also a founding member of The Art Commune and owner of a travel agency in Malaysia for more then 30 years ventured into a boutique hotel business in Melaka. Together, they wished to share Ping Lian's story and art with the world via Melaka as Melaka is an Historic City of Malaysia.

The significance of this accomplishment for Ping Lian is beyond belief.

"The story of Melaka[36], also known as Malaysia's Historic City, starts of with the fascinating tale of the origin of its name. Founded in 1400 by Parameswara, a Palembang Prince who, inspired by the show of bravery of a mousedeer that kicked one of his hunting dogs into a river, decided to establish a city on the ground he was sitting on. As he was resting under the shade of

---

36 Historical extract cited from The Settlement Hotel website (2016).

the Melaka tree, so the city was named.

Situated at a point of strategic importance, Melaka boomed into a prosperous international trading port for spices, porcelain, tea and silk – luring Chinese, Javanese, Indian and Arab merchants. As Malacca's fame and wealth grew, it soon fell under the covetous eyes of emerging European powers, and was colonised by the Portuguese, Dutch and British. The imprints of all the different influences are still visible in the architecture, heritage buildings and colonial structures we see in Melaka.

The Settlement Hotel Melaka[37] seeks to capture and preserve Melaka's illustrious history, and to weave our guests through an evolution of cultures and hospitality. After two years of fervent restoration, the once tired-looking 1960's 4-storey government building located at the fringe of the Portuguese Settlement along Jalan Ujong Pasir, World UNESCO Heritage City Melaka, has now come alive in the form of an intimate boutique hotel that showcases the unique intertwined cultures and the rich heritage of Melaka." (https://thesettlementhotel.com/about-us)

I cannot thank Billy enough for establishing the Ping Lian Gallery at The prestigious Settlement Hotel in Melaka." With the more than 25 artworks on loan by Ping Lian at the hotel, we feel as though we are part of this amazing history.

---

37 Historical extract cited from The Settlement Hotel website (2016).

THE "SUPERWOMAN" IN PING LIAN'S JOURNEY
By Dr Rosa Martinez, in year 2012

Ping Lian has been so very blessed to have his "Mummy". Sarah Lee was obviously extremely dedicated, putting her own life on hold for the sake of her autistic son and her family's future. She took care of him, trained him, nurtured him, and of course to use her own words "brainwashed" him to prepare him to be the best that he could be. Even after Ping Lian's father passed away, it just made her stronger and more determined to find her son's strength and "train his talent".

In 2012, Sarah Lee was honored and recognized by Dr. Temple Grandin (along with Dr. Rosa C. Martinez and Stuart Flaum of Strokes of Genius)[38] as an outstanding parent for her pioneering efforts in nurturing and advocating for her son. Her tireless effort, encouragement and success have shaped Ping Lian's outstanding abilities. We hope that this story will empower others to be as innovative, intuitive and determined to cultivate interests and to acknowledge that every human being deserves an opportunity to contribute to society.

---

38 Strokes of Genius, Inc is a non-profit 501(c)3 organization that empowers individuals with autism www.strokesofgeniusinc.org

09502 FLOWERS

Ping Lian painted this after the official opening of the galley, by referring to the flowers that were sent in as a gift for the official opening - August 2009.

PING LIAN AND MOM AT SYDNEY - PHOTO BY DIANE MACDONALD

Ping Lian at The Rocks Market with sisters.

Ping Lian at The Rock Market with mom and aunties from left, Sarah 6th sister Siew Ing, 3rd sister Swee Eng, elder sister Choo Ing, Ping Lian and Sarah.

CHAPTER 16
What Does the Future Hold...?

Ping Lian, now in 2012 is known as a prodigious autistic savant artist around the world. In 2003 he out-grew tracing and seemed to suddenly acquire an obsession in drawing. He has not stopped drawing since. From simple, childish sketches, Ping Lian's style evolved to a more sophisticated level. Ping Lian's artistic journey has been very exciting and we are still constantly amazed by his artistic skill. Over the last several years, his talent has rapidly attracted local and international interest. Ping Lian continues to create magnificent works of art using charcoal, acrylic, watercolor, ink, oil and oil pastels. He has a signature style that has won over many art enthusiasts and collectors. His art works have been featured in exhibitions in the United States, UK, Germany, Japan, Australia and Malaysia. Ping Lian continues to exhibit across continents. He has been featured in various documentaries and his art works and story have been published in major newspapers, magazines, and books. Ping Lian continues to contribute to society by donating artworks to special organizations and charity events.

While reading through my journal, in preparation for writing this book, I noticed the many times that I referred to my son as "cute". He is now eighteen and I still refer to him as "Cute"! I take joy in every bit of progress my son makes, no matter how big or small, it is a victory. To others, from the outside looking in, I'm sure many of Ping Lian's behaviors would be viewed as ridiculous looking for an eighteen-year old. However, for me, each step in Ping Lian's development is like the milestone of a toddler's development. So, I enjoy his cuteness, just like all parents enjoy their baby's progress.

Throughout my life and this journey, I have upgraded Ping Lian's Dream many times. I always strive for 'a next step'; a 'new goal'. I still continue to work on his Dream and to aim for higher levels of achievement. However, with autism in our lives, the definition of the "Ultimate Dream" escapes me. I am just an ordinary mother, still always praying that Ping Lian will one day no longer have autism. I don't care how long it takes, I don't care if it is realistic or not, I don't care what my brain tells me......deep inside my heart, I never give up this hope. I prefer to hope, knowing that at least it motivates me to keep moving along in this journey. I am not expecting a scientific or even a medical breakthrough to cure autism. My hope and prayer is simply that one day, Ping Lian will be able to live independently, with reasonable social and communication skills. Ping Lian has severe autism and I continue to pray desperately that my hard work and Ping Lian's hard work together with the Grace of God can make that Ultimate Dream a reality.

My earlier prayers about Ping Lian's autism were not that specific. I used to pray for a miracle healing for Ping Lian for many years. For many years, every day I would pray for a miracle healing and say "immediately", "right now", and "at this moment". After many years of prayer, God did indeed grant Ping Lian a miracle – the miracle of his art ability. At some point after enjoying his miracle artistic gift for a while, my prayers did indeed become more specific. I continued praying for a miracle healing in which God would get rid of the autism in Ping Lian and make him *normal* .... like my nephews. Many times, in my head I imagine Ping Lian acting, talking and behaving as my sister's son's behaved. That is the Ultimate Level that I pray for, yet I still ask myself "Can it happen?"

After many years of working hard and praying, Ping Lian has definitely made tremendous progress in his personal development. He has shown marked improvement in some basic independence skills and basic communication skills. While he has become quite flexible, with a lot of affection, and no longer lives in his own world; he is still a very long way from being normal. I later started to view the causal factor of Ping Lian's developmental delays to be his IQ, and the autism as a secondary issue. Throughout the years, Ping Lian has become very obedient and always happy to learn. Yet, his cognitive limitations affect what he is able to comprehend (input) and what he is able to communicate (output). Ping Lian has always shown an eagerness and willingness to learn and to perform. He is a very hard working boy, but often he is unable to cope or understand situations and directions. I have spent countless hours teaching and guiding him. He is very slow in learning and understanding most new things I teach him. As Ping Lian grows older, I have become more doubtful about an autism healing.

Ping Lian still communicates with very limited spoken words or phrases. He does make attempts to initiate communication and will sometimes rely on his body gestures and a single word or a few words, to try to get his family members to understand him. I can understand him quite well but others who know him are just starting to understand him, and strangers or people who do not know him would not understand him at all. Currently Ping Lian's overall behavior is good. He does not have many incidents of obsessive or compulsive behaviors, rigidity, tantrum, self-injury or aggression. As a matter of fact, he is very obedient and can also be quite flexible. Ping Lian has a low IQ, which has restricted his ability to learn and integrate into society as other people do. I would not say that *communication* is his major problem. Ping Lian's major problem is comprehension. I would teach and re-teach to the point where I thought I was ready to "vomit blood", but Ping Lian still would not 'get it'! Now that he is a teenager, my main concerns are whether he can still develop further, and if a rapid pace of progress can be maintained into his adult hood.

After so many years of hard work and prayer, Ping Lian is still so very far away from being normal. There is still such a long way to go to achieve the Ultimate Dream. Do I give up? Even though I started to doubt that the miracle healing would ever happen, I never did actually give up totally and I never felt really disappointed by God. Instead, I changed the focus of my prayer. Instead of praying for a miracle healing to get rid of the autism in Ping Lian, I prayed to God for a miracle healing to provide Ping Lian with a higher IQ and a higher EQ (emotional intelligence). I prayed for Ping Lian to be able to understand life better and to function better.

I say "Thank you" to God for all he has provided and "Thank you" for all the miracles, grace and favors he has granted in Ping Lian's Journey, especially his Artistic Journey. Yet, I constantly tell God that I need more…. I desperately need more… to heal my Ping Lian and I desperately needed him to provide Ping Lian with a higher EQ. I also need Him to give me wisdom for teaching Ping Lian and guiding Ping Lian to move forward in this journey toward improved success.

I tell God… if asking for Ping Lian to get out from under autism is too ambitious for now (I guess all mothers' hope for that), then heal him in any way HE can grant for now…grant him higher intelligence…As I most desperately want my Ping Lian to function as normal as possible….

Anyway I will do my best and search for the next level of specific plans and actions for Ping Lian. I need to decide what is next and take action again…. So with *autism in our lives, which is not totally within our control, what can be the Ultimate Level? We do not know.… So I can only choose to go one step at a time.*

EXCERPT FROM SARAH SH LEE:

"About Ping Lian Yeak - His journey and gallery..." (August 2009)

"…. I can only go by attitude of doing my best and focusing on what he can and not what he can't do… so I believe that in order for all of us to achieve a happy life (with an autistic child at home) …. we need to respect him by appreciating what he can do (even a single small ability). To help him, we need to focus on what he CAN do while not denying his disability. We must maintain the attitude that as long as we do our best, the situation will be better and we will see improvements day by day in his future progress. So to remain happy, let us learn to appreciate, learn to be happy with whatever we have NOW while looking forward and working toward, what CAN be better."

I THOUGHT PING LIAN WAS GONE

March 16, 2010 my e-mail to Dr. Rosa Martinez:

" …. Last Wednesday, 10 March evening ……Accordingly, Ping Lian had a first generalized tonic-chronic seizure. While we were having dinner with Ping Lian in front of TV, he collapsed on the floor... I think he fainted (like unconscious) and later he shook his body and fainted (like unconscious) again.... (I am very panic... not very sure what happen...) at that time I did not know what happen... I am not sure of he is having a seizure or not... as he did not seem to shake so much. The scariest part is he is unconscious.... Ping Lian had complained of stomach pain on and off since Chinese new year holiday at Malaysia for the last few weeks (that is what happened to my husband during 2004 Chinese New Year and later he get heart attack, and then I was told stomach discomfort could be a sign of heart problem.... and my husband's family does have heart issues....). At that moment I thought he was dying....I do not know what can I do, only to call ambulance....when he is unconscious, my heart scream that; ...I can't lose him, he is too young...no way ...Oh! I can't live without him... he must come back......suddenly I remember that I need Gods help...I keep calling Ping Lian come back, Ping Lian come back... and I called God for help, I keep calling God to get him back... he must come back.... I desperately need him to come back.... Later before the ambulance arrived, he woke up....

While in the hospital.... whenever I thought of that moment scene, I just can't stop crying.... I can't lose him...I can't get over that scary moment (in 2005, my mother in-law fell down, also unconscious in front of me, and never got up again)..... But later I am OK.... As I tell myself, why should I be sad again....as Ping Lian is still a happy boy, in front of me.... I should be happy and I should thank God for that.... so I get back to my normal self again. And try to get rid of that sad scene..."

We stayed in the hospital for two days. Ping Lian had an EEG test, etc.... By Saturday Ping Lian happily start helping out at the art market again. The thought of losing Ping Lian has severely impacted and changed my life. The experience at that moment was like I lost him and now he is back again. It is too difficult to try to explain what I experienced. I cannot even describe it further.

Since that incident, Ping Lian has not had any further seizures. Yet, my outlook regarding Ping Lian's Ultimate Dream was definitely altered after the day I thought I was losing him. Our family treasures every moment

Chapter 16: What Does the Future Hold…?

with him regardless of what level of ability he is on. I also, came to realize that it had been a very long time since I viewed him as my burden. Seeing my son collapse and unconscious before my eyes, all I could think at that moment was "I can't live without him." We already knew that we loved Ping Lian more than anything, but we now appreciated and were grateful he was in our lives even more. As a family, we became even more determined to work together happily to achieve our New Upgraded Dream to make our journey in this world more meaningful.

DID GOD HAVE A PURPOSE FOR ME AND MY SON?

I have made many references to God in this story. Having read the entire journey as I and my family have experienced it, wouldn't you agree that it has been a miraculous journey?

Looking way back, to when I first confirmed that my son had autism and was constantly asking myself "Why me? God why are you punishing me?" I feel the need to share the first time that I was told "God has a plan for you!" ….

Many years ago, for the first time I joined a gathering for autistic families. It was a Christmas gathering and the parent of an autistic child knowing that I was a new parent to the group, began sharing stories with me about her autistic son. I understood that her intention was try to encourage me so that I did not feel so sad about having a son with autism. One of the last things she said to me before she walked off was "God has a purpose for you, your son and for everyone". At the time, I was wondering, who is this Christian lady to tell me about having a son with autism. Her son's behaviors are worse than Ping Lian's. How can she take it so easily? I was very puzzled and wondered if she knew what she was talking about. I actually remember saying to myself at that moment "Why has God chosen me?" "Why has God given me an autistic son?" "What have I done wrong that I deserve this?"

I have always believed myself to be a good person. I was kind hearted and unselfish. I was a good lady – so why had God chosen me? The comment just made me angry!

Another time, soon after that Christmas gathering, a friend and colleague from work knew of my sadness and frustration having learned that my son had autism. She was also a faithful Christian. One day she came to me and said "….. God has a purpose for you and he has a purpose for your son… ". It was the second time I heard this in a few short weeks. I couldn't take it anymore. This time I felt so offended and I couldn't believe that my own friend would say such a thing to me. Knowing, that she probably had good intentions I ignored her, but inside I was screaming "I don't want to hear that any more!!! Why? Why does God have a purpose for me?" I felt cheated. I felt it was insensitive for her to talk to me about my son with autism in such a way at all. She was "lucky". She did not have to go through what I was going through. She would never know what it would be like to have an autistic child. I was so angry as I continued thinking to myself "That is very easy for you to say. Wait till if one day you have an autistic child, then you will know, and you would not dare say that again to me. I felt insulted!!"

Till today, the feelings that were stirred when those two people told me "God had a purpose for you" are still imprinted in my brain. I must now say that I understand. Yes! God had a purpose for me and for my son, Ping Lian. There is a reason He chose me. Somewhere along this journey I started to trust in God, knowing that if He chose me, He knew I could handle it well. He would walk with me in this special journey and He would not let me suffer. . I am happy that I eventually decided to move forward and chose to trust, lean and depend on God's power rather than to blame Him. In reality, I chose to *hope*. Knowing that my own power and strength would not be enough. I chose to lean, depend and trust in God. I sought wisdom to be able to handle all situations and I asked God for miracles. Mostly I chose to trust in God to bring us happiness.

WHAT DOES THE FUTURE HOLD FOR PING LIAN AND HIS MOM?
(Update written in December 2012)

I recall the moments, a long time ago when Min Seng told me he was anxious about my safety and health, as I would prepare to give birth to our baby. He was referring to the fact that all of my previous births required a caesarean delivery. When our baby would be born, he said he would first make sure that I was safe, and then only would he look at our baby. He would then look at our baby's face, then his body, his legs and his hands. Once he sees that our baby is fine and healthy, and I am also okay, he will be happy. However, at that time we both only knew of physical disabilities and Down Syndrome. Min Seng always said that he wanted our baby to look like me because I "have a beautiful face." Ping Lian was indeed a very handsome baby, but we eventually learned that "fine and healthy" had to do with so much more than just physical appearance.

As autism entered into our existence and our understanding of autism grew, we initially thought there would be no hope for our Ping Lian. He would be our burden and will make us suffer. Now I am very happy with Ping Lian's progress so far and he is a wonderful, loving young man, who loves to be a "good helper". My two daughters love him a lot and I love him dearly. He is a wonderful "baby" at home. He is so cute, so loving and helpful; so eager to help us, to serve us and to contribute at home in many areas of the house chores. He makes us all feel so good and we love him so much. He is a blessing in disguise, not a burden.

On any given, ordinary day, Ping Lian attempts to take the responsibility of doing the basic household chores as best he can. He likes to vacuum the house (although he is not yet very thorough). When I prepare to cook, he helps in the kitchen by cutting the vegetables and he cleans the dishes after our meals. He also hangs the clothes on the line and collects and folds the laundry to put it back into the cabinet. Above all else, his favorite chore seems to be loading and unloading the car, with all the art stuff that needs to be taken to and brought back from The Rocks Market. After many years of training, he has also become very good in helping to set up the stall at The Rocks Market. He hangs his artwork at the art market with so much pride and joy. Most weekend mornings, I can hear him singing and making lots of "happy sounds" at the market while he is helping to set up the stall and hang his artwork. Many autistic people make certain sounds regularly, that I believe are self-stimulatory. Ping Lian makes such sounds a lot too. I can decipher whether he is happy, sad, anxious, etc.; by the tone of his self-stimulatory vocalizations.

As a young man, Ping Lian physically possesses the strength necessary enabling him to help out with all the heavy physical duties needing to be done at home and at the market. Yet, in many ways, in most areas, Ping Lian is like a small boy - so cute but so helpful and eager to please us, while still needing a lot of supervision and care from us. Though Ping Lian is very eager to contribute in doing a lot of house work, he still has many limitations, especially in novel situations and circumstances. He can easily perform all the basic tasks that took so long to teach him. However, once he learns the task, he is very hard working. He requires no reminders as he is always eager to do chores with much pride. Ping Lian's improved overall obedience and behavior have greatly contributed to his ability to be more independent. This improved level of functioning has also allowed me to have some time for myself. Although Ping Lian is still unable to be alone outside of the house environment, in a *trained* environment like home,

Chapter 16: What Does the Future Hold...?

he can remain alone and function independently. He will occupy himself for several hours by reading (although I am still not sure how much he understands of what he reads), playing piano, painting, doing house work, using his ipad and even taking a nap. Ping Lian does not play games on his ipad. He mainly uses his ipad to search for Google images, especially subjects he is obsessed with at the time, or subjects he love to draw. He also often Google searches foods that he likes and searches on YouTube for children's songs he enjoys.

With all this progress, I have begun to feel that I do have a life and some freedom to live it. This is not something I ever really experienced while I was raising my son. Although, independent living is something still very far from Ping Lian's reach, my own restrictions have been narrowed. I love my son unconditionally. He is my great "companion"; and enjoys accompanying me anywhere I go. So what does the future hold... for Ping Lian and his family; his mom and his sisters? I do not know.... but I will just commit to continue allowing God to lead us and give us the wisdom to walk this Journey. Let God protect us, lead us and provide for us abundantly. Let God reveal to us in stages, "How?" and "Who?" Ping Lian will become??? Will God send Ping Lian's Mom a wonderful life partner who will love her dearly but also accept and love Ping Lian dearly??? This, cannot be overlooked, as Ping Lian will be forever be living with his mom while she is on this earth.

As we progress on this journey with Ping Lian, we continuously experience more good happenings and many "coincidences" which (big or small) I believe are created by God. Too many times I have said; "Oh! I can't believe this can happen." Initially, as my family constantly experienced these "coincidences" I told myself that one day I may write another book detailing with many short stories all of these experiences that resulted from events that coincided.. However, in 2010, so many amazing things kept happening that I felt the need, like *a calling* to write a second book. I will write about how and why, I refer to these instances as special "coincidences" that show "God's hand at work" and resulted in many positive outcomes. Since then, I have become more dedicated in keeping a journal, so that I can write additional accurate testimonies of the events. Many are so inexplicable and unexpected and may be referred to as "God's incidents" since I can't explain them. My second book will also include details of how Ping Lian's life was in danger on two separate occasions and the special coincidences and voice in my head that lead to me able to help him. Writing a book is difficult for me because I read and write in English very, very slowly. I am not absolutely sure how efficiently I can do it again, but I am compelled to do so. For me it is God's intention. I believe that God has chosen me and has a purpose for me, so He will help me and bless me to get it done. Hopefully, by then we will have a clearer picture of what the future holds for Ping Lian and His mom.

    Good Bye!!!

IMPORTANT NOTE

This book was written and completed in approximately 2012, when Ping Lian was nineteen years old. The last chapter was originally Chapter 16, but the book was not submitted for publication until now (several years later). Many of the stories shared by Sarah Lee, were extremely difficult for her to write down on paper, as she was sharing a very personal story with the world. Ping Lian is now twenty-two years old – It is time.

During this period, Sarah Lee encountered new changes from Ping Lian which she did not expect. With these changes she realised that this Journey with Ping Lian is a continuous learning process, constantly in need of new strategies for dealing with Ping Lian at his many different stages of development. She has experienced a new alertness to understand the changes in his development and to experiment and discover new methods for taking action. Coupled with her positive mental attitude, Ping Lian's intellectual progress required yet new expectations and new approaches. Regression was not an option. Thus, Sarah Lee has added some updated information in the following epilogue, as a summary of her new realisation during these past few years of their journey.

PING LIAN- EXHIBITION AT DBS AUDITORIUM, MARINA BAY, SINGAPORE (2015)

EPILOGUE

Four years after the book was completed – New updates: Summary Update 2015/2016

PING LIAN'S PERSONAL DEVELOPMENT:

Chapter 16 of this book was intended to be the last chapter. It was completed in 2012, when Ping Lian was 19 years old. In some of the book chapters Ping Lian was described as "cute", "baby", and as a "beautiful angel". For a few years he was obedient and tantrum free. He appeared relaxed, happy, compliant and easy to monitor. He developed to a point where he would follow most directions I gave him, with the absence of negative behavior. Up until the age of 19, Ping Lian was still *cute like a baby* and easy to manage. Although the praise we delivered to Ping Lian as a family was unsurmountable, I still wondered how he became so "easy" with regard to behaviors. Much of his complacency was derived from the rewards, love and attention that we provided him daily, consistently and constantly. Of even greater importance may be the effort spent on teaching Ping Lian to have emotion. I now refer to this as *character building*. Having taught Ping Lian at a very early age to love God, love others, love himself, care for others, oblige others, to be grateful, patient, to share, to not waste money, not waste people's time, etc ; have all contributed to strengthening his character. These are lessons instilled in my son that will always remain with him.

More recently, as Ping Lian is approaching the age of 21, he has shown much growth, maturity and awareness. His acquisition of day to day life skills and his general level of comprehension has tremendously increased in comparison to his overall development by age 19. Ping Lian can now actually anticipate our plans. The days of repeating myself over and over and over again are *OVER*! I can say something once and he will remember it. He is now also able to contemplate the activities for any given day of the week. Monday to Sunday now holds meaning for Ping Lian, as he is aware of his plans and routines throughout the week. Words like "tomorrow" that were once so abstract and inconsequential to him, now had significance. For example, he can return from his Day Center and tell me that next Monday is a holiday, understanding that he will not be attending the Day Center on that day. He also displays a very good memory now. He always displayed a good memory for detail, as evident in his drawings, but this is very different. He now often reminds me on a given day, if I had previously made a promise to him to take him somewhere that day. Ping Lian now selects his own food from a menu. He is *thinking* and making choices independently. All of these advances appeared within the last few years (after my completion of Chapters 1-16).

Ping Lian continues to have severe deficits in the areas of socialization and verbal communication. Nevertheless, the pace of his development has been astounding and although chronologically, his overall developmental level is still well below the skill level of a typically developing 21 year old, for Ping Lian the maturity and growth have been amazing.

Our family is extremely happy with his progress. However, we have witnessed, that with this progress have come some behavioral setbacks. We have seen the re-occurrence of sudden and drastic negative behaviors. I have found myself now having to deal with an *adult* son with autism. A son who can *think* for himself, but cannot functionally express himself. Ping Lian is demonstrating negative behavior due to his frustrations and anxieties. He, like many other adults with autism has a mind full of thoughts he is unable to express, a heart full of emotions he cannot share, and a body wrought with feelings he may not understand.

I do not view these newly emerging behavioral setbacks as regression. It is important to understand that my son has emotionally and developmentally matured within the last three years. This maturity encompasses a higher intellect in Ping Lian's understanding of the world he lives in. Thus, he is obviously faced with many new challenges, disappointments and frustrations that he is yet unable to grasp or navigate. He has new, more advanced thought processes requiring new needs and new expectations, yet coupled with the inability to communicate his new understanding and advanced perspective of life. In my view, this is not regression for my son. It is regression for those around him, including myself.

The strategies I used with Ping Lian when he was younger, are not effective for him at this point in his life. What worked when he was less intellectually developed, less involved and unaware of choice making, etc, is no longer applicable. Thus, the more Ping Lian has become immersed in higher level activities and relationships, the more entangled his life has become. He tries very hard to communicate and the end result is currently frustration.

I see him close his eyes...... "Is he attempting to concentrate? ... Is he trying to control his anxiety? ... Is he trying to block out stimuli? ... Is he attempting to figure something out by digesting the information?" I have found myself back in a situation where I have not been for many years. "My poor son. What is he trying to say?" The bottom line, is that I have not lost Faith. I am in the process of refreshing myself with prayer.

I continue to develop new strategies to deal with my now, much taller and much stronger boy. However, I imagine how impossible this might be, if Ping Lian did not experience the character building lessons from a young age. Ping Lian's responses in the future will largely depend on his character. I expect that the choices and reactions he will display as he continues to mature will be triggered by the values that have been instilled upon him in the past. Based on my beliefs and family values, we lived by a set of principles and rules that were not so different for Ping Lian. I thank God for the wisdom with which I imparted these values to my son when he was just a small boy. Imagine trying to suddenly instill good character to a behaviorally challenged autistic adult. For individuals on the autism spectrum we know that routines are important, but more importantly routines become habits that are hard to break for EVERYONE! Instil good character from the very beginning.

At some point in 2013, I developed a plan for my adult son and called it Ping Lian's *Independent Living Skills Plan.* This was a 5 to 15-year plan that would address his personal development. One day, while I was jogging, the idea for this plan popped into my head. Basically, it was a replica of the plan I initially developed to train Ping Lian to become an artist. Only, now I applied the tactics to his personal development. With God's help, I am no longer regressing when it comes to Ping Lian. My hope is to be able to chronicle the positive effects of this plan in my second book.

By 2012, having aged-out of the school system, Ping Lian began attending Studio Artes community participation program (a Day Center for people with disabilities). After years of painting and drawing on his own without any professional guidance or professional tutoring since moving to Sydney in 2006, we were blessed to have access to Studio Artes. Through this association, Ping Lian met artist Greg Warburton, who later helped guide Ping Lian with painting portraits. Warburton is a six time Archibald Prize finalist who has worked with challenged individuals for many years. His work is held in the permanent collection of the National Portrait Gallery in Canberra. After guiding Ping Lian and watching Ping Lian's unique style of painting Warburton stated:

> "I am very aware of the importance of Ping Lian maintaining the expressive spontaneity and individuality of his images while at the same time adapting to a new medium. Making portraits that capture a likeness of the subject and convey human emotions within Ping Lian's unique style will produce remarkable work we

can all celebrate. It is a privilege to be a part of this young man's artistic journey".

The opportunities at Studio Artes further helped to upgrade Ping Lian's skills as he learned about various media; especially oil paint which he had only used briefly before moving to Sydney. Studio Artes also served as a good professional art studio for him to do his painting. Since he was a very young child, Ping Lian was always very motivated to paint at exhibition spaces and art environments.

In August 2016, Ping Lian joined another program at Dulkara Center For Life Skills and Art. There he began to explore his talent in pottery. As I always suspected, he had this area of talent that I had accidentally discovered just before we flew to New York in 2006. Knowing I was not "supermom", I was unable to pursue this discovery at the time. My decision was to set this area aside for nurturing t a latter date. It would have to be a project to nurture at another time. The time would come when it is right and when it is right, it will happen. Well, on his first day of pottery class.... He was excellent!

To date, judging by my son's successes, I have been very effective with my brain-washing approach in helping Ping Lian attain status as an Artist. I *brainwashed* him for years, and now he is not only an artist but he loves to go to The Rocks Market to "work". He does not have a single friend, but he is integrated in the community and contributes to society every time he is at work. He enjoys the recognition and many praises of his ability. I think being at The Rocks Market and at his art exhibitions makes him feel significant. So for now, going to the Rocks Market is still an important life style for him. The groundwork has been done, but what the future holds, remains an unknown. I will continue to work toward achieving our Dream and Goals; both big and small, while sharing Ping Lian's inspiring story.

At present (August 2016), Ping Lian still has limited communication and social skills but we are happy that art has provided him with an outlet of expression and countless opportunities to further his development. I can only pray for the best, while doing *my* best. I remember a pastor who once said, "…Holy spirit will lead, but you need to do the work …"

END

Ping Lian at work at Dulkara Center for Life Skills - August 2016.

ABOUT THE AUTHOR
Sarah Sh Lee

"While putting her own career and social life on hold, Sarah Lee managed to create a *special talent* and a meaningful life for her severely autistic son."

Sarah Lee possesses a Bachelor's degree in Economics. She majored in Business Administration at the University of Malaya, Malaysia. She was a Senior Sales and Marketing Manager in a business software solutions and a telecommunications company. Sarah Lee was extremely successful in attaining numerous high profile corporate clients, bringing the company of one of her employers, from loss to profit in a short period. In a very competitive corporate environment, Sarah Lee's intuitive drive consistently generated the highest level of individual sales whilst recruiting, nurturing and developing the sales team.

At the age of 42, Sarah Lee became a widow leaving her to single handedly raise three dependent children; the youngest (Ping Lian Yeak) 10 with severe autism. Only two years later, in 2006, Sarah Lee left her illustrious career behind and uprooted her family from Malaysia to Sydney, Australia. Without a single relative or friend in Sydney, she set off to start their new lives, with an extreme focus to create a meaningful life for her son. Refusing to accept that Ping Lian living in his own world had "no affect"; "no emotion" and would "look right through" her; this brave lady's determination and practice to develop, maintain and live with a positive mental attitude and a happy personality has resulted in this remarkable book of Ping Lian's journey. His success not only as an artist, but as a young man full of emotions who interacts meaningfully with his family is a miraculous testament to his mother's will. *"He has matured into an obedient, hard-working and grateful boy," reflects Lee. "He is my good helper at home and when we go shopping."*

As a business woman; but first and foremost, as a Mother, Sarah Lee's commitment to "feeding the mind and soul" is unceasing. She has a never-ending drive to improve and expand upon her positive outlook; constantly reading and attending seminars.

In 2012, she received the "Parent's Certificate of Recognition" from Temple Grandin, for her pioneering efforts in Training The Talent and nurturing the artistic abilities and interests of her son Ping Lian Yeak. Her achievements, chronicled in Ping Lian's uniquely touching story have been noted and acclaimed in various documentaries, text books and news articles throughout this journey.

- 2005 – Korean Broadcasting System: *Savant Syndrome* documentary alongside Kim Peek (real Rain Man) and Kodi Lee.
- 2005 – TV8 Malaysia: *Eve's Diary*
- 2006 – United Kingdom Focus Productions *Painting the Mind* aired on Channel 4, Four Corners, ABC TV Australia, Scandinavia
- 2008 - EBS Korea: *Uncovering the Secret of Childhood*
- 2009 – CNA International and CNA Singapore: *Asia's Wonder Kids*
- 2011 – "'Real Reading 3" – English textbook published by PEARSON Longman; Chapter 24- *Through the Eye of Love*.

- 2011 – "Adventures in Autism" by the master of motivation, Peter A. LaPorta (USA).
- 2012 – *Positively Remarkable Women* – 50 Portraits - by Diane Macdonald
- 2014 – The Sydney Morning Herald: *Ping Lian Yeak: the autistic savant who is a prodigious artist*
- 2016 - "The Prodigy's Cousin: The Family Link Between Autism and Extraordinary Talent" - Joanne Ruthsatz and Kimberly Stephens

ABOUT THE EDITOR
Dr. Rosa C. Martinez

Dr. Martinez has a B.S. in Special Education from CCNY, a Masters degree in Adolescent Autism, a Masters of Philosophy, and a Doctorate in Behavioral Disorders from Columbia University. She is also a Board Certified Behavior Analyst currently working for the NYS Department of Education.

Dr. Martinez is the President and Founder of Strokes of Genius, Inc. After meeting Ping Lian Yeak in 2006, Dr. Rosa C. Martinez created her vision for Strokes of Genius, Inc. She soon became a collaborator with Sarah SH Lee and began promoting Ping Lian Yeak's artworks here in the United States. She organizes art exhibitions throughout the United States and internationally featuring the artworks of savants and individuals on the autism spectrum. She has curated art shows at the The United Nations, Carnegie Hall, Cooper Union, The Michael Schimmel Arts Center and the prestigious Salmagundi Historical Art Club.

Dr. Martinez has taught Education courses at Hunter College, the College of Staten Island, Long Island University, Touro College and the University of Maryland and also teaches literacy and communication skills to behaviorally challenged adolescents with autism and other developmental disabilities. She was instrumental in establishing various ABA programs for young children with PDD and Autism in New York City and has been working with individuals on the autism spectrum ranging from infants to adult populations for more than 30 years.

PING LIAN WITH DR ROSA MARTINEZ AT HENRY GREG GALLERY, NEW YORK - JANUARY 2006

Publications include:
- Hosseini, D. & Martinez, R.C. (2011) The Art of Autism: Shattering 7 Myths about autism through the voices and art of those on the spectrum
- Treffert, D. (2011) Islands of Genius: The Bountiful Mind of the Autistic, Acquired and Sudden Savant (Martinez, R.C. - Ch. 26 – *Training the Talent in Art: An Educators Approach*)
- Greenberg, J. & Martinez, R.C. (2008). Starting Off on the Right Foot: One Year of Behavior Analysis in Practice and Relative Cost
- International Journal of Behavioral Consultation and Therapy, Vol.4
- Martinez, R.C. (2014) Video presentation: Training The Talent in Individuals With Autism . A video presentation featuring Temple Grandin. Pace University, 2014

Ping Lian Yeak

My Artistic Journey

www.pinglian.com
Born in Malaysia – 18 November 1993
Residing in Sydney, Australia, since May 2006

PRODIGIOUS SAVANT ARTIST (AUTISTIC)

Initially Ping Lian was hyperactive, living in his own world, not showing affection or awareness of danger, unable to hold a pencil to write or use scissors to cut. In order to strengthen and develop Ping Lian's fine motor skills, his home program focused on tracing and coloring activities. These activities also served as a way for Ping Lian to occupy himself, given his inability to appropriately engage in any leisure or socialization skills. Ping Lian also had very poor imitation skills. Guiding him through tracing and drawing activities, stroke by stroke, was also one of the ways to develop his imitation skills. Ultimately, tracing became a catalyst for discovering his exceptional artistic talent.

At the age of 8 (mid-2002), Ping Lian out-grew tracing and seemed to suddenly acquire an obsession for drawing. The transition from tracing to drawing happened almost instantly. One day after he had finished eating an ice-cream cone, he just started drawing the pictures that were printed on the ice cream wrapper. He has not stopped drawing since then. The quality of his drawings has rapidly advanced and his rate of progress was fascinating. Now, Ping Lian is a talented artist full of love and affection. Due to his mother's perseverance he has also matured into an obedient, hardworking, and grateful boy. Ping Lian still has limited communication and social skills. Art has provided him with an outlet of expression.

His unique style of bold strokes and cheerful colors has won over many art enthusiasts and collectors. (written in 2008)

- **March 2003** - Ping Lian's mother wrote in her diary "I want to develop Ping Lian to be an Artist….. I got Ping Lian to say "I Want to be an Artist" every day…… I know he will be an Artist one day……. "

- **Feb 2004** - Ping Lian's father passed away due to a sudden heart attack. Ping Lian not only lost his dad but his only male friend.

- **April 2, 2012** – his mother Sarah SH Lee was awarded a certificate of recognition for her pioneering efforts to "Train the Talent" signed by Temple Grandin and presented at The Strokes of Genius World Autism Awareness ceremony at United Nations Plaza, New York.

- A book about Ping Lian titled **"I Want To Be Artist": An Autistic Savant's Voice and a Mother's Dream Transformed Onto Canvas** is scheduled to be published in 2016 (written by Ping Lian's mom, edited by Dr Rosa C. Martinez from New York).

"Ping Lian's art is really very amazing. I would certainly put him into the category of 'savants'… I really like his art…. **They are national treasures wherever they are located…..**" - Sept 2004

"Ping Lian's artwork stands on its own demonstrating a remarkable artistic ability. His artworks take on an added significance when one sees such ABILITY CO-EXIST with DIS– ABILITY. He is a natural artist whose work draws immediate attention, and appreciation. His works are a spark of joy and flame, talent and enthusiasm."… 2008

Darold A. Treffert, MD, author of "Extraordinary People: Understanding the savant syndrome" and "Islands of GENIUS", has been studying savant syndrome for the last 45 years, and was a consultant to the award winning movie Rain Man.

To view Ping Lian's artwork painted from age 10 to 20

In Malaysia, visit **Ping Lian Gallery @ The Settlement Hotel**, Historic Melaka, Malaysia. Address: No 63, Jalan Ujong Pasir, World UNESCO Heritage City Melaka, 75050, Melaka, Malaysia. Tel: +606-2921133 www.thesettlementhotel.com

In Sydney – Argyle Gallery, Playfair St, The Rocks, Sydney NSW, 2000, Australia. Tel: +61 2 92474427 (Monday - Sunday) or The Rocks Market (Saturday and Sunday only)

TV COVERAGE, EXHIBITIONS AND BOOKS

Upcoming Exhibition: March 10th – March 30th 2017 at Agora Gallery; a contemporary fine art gallery in New York's Chelsea art district. www.agoragallery.com/artistpage/Ping_Lian_Yeak.aspx

- **At age 11 (2005)** – Filmed for Korea Broadcasting System's 60-minutes savant syndrome documentary alongside Kim Peek (real Rain Man) and Kodi Lee. 'Eve's Diary' (TV8 – Malaysia) featured Ping Lian and his solo exhibition at ABWM House. In November 2004, Ping Lian's work, "Ubudiah Mosque 1" was donated to Riding for the Disabled Association, Malaysia for charity auction. It sold for MYR100,000.00 (100% of the proceeds were donated).

- **At age 12** – Focus Productions from UK, filmed Ping Lian at his exhibition at Henry Gregg Gallery, Brooklyn, New York for documentary, 'Painting the Mind' a documentary for Channel 4, that also aired on Four Corners, ABC TV Australia(April 2007), and in Scandinavia. Ping Lian's family moved to Sydney.

- **At age 13** – EBS from Korea filmed Ping Lian with Dr Darold Treffert in a documentary entitled "Uncovering the Secret of Childhood" during the "Windows of Genius: Artworks of the Prodigious Savant" art exhibition in Wisconsin, USA.

- **At age 14** – 'Don't 'dis' the ability' – artworks featured at the United Nations Headquarters in New York (April 2008) in honor of the inaugural World Autism Awareness Day.

- **At age 15** – Official opening of his personal gallery in Malaysia – 'Ping Lian @ The Art Commune' featuring a permanent showcase of his works in Malaysia, established by The Art Commune and supported by JPMorgan Chase Foundation (for 2009) in collaboration with ABWM. Ping Lian was also filmed at the official opening of the gallery for a documentary, 'Asia's Wonder Kids' for Channel News Asia (CNA International and CNA Singapore).

- **At age 16** – Featured in three books that were published in the USA – 'Islands of Genius' by Dr. Darold Treffert, 'Real Reading 3 – English textbook published by PEARSON Longman (one chapter about Ping Lian), and 'Drawing Autism' by Jill Mullin. Solo art exhibition at The Malaysia Tourism Centre (Matic).

- **At age 17** – Featured in the book published in Korea, titled 'Knowledge', which also included the Real Rain Man (Kim Peek), Albert Einstein, Abraham Lincoln, Warren Edward Buffett, William H. Gate, etc. Also featured in the book "Artism: The Art of Autism" (U.S. 2011). Participated in exhibitions "The Genius of Autism" at Carnegie Hall (New York), "Strokes of Genius" at The Salmagundi Art Society, New York and "Savant Art" at The Rocks Pop - Up Project, Sydney.

- **At age 18** – Ping Lian's story was featured in one chapter of the book "Adventures in Autism" by the master of motivation, Peter A. LaPorta (USA).

- **At age 20 n 21** – "Ping Lian @ The Art Commune" relocated to "Ping Lian Gallery @ The Settlement Hotel", Melaka. Dec 2014- "Architectural Impressions", a two month long art exhibition of Ping Lian's Architectural Landscapes artworks at Port Authority, New York City.

- **At age 22** - Exhibited at Agora Gallery; a contemporary fine art gallery in New York's Chelsea art district. Featured in the book "The Prodigy's Cousin" by Joanne Ruthsatz n Kimberly Stephens.

Ping Lian continues to create magnificent works of art using charcoal, acrylic, water color, ink and oil. He also continues to donate his works to organisations and charities. His art works have been featured in exhibitions in the United States, UK, Australia, Germany, Japan, Korea, Singapore and Malaysia.

> *"Let us celebrate and focus on what autistic people can do, not what they can't do, and not label them as DISABLED."*
>
> *Sarah SH Lee*

Revision June 2016

2011 JULY - PING LIAN AT SYDNEY- "THE ROCKS POP - UP PROJECT" PHOTO BY DIANE MACDONALD

www.ingramcontent.com/pod-product-compliance
Lightning Source LLC
Chambersburg PA
CBHW062055290426
44110CB00022B/2599